Horse-Drawn Carriage Catalog, 1909

Elkhart Manufacturing Company

DOVER PUBLICATIONS, INC.
Mineola, New York

Published in Canada by General Publishing Company, Ltd., 30 Lesmill Road, Don Mills, Toronto, Ontario.

Bibliographical Note

This Dover edition, first published in 2001, is an unabridged republication of Catalog No. 63, originally published in 1909 by the Elkart Carriage & Harness Manufacturing Co., Elkhart, Indiana.

DOVER *Pictorial Archive* SERIES

Library of Congress Cataloging-in-Publication Data

Elkhart Carriage and Harness Manufacturing Co.
    Horse-drawn carriage catalog, 1909 / Elkhart Manufacturing Company.
        p. cm.
    Originally published: Elkhart, Ind., 1909.
    ISBN 0-486-41531-7 (pbk.)
        1. Elkhart Carriage and Harness Manufacturing Co.—Catalogs. 2. Carriages and carts—Indiana—Elkhart—Catalogs. I. Title.

TS2033 .E45 2001
688.6—dc21

00-049388

Manufactured in the United States of America
Dover Publications, Inc., 31 East 2nd Street, Mineola, N.Y. 11501

ELKHART
CARRIAGE & HARNESS
MANUFACTURING CO.

THE LARGEST MANUFACTURERS
OF VEHICLES AND HARNESS IN
THE WORLD SELLING TO THE
CONSUMER EXCLUSIVELY

"We have no agents but sell direct to you"

SHIP ANYWHERE FOR EXAMINATION

ELKHART INDIANA

1909

Catalog No. 63

This is our catalog No. 63 for the season of 1909. It is our only salesman, and you will find the following paragraphs well worth reading.

36 Years Experience

For 36 years we have been manufacturing and selling vehicles and harness to the individual user from our factory here in Elkhart at factory prices. Instead of having expensive salesmen on the road to sell our product to the dealer, who in turn would sell to the user at an advance of anywhere from $20.00 to $40.00 per vehicle, we have always sold direct from our factory, and our prices represent at all times the actual cost of the material and making, plus our small profit.

No Agents or Dealers to Protect

We have no agents or dealers in any locality to protect and in making our prices we do not have to consider them in any way. We not only save the salaries paid to high salaried traveling men but their expenses, losses due to failures and dealers' profits and expenses. We have succeeded from the beginning of our business, and the fact that we have on our books now customers who have dealt with us for years and whose sons are dealing with us today, is the best evidence we could produce that we are building first class work and saving our patrons money.

The Largest in the World

We are by far the largest manufacturers of vehicles and harness in the world selling exclusively to the consumer. Our large factories here in Elkhart are the most up-to-date plants to be found anywhere, and are equipped throughout with modern machinery which not only enables us to produce better work than with old style equipments, but to produce it at the lowest possible cost. It has always been our desire to keep our line up-to-date, and you will find in this catalog the largest variety of strictly up-to-date first class work on the market today. Regardless of the superiority and up-to-dateness of our work we have always added to the actual cost of the vehicles and harness, only a reasonable profit.

We Guarantee Absolutely to Save you Money

We are willing always to ship our work anywhere for full examination and approval without one penny being paid in advance, and if you do not feel, after making a careful examination, that you are getting a better article for the money than you could possibly procure elsewhere, all that is necessary for you to do is to write us and say that you do not want the shipment. There will be no unpleasantness about it. We will simply order the shipment back at our expense and you will be nothing out.

No Money in Advance

We have been in this business for so many years (36) and have so much confidence in our ability to satisfy our patrons, that we do not even require a deposit placed with us or with the bank or express agent in your town as is the case with all other companies, on orders that are not paid for in full in advance. We are willing to ship on our C. O. D. plan, if you prefer to order in that way, without your making either any deposit or payment in advance.

When Cash is Sent With Order

When the full amount of money is sent in advance, we ship just the same as we do on C. O. D orders; that is, with the distinct understanding that if everything is not found perfectly satisfactory and you do not feel that you are saving money in buying from us, you need not accept the shipment, and we will order it returned and refund the entire amount of your remittance. In other words, you are nothing out if you are not pleased and perfectly satisfied.

Dealers May Try to Mislead You

Remember, if you want our quality at our price, the only way you can secure it is direct from our factory, unless some dealer is so anxious to sell you that he is willing to buy from us, for you, without any profit for himself. Our prices are the same to all. It makes no difference whether the order is for one or a dozen vehicles we do not vary from our catalog prices and the dealer can obtain our work only by paying what you would pay us. Frequently our friends write us that their local dealer has informed them that our vehicles are sold through dealers as well as direct and that if they want our make he will order it for them at a reduction from our catalog prices. This is not true, and such talk is resorted to in order to divert your attention from our work. We do not hesitate to sell to dealers at our regular catalog prices and many dealers buy from us on this plan, but they have us ship less our name plate and with plain shipping tags and the vehicle is not known as our make when they sell it at an advanced price over our regular catalog price. We have for many years proved and are all the time proving that there is no reason or excuse for the additional profit between the manufacturer and the consumer which you have to pay when you buy from the dealer.

How to Order

We send with each catalog an order blank which will assist you in making out your order and simplify the entering of same here in our office. It is not necessary to use this order blank, however, unless you wish. In ordering, say whether you want pole or shafts or both, regular 4 foot 8 inch track, or the wide 5 foot 2 inch track. We carry these two widths in stock and gladly make other widths when ordered. The track is measured from outside to outside of tire along the ground. When reference to the track is overlooked and there is any question at all with us regarding width of track that is necessary, or regarding anything else about your order, we always write before shipping.

How We Ship

When the order is paid for in full in advance, we ship direct to you and you save the difference between our C. O. D. and our cash with order price, and also the small charge made by bank or express company on C. O. D. shipments for collecting and returning money. When the order is for C. O. D. shipment; that is, collect on delivery, we bill to our order, sending you a written order on the freight agent to allow you to fully examine the goods, making collection with bill of lading attached through any bank you may name, or express company. If after examination you find everything satisfactory you simply step into the bank or express office and pay the bill, securing the freight bill which gives you possession of the shipment.

In sending money in advance you can send bank draft, P. O. money order, express money order, money in registered letter or your personal check. We name two prices, as you will see upon referring to catalog; the first, a cash in advance price; the second, a C. O. D. price.

We do not Vary

We are frequently asked to make our cash in advance price on a C. O. D. shipment. It is useless to ask us to vary from our prices or our terms of shipment. When the order is not paid for in advance we always adhere strictly to our C. O. D. price, shipping on our regular C. O. D. plan. Over three-fourths of our customers send money in advance, and it would not be fair to those who pay in advance for us to allow our cash with order prices on any C. O. D. orders. We treat all alike and do not, under any circumstances, vary. Our system is very simple and very satisfactory when understood. The day the goods are shipped we always notify you, and if sent C. O. D. we enclose an order on the freight agent to allow you to fully examine. We also name the bank or express office where the papers are sent, if it is a C. O. D. shipment.

We Guarantee Safe Delivery

We use regulation sizes of crating lumber, as demanded by railroad companies, and we crate all of our work in the regulation manner as agreed upon by shippers and railroad companies. We cover every vehicle before it is crated with a heavy waterproof paper bag. Our vehicles go in nice shape to all parts of the United States. There is no extra charge for the crating and putting on board cars here, and we guarantee safe delivery. If anything is in any way damaged while in transit, we hold ourselves responsible and take our chances with the railroad company adjusting the matter with us after we have satisfied you. In fact, you are just as safe in placing your order with us at any distance as you would be if you were here at our factory to take the buggy out of our repository, because we agree positively to deliver it to you in as good shape.

Freight Charges

Very often the local retail dealer will talk about the freight charges to a prospective buyer, as though it amounted to a great deal, whereas the local dealer always pays exactly the same rate of freight that you would pay, as there positively cannot be any discrimination by railroad companies with regard to freight rates. Unless shipped in car load lots (and very, very few dealers buy that way) there is no difference whatever. The difference per vehicle between carload shipment and single shipment is very small indeed. It is not one-fourth the smallest profit that is usually made by the local dealer. When you buy from the dealer he adds the freight to the manufacturer's price and that makes the net cost to him; then to this cost he will add anywhere from $20.00 to $40.00 as his profit. That you may be able to tell within a very small amount what the freight will be to almost any place in the United States we give freight to a few principal points in every state and territory in the Union (see page 147) on a single top buggy and on an open single seat road wagon or runabout. Do not say you live too far away to order a carriage from us for the freight is not as much as you may think. We agree positively to save you money with the freight added to our price and you need not accept the shipment if you do not feel you have saved money. If you are at all in doubt about the freight write us and we will tell you just what we will guarantee the freight to be on any style or styles you may be thinking of buying.

Our Two Years Warranty

Our vehicles and harness are fully warranted for two years, and if anything gives out within that length of time, caused by any imperfection in workmanship or material, we will make it good, free of expense to you. Our guarantee is very broad and liberal. We are always ready and willing to do the fair thing by our customers when any imperfection in workmanship or material develops, even though the time limit on our guarantee has expired. We send a two-year signed guarantee by mail with every shipment. Our vehicles very seldom cause the user trouble, and the chances for repairs are always small. We want our customers to write us, however, whenever they have what they feel is a just cause for complaint, for it is our desire at all times to have everyone with whom we deal perfectly satisfied.

Had we not followed a policy of using good honest material throughout in the construction of our vehicles and employed the best workmen possible to secure, we would not have succeeded as we have and established the reputation we enjoy today as manufacturers of high grade vehicles. If there is any question regarding any piece or part used in the construction of our vehicles or regarding our system of manufacturing that is not made clear in the following description of material and manufacture, do not hesitate to write us.

Bodies and Seats

We do not buy our bodies and seats from outside body manufacturers as most builders of vehicles do, but we have a large, modern equipped wood working machinery department and body shop where we build every body and seat used in the construction of our work. We are not, therefore, obliged to use styles of bodies and seats that are the same as those used by other manufacturers, but we have our own designers and we design our own styles and they are distinctive. We guarantee our bodies and seats to be much better constructed throughout than those made by most exclusive body and seat manufacturers. We have in our body department workmen who have been with us from 20 to 30 years, and they are all skilled mechanics. We use none but high grade thoroughly seasoned stock in the construction of our bodies and seats and they are all well glued, screwed, plugged and ironed, and guaranteed absolutely not to open at the joints, no matter in what climate used.

Gears

Our gear woods are all made from thoroughly seasoned, straight grain white hickory. We use the best grades and styles of wrought fifth wheels for our different styles. Our axles are fine steel, bell collar, dust proof long distance pattern, with groove and felt oil pad. Axle beds are selected straight grain hickory, securely cemented and clipped to axles, and when they are smoothed up for painting the axle and the wood bed are the same as one piece. On all driving wagons, buggies, Stanhopes, traps, surreys and carriages we use fine oil tempered French pattern open head springs, which are especially graded for the different style vehicles they are used on, and are soft and very easy riding. All reaches are fine straight grain hickory, and they are thoroughly well ironed and braced. Stanhope reaches, buggy reaches and runabout reaches have channel reach irons and they are bolted and well braced. Wrought Bailey loops are used on runabouts, top buggies, etc. We furnish on nearly all vehicles the celebrated Bradley quick shifting shaft coupler, which is one of the most popular and most successful couplers on the market. It is a quick shifting coupler in the true sense of the word, because all that is

necessary to make the change from pole to shafts is the hand. This is the coupler that is used on high grade work.

The gear is one of the most important parts of a vehicle, and it has always been our aim to make our gears in a thoroughly substantial manner and at the same time have them neat and trim in appearance. All steps, clips, bolts, etc., are the best grades and in keeping with the style of the vehicle.

Pole and Shafts

Our poles and shafts are made from thoroughly seasoned straight grain hickory. They are the correct shapes for the different styles of vehicles they are used on, and are well ironed and braced throughout. All poles, except for spring wagons, etc., are equipped with nickel neck yoke tips and pole tip. All carriage, surrey, Stanhope, buggy and driving wagon shafts are full patent leather trimmed with long patent leather tips. We take a great deal of pains in our pole and shaft department to have these parts well made and neatly finished and trimmed.

Wheels

Our wheels are all made from fine selected straight grain white hickory. We specify the style of wheels used on the different styles listed in the catalog, but give choice of either Sarven patent or banded hub, as you will notice. Most companies make an additional charge for the banded hub style, but we have an arrangement with our wheel factory which enables us to furnish the banded hub style at the same price as the Sarven patent, and we give our customers the benefit of this advantage. The Sarven patent wheel is considered by many users the most substantial wheel. It has sixteen spokes, while the banded hub has fourteen spokes. The wheel is the life of the vehicle, and we consider the tiring of the wheel one of the most important features of wheel construction. In tiring our wheels we pay special attention to the dish as it is very important that wheels be properly dished. Our steel tire is the round edge planished tire, and our channel tire for rubber tired wheels the standard section channel steel. Our tires are all set hot by hand and not by machine; they are bolted between every spoke and the felloes have screws through them on each side of every spoke. Every wheel that leaves our factory is fully warranted for two years.

Trimmings and Upholstering

These are important features in the construction of first class vehicles. It is very important in the first place that the fabrics used in trimming seats and tops be made of the right quality of wool. Our all wool broadcloths are the grade made to withstand hard usage. They are guaranteed absolutely fast color. Our whipcords are all the best patterns and good heavy unfading fabrics. When leather is ordered instead of all wool broadcloth, we use fine, soft, genuine trimming leather at the additional charges specified in descriptions. Cushions and backs are upholstered with the best of material, including hair and felt with the finest grade upholstering springs in both cushion and back. Seat ends are always trimmed to match cushion and back. Every vehicle listed in our catalog has all the necessary extras to make it a complete finished vehicle, such as carpet, apron, boot, etc., as you will find upon referring to the different descriptions of our styles.

Tops

Our buggy tops and surrey extension tops are made of good material. throughout. We use only nice, soft, pliable enameled top leather. The rubber used in our leather quarter and full rubber tops is the best make known and is heavier than is used by most other companies. We take pride in the construction of our tops because the top can spoil the appearance of the buggy or improve it wonderfully as a complete vehicle. On all our rubber tops and leather quarter tops we use the finest enamel steel bows we can secure; also the finest enameled joints, and our buggy tops can all be removed from the seats, to which they are attached with shifting rails.

On full leather tops with leather covered bows, we use the finest leather covered sockets made. The side curtains on leather tops, unless ordered leather, are made of heavy rubber. We are also using one of the best pattern curtain roll up straps made, although these straps do not show just as they are on all our different styles. Our tops are always lined to match cushion and back. Canopy top used on surreys are lined with the same color material as the seats, and the fringe matches the trimming. All canopy tops have finely enameled standards and are complete with side curtains all around, and storm apron.

Painting

We employ in our paint shop none but skilled painters. Our foremen in these departments have been with us for 25 years. In fact, we have a good many men in this department who have been with us for years, and they are all skilled workmen in the different positions they fill. We use the best and most durable system of painting known. We have ample capacity in our large factories to enable us to carry the work in our paint department the length of time it should be carried. Each coat is therefore treated properly and given the required length of time to season before another coat is applied. The filler coats are properly rubbed down so that all surfaces are perfectly smooth before the different color varnish coats are put on. The different color varnish coats are rubbed down with powdered pumice and each coat of color varnish is made perfectly smooth before another coat is applied. Finally the last rubbing varnish coat is rubbed down and all surfaces are polished and made perfectly smooth for the last coat of finishing varnish. We use high grade material from the foundation coats to the last finishing coat and we guarantee our painting high grade.

OUR REFERENCES

Our thirty-six years of business success has made us so well and favorably known throughout the United States that we feel it almost unnecessary to give references. However, for the benefit of anyone not acquainted with us and our manner of doing business, we publish the following bankers' testimonial and refer you to these banks:

"The proprietors of the Elkhart Carriage & Harness Manufacturing Company are personally known to the undersigned, and are thoroughly reliable, straightforward business men. Anyone is safe in sending them money in advance. They have built up a very large business during the past thirty-six years by their fair method of dealing."

W. H. KNICKERBOCKER,   W. S. HAZLETON,   CHAS. T. GREENE.
Cashier First National Bank, Elkhart.   Cashier St. Joseph Valley Bank, Elkhart.   Cashier First State Bank, Elkhart.
HOWARD H. HITCHCOCK, Vice-President First National Bank, Chicago.

We also refer you to our commercial rating in the R. G. Dun & Co.'s or Bradstreet's Reference Books.

INDEX

THE ABOVE PICTURE ILLUSTRATES OUR FACTORY NO. 1 ON BEARDSLEY AVENUE, ELKHART, IND.

THE ABOVE PICTURE ILLUSTRATES OUR FACTORY NO. 2 ON PRATT STREET, ELKHART, IND.

WE ARE THE LARGEST MANUFACTURERS OF VEHICLES AND HARNESS IN
THE WORLD SELLING EXCLUSIVELY TO THE CONSUMER

RUBBER TIRES

Our experience has taught us that it is economy for both manufacturer and consumer to use the best grade rubber tires that it is possible to buy. We have watched this rubber tire problem closely for a number of years, and we hold today the same opinion that we have always held that in the long run, the most economical rubber tire to buy is the best grade made, even though the price at first is a little higher than for a second grade tire. We have done some experimenting during past years and know positively that a good rubber tire is worth three or four times as much as a poor tire.

With the manufacturer who wants to use the highest grade tires possible, it is a matter of knowing where to get them and then paying the extra price for high grade rubber. We are using the Goodyear celebrated wing tire, which is high grade and should be sold at higher prices than we are charging. We do not, however, consider it policy to list two grades of rubber tire, as some companies do, and under the circumstances have figured our prices just about the same as is usually charged for medium grade tires. We do not want our customers to take any chances on a second grade tire, and therefore give them the benefit of these low prices on the high grade Goodyear wing tire. A cheap tire will rarely wear over a year. A high grade tire will give good service for several years and are easily worth, from an investment standpoint, from two to four times as much as a cheap tire.

We have, as stated above, done some experimenting with rubber tires, as have all manufacturers, but we can safely say now that as long as we are in the vehicle business we will not try to use a medium grade tire, and if you will take our advice you will never buy a low priced rubber tire.

Although our prices on this fine Goodyear wing tire are as low as usually charged for second grade tire, we feel that if we give you the best grade rubber tire made, at lower prices than other manufacturers, it is an additional inducement for you to give us your order. Our warranty on tires is broad and liberal. Every set that we send out is fully warranted for one year, and if a tire shows no defects and is not worn down enough to seem defective within a year after put in use, you can rest assured that they are good for several years of satisfactory service. The wing feature of this tire is a good one as it prevents sand and pebbles from working in between the tire and the side of the channel, which often occurs on the ordinary tire, and thus injures the rubber.

While we recommend the Goodyear wing tire over all others, we will gladly furnish any other make of tire that may be preferred at the same price as quoted on the high grade wing tire. Remember, rubber tires lengthen materially the life of a vehicle. They are considered today almost a necessity to the completion of a pleasure vehicle.

PRICES ON GOODYEAR WING SOLID RUBBER TIRES:

On ¾ inch wheels per set of four tires	$13.00
On ⅞ inch wheels per set of four tires	15.00
On 1 inch wheels per set of four tires	17.50
On 1⅛ inch wheels per set of four tires	22.50

CUSHION TIRES

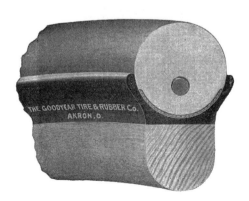

Our cushion tires are of the Goodyear make and are of the same high grade quality as the solid wing tire. This cushion tire is constructed under special patents owned exclusively by the Goodyear company. It is made, as you will see from the illustration, with the hole for the retaining wire below the center, thus giving more wearing surface and making this particular cushion tire superior to the ordinary style, which has the hole through the center. Our cushion tires are fully warranted, the same as our solid wing tire, and you can be assured if a tire shows no defects within a year from the time it is put in use it will give you several years of satisfactory service. We guarantee these tires to give the best of satisfaction in every respect. One-inch cushion tire is used largely on high wheeled buggies, where the wheels are 40 inches front and 44 inches rear, and the 1⅛-inch cushion tires on bike gear buggies with lower wheels.

PRICES ON GOODYEAR CUSHION TIRES:

1 inch cushion tires per set of four	$17.50
1⅛ inch cushion tires per set of four	20.00

Bradley Couplers

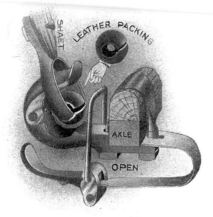

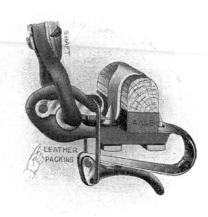

The accompanying illustrations show the Bradley Quick Shifting Pole and Shaft Coupler. This is acknowledged by all as the most satisfactory quick shifting shaft coupler made. The hand is all that is required with this coupler to change from pole to shafts or vice versa. Often it is very convenient if shafts can be taken out of the buggy after it has been run in the shed, and with the Bradley couplers the shafts can be removed in an instant. There are leather bushings, as illustration shows, and this bushing forms a perfect anti-rattler. The coupler takes up its own wear. You will find upon investigation that the Bradley Quick Change Shaft Coupler is the style coupler that is used everywhere on first class work. We furnish, as you will see from our descriptions, Bradley couplers on nearly all vehicles.

Our Dust Proof Bell Collar Long Distance Axle

This illustration shows our dust proof bell collar long distance axle which has groove in the spindle for felt oil pad. These spindles are absolutely dust proof and are long distance in every sense of the term. They are made from the best of axle steel and warranted in every way.

Timken Roller Bearing Axles

We are prepared to offer our customers the celebrated Timken Roller Bearing Axle at very low prices. While at these prices they may seem somewhat of a luxury, we would say to those who prefer a roller bearing axle to the regular dust proof long distance axle, that the Timken Axle is the king of all roller bearing axles. It is simple and durable, noiseless and dust proof and reduces the draft fully 50 per cent.

These axles are covered with our two years' warranty, as well as the binding two years' guarantee given by the Timken Axle Co.

We furnish these axles on any of our vehicles instead of the regular axles at the following extra charges:

For 7/8-inch and 1-inch axles on open driving wagons, top buggies, Stanhopes, phaetons and spiders..........$15.00
For 1 1/16-inch axles on surreys, etc...................... 16.25
For 1 1/8-inch axles 17.50

Sarven Patent and Banded Hub Wheels

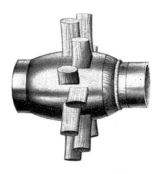

The illustration to the right shows our Sarven patent wheel hub. A good many users consider the Sarven patent wheel the most durable wheel made. It has 16 spokes while the banded hub has 14.

The illustration to the left shows our banded wheel hub. Our wheels are all made from selected straight grain white hickory, and are fully warranted for two years.

Banded Hub Wheel

Sarven Patent Wheel

Combination Storm Protector and Rain Apron

A Protector That Protects

This protector can be used as a regular storm apron as well as storm front. During ordinary rainy weather the storm front part of the Protector is rolled down to the hooks which attach the apron to the bow, and buckles under the apron with small straps. It is always convenient to be unrolled and attached to top in case of severe storm. It is attached to the top by two hooks placed in the bow and there are metal eyelets in the Protector which attach to these hooks. We furnish extra large Protectors for phaetons and Stanhopes.

In putting on the Storm Protector, all that is necessary is to place the apron on the dash, hook the storm curtain to the top and then fasten the side hooks to the bows. It can be put on in a few seconds. It is made from good heavy rubber and all corners are reinforced.

Price for Storm Protector complete, $2.50. Extra when furnished with one of our buggies in place of the regular storm apron which is priced with the buggy, $1.50.

Screwed Rims

The felloes, or rims, on all our wheels are screwed on either side of each spoke, as shown in cut above. This prevents the rims from checking or splitting at the spokes, which is often the case where the rims do not have screws in them. The screws do not show after the wheels are painted.

Steel Tire

The above cut shows our round edge planished steel tire You will note that the edges on this tire oval enough to pro ject over the sides of the felloe and thus protect the felloe.

Handy Style Top

The above illustration shows what is known as the Handy style buggy top. This illustration represents the 2½ bow top. We furnish 3½ bow if desired. We can furnish this top on any of our top buggies instead of the regular style top without extra charge.

Cately Top Lever

The above cut shows the location of the Cately lever for throwing the top back, also the self-acting spring which lowers the top gradually. This device enables you to lower the top while the side curtains are on and without getting up from the seat. Our additional charge for Cately top levers on top buggies is $1.00.

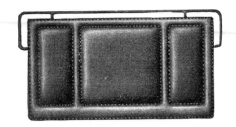

Special Dash with Line Rail

This illustration shows our straight four bar padded dash with fine japanned line rail with hand holds. This rail is made solid with the regular dash frame and is therefore a part of the dash. We furnish it on any of our piano body buggies instead of regular dashes without additional charge.

Padded Dash

Roller Rub Iron

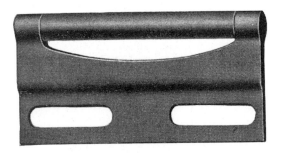

The above cut illustrates the style roller rub iron we use on piano bodies. On surreys, phaetons, etc., we have to use different styles of iron suitable for the different style vehicles. We furnish roller rub irons on almost every vehicle we make, as you will notice upon referring to our detailed descriptions.

The above cut illustrates one of our padded wing piano body buggy dashes. The patent leather on unpadded dashes invariably bags or sags, making a very bad looking dash. A padded dash will hold its shape for years and look well. It is practically impossible for the patent leather in a good padded dash to sag. You will note from our descriptions that all of our dashes are padded.

Fifth Wheel

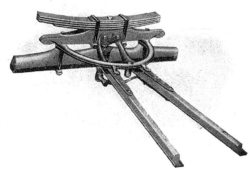

The above cut shows our fine full circle wrought Brewster slotted fifth wheel, which is one of the ear marks of quality on all high grade buggies. This fifth wheel has the regulation style clip king bolt, which does not pass through the axle but clips around it and goes through the head block into the spring.

We use this fine wrought Brewster fifth wheel on Stanhopes, top buggies, open driving wagons, etc., as you will see upon referring to our descriptions. It is one of the finest full circle wrought fifth wheels made, and is the style wheel used by all high grade builders. There is absolutely no better fifth wheel made. On all surreys with single reaches, we use the regulation heft single reach full circle wrought surrey fifth wheel.

Channel Reach Iron

STEEL CHANNEL PLATE

The above illustration represents our channel reach iron which is the style reach iron we use on all Stanhopes, top buggies, open driving wagons, etc., as per descriptions in catalog. These reach irons are bolted full length and all reaches are well braced.

Three Prong Step

The above cut illustrates our fine three prong step. This is one of the best style steps made.

Axles

The five illustrations of axles represent the different styles of axles used on our buggies, driving wagons, Stanhopes, etc.

No. 1 is our regulation slightly arched buggy axle.

No. 2 is the new style true sweep arched axle which arches just a little more than No. 1.

No. 3 is our regulation drop style axle which is very popular in many localities and especially with users who prefer a buggy hung a little lower than with arched axles.

No. 4 is the new style true sweep bike axle which is one of the most popular bike style axles made.

No. 5 is the Roman bike style axle which is called by some the naked axle as it has only short wood beds in the center, as illustration shows. The wood beds used on all these axles are made from selected white hickory and when they are smoothed up for finishing the axle and the bed are the same as one piece.

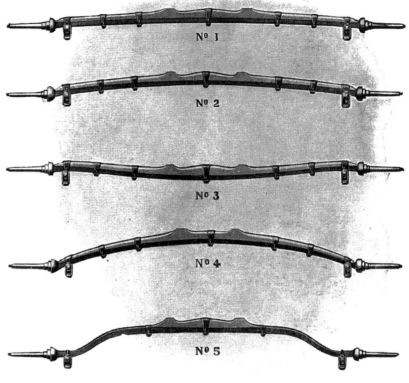

High Grade Steel Wire Wheels

Furnished on any of our Bike Gears

The accompanying illustration shows our fine high grade steel wire wheel. These wheels are made from the finest of steel. The rims are made from steel especially rolled for this style wheel. The spokes are made from fine Swedish steel rods imported especially for this make of wheel. We guarantee our wire wheels to be high grade in quality of material and workmanship throughout. We furnish these wheels on any of our top buggies or open driving wagons which are regular with bike style gears, complete with 1⅛-inch guaranteed cushion rubber tires for $25.00 additional charge to the price quoted with wood wheels and steel tires. On surreys and traps with bike gears, $27.50 additional charge, including 1⅛-inch cushion tires, to the price quoted with wood wheels and steel tires.

Ball Bearing Wheel

If ball bearing wire wheels are preferred to the long distance, the extra charge for the ball bearing over the additional charges quoted above is $10.00.

W. S. Shuler Patent Roller Bearing Spring

We regularly use the Shuler Roller Bearing Spring on our No. 329 Buckboard, page 40, and No. 953 Top Buggy, page 85, and can furnish them on any of our buggies in place of the regular end springs without additional charge. A good many users prefer this spring over others, as they consider them the easiest riding springs made. They are made from the highest grade material, and are guaranteed not to break during the life of the vehicle, and to give perfect satisfaction. We can unhesitatingly recommend this spring, if something of this style is preferred to the end spring.

ROLLER BEARING

Money Saved is Money Made.

Edinburg, Ill., April 10, 1908.
Elkhart Carriage & Harness Mfg. Co., Elkhart, Ind.,
Gentlemen:—Received top buggy in good condition and am more than pleased with same, and believe that I have saved $25.00 by buying from your company.
Thanking you for your prompt delivery, I remain,
Yours truly, IRWIN REIMER.

Caledonia, Mich., April 3, 1908.
Elkhart Carriage & Harness Mfg. Co., Elkhart, Ind.,
Gentlemen:—I received my buggy and harness all in good condition today and am well pleased with them. Think I saved at least $30.00 on same.
Please accept my thanks.
Yours truly, WELLINGTON BERGY,

Neosho, Wis., June 11, 1908.
Elkhart Carriage & Harness Mfg. Co., Elkhart, Ind.,
Gentlemen:—I received surrey in fine shape and am more than pleased. I am sure that I saved about $35.00 in ordering from you. I remain,
Yours truly, GEO. BERTZ.

Nace, Va., June 1, 1908.
Elkhart Carriage & Harness Mfg. Co., Elkhart, Ind.,
Gentlemen:—I received my buggy and harness all O. K. May 8th and many thanks for your promptness.
I consider that I just saved $25.00 on my buggy and $8.00 on my harness according to what our local dealers are selling for around here, and besides having one of the best and nicest buggies in this locality. Everything is exactly as I ordered and better than I expected or you claimed.
Thanking you again, I am yours for future business,
C. L. SIFFORD.

Houston, Tex., June 29, 1908.
Elkhart Carriage & Harness Mfg. Co., Elkhart, Ind.,
Gentlemen:—The goods ordered of you to be shipped to San Angelo arrived here on the 24th inst. and I must say that I am more than pleased, as the same buggy here would cost me almost double, and harness, too. In fact, a friend of mine saw me put it together and I asked him for an estimate of what it cost me. He guessed $225.00, and when I told him the whole outfit cost me $87.60 he was amazed.
I thank you very much for the promptness in handling the order and assure you of my desire to be commanded if I can serve you. I remain,
Yours truly, G. M. BRITAIN.
2014 Jackson Street.

New Weston, Ohio, March 2, 1908.
Elkhart Carriage & Harness Mfg. Co., Elkhart, Ind.,
Gentlemen:—Since nearly a year's use of one of your buggies I find that it is just as represented and have found that you will do all and even more than you say. I know that I saved more than $25.00 by buying from you, and wish you future success.
Yours truly, A. F. McCLANNAN.

Batavia, N. Y., May 20, 1908.
Elkhart Carriage & Harness Mfg. Co., Elkhart, Ind.,
Gentlemen:—I received my buggy this morning and am well pleased with it. I think I saved $30.00 by ordering from you.
Thanking you for your prompt shipment, I remain,
Yours very truly, EDWIN D. PATTERSON.

Charlestown, W. Va., May 1, 1908.
Elkhart Carriage & Harness Mfg. Co., Elkhart, Ind.,
Gentlemen:—My buggy arrived all O. K. in fine condition. I am well pleased with it. I am safe in saying I saved $25.00 by placing my order with you.
Please accept my sincere thanks for your prompt shipment, and if I ever need anything in your line of business you can rest assured of my order.
Yours respectfully, C. PRESTON ENGLE.

Sandford, Ind., June 11, 1908.
Elkhart Carriage & Harness Mfg. Co., Elkhart, Ind.,
Gentlemen:—I received the buggy on the 5th and it proved out very well. I am well pleased with it and am sure I saved $25.00 on the buggy and I will recommend it to my friends.
Yours truly, ALBERT PIPER.
R. F. D. No. 1.

Lime Springs, Ia., June 1, 1908.
Elkhart Carriage & Harness Mfg. Co., Elkhart, Ind.,
Gentlemen:—I received the buggy which you shipped me. It reached here in good shape. I am well pleased with same and think that I have saved $25.00 in ordering from you.
Yours truly, M. H. JONES.
P. S.—I will do all that I can to advertise your goods.

Once a Customer Always a Customer. There are Reasons for this.

Stittville, N. Y., May 18, 1908.
Elkhart Carriage & Harness Mfg. Co., Elkhart, Ind.,
Gentlemen:—I received the buggy all right and am very much pleased with it. We think it is all right. If I can help you in any way I will do so. My brother-in-law, John Whitaker, bought a buggy of you a few years ago and it is a good buggy yet. We are all perfectly satisfied.
Yours respectfully, MR. CHAS. JEPSON.

Norway, Ia., April 9, 1908.
Elkhart Carriage & Harness Mfg. Co., Elkhart, Ind.,
Gentlemen:—We received the buggy and harness all O. K. and are very much pleased with them. This is the third buggy and also harness we have received from you and we have saved money on all of them.
Thanking you very much for your prompt shipment, we remain,
Yours truly, MRS. LEONARD BRECHT.

Clinton, Ind., March 30, 1908.
Elkhart Carriage & Harness Mfg. Co., Elkhart, Ind.,
Gentlemen:—I received the top buggy on the 28th inst. and am more than well pleased. I know that your vehicles have the timber in them for there are five of them in my neighborhood that convinced me to let you have my order by their durability and style.
Yours truly, W. G. CAMPBELL.

Table Grove, Ill., June 26, 1908.
Elkhart Carriage & Harness Mfg. Co., Elkhart, Ind.,
Gentlemen:—I received my rig last Monday and was well pleased with it. This is my second Elkhart rig and I like them both.
Yours respectfully, OTIS F. MERRITT.

Hartford Pa., July 1, 1908.
Elkhart Carriage & Harness Mfg. Co., Elkhart, Ind.,
Gentlemen:—I received your shipment of June 22d of wagon and have found it all O. K. I would also say that all the vehicles and harness I have had from your firm have been perfectly satisfactory.
Very respectfully yours, LELAND A. WILLIAMS.

Kewanee, Ill., March 3, 1908.
Elkhart Carriage & Harness Mfg. Co., Elkhart, Ind.,
Gentlemen:—Harness received in due time. Am well satisfied. It is what I wanted. I think this is the fourth harness and about 25 or 30 halters and one surrey and can't complain of any deal I have had with firm as yet.
Best regards and well wishes to your firm.
Yours truly, J. H. HADSELL.

Grand Rivers, Ky., January 9, 1908.
Elkhart Carriage & Harness Mfg. Co., Elkhart, Ind.,
Gentlemen:—I have just received your spring wagon. I find it to be just the style and weight in every particular that I ordered. As this is the third wagon bought of you I may be considered partial to your duplex gear.
Thanking you for your courteous treatment, I beg to remain,
Yours truly, JOSEPH M. CHAUDET.

Milwaukee, Wis., July 25, 1908.
Elkhart Carriage & Harness Mfg. Co., Elkhart, Ind.,
Gentlemen:—The Physician's Stanhope bought of you came to hand yesterday and was found just as represented in every way. The work is first class even to the minutest detail, a thing which is characteristic of the Elkhart make. This is the third rig bought of you, the other two are still in first class shape.
Thanking you for your fairness, we beg to remain,
Yours truly, DRS. ROSENHEIMER.

Natchez, Miss., March 26, 1908.
Elkhart Carriage & Harness Mfg. Co., Elkhart, Ind.,
Gentlemen:—I take this method to inform you that my buggy reached me in good condition, and to say that I am well pleased with the job is to express it mildly. If it proves as durable as the one I bought of you a few years ago I will be satisfied. Everybody who has seen it admires it very much.
Respectfully, A. W. DUMAS, M. D.

Andover, N. Y., July 21, 1908.
Elkhart Carriage & Harness Mfg. Co., Elkhart, Ind.,
Gentlemen:—The driving wagon received in good shape. If it proves to be as good as the surrey and covered buggy that I bought of you eight years ago I shall be well pleased with it.
Yours truly, S. MEAD.

The above cut illustrates No. 201 which is the same as No. 200, only it has canopy top instead of extension top. Price of No. 201, with canopy top, $20.00 less than No. 200.

No. 200—FINE LEATHER TOP CABRIOLET WITH LEATHER COVERED BOWS

PRICE
- Cash with order with steel tires and pole or shafts.........................$190.00
- C. O. D. with steel tires and pole or shafts................................195.00
- Cash with order with 1-inch guaranteed rubber tires and pole or shafts........207.50
- C. O. D with 1-inch guaranteed rubber tires and pole or shafts...............212.50

No. 200 is one of the best selling carriages we have ever made. It is one of the finest styles to be found anywhere and is strictly first class both in quality of workmanship and material throughout. We are very glad to ship No. 200 for examination and approval with the understanding that it is to be considered all we claim and you are to feel you are saving $50.00, or we will take the shipment back at our expense and you will be nothing out. This carriage gives our patrons entire satisfaction, we can unhesitatingly recommend it.

BODY—Is one of the finest style carriage bodies made. We use in the construction of this body high grade stock throughout. Seats are very roomy and comfortable and have good high backs. There is plenty of room between the seats, making it easy to get into and out of rear seat. There are heavy steel sill or rocker plates laid in white lead and screwed full length of sills.

GEAR—1¹⁄₈-inch dust proof bell collar long distance axles, with felt oil pads. The front axle drops slightly as picture shows and has wood axle bed cemented and fully clipped to axle. Rear axle is coach pattern. Springs are fine oil tempered French pattern open head, well graded and easy riding. Reach is ironed full length on bottom and sides and is well bolted and braced. Fine full circle wrought carriage fifth wheel. Bradley quick shifting shaft couplers, which are the best quick shifting couplers made and are used on all high grade work. Regulation carriage shafts made from selected straight grain white hickory, full patent leather trimmed with 36-inch tips. Pole, regulation carriage style made from selected straight grain white hickory properly ironed and braced, with nickel pole tip and neck yoke tips. We furnish both pole and shafts for $5.00 extra.

WHEELS—Fine selected straight grain white hickory, 1-inch banded hub style, equipped with 1-inch round edge planished steel tire which is bolted between every spoke. Tires are ¼-inch thick and are set hot by hand and not by machine. Felloes have screws through them on each side of every spoke which insures them

against checking at the spokes. Wheels are 36 inches front, 47 inches rear, which is the correct height for this style carriage. We furnish Sarven patent style wheels if preferred to the banded hub, but the banded hub is what is used almost entirely on work of this style and grade.

TRIMMINGS—Seats are trimmed with fine dark green all wool broadcloth, guaranteed absolutely fast color. We will trim with fine dark blue all wool broadcloth or whipcord, if preferred. The ends of seats are pleated and trimmed to match cushions and backs, and both cushions and backs are upholstered with hair and upholstering springs, and the seats are very comfortable and easy riding. We furnish special colors in broadcloth trimmings, if desired, at a small additional charge. Fine genuine leather trimmings in dark green, maroon or russet instead of broadcloth trimmings, $5.00 extra. Fine full padded patent leather wing dash. Oil burner lamps and velvet carpets.

TOP—Fine full leather top with very best leather covered bow sockets. Heavy rubber side curtains and storm apron. Top is lined with all wool broadcloth to match seat trimmings. We furnish No. 200 with canopy top, as shown by small cut in corner of page, for $20.00 less than with leather extension top.

PAINTING—The body is black; gear, Brewster green, correctly striped. We will furnish New York red gear or make any changes in painting desired. Our painting is all fully guaranteed. For system of painting, see page 5.

13

The above cut shows No. 203 without top. Price $15.00 less than with top.

No. 203—FINE DEEP PANEL, CANOPY TOP, CUT-UNDER SURREY

PRICE

Cash with order, with steel tires and pole or shafts..........................$147.00
C. O. D., with steel tires and pole or shafts................................ 150.00
Cash with order, with 1-inch guaranteed rubber tires and pole or shafts....... 164.50
C. O. D., with 1-inch guaranteed rubber tires and pole or shafts.............. 167.50

No. 203 is one of the most stylish and up-to-date surreys we have ever made. It is very fine throughout; is well proportioned, light running and most comfortable riding. We are glad of an opportunity to ship No. 203 for examination and approval, and if it is not found all we claim and considered as good as usually sells for $40.00 to $50.00 more than our price, it may be returned at our expense.

BODY—Is one of the finest cut-under surrey bodies made. Seats are well shaped, have high backs and are very comfortable. We use high grade stock throughout in the construction of this body and it is made in a manner that insures perfect satisfaction. There are heavy steel sill or rocker plates laid in white lead and screwed full length of sills and over the wheel house.

GEAR—1 $\frac{1}{8}$-inch dust proof bell collar long-distance axles, with felt oil pads. Axles are fitted with selected straight grain white hickory beds, which are cemented and fully clipped full length of axles. When these axle beds are finished up the beds and axles are the same as one piece. Fine oil tempered French pattern open head springs, well graded and very easy riding. Reach is well ironed full length, bolted and properly braced. Fine full circle wrought surrey fifth wheel. Bradley quick shifting shaft couplers, which are the best quick shifting couplers on the market, and are used on all high grade work. Roller rub irons. Regulation cut-under surrey shafts made from straight grain selected hickory, full patent leather trimmed with long 36-inch tips. Pole is made from fine selected straight grain hickory, well ironed and properly braced, has nickel pole tip and nickel neck yoke tips. Both pole and shafts, $5.00 extra.

WHEELS—Fine selected straight grain white hickory, 1-inch banded hub style, 36 inches front and 44 inches rear, equipped with 1-inch round edge planished steel tire which is bolted between every spoke. Tires are set hot by hand and not by machine. Felloes have screws through them on each side of every spoke, which insures them against checking at the spokes. The wheels we regularly furnish are the correct height for this style gear, but

we can lower the height of wheels, if desired. They could not be raised without there being danger of the front wheels striking the wheel house in turning and the rear wheels the fenders. We also furnish Sarven patent wheels instead of banded hub, if preferred.

TRIMMINGS—Seats are trimmed with fine dark green all wool broadcloth, guaranteed fast color. We will trim with fine dark blue all wool broadcloth or fine whipcord, if preferred. The ends of the seats are pleated and trimmed to match the cushions and backs, and both cushions and backs are upholstered with hair and fine upholstering springs. They are very comfortable and most easy riding. We can furnish special colors in broadcloth trimmings, if desired, at a small additional charge. Fine genuine leather trimmings, in dark green, maroon or russet instead of broadcloth, $5.00 extra. Fine full padded dash. Velvet carpet in bottom of body, or rubber mat, if preferred to the carpet. Oil burner lamps.

TOP—Fine canopy top style, lined with all wool broadcloth to match seat trimmings, and with fine fringe all around. Standards are finely enameled. There are heavy rubber side curtains all around, also heavy rubber storm apron for the dash. We furnish No. 203 equipped with fine leather quarter extension top instead of canopy top for $10.00 additional charge. We also furnish it without top, as shown by small cut in corner of page, and the price is $15.00 less than with canopy top.

PAINTING—Body is finely finished in black, correctly striped; gear, Brewster green, properly striped. We will make any changes in color of painting desired. For system of painting, see page 5.

The above cut illustrates No. 211 with leather quarter extension top and hung on three spring gear instead of two spring. We furnish three spring gear under No. 211 for $5.00 additional charge. Leather quarter extension top, instead of canopy top, $10.00 additional charge. If full rubber extension top is desired, the extra charge is $5.00.

No. 211—FINE FULL PANEL, CANOPY TOP, CUT-UNDER SURREY

PRICE
- Cash with order, with steel tires and pole or shafts..........................$132.00
- C. O. D., with steel tires and pole or shafts.................................. 135.00
- Cash with order, with 1-inch guaranteed rubber tires and pole or shafts....... 149.50
- C. O. D., with 1-inch guaranteed rubber tires and pole or shafts.............. 152.50

Our No. 211 is a very desirable style full panel cut-under surrey. It has become a very popular seller with us and is made in the same grade and style throughout as usually sells for $30.00 to $40.00 more than our price. We are glad of an opportunity to ship this surrey for examination and approval with the understanding that it is to be found all we claim and satisfactory in every respect, or it may be returned at our expense.

BODY—Is one of the best full panel cut-under designs we have ever made. The panels are in one piece from the arms to the sills, permitting of a fine effect in finishing. We use in the construction of this body high grade stock throughout and every piece is fully warranted. There are heavy steel sill or rocker plates laid in white lead and screwed full length of sills.

GEAR—$1\frac{1}{16}$-inch dust proof bell collar long distance axles, with felt oil pads. Axles are fitted with selected straight grain white hickory beds, which are cemented and fully clipped full length of axles. When these axle beds are finished up the beds and axles are the same as one piece. Fine oil tempered French pattern open head springs, well graded and very easy riding. Reach is well ironed full length, bolted and properly braced. Fine full circle wrought surrey fifth wheel. Bradley quick shifting shaft couplers, which are the best quick shifting couplers on the market and are used on all high grade work. Roller rub irons. Regulation cut-under surrey shafts, made from straight grain selected hickory, full patent leather trimmed with long 36-inch tips. Pole is made from fine selected straight grain hickory, well ironed and properly braced, has nickel pole tip and nickel neck yoke tips. Both pole and shafts, $5.00 extra.

WHEELS—Fine selected straight grain white hickory, 1-inch banded hub style, 36 inches front and 44 inches rear, equipped with 1-inch round edge planished steel tire which is bolted between every spoke. Tires are set hot by hand and not by machine. Felloes have screws through them on each side of every spoke, which insures them against checking at the spokes. The wheels we regu-

larly furnish are the correct height for this style gear, but we can lower the height of wheels, if desired. They could not be raised without there being danger of the front wheels striking the wheel house in turning and the rear wheels the fenders. We also furnish Sarven patent wheels instead of banded hub, if preferred.

TRIMMINGS—Seats are trimmed with fine dark green all wool broadcloth, guaranteed fast color. We will trim with fine dark blue all wool broadcloth or fine whipcord, if preferred. The ends of the seats are pleated and trimmed to match the cushions and backs, and both cushions and backs are upholstered with hair and fine upholstering springs. They are very comfortable and most easy riding. We can furnish special colors in broadcloth trimmings, if desired, at a small additional charge. Fine genuine leather trimmings in dark green, maroon or russet instead of broadcloth, $5.00 extra. Fine full padded dash. Velvet carpet in bottom of body, or rubber mat is preferred to the carpet. Oil burner lamps.

TOP—Fine canopy top style, lined with all wool broadcloth to match seat trimmings, and with fine fringe all around. Standards are finely enameled. There are heavy rubber side curtains all around, also heavy rubber storm apron for the dash. We furnish No. 203 equipped with fine leather quarter extension top instead of canopy top for $10.00 additional charge.

PAINTING—Body is finely finished in black, correctly striped; gear, Brewster green, properly striped. We will make any changes in color of painting desired. For system of painting, see page 5.

15

The above cut shows No. 213 with leather quarter extension style top. Our price with extension top is $10.00 more than with canopy top.

No. 213—FINE CUT-UNDER SURREY, WITH SPECIAL AUTO STYLE SEATS

PRICE
{ Cash with order, with steel tires and pole or shafts..........................$122.50
C. O. D., with steel tires and pole or shafts.................................. 125.00
Cash with order, with 1-inch guaranteed rubber tires and pole or shafts....... 140.00
C. O. D., with 1-inch guaranteed rubber tires and pole or shafts.............. 142.50

Our No. 213 is an up-to-date style surrey. It is made in our best grade throughout and is equal in quality of workmanship and material to similar surreys sold by others for $35.00 to $40.00 more than our price. We are glad to ship this surrey for examination and approval, and if it is not found all we claim and a very satisfactory surrey in every way, we are willing to take it back at our expense.

BODY—Is one of our best grades and a very desirable style. The seats are large and roomy and have extra high backs. They are very comfortable. We use in the construction of body and seats high grade stock. There are heavy steel sill or rocker plates laid in white lead and screwed full length of sills.

GEAR—1$\frac{1}{8}$-inch dust proof bell collar long distance axles, with felt oil pads. Axles are fitted with selected straight grain white hickory beds, which are cemented and fully clipped full length of axles. When these axle beds are finished up the beds and axles are the same as one piece. Fine oil tempered French pattern open head springs, well graded and very easy riding. Reach is well ironed full length, bolted and properly braced. Fine full circle wrought surrey fifth wheel. Bradley quick shifting shaft couplers, which are the best quick shifting couplers on the market and are used on all high grade work. Roller rub irons. Regulation cut-under surrey shafts made from straight grain selected hickory, full patent leather trimmed with long 36-inch tips. Pole is made from fine selected straight grain hickory, well ironed and properly braced, has nickel pole tip and nickel neck yoke tips. Both pole and shafts, $5.00 extra.

WHEELS—Fine selected straight grain white hickory, 1-inch banded hub style, 36 inches front and 44 inches rear, equipped with 1-inch round edge planished steel tire which is bolted between every spoke. Tires are set hot by hand and not by machine. Felloes have screws through them on each side of every spoke, which insures them against checking at the spokes. The wheels we regu-

larly furnish are the correct height for this style gear, but we can lower the height of wheels, if desired. They could not be raised without there being danger of the front wheels striking the wheel house in turning and the rear wheels the fenders. We also furnish Sarven patent wheels instead of banded wood hubs, if preferred.

TRIMMINGS—Seats are trimmed with fine dark green all wool broadcloth, guaranteed fast color. We will trim with fine dark blue all wool broadcloth or fine whipcord, if preferred. The ends of the seats are pleated and trimmed to match the cushions and backs and both cushions and backs are upholstered with hair and fine upholstering springs. They are very comfortable and most easy riding. We can furnish special colors in broadcloth trimmings, if desired, at a small additional charge. Fine genuine leather trimmings in dark green, maroon or russet leather instead of broadcloth, $5.00 extra. Fine full padded dash. Velvet carpet in bottom of body, or rubber mat if preferred to the carpet. Oil burner lamps.

TOP—Fine canopy top style lined with all wool broadcloth to match seat trimmings and with fine fringe all around. Standards are finely enameled. There are heavy rubber side curtains all around, also heavy rubber storm apron for the dash. We furnish No. 213 equipped with fine leather quarter extension top instead of canopy top for $10.00 additional charge.

PAINTING—Body is finely finished in black, correctly striped; gear, Brewster green, properly striped. We will make any changes in painting desired. For system of painting, see page 5.

The above cut shows No. 214 with canopy top instead of extension. Price with canopy top, $10.00 less than with extension.

No. 214—FINE THREE SPRING, EXTENSION TOP, CUT-UNDER SURREY

PRICE
Cash with order, with steel tires and pole or shafts.........................$113.00
C. O. D., with steel tires and pole or shafts................................. 115.00
Cash with order, with 1-inch guaranteed rubber tires and pole or shafts....... 130.50
C. O. D., with 1-inch guaranteed rubber tires and pole or shafts............. 132.50

Our No. 214 is one of the best three spring cut-under surreys ever offered for the money. It is very roomy and on the order of a three spring carriage. The seats, as the picture shows, are made up with handles which is a very desirable feature with many buyers and adds materially to the appearance of the carriage. We are glad to ship our No. 214 anywhere for examination and approval, and if it is not found equal to similar surreys or carriages sold by others for $30.00 to $40.00 more than our price we will take the shipment back at our expense. It is a light running, very comfortable riding surrey.

BODY—Is one of our best styles and a design that pleases our patrons. The seats are roomy, have good high backs and are very comfortable. They have seat handles, as picture shows, which gives the surrey the appearance of a carriage body. There are heavy steel sill or rocker plates laid in white lead and screwed full length of sills. We use high grade stock throughout in the construction of body and seats.

GEAR—Three spring style with 1⅛-inch dust proof bell collar long distance axles, with felt oil pads. Axles are fitted with selected straight grain white hickory beds, which are cemented and clipped full length of axles. When these axle beds are smoothed up for finishing the beds and axles are the same as one piece. Fine oil tempered French pattern open head springs, well graded and very easy riding. Reach is well ironed full length, bolted and properly braced. Fine full circle wrought surrey fifth wheel. Bradley quick shifting shaft couplers, which are the best quick shifting couplers on the market and are used on all high grade work. Roller rub irons. Regulation cut-under surrey shafts, made from straight grain selected hickory, full patent leather trimmed with long 36-inch tips. Pole is made from fine selected straight grain hickory, well ironed and properly braced, has nickel pole tip and nickel neck yoke tips. Both pole and shafts, $5.00 extra.

WHEELS—Fine selected straight grain white hickory, 1-inch banded hub style, 36 inches front and 44 inches rear, equipped with 1-inch round edge planished steel tire which is bolted between every spoke. Tires are set hot by hand and not by machine. Felloes have screws through them on each side of every spoke which insures them against checking at the spokes. The wheels we regularly furnish are the correct height for this style gear, but we

can lower the height of wheels, if desired. They could not be raised without there being danger of the front wheels striking the wheel house in turning and the rear wheels the fenders. We also furnish Sarven patent wheels instead of banded hub, if preferred.

TRIMMINGS—Seats are trimmed with fine dark green all wool broadcloth, guaranteed fast color. We will trim with fine dark blue all wool broadcloth or fine whipcord, if preferred. The ends of the seats are pleated and trimmed to match the cushions and backs, and both cushions and backs are upholstered with hair and fine upholstering springs. They are very comfortable and easy riding. We can furnish special colors in broadcloth trimmings. if desired, at a small additional charge. Fine genuine leather trimmings in dark green, maroon or russet instead of broadcloth, $5.00 extra. Fine full padded dash. Velvet carpet in bottom of body, or rubber mat if preferred to the carpet. Oil burner lamps.

TOP—Fine leather quarter with heavy rubber side curtains and storm apron. Bow sockets are the best grade enameled steel sockets we can buy, and top joints are the best grade enameled joints made. There are heavy rubber side curtains and storm apron for the dash. We will furnish full leather top with best grade leather covered bow sockets and heavy rubber side curtains for $10.00 additional charge. We also furnish with canopy top instead of extension top, as shown by small cut in corner of page, for $10.00 less than with extension top.

PAINTING—The body is black; gear, Brewster green, correctly striped. We will make any changes in painting desired. Our painting is all fully guaranteed. For system of painting, see page 5.

The above cut illustrates No. 217 with leather quarter extension top instead of canopy. Price with extension top, $10.00 more than with canopy.

No. 217—FINE CANOPY TOP, CUT-UNDER SURREY

PRICE
Cash with order, with steel tires and pole or shafts.........................$ 98.00
C. O. D., with steel tires and pole or shafts................................. 100.00
Cash with order, with 1-inch guaranteed rubber tires and pole or shafts...... 115.50
C. O. D., with 1-inch guaranteed rubber tires and pole or shafts............. 117.50

No. 217 is one of our best selling canopy top cut-under surreys and is a style that always gives entire satisfaction wherever shipped. The body and seats are roomy and the surrey is a very comfortable riding one. There are handles on the seats, as picture shows, and they aid very much in getting into and out of the surrey. We unhesitatingly recommend our No. 217 and are glad to ship it anywhere for examination and approval with the understanding that it is to be found as good in quality of workmanship and material throughout as usually sells for $35.00 to $40.00 more than our price, or we will take it back at our expense.

BODY—Is one of the best made styles and a design that pleases our patrons. The seats are roomy, have good high backs and are very comfortable. They have seat handles, as picture shows, which gives the surrey the appearance of a carriage body. There are heavy steel sill or rocker plates laid in white lead and screwed full length of sills. We use high grade stock throughout in the construction of body and seats.

GEAR—1⅛-inch dust proof bell collar long distance axles, with felt oil pads. Axles are fitted with selected straight grain white hickory beds, which are cemented and clipped full length of axles. When these axle beds are finished up the beds and axles are the same as one piece. Fine oil tempered French pattern open head springs, well graded and very easy riding. Reach is well ironed full length, bolted and properly braced. Fine full circle wrought surrey fifth wheel. Bradley quick shifting shaft couplers, which are the best quick shifting couplers on the market and are used on all high grade work. Roller rub irons. Regulation cut-under surrey shafts made from straight grain selected hickory, full patent leather trimmed with long 36-inch tips. Pole is made from fine selected straight grain hickory, well ironed and properly braced, has nickel pole tip and nickel neck yoke tips. Both pole and shafts, $5.00 extra.

WHEELS—Fine selected straight grain white hickory, 1-inch banded hub style, 36 inches front and 44 inches rear, equipped with 1-inch round edge planished steel tire which is bolted between every spoke. Tires are set hot by hand and not by machine. Felloes have screws through them on each side of every spoke, which

insures them against checking at the spokes. The wheels we regularly furnish are the correct height for this style gear, but we can lower the height of wheels, if desired. They could not be raised without there being danger of the front wheels striking the wheel house in turning and the rear wheels the fenders. We also furnish Sarven patent wheels instead of banded hub, if preferred.

TRIMMINGS—Seats are trimmed with fine dark green all wool broadcloth, guaranteed fast color. We will trim with fine dark blue all wool broadcloth or fine whipcord, if preferred. The ends of the seats are pleated and trimmed to match the cushions and backs, and both cushions and backs are upholstered with hair and fine upholstering springs. They are very comfortable and easy riding. We can furnish special colors in broadcloth trimmings, if desired, at a small additional charge. Fine genuine leather trimmings in dark green, maroon or russet instead of broadcloth, $5.00 extra. Fine full padded dash. Velvet carpet in bottom of body, or rubber mat if preferred to the carpet. Oil burner lamps.

TOP—Fine canopy top style lined with all wool broadcloth to match seat trimmings and with fine fringe all around. Standards are finely enameled. There are heavy rubber side curtains all around, also heavy rubber storm apron for the dash. We furnish No. 217 equipped with fine leather quarter extension top instead of canopy top for $10.00 additional charge.

PAINTING—The body is black; gear, Brewster green, correctly striped. We will make any changes in painting desired. Our painting is all fully guaranteed. For system of painting, see page 5.

18

The above cut shows No. 222 with fine half spindle style seats, bike gear and English canopy top. Price, same as No. 222.

No. 222—FINE, LIGHT, ONE HORSE, CUT-UNDER, CANOPY TOP SURREY

PRICE
{
Cash with order, with steel tires and shafts..................................$ 98.00
C. O. D., with steel tires and shafts.. 100.00
Cash with order, with ⅞-inch guaranteed rubber tires and shafts.............. 113.00
C. O. D., with ⅞-inch guaranteed rubber tires and shafts.................. 115.00
}

If 1-inch guaranteed rubber tires are preferred, add $2.50 to the price quoted with ⅞-inch rubber tires.

Our No. 222 we consider one of the best light one horse cut-under surreys ever made. There is a large demand for light weight surreys with sufficient room for carrying four adults comfortably, and our No. 222 fills the bill exactly. Although it is a light weight surrey and intended for one horse, it is all right to be used with two horses. We know our No. 222 is as good in quality of workmanship and material throughout as usually sells for $25.00 more than our price. We are very glad to ship it for full examination and approval.

BODY—Light cut-under style made from the best body stock throughout. The seats are our best auto style, have good high backs and are roomy and comfortable. Furnished with seats style of No. 225, page 24, if desired. There are heavy steel sill or rocker plates laid in white lead and screwed full length of sills.

GEAR—1-inch dust proof bell collar long distance axles with felt oil pads. Axles are fitted with light wood beds, which are cemented and fully clipped. Fine oil tempered French pattern open head springs, very elastic and easy riding. Reach is ironed full length, bolted and well braced. Full circle wrought surrey fifth wheel. Bradley quick shifting shaft couplers, which are the best quick shifting couplers made, and are used on all high grade work. Roller rub irons. Regulation cut-under surrey shafts made from straight grain selected hickory, full patent leather trimmed with long 36-inch patent leather tips. Pole instead of shafts, $1.00 extra. Pole in addition to shafts, $5.00 extra.

WHEELS—Fine selected straight grain white hickory, ⅞-inch Sarven patent style, 36 inches front, 44 inches rear, with ⅞-inch round edge planished steel tire bolted between every spoke. Tires are ¼-inch thick and are set hot by hand and not by machine. Felloes have screws through them on each side of every spoke, which insures absolutely against checking at the spokes. The height of wheels we furnish is correct for this style gear, but we can make any change in height desired. We furnish 1-inch wheels

instead of ⅞-inch, if preferred. Also banded hub style, if desired, instead of Sarven patent.

TRIMMINGS—Seats are trimmed with fine dark green all wool broadcloth, guaranteed absolutely fast color. Will trim with fine dark blue wool broadcloth or fine whipcord, if preferred. The ends of seats are pleated and trimmed to match cushions and backs, and both cushions and backs are upholstered with hair and upholstering springs and the seats are very comfortable and easy riding. We can furnish special colors in broadcloth trimmings, if desired, at a small additional charge. Genuine leather trimmings in dark green, maroon or russet instead of broadcloth, $5.00 extra. Fine full padded patent leather dash. Fine velvet carpet in bottom of body, or if rubber mat is preferred to the carpet we furnish mat. Oil burner lamps.

TOP—Fine canopy style lined with all wool broadcloth to match seat trimmings, and with fine fringe all around. Standards are finely enameled. There are heavy rubber side curtains all around and heavy rubber storm apron for the dash. We furnish No. 222 equipped with fine leather quarter extension top instead of canopy top, for $10.00 extra.

PAINTING—The body is black; gear, Brewster green, correctly striped. We will furnish New York red gear or make any changes in painting desired. Our painting is all fully guaranteed. For system of painting, see page 5.

19

The above cut shows No. 222½ equipped with our new twin style auto seat. The divided effect is in the backs of the seat only. The upholstering on the backs and the cushions are the same as No. 222½ and are not divided. We furnish the twin style seats instead of the regular tulip pattern seats as shown on No. 222½ for $2.00 extra charge.

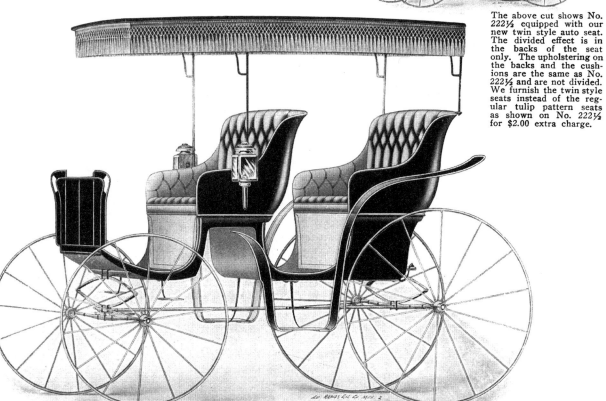

No. 222½—FINE, LIGHT, ONE HORSE, CUT-UNDER SURREY, WITH AUTO SEATS

PRICE
Cash with order, with steel tires and shafts..................................$108.00
C. O. D., with steel tires and shafts... 110.00
Cash with order, with ⅞-inch guaranteed rubber tires and shafts.............. 123.00
C. O. D., with ⅞-inch guaranteed rubber tires and shafts..................... 125.00

If 1-inch guaranteed rubber tires are preferred, add $2.50 to the price quoted with ⅞-inch rubber tires.

Our No. 222½ cut-under surrey is one of the most up-to-date surreys on the market today. Although it is a light weight surrey and is built especially for one horse, it is all right for two horses, and there is plenty of room in the surrey for seating four persons very comfortably. Seats on No. 222½ are our latest tulip pattern auto seats. They are very roomy and have extra high backs, which are luxuriously upholstered. We know our No. 222½ is as good in quality of workmanship and material throughout as sold by others for $25.00 to $35.00 more than our price. We are glad to ship this surrey for full examination and approval with the distinct understanding that it is to be found all we claim and highly satisfactory or it may be returned at our expense.

BODY—Is one of the best cut-under styles we are making. The body as well as the seats are made from high grade body stock. There are heavy steel rocker plates laid in white lead and screwed full length of sills and over the wheel house. The seats are the finest auto style seats we have ever made. They are very roomy and have extra high backs.

GEAR—1-inch dust proof bell collar long distance axles with felt oil pads. Axles are fitted with light wood beds, which are cemented and fully clipped. Fine oil tempered French pattern open head springs, very elastic and easy riding. Reach is ironed full length and bolted and well braced. Full circle wrought surrey fifth wheel. Roller rub irons. Bradley quick shifting shaft couplers, which are the best quick shifting couplers made, and are used on all high grade work. Regulation cut-under surrey shafts made from straight grain selected hickory, full patent leather trimmed with long 36-inch patent leather tips. Pole in addition to shafts, $5.00 extra. Furnished with bike gear style of No. 223, if desired.

WHEELS—Fine selected straight grain white hickory, ⅞-inch Sarven patent style, 36 inches front, 44 inches rear, with ⅞-inch round edge planished steel tire, bolted between every spoke. Tires are ¼-inch thick and are set hot by hand and not by machine. Felloes have screws through them on each side of every spoke, which insures absolutely against checking at the spokes. The height of wheels we furnish is correct for this style gear, but we can make any change in height desired. We furnish 1-inch wheels instead of ⅞-inch, if preferred. Also banded hub style, if desired instead of Sarven patent.

TRIMMINGS—Seats are trimmed with fine dark green all wool broadcloth, guaranteed absolutely fast color. Will trim with fine dark blue wool broadcloth or fine whipcord, if preferred. The ends of the seats are pleated and trimmed to match cushions and backs, and both cushions and backs are upholstered with hair and upholstering springs, and the seats are very comfortable and easy riding. We can furnish special colors in broadcloth trimmings, if desired, at a small additional charge. Genuine leather trimmings, in dark green, maroon or russet instead of broadcloth, $5.00 extra. Fine full padded patent leather dash. Fine velvet carpet in bottom of body, or if rubber mat is preferred to the carpet we furnish mat.

TOP—Fine canopy style lined with all wool broadcloth to match seat trimmings, and with fine fringe all around. Standards are finely enameled. There are heavy rubber side curtains all around and heavy rubber storm apron for the dash. We furnish No. 222½ equipped with fine leather quarter extension top instead of canopy top, for $10.00 extra.

PAINTING—The body is black; gear, Brewster green, correctly striped. We will make any changes in painting desired. Our painting is all fully guaranteed. For painting system, see page 5.

20

The above cut illustrates No. 223 without top. Price $15.00 less than with top.

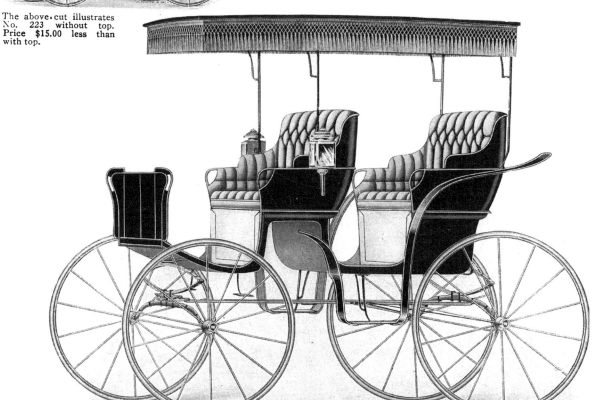

No. 223—FINE, LIGHT, ONE HORSE, CUT-UNDER SURREY, WITH BIKE GEAR AND AUTO STYLE SEATS

PRICE
{
Cash with order, with steel tires and shafts...............................$105.00
C. O. D., with steel tires and shafts... 107.00
Cash with order, with 1⅛-inch guaranteed cushion tires and shafts........... 125.00
C. O. D., with 1⅛-inch guaranteed cushion tires and shafts.................. 127.00
}

If ⅞-inch guaranteed rubber tires are preferred, deduct $5.00 from the price quoted with 1⅛-inch cushion tires.

Our No. 223 is one of the most popular light one horse surreys we have ever made. While it is built especially for one horse it is all right to be used with two horses, if desired. This surrey is roomy and comfortable for four adults. We know No. 223 will please, and we are glad to ship it for examination and approval with the understanding that it is to be found all we claim and a highly satisfactory surrey or it may be returned at our expense. We guarantee it as good as usually sells for $25.00 to $35.00 more than our price.

BODY—Fine light cut-under design with auto seats. Body and seats are made from high grade stock throughout. Backs of the seats are high and they are very comfortable. There is plenty of room between the seats. There are heavy steel sill or rocker plates laid in white lead and screwed full length of sills.

GEAR—1-inch true sweep dust proof bell collar long distance bike axles, with felt oil pads. Axles are fitted with light wood beds, which are cemented and clipped to the axles. Fine oil tempered French pattern open head springs, very elastic and easy riding. The reaches have channel iron full length and they are bolted and well braced. Roller rub irons. Full circle wrought Brewster slotted fifth wheel with king bolt clipped around axle. It is the style fifth wheel used on all strictly high grade work. Wrought Bailey body loops clipped to springs. Will furnish wood spring bar if preferred to the Bailey loops. Bradley quick change shaft couplers, which are the most practical quick shifting couplers made. They are usually used on all high grade work. Shafts are regular surrey style. They are made from selected hickory, full patent leather trimmed. They are also well braced. Pole instead of shafts, $1.00 extra. Will furnish pole in addition to shafts for $5.00 extra.

WHEELS—Fine selected straight grain white hickory, ⅞-inch Sarven patent, 38 inches front and 40 inches rear, with ⅞-inch round edge planished steel tire bolted between each spoke. Tires are ¼-inch thick and are set hot by hand and not by machine. Felloes have screws through them on each side of every spoke, which insures absolutely against checking at the spokes. The height of the wheels we furnish is correct for this style gear, but we can make any change in height desired. We furnish 1-inch wheels instead of ⅞-inch, if preferred. Also banded hub style instead of Sarven patent. Furnished with fine steel wire wheels and 1⅛-inch guaranteed cushion tires for $25.00 additional charge to price quoted with wood wheels and steel tires.

TRIMMINGS—Seats are trimmed with fine dark green all wool broadcloth, guaranteed absolutely fast color. Will trim with fine dark blue all wool broadcloth or fine whipcord, if preferred. The ends of the seats are pleated and trimmed to match cushions and backs, and both cushions and backs are upholstered with hair and upholstering springs, and the seats are very comfortable and easy riding. We can furnish special colors in broadcloth trimmings, if desired, at a small additional charge. Genuine leather trimmings in dark green, maroon or russet instead of broadcloth, $5.00 extra. Fine full padded patent leather dash. Fine velvet carpet in bottom of body, or if rubber mat is preferred to the carpet we furnish mat. Oil burner lamps.

TOP—Fine canopy style lined with all wool broadcloth to match seat trimmings, and with fine fringe all around. Standards are finely enameled. There are heavy rubber side curtains all around and heavy rubber storm apron for the dash. We furnish No. 223 equipped with fine leather quarter extension top instead of canopy top for $10.00 extra.

PAINTING—The body is black; gear, Brewster green, correctly striped. We will make any changes in painting desired. For painting system, see page 5.

21

The above cut shows No. 224 with full rubber extension top. Price, $5.00 more than with canopy top.

No. 224—LIGHT, CUT-UNDER SURREY, WITH CANOPY TOP

PRICE
{
Cash with order, with steel tires and shafts.................................$ 83.00
C. O. D., with steel tires and shafts.. 85.00
Cash with order, with ⅞-inch guaranteed rubber tires and shafts............ 98.00
C. O. D., with ⅞-inch guaranteed rubber tires and shafts................... 100.00
}

If 1-inch guaranteed rubber tires are preferred, add $2.50 to the price quoted with ⅞-inch rubber tires.

Our No. 224 is as good in style, quality of workmanship and material throughout as similar surreys sold by others for fully **$30.00** more than our price. Although it is a light weight surrey, especially adapted for one horse use, it is very suitable for two horses if team is desired. It is sufficiently roomy to seat four persons comfortably. We are very glad to ship No. 224 for full examination and approval.

BODY—Is good style cut-under design with roomy, comfortable, high backed seats. We use in the construction of body and seats high grade stock throughout. There are heavy steel sill or rocker plates laid in white lead and screwed full length of sills. There is plenty of room in this surrey for seating four adults with perfect comfort.

GEAR—1¹⁄₁₆-inch dust proof bell collar long distance axles, with felt oil pads. Axles are equipped with selected straight grain white hickory beds, which are clipped full length of axles. Fine oil tempered French pattern open head springs, properly graded and very easy riding. Reaches are ironed full length, bolted and well braced. Roller rub irons. Full circle wrought surrey fifth wheel, which is one of the best and strongest fifth wheels made. Bradley quick shifting shaft couplers, the style used on all first class work. Regulation cut-under shafts made from selected straight grain white hickory, full patent leather trimmed, and heel braces. We will furnish pole in place of shafts for $1.00 additional charge. Pole in addition to shafts, $5.00 additional charge.

WHEELS—Fine selected straight grain white hickory, ⅞-inch Sarven patent, 36 inches front, 44 inches rear, equipped with ⅞-inch round edge planished steel tire, bolted between every spoke. Our tires are set hot by hand and not by machine. Felloes have

screws through them on each side of every spoke, which insures them against checking at the spokes. We will furnish banded hub style wheels, if desired; also 1-inch instead of ⅞-inch.

TRIMMINGS—Seats are trimmed with dark green all wool broadcloth, guaranteed fast color. We will trim with dark blue all wool broadcloth or fine whipcord, if preferred. The ends of the seats are pleated and trimmed to match cushions and backs, and there are fine upholstering springs in both cushions and backs. Seats are very comfortable. We furnish special colors in broadcloth trimmings, if desired, at a small additional charge. Fine genuine leather trimmings in dark green, maroon or russet, $5.00 extra. Full padded patent leather dash. Velvet carpet in bottom of body, or rubber mat if preferred to the carpet. Oil burner lamps.

TOP—Is canopy style lined with wool cloth to match seat trimmings, and with fringe all around. Rubber side curtains all around, and good rubber storm apron for the dash. We furnish full rubber extension top instead of canopy top for $5.00 additional charge. (See small cut above.)

PAINTING—The body is black; gear, Brewster green, correctly striped. We will make any changes in painting desired. Our painting is all fully guaranteed. For system of painting, see page 5.

No. 224½—LIGHT, ONE HORSE SURREY, WITH BIKE GEAR AND AUTO SEATS

PRICE
- Cash with order, with steel tires and shafts.................................$ 93.00
- C. O. D., with steel tires and shafts.. 95.00
- Cash with order, with ⅞-inch guaranteed rubber tires and shafts............. 108.00
- C. O. D., with ⅞-inch guaranteed rubber tires and shafts.................... 110.00

If 1⅛-inch guaranteed cushion tires are preferred, add $5.00 to the price quoted with ⅞-inch solid tires.

Our No. 224½ is one of the best style light cut-under surreys we are making. It is just the thing for one horse, yet is suitable for **two**. Although the surrey is light it is sufficiently roomy to seat four persons comfortably. We know our No. 224½ is as good as usually **sells** for $25.00 to $35.00 more than our price. We are very glad to ship it for full examination and approval, and it may be returned at our expense if not found perfectly satisfactory.

BODY—Is a good style cut-under design with roomy, comfortable, high backed seats. We use in the construction of body and seats high grade stock throughout. There are heavy steel sill or rocker plates laid in white lead and screwed full length of sills. There is plenty of room in this surrey for seating four adults with perfect comfort.

GEAR—Roman bike style dust proof bell collar long distance axles, with felt oil pads. Axles are equipped with short straight grain hickory beds, which are cemented and clipped to center of axles. Fine oil tempered French pattern open head springs, properly graded and very easy riding. Reaches are ironed full length, bolted and well braced. Roller rub irons. Full circle wrought Brewster fifth wheel, which is one of the best and strongest fifth wheels made. Bradley quick shifting shaft couplers, the style used on all first class work. Regulation cut-under shafts made from selected straight grain white hickory, full patent leather trimmed, and heel braces. We will furnish pole in place of shafts for $1.00 additional charge. Pole in addition to shafts, $5.00 additional charge.

WHEELS—Fine selected straight grain white hickory, ⅞-inch Sarven patent, 38 inches front, 40 inches rear, equipped with ⅞-inch round edge planished steel tire, bolted between every spoke. Our tires are set hot by hand and not by machine. Felloes have

screws through them on each side of every spoke, which insures them against checking at the spokes. We will furnish banded hub style wheels, if desired; also 1-inch instead of ⅞-inch.

TRIMMINGS—Seats are trimmed with dark green all wool broadcloth, guaranteed fast color. We will trim with dark blue all wool broadcloth or fine whipcord, if preferred. The ends of the seats are pleated and trimmed to match cushions and backs, and there are fine upholstering springs in both cushions and backs. Seats are very comfortable. We furnish special colors in broadcloth trimmings, if desired, at a small additional charge. Fine genuine leather trimmings in dark green, maroon or russet, $5.00 extra. Full padded patent leather dash. Velvet carpet in bottom of body, or rubber mat if preferred to the carpet. Oil burner lamps.

TOP—Is canopy style lined with wool cloth to match seat trimmings, and with fringe all around. Rubber side curtains all around and good rubber storm apron for the dash. We furnish full rubber extension top instead of canopy top for $5.00 additional charge.

PAINTING—The body is black; gear, New York red, correctly striped. We will furnish Brewster green gear or make any changes in painting desired. Our painting is all fully guaranteed. For system of painting, see page 5.

23

The above cut shows No. 225 with extension style top. We furnish this leather quarter extension top instead of canopy top for $10.00 additional charge.

No. 225 FINE, LIGHT, ONE HORSE, CANOPY TOP SURREY

PRICE
{
Cash with order, with steel tires and shafts.................................$ 93.00
C. O. D., with steel tires and shafts.. 95.00
Cash with order, with ⅞-inch guaranteed rubber tires and shafts............ 108.00
C. O. D., with ⅞-inch guaranteed rubber tires and shafts................... 110.00
}

If 1-inch guaranteed rubber tires are preferred, add $2.50 to the price quoted with ⅞-inch rubber tires.

Our No. 225 is a light weight, four passenger surrey, made especially for one horse, yet it is suitable to be used with two horses. It is one of the best style light surreys we have ever made, and we can unhesitatingly recommend it. We know No. 225 is made as good in quality of workmanship and material throughout as usually sells for $25.00 to $35.00 more than our price. We are glad to ship it for examination and approval with the understanding that it is to be found all we claim and you are to feel you have saved money or it may be returned at our expense.

BODY—Is light weight, straight sill design with good steel sill or rocker plates laid in white lead and screwed full length of sills. We use high grade stock in the construction of body and seats, and we guarantee the panels not to open at the corners no matter in what climate used. Seats have good high backs and are roomy and comfortable. Furnished with auto seats, style of No. 226, if desired. Roller rub irons.

GEAR—1-inch dust proof bell collar long distance axles, with felt oil pads. Axles are fitted with light wood beds, which are cemented and fully clipped. Fine oil tempered French pattern open head springs, very elastic and easy riding. Reach is ironed full length and bolted and well braced. Full circle wrought surrey fifth wheel. Bradley quick shifting shaft couplers, which are the best quick shifting couplers made, and are used on all high grade work. Regulation surrey shafts made from straight grain selected hickory, full patent leather trimmed. Pole instead of shafts, $1.00 extra. Pole in addition to shafts, $5.00 extra.

WHEELS—Fine selected straight grain white hickory, ⅞-inch Sarven patent style, 40 inches front, 44 inches rear, with ⅞-inch round edge planished steel tire bolted between every spoke. Tires are ¼-inch thick and are set hot by hand and not by machine. Fellows have screws through them on each side of every spoke, which insures absolutely against checking at the spokes. The height of wheels we furnish is correct for this style gear, but we can make any change in height desired. We furnish 1-inch wheels

instead of ⅞-inch, if preferred. Also banded hub style, if desired instead of Sarven patent.

TRIMMINGS—Seats are trimmed with fine dark green all wool broadcloth, guaranteed absolutely fast color. Will trim with fine dark blue wool broadcloth or fine whipcord, if preferred. The ends of seats are pleated and trimmed to match cushions and backs, and both cushions and backs are upholstered with hair and upholstering springs, and the seats are very comfortable and easy riding. We can furnish special colors in broadcloth trimmings if desired at a small additional charge. Genuine leather trimmings in dark green, maroon or russet instead of broadcloth, $5.00 extra. Fine full padded patent leather dash. Fine velvet carpet in bottom of body, or if rubber mat is preferred to the carpet we furnish mat. Oil burner lamps.

TOP—Fine canopy style lined with all wool broadcloth to match seat trimmings, and with fine fringe all around. Standards are finely enameled. There are heavy rubber side curtains all around and heavy rubber storm apron for the dash. We furnish with fine leather quarter extension top instead of canopy top, for $10.00 extra.

PAINTING—The body is black; gear, Brewster green, correctly striped. We will make any changes in painting desired. Our painting is all fully guaranteed. For system of painting, see page 5.

24

The above cut illustrates No. 226 with fine half spindle style seats, as picture shows. These are especially desirable seats when extra lightness in appearance is desired. Seats are just as roomy as the No. 226 seat. Price same as No. 226.

No. 226—FINE, LIGHT, ONE HORSE SURREY, WITH BIKE GEAR AND AUTO SEATS

PRICE
- Cash with order, with steel tires and shafts...................................$100.00
- C. O. D., with steel tires and shafts.. 102.00
- Cash with order, with ⅞-inch guaranteed rubber tires and shafts............ 115.00
- C. O. D., with ⅞-inch guaranteed rubber tires and shafts.................. 117.00

If 1⅛-inch guaranteed cushion tires are preferred, add $5.00 to the price quoted with ⅞-inch solid tires.

No. 226 is one of our most up-to-date style light one horse surreys. Although it is a regular one horse surrey it is suitable to be used with two horses. Seats are sufficiently roomy to seat four adults with perfect comfort. The backs are high. We know No. 226 is as good in style, quality of workmanship and material throughout as similar surreys sold by others for fully $35.00 more than our price. We are very glad to ship it for full examination and approval.

BODY—Is one of our best light straight sill designs. Body and seats are made from high grade stock throughout and they are so constructed that we guarantee them not to open at the corner no matter in what climate they are used. The seats are a very popular auto design and are roomy and comfortable. There are steel rocker plates laid in white lead and screwed full length of body sills. Roller rub irons.

GEAR—1-inch true sweep dust proof bell collar long distance bike axles, with felt oil pads. Axles are fitted with light wood beds, which are cemented and clipped to the axles. Fine oil tempered French pattern open head springs, very elastic and easy riding. The reaches have channel iron full length and they are bolted and well braced. Full circle wrought Brewster slotted fifth wheel with king bolt clipped around axle. It is the style fifth wheel used on all strictly high grade work. Wrought Bailey body loops clipped to springs. Will furnish wood spring bar if preferred to the Bailey loops. Bradley quick change shaft couplers, which are the most practical quick shifting shaft couplers made. They are usually used on all high grade work. Shafts are regular bike surrey style. They are made from selected straight grain hickory, full patent leather trimmed and well braced. Will furnish pole in addition to shafts for $5.00 extra.

WHEELS—Fine selected straight grain white hickory, ⅞-inch Sarven patent, 38 inches front and 40 inches rear, with ⅞-inch round edge planished steel tire, bolted between each spoke. Tires are ¼-inch thick and are set hot by hand and not by machine. Felloes have screws through them on each side of every spoke, which insures absolutely against checking at the spokes. The

height of the wheels we furnish is correct for this style gear, but we can make any change in height desired. We furnish 1-inch wheels instead of ⅞-inch, if preferred. Also banded hub style instead of Sarven patent. Furnished with fine steel wire wheels and 1⅛-inch guaranteed cushion tires for $25.00 additional charge to the price quoted with wood wheels and steel tires.

TRIMMINGS—Seats are trimmed with fine dark green all wool broadcloth, guaranteed absolutely fast color. Will trim with fine dark blue all wool broadcloth or fine whipcord, if preferred. The ends of the seats are pleated and trimmed to match cushions and backs, and both cushions and backs are upholstered with hair and upholstering springs, and the seats are very comfortable and easy riding. We can furnish special colors in broadcloth trimmings, if desired, at a small additional charge. Genuine leather trimmings in dark green, maroon or russet instead of broadcloth, $5.00 extra. Fine full padded patent leather dash. Fine velvet carpet in bottom of body, or if rubber mat is preferred to the carpet we furnish mat. Oil burner lamps.

TOP—Fine canopy style lined with all wool broadcloth to match seat trimmings, and with fine fringe all around. Standards are finely enameled. There are heavy rubber side curtains all around and heavy rubber storm apron for the dash. We furnish with fine leather quarter extension top instead of canopy top for $10.00 extra.

PAINTING—Body is finely finished in black, correctly striped; gear, Brewster green, properly striped. We will make any changes in color of painting desired. For system of painting, see page 5.

25

The above cut shows No. 226½ without top. Price, $12.00 less than with top.

No. 226½—FINE, LIGHT, ONE HORSE SURREY, WITH BIKE STYLE GEAR

PRICE
Cash with order, with steel tires and shafts.................................$103.00
C. O. D., with steel tires and shafts.. 105.00
Cash with order, with 1⅛-inch guaranteed cushion tires and shafts........... 123.00
C. O. D., with 1⅛-inch guaranteed cushion tires and shafts................. 125.00

If ⅞-inch guaranteed rubber tires are preferred, deduct $5.00 from the price quoted with 1⅛-inch cushion tires.

No. 226½ is a new design and is one of the most beautiful straight sill bike gear surreys made. It is so good in quality of workmanship and material throughout that we are glad to ship it anywhere for examination and approval, and if the purchaser does not feel that he is saving money in buying from us, we will take the shipment back at our expense. We unhesitatingly recommend this surrey and guarantee it equal in quality of workmanship and material throughout to similar surreys sold for $25.00 to $35.00 more than our price.

BODY—Is one of our best straight sill designs with our new tulip pattern auto seats, which have extra high backs and are luxuriously upholstered and very comfortable. Both body and seats are made from high grade body and seat material and are constructed in such a manner that we guarantee them not to open at the corners, no matter in what climate they are used. There are good steel rocker plates laid in white lead and screwed full length of sills. Roller rub irons.

GEAR—1-inch true sweep dust proof bell collar long distance bike axles, with felt oil pads. Axles are fitted with light wood beds, which are cemented and clipped to the axles. Fine oil temperd French pattern open head springs, very elastic and easy riding. The reaches have channel iron full length and they are bolted and well braced. Full circle wrought Brewster slotted fifth wheel with king bolt clipped around axle. It is the style fifth wheel used on all strictly high grade work. Wrought Bailey body loops clipped to springs. Will furnish wood spring bar, if preferred to the Bailey loops. Bradley quick change shaft couplers, which are the most practical quick shifting couplers made. They are usually used on all high grade work. Shafts are regular bike surrey style. They are made from selected hickory, full patent leather trimmed and well braced. Will furnish pole in addition to shafts for $5.00 extra.

WHEELS—Fine selected straight grain white hickory, ⅞-inch Sarven patent, 38 inches front and 40 inches rear, with ⅞-inch round edge planished steel tire bolted between each spoke. Tires are ¼-inch thick and are set hot by hand and not by machine. Felloes have screws through them on each side of every spoke,

which insures absolutely against checking at the spokes. The height of the wheels we furnish is correct for this style gear, but we can make any change in height desired. We furnish 1-inch wheels instead of ⅞-inch, if preferred. Also banded hub style instead of Sarven patent. Furnished with fine steel wire wheels and 1⅛-inch guaranteed cushion tires for $25.00 additional charge to price quoted with wood wheels and steel tires.

TRIMMINGS—Seats are trimmed with fine dark green all wool broadcloth, guaranteed absolutely fast color. We will trim with fine dark blue all wool broadcloth or fine whipcord, if preferred. The ends of the seats are pleated and trimmed to match cushions and backs, and both cushions and backs are upholstered with hair and upholstering springs, and the seats are very comfortable and easy riding. We can furnish special colors in broadcloth trimmings, if desired, at a small additional charge. Genuine leather trimmings in either dark green, maroon or russet instead of broadcloth, $5.00 extra. Fine full padded patent leather dash. Fine velvet carpet in bottom of body, or if rubber mat is preferred to the carpet we furnish mat. Oil burner lamps.

TOP—Fine canopy style lined with all wool broadcloth to match seat trimmings, and with fine fringe all around. Standards are finely enameled. There are heavy rubber side curtains all around and heavy rubber storm apron for the dash. We furnish with fine leather quarter extension top instead of canopy top for $10.00 extra.

PAINTING—The body is black; gear, Brewster green, correctly striped. We will furnish New York red gear or make any changes in painting desired. For system of painting, see page 5.

We make any changes in our vehicles necessary to suit your ideas, and where the change represents only a small extra expense to us we make no additional charge for same.

No. 227½—FINE, LIGHT, ONE HORSE SURREY, WITH OUR NEW TWIN AUTO SEATS AND BIKE GEAR

PRICE
{
Cash with order, with steel tires and shafts.................................$108.00
C. O. D., with steel tires and shafts... 110.00
Cash with order, with 1⅛-inch guaranteed cushion tires and shafts........... 128.00
C. O. D., with 1⅛-inch guaranteed cushion tires and shafts.................. 130.00
}

If ⅞-inch guaranteed rubber tires are preferred, deduct $5.00 from the price quoted with cushion tires.

Our No. 227½ is a new design for this season and one of the best surreys we are making. Although it is lighter and a little more compact than the regular two horse surrey, it is sufficiently roomy to seat four persons with perfect comfort. The divided effect in the seats is shown in the back only and does not affect the seating capacity of the seat, as the cushion and back trimmings are just the same as on the regular style seat. Although No. 227½ is a one horse surrey it is all right for two horses, if desired. We guarantee this surrey as good as usually sells for $35.00 more than our price, and we are very glad to ship it for full examination and approval.

BODY—Is one of our best straight sill designs with our new twin pattern auto seats, which have extra high backs and are luxuriously upholstered and very comfortable. Both body and seats are made from high grade body and seat material and are constructed in such a manner that we guarantee them not to open at the corners, no matter in what climate they are used. There are good steel rocker plates laid in white lead and screwed full length of sills. Roller rub irons.

GEAR—1-inch true sweep dust proof bell collar long distance bike axles, with felt oil pads. Axles are fitted with light wood beds, which are cemented and clipped to the axles. Fine oil tempered French pattern open head springs, very elastic and easy riding. The reaches have channel iron full length and they are bolted and well braced. Full circle wrought Brewster slotted fifth wheel with king bolt clipped around axle. It is the style fifth wheel used on all strictly high grade work. Wrought Bailey body loops clipped to springs. Will furnish wood spring bar, if preferred to the Bailey loops. Bradley quick change shaft couplers, which are the most practical quick shifting couplers made. They are usually used on all high grade work. Shafts are regular bike surrey style. They are made from selected hickory, full patent leather trimmed and well braced. Will furnish pole in addition to shafts for $5.00 extra.

WHEELS—Fine selected straight grain white hickory, ⅞-inch Sarven patent, 38 inches front and 40 inches rear with ⅞-inch round edge planished steel tire bolted between each spoke. Tires are ¼-inch thick and are set hot by hand and not by machine. Felloes have screws through them on each side of every spoke,

which insures absolutely against checking at the spokes. The height of the wheels we furnish is correct for this style gear, but we can make any change in height desired. We furnish 1-inch wheels instead of ⅞-inch, if preferred. Also banded hub style instead of Sarven patent. Furnished with fine steel wire wheels and 1⅛-inch guaranteed cushion tires for $25.00 additional charge to price quoted with wood wheels and steel tires.

TRIMMINGS—Seats are trimmed with fine dark green all wool broadcloth, guaranteed absolutely fast color. Will trim with fine dark blue all wool broadcloth or fine whipcord, if preferred. The ends of the seats are pleated and trimmed to match cushions and backs, and both cushions and backs are upholstered with hair and upholstering springs, and the seats are very comfortable and easy riding. We can furnish special colors in broadcloth trimmings, if desired, at a small additional charge. Genuine leather trimmings in dark green, maroon or russet instead of broadcloth, $5.00 extra. Fine full padded patent leather dash. Fine velvet carpet in bottom of body, or if rubber mat is preferred to the carpet we furnish mat. Oil burner lamps.

TOP—Fine canopy style lined with all wool broadcloth to match seat trimmings, and with fine fringe all around. Standards are finely enameled. There are heavy rubber side curtains all around and heavy rubber storm apron for the dash. We furnish with fine leather quarter extension top instead of canopy top for $10.00 extra.

PAINTING—Body is finely finished in black, correctly striped; gear, Brewster green, properly striped. We will make any changes in color of painting desired. For system of painting, see page 5.

The above cut shows No. 229 with three spring gear instead of two spring and with extension top. With three spring gear, $5.00 extra. With extension top, $10.00 extra.

No. 229—FINE, FULL PANEL, CANOPY TOP SURREY

PRICE
- Cash with order, with steel tires and pole or shafts.........................$117.50
- C. O. D., with steel tires and pole or shafts................................. 120.00
- Cash with order, with 1-inch guaranteed rubber tires and pole or shafts....... 135.00
- C. O. D., with 1-inch guaranteed rubber tires and pole or shafts.............. 137.50

Our No. 229 is one of the finest style full panel surreys made. There are few companies manufacturing these full panel surreys, because the wide panel stock necessary in their construction is very difficult to secure. Those who do make anything on this order charge anywhere from $40.00 to $50.00 more than our price. We are very glad of an opportunity to ship No. 229 for examination and approval with the understanding that it is to be found all we claim and perfectly satisfactory in every respect or it may be returned at our expense.

BODY—Is one of the finest full panel straight sill surrey bodies made. Side panels are in one piece from arms to sills, making it possible for a very beautiful effect in finishing. Seats have good high backs and are large and very comfortable. There are heavy steel sill or rocker plates laid in white lead and screwed full length of sills. We use in the construction of these bodies high grade stock throughout. We guarantee them not to open at the corners, no matter in what climate they are used.

GEAR—1¼-inch dust proof bell collar· long distance axles, with felt oil pads. Axles are fitted with selected straight grain white hickory beds, which are cemented and fully clipped full length of axles. When these beds are finished up the beds and axles are the same as one piece. Fine oil tempered French pattern open head springs, well graded and very easy riding. Reach is well ironed full length, bolted and properly braced. Fine full circle wrought surrey fifth wheel. Bradley quick shifting shaft couplers, which are the best quick shifting couplers on the market and are used on all high grade work. Roller rub irons. Regulation surrey shafts made from straight grain selected hickory, full patent leather trimmed with long 36-inch tips. Pole is made from fine selected straight grain hickory, well ironed and properly braced, has nickel pole tip and nickel neck yoke tips. Both pole and shafts, $5.00 extra.

WHEELS—Fine selected straight grain white hickory, 1-inch banded hub style, 40 inches front and 44 inches rear, equipped with 1-inch round edge planished steel tire which is bolted between every spoke. Tires are set hot by hand and not by machine Felloes have screws through them on each side of every spoke, which insures them against checking at the spokes. The wheels we regularly furnish are the correct height for this style gear, but we can change the height of wheels, if desired. We also furnish Sarven patent wheels instead of banded hub, if preferred.

TRIMMINGS—Seats are trimmed with fine dark green all wool broadcloth, guaranteed fast color. We will trim with fine dark blue all wool broadcloth or fine whipcord, if preferred. The ends of the seats are pleated and trimmed to match the cushions and backs, and both cushions and backs are upholstered with hair and fine upholstering springs. They are very comfortable and most easy riding. We can furnish special colors in broadcloth trimmings, if desired, at a small additional charge. Fine genuine leather trimmings in dark green, maroon or russet instead of broadcloth, $5.00 extra. Fine full padded dash. Velvet carpet in bottom of body, or rubber mat if preferred to the carpet. Oil burner lamps.

TOP—Fine canopy top style lined with all wool broadcloth to match seat trimmings, and with fine fringe all around. Standards are finely enameled. There are heavy rubber side curtains all around, also heavy rubber storm apron for the dash. We furnish No. 229 equipped with fine leather quarter extension top instead of canopy top for $10.00 additional charge.

PAINTING—Body is finely finished in black, correctly striped; gear, Brewster green, properly striped. We will make any changes in color of painting desired. For system of painting, see page 5.

28

The above cut shows No. 231 which is just the same as No. 230 only with canopy top. Price, $10.00 less than with extension top.

No. 230—FINE EXTENSION TOP SURREY, WITH SPECIAL AUTO STYLE SEATS

PRICE
{
Cash with order, with steel tires and pole or shafts..........................$122.50
C. O. D., with steel tires and pole or shafts.................................. 125.00
Cash with order, with 1-inch guaranteed rubber tires and pole or shafts....... 140.00
C. O. D., with 1-inch guaranteed rubber tires and pole or shafts............. 142.50
}

No. 230 is a light running, roomy, comfortable riding and attractive surrey. It is one of our best grades and a style that gives universal satisfaction. We are glad of an opportunity to ship No. 230 anywhere for examination and approval, and if it is not considered all we claim and equal to similar surreys sold for $30.00 to $40.00 more than our price, we will take it back at our expense.

BODY—Regulation size straight sill design with large, roomy, high backed, comfortable seats. There is plenty of room in front and between the seats for comfort. We use high grade stock throughout in their construction. There are good heavy steel sill or rocker plates laid in white lead and screwed full length of sills.

GEAR—1⅛-inch dust proof bell collar long distance axles, with felt oil pads. Axles are fitted with selected straight grain white hickory beds, which are cemented and clipped full length of axles. Fine oil tempered French pattern open head springs, well graded and very easy riding. Reach is well ironed full length, bolted and properly braced. Fine full circle wrought surrey fifth wheel. Bradley quick shifting shaft couplers, which are the best quick shifting couplers on the market and are used on all high grade work. Roller rub irons. Regulation surrey shafts made from straight grain selected hickory, full patent leather trimmed with long 36-inch tips. Pole is made from fine selected straight grain hickory, well ironed and properly braced, has nickel pole tip and nickel neck yoke tips. Both pole and shafts, $5.00 extra.

WHEELS—Fine selected straight grain white hickory,1-inch banded hub style, 40 inches front and 44 inches rear, equipped with 1-inch round edge planished steel tire which is bolted between every spoke. Tires are set hot by hand and not by machine. Felloes have screws through them on each side of every spoke, which insures them against checking at the spokes. The wheels we regularly furnish are the correct height for this style gear, but we can change the height of wheels, if desired. We also furnish Sarven patent wheels instead of banded hub, if preferred.

TRIMMINGS—Seats are trimmed with fine dark green all wool broadcloth, guaranteed fast color. We will trim with fine dark blue all wool broadcloth or fine whipcord, if preferred. The ends of the seats are pleated and trimmed to match the cushions and backs, and both cushions and backs are upholstered with hair and fine upholstering springs. They are very comfortable and most easy riding. We can furnish special colors in broadcloth trimmings, if desired, at a small additional charge. Fine genuine leather trimmings in dark green, maroon or russet instead of broadcloth, $5.00 extra. Fine full padded dash. Velvet carpet in bottom of body, or rubber mat if preferred to the carpet. Oil burner lamps.

TOP—Fine leather quarter with heavy rubber side curtains and storm apron. Bow sockets are the best grade enameled steel sockets we can buy, and top joints are the best grade enameled joints made. There are heavy rubber side curtains and storm apron for the dash. We will furnish full leather top with best grade leather covered bow sockets and heavy rubber side curtains for $10.00 additional charge. We also furnish with canopy top instead of extension top, as shown by small cut in corner of page, for $10.00 less than with extension top.

PAINTING—The body is black; gear, Brewster green, correctly striped. We will make any changes in painting desired. Our painting is all fully guaranteed. For system of painting, see page 5.

29

The above cut shows No. 232 with canopy top instead of extension. Price, $10.00 less than with extension top.

No. 232—FINE THREE SPRING, EXTENSION TOP SURREY

A good many users prefer three spring gear for surrey use, and our No. 232 is one of the most desirable style straight sill surreys we are making. It is equipped with regular three spring carriage style gear. The handles on the seats of this surrey are a very desirable feature as they aid materially in getting into and out of the surrey. We know No. 232 is as good in quality of workmanship and material throughout as usually sells for $35.00 to $40.00 more than our price. We are glad to ship it for examination and approval, and if it is not found all we claim and satisfactory, it may be returned at our expense.

BODY—Is one of our best straight sill styles and a design that has always pleased our patrons. The seats are roomy, have good high backs and are very comfortable. They have seat handles, as picture shows, which gives the surrey the appearance of a carriage body. There are heavy steel sill or rocker plates laid in white lead and screwed full length of sills. We use high grade stock throughout in the construction of this body and seats.

GEAR—Three spring style, with 1 1/16-inch dust proof bell collar long distance axles, with felt oil pads. Axles are fitted with selected straight grain white hickory beds, which are cemented and clipped full length of axles. When these axle beds are finished up the beds and axles are the same as one piece. Fine oil tempered French pattern open head springs, well graded and very easy riding. Reach is well ironed full length, bolted and properly braced. Fine full circle wrought surrey fifth wheel. Bradley quick shifting shaft couplers, which are the best quick shifting couplers on the market and are used on all high grade work. Roller rub irons. Regulation surrey shafts made from straight grain selected hickory, full patent leather trimmed with long 36-inch tips. Pole is made from fine selected straight grain hickory, well ironed and properly braced, has nickel pole tip and nickel neck yoke tips. Both pole and shafts, $5.00 extra.

WHEELS—Fine selected straight grain white hickory, 1-inch banded hub style, 40 inches front and 44 inches rear, equipped with 1-inch round edge planished steel tire which is bolted between every spoke. Tires are set hot by hand and not by machine. Felloes have screws through them on each side of every spoke, which insures them against checking at the spokes. The wheels we regu-

larly furnish are the correct height for this style gear, but we can change height of wheels, if desired. We also furnish Sarven patent wheels instead of banded hub, if preferred.

TRIMMINGS—Seats are trimmed with fine dark green all wool broadcloth, guaranteed fast color. We will trim with fine dark blue all wool broadcloth or fine whipcord, if preferred. The ends of the seats are pleated and trimmed to match the cushions and backs, and both cushions and backs are upholstered with hair and fine upholstering springs. They are very comfortable and most easy riding. We can furnish special colors in broadcloth trimmings, if desired, at a small additional charge. Fine genuine leather trimmings in dark green, maroon or russet instead of broadcloth, $5.00 extra. Fine full padded dash. Velvet carpet in bottom of body, or rubber mat if preferred to the carpet. Oil burner lamps.

TOP—Fine leather quarter extension top, with heavy rubber side curtains and storm apron. Bow sockets are the best grade enameled steel sockets we can buy and top joints are the best grade enameled joints made. There are heavy rubber side curtains and storm apron for the dash. We will furnish full leather top with best grade leather covered bow sockets and heavy rubber side curtains for $10.00 additional charge. We also furnish with canopy top instead of extension top, as shown by small cut in corner of page, for $10.00 less than with extension top.

PAINTING—The body is black; gear, Brewster green, correctly striped. We will make any changes in painting desired. Our painting is all fully guaranteed. For system of painting, see page 5.

The above cut shows No. 233 with extension top instead of canopy. Price, with leather quarter extension top, $10.00 more than canopy.

No. 233—FINE CANOPY TOP, TWO SPRING SURREY

PRICE

Cash with order, with steel tires and pole or shafts	$ 93.00
C. O. D., with steel tires and pole or shafts	95.00
Cash with order, with 1-inch guaranteed rubber tires and pole or shafts	110.50
C. O. D., with 1-inch guaranteed rubber tires and pole or shafts	112.50

No. 233 is one of the best selling straight sill surreys we are making. It is a light running, comfortable riding vehicle, and a style that gives our customers the very best of satisfaction. The body hangs low and it is easy to get into and out of. We are glad to ship No. 233 for full examination and approval, with the understanding that it is to be found perfectly satisfactory in every particular and equal to similar styles of surreys sold for fully $30.00 more than our price, or it may be returned at our expense. In dealing with us you are out nothing if not perfectly satisfied.

BODY—Is one of the finest straight sill surrey bodies made. Seats have handles as picture shows. They have good high backs and are roomy and very comfortable. There are heavy steel sill or rocker plates laid in white lead and screwed full length of sills. We use in the construction of these bodies and seats high grade stock throughout and guarantee them not to open at the corners, no matter in what climate they are used.

GEAR—1⅛-inch dust proof bell collar long distance axles, with felt oil pads. Axles are fitted with selected straight grain white hickory beds, which are cemented and fully clipped full length of axles. When these beds are smoothed up the beds and axles are the same as one piece. Fine oil tempered French pattern open head springs, well graded and very easy riding. Reach is well ironed full length, bolted and properly braced. Fine full circle wrought surrey fifth wheel. Bradley quick shifting shaft couplers, which are the best quick shifting couplers on the market and are used on all high grade work. Roller rub irons. Regulation surrey shafts made from straight grain selected hickory, full patent leather trimmed with long 36-inch tips. Pole is made from fine selected straight grain hickory, well ironed and properly braced, has nickel pole tip and nickel neck yoke tips. Both pole and shafts, $5.00 extra.

WHEELS—Fine selected straight grain white hickory, 1-inch banded hub style, 40 inches front and 44 inches rear, equipped with 1-inch round edge planished steel tire, which is bolted between every spoke. Tires are set hot by hand and not by ma-

chine. Felloes have screws through them on each side of every spoke, which insures them against checking at the spokes. The wheels we regularly furnish are the correct height for this style gear, but we can change height of wheels, if desired. We also furnish Sarven patent wheels instead of banded hub, if preferred.

TRIMMINGS—Seats are trimmed with fine dark green all wool broadcloth, guaranteed fast color. We will trim with fine dark blue all wool broadcloth or fine whipcord, if preferred. The ends of the seats are pleated and trimmed to match the cushions and backs, and both cushions and backs are upholstered with hair and fine upholstering springs. They are very comfortable and most easy riding. We can furnish special colors in broadcloth trimmings, if desired, at a small additional charge. Fine genuine leather trimmings in dark green, maroon or russet instead of broadcloth, $5.00 extra. Fine full padded dash. Velvet carpet in bottom of body, or rubber mat if preferred to the carpet. Oil burner lamps.

TOP—Fine canopy top style lined with all wool broadcloth to match seat trimmings and with fine fringe all around. Standards are finely enameled. There are heavy rubber side curtains all around, also heavy rubber storm apron for the dash. We furnish with fine leather quarter extension top instead of canopy top for $10.00 additional charge.

PAINTING—Body is finely finished in black, correctly striped; gear, brewster green, properly striped. We will make any changes in color of painting desired. For system of painting, see page 5.

31

The above cut shows No. 311 with full rubber extension style top. Price, $5.00 more than with canopy top.

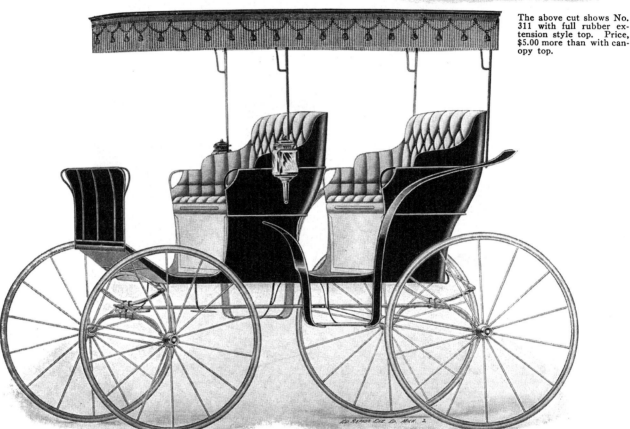

No. 311—LIGHT, ONE HORSE SURREY, WITH BIKE GEAR AND AUTO SEATS

PRICE
Cash with order, with steel tires and shafts.................................$ 83.00
C. O. D., with steel tires and shafts.. 85.00
Cash with order, with ⅞-inch guaranteed rubber tires and shafts............. 98.00
C. O. D., with ⅞-inch guaranteed rubber tires and shafts.................... 100.00
If 1⅛-inch guaranteed cushion tires are preferred, add $5.00 to the price quoted with ⅞-inch solid tires.

Our No. 311 is an up-to-date, light one horse surrey, and as good in quality of workmanship and material throughout as usually sells for $30.00 more than our price. It is equipped with automobile style seats and bike gear. We know our No. 311 will please, and are glad to ship it anywhere for full examination and approval.

BODY—Is a very desirable design. Seats are one of the most popular auto styles made and the backs are high and very comfortable. We use high grade stock throughout in the construction of the body and seats, and we guarantee the panels not to open at the joints, no matter in what climate they are used. There are good steel sill or rocker plates laid in white lead and screwed full length of body. Roller rub irons.

GEAR—Roman bike style dust proof bell collar long distance axles, with felt oil pads. Axles are equipped with short straight grain white hickory beds, which are cemented and clipped to center of axles. Fine oil tempered French pattern open head springs, properly graded and very easy riding. Reaches are ironed full length, bolted and well braced. Full circle wrought Brewster fifth wheel, which is one of the best and strongest fifth wheels made. Bradley quick shifting shaft couplers, the style used on all first class work. Regulation shafts made from selected grain white hickory, full patent leather trimmed, and heel braces. We will furnish pole in place of shafts for $1.00 additional charge. Pole in addition to shafts, $5.00 additional charge.

WHEELS—Fine selected straight grain white hickory, ⅞-inch Sarven patent, 38 inches front, 40 inches rear, equipped with ⅞-inch round edge planished steel tire, bolted between every spoke. Our tires are set hot by hand and not by machine. Felloes have screws through them on each side of every spoke, which insures them against checking at the spokes. The height of wheels furnished is correct for this style gear, but will change height, if desired. We will furnish banded hub style wheels, if desired; also 1-inch instead of ⅞-inch.

TRIMMINGS—Seats are trimmed with dark green all wool broadcloth, guaranteed fast color. We will trim with dark blue all wool broadcloth or fine whipcord, if preferred. The ends of the seats are pleated and trimmed to match cushions and backs, and there are fine upholstering springs in both cushions and backs. Seats are very comfortable. We furnish special colors in broadcloth trimmings, if desired, at a small additional charge. Fine genuine leather trimmings in dark green, maroon or russet, $5.00 extra. Full padded patent leather dash. Velvet carpet in bottom of body, or rubber mat if preferred to the carpet. Oil burner lamps.

PAINTING—Body is plain black; gear, New York red, neatly striped. We will furnish Brewster green gear, correctly striped, or will paint any color you desire. For system of painting, see page 5.

32

The above cut shows our No. 313 without top. Price, $10.00 less than with top.

No. 313—LIGHT CANOPY TOP SURREY, WITH AUTO SEATS

PRICE
Cash with order, with steel tires and shafts.................................$ 83.00
C. O. D., with steel tires and shafts.. 85.00
Cash with order, with 7⁄8-inch guaranteed rubber tires and shafts............ 98.00
C. O. D., with 7⁄8-inch guaranteed rubber tires and shafts................... 100.00
If 1-inch guaranteed rubber tires are preferred, add $2.50 to the price quoted with 7⁄8-inch solid tires.

Our No. 313 is one of the most up-to-date style light surreys made. It is equipped with our late automobile style seats, which are very roomy and comfortable. It is light weight and just right for one horse, yet it is suitable for two horses. We are glad of an opportunity to ship No. 313 for examination and approval, and if not found all we claim and well worth $25.00 to $30.00 more than our price, it may be returned at our expense.

BODY—Is a very desirable design. Seats are one of the most popular auto styles made, and the backs are high and very comfortable. We use high grade stock throughout in the construction of the body and seats, and we guarantee the panels not to open at the joints, no matter in what climate they are used. There are good steel sill or rocker plates laid in white lead and screwed full length of body. Roller rub irons.

GEAR—1 1⁄8-inch dust proof bell collar long distance axles, with felt oil pads. Axles are equipped with selected straight grain white hickory beds, which are clipped full length of axles. Fine oil tempered French pattern open head springs, properly graded and very easy riding. Reaches are ironed full length, bolted and well braced. Full circle wrought surrey fifth wheel, which is one of the best and strongest fifth wheels made. Bradley quick shifting shaft couplers, the style used on all first class work. Regulation shafts made from selected straight grain white hickory, full patent leather trimmed, and with heel braces. We will furnish pole in place of shafts for $1.00 additional charge. Pole in addition to shafts, $5.00 additional charge.

WHEELS—Fine selected straight grain white hickory, 7⁄8-inch Sarven patent, 40 inches front, 44 inches rear, equipped with 7⁄8-inch round edge planished steel tire, bolted between every spoke. Our tires are set hot by hand and not by machine. Felloes have screws through them on each side of every spoke, which insures them against checking at the spokes. Wheels we furnish are correct height, but will change height if desired. We will furnish banded hub style wheels, if desired; also 1-inch instead of 7⁄8-inch.

TRIMMINGS—Seats are trimmed with dark green all wool broadcloth, guaranteed fast color. We will trim with dark blue all wool broadcloth or fine whipcord, if preferred. The ends of the seats are pleated and trimmed to match cushions and backs, and there are fine upholstering springs in both cushions and backs. Seats are very comfortable. We furnish special colors in broadcloth trimmings, if desired, at a small additional charge. Fine genuine leather trimmings in dark green, maroon or russet, $5.00 extra. Full padded patent leather dash. Velvet carpet in bottom of body, or rubber mat if preferred to the carpet. Oil burner lamps.

TOP—Is canopy style lined with wool cloth to match seat trimmings, and with fringe all around. Rubber side curtains all around and good rubber storm apron for the dash. We furnish full rubber extension top instead of canopy top for $5.00 additional charge.

PAINTING—The body is black; gear, Brewster green, correctly striped. We will make any changes in painting desired. Our painting is all fully guaranteed. For system of painting, see page 5.

33

The above cut illustrates No. 315 with canopy top. Price, $5.00 less than with extension top.

No. 315—LIGHT EXTENSION TOP SURREY

PRICE
Cash with order, with steel tires and shafts....................................$78.00
C. O. D., with steel tires and shafts... 80.00
Cash with order, with ⅞-inch guaranteed rubber tires and shafts.............. 93.00
C. O. D., with ⅞-inch guaranteed rubber tires and shafts..................... 95.00
If 1-inch guaranteed rubber tires are preferred, add $2.50 to the price quoted with ⅞-inch rubber tires.

We offer in our No. 315 a very desirable style medium weight surrey, which is just the thing for one horse. We know our No. 315 is as good in every particular as usually sells for $25.00 to $35.00 more than our price. We have so much confidence in this surrey that we are glad to ship it for full examination and approval, with the understanding that it is to be found all we claim and a highly satisfactory surrey for the money, or it may be returned at our expense.

BODY—Is a style that has always been very popular. There is plenty of room in front and between the seats, and the seats are roomy and have good high backs. We use in the construction of body and seats high grade stock throughout, and they are so constructed that we guarantee the joints not to open, no matter in what climate they are used. There are good steel sill or rocker plates laid in white lead and screwed full length of sills.

GEAR—1⅛-inch dust proof bell collar long distance axles, with felt oil pads. Axles are equipped with selected straight grain white hickory beds, which are clipped full length of axles. Fine oil tempered French pattern open head springs, properly graded and very easy riding. Reaches are ironed full length, bolted and well braced. Full circle wrought surrey fifth wheel, which is one of the best and strongest fifth wheels made. Bradley quick shifting shaft couplers, the style used on all first class work. Regulation surrey shafts made from selected straight grain white hickory, full patent leather trimmed, and heel braces. We will furnish pole in place of shafts for $1.00 additional charge. Pole in addition to shafts, $5.00 additional charge.

WHEELS—Fine selected straight grain white hickory, ⅞-inch Sarven patent, 40 inches front, 44 inches rear, equipped with ⅞-inch round edge planished steel tire, bolted between every spoke. Our tires are set hot by hand and not by machine. Felloes have

screws through them on each side of every spoke, which insures them against checking at the spokes. We will furnish banded hub style wheels, if desired; also 1-inch instead of ⅞-inch.

TRIMMINGS—Seats are trimmed with dark green all wool broadcloth, guaranteed fast color. We will trim with dark blue all wool broadcloth or fine whipcord, if preferred. The ends of the seats are pleated and trimmed to match cushions and backs, and there are fine upholstering springs in both cushions and backs. Seats are very comfortable. We furnish special colors in broadcloth trimmings, if desired, at a small additional charge. Fine genuine leather trimmings in dark green, maroon or russet, $5.00 extra. Full padded patent leather dash. Velvet carpet in bottom of body, or rubber mat if preferred to the carpet. Oil burner lamps.

TOP—Good full rubber extension top with rubber side curtains and storm apron. Top is lined with wool cloth to match seat trimmings. We furnish leather quarter top instead of full rubber for $5.00 additional charge. Canopy top instead of extension top, $5.00 less than regular price.

PAINTING—The body is black; gear, Brewster green, correctly striped. We will make any changes in painting desired. Our painting is all fully guaranteed. For system of painting, see page 5.

The above cut illustrates
No. 318 with full rubber
extension top instead of
canopy. Price, $5.00
more than with canopy.

No. 318—CANOPY TOP, PIANO BODY SURREY

PRICE
{
Cash with order, with steel tires and shafts.................................$73.00
C. O. D., with steel tires and shafts.. 75.00
Cash with order, with ⅞-inch guaranteed rubber tires and shafts.............. 88.00
C. O. D., with ⅞-inch guaranteed rubber tires and shafts..................... 90.00
}
If 1-inch guaranteed rubber tires are preferred, add $2.50 to the price quoted with ⅞-inch rubber tires.

Our No. 318 is a splendid carriage, and is desired by many users because of the style of the body. We know our No. 318 is as good in quality of workmanship and material throughout as usually sells for $25.00 more than our price. We are glad to ship it for full examination and approval, and if not found all we claim it may be returned at our expense.

BODY—Is 5 feet 8 inches long by 29 inches wide. Seats are regular surrey style, the backs are high and they are very comfortable. The front seat is stationary. Rear seat is removable and can be taken out without removing the top. We use high grade stock in the construction of the body and seats and guarantee them not to open at the joints, no matter in what climate they are used.

GEAR—1¼-inch bell collar long distance axles, with felt oil pads. Axles are equipped with selected straight grain white hickory beds, which are cemented and clipped full length of axles. Fine oil tempered French pattern open head springs, properly graded and very easy riding. Reaches are ironed full length, bolted and well braced. Bradley quick shifting shaft couplers, the style used on all first class work. Regulation shafts made from selected grain white hickory, full patent leather trimmed, and with heel braces. We will furnish pole in place of shafts for $1.00 additional charge. Pole in addition to shafts, $5.00 additional charge.

WHEELS—Fine selected straight grain white hickory, ⅞-inch Sarven patent, 40 inches front, 40 inches rear, equipped with ⅞-inch round edge planished steel tire, bolted between every spoke. Our tires are set hot by hand and not by machine. Felloes have screws through them on each side of every spoke, which insures them against checking at the spokes. The wheels we furnish are the correct height, but will change height, if desired. We will furnish banded hub style wheels, if desired; also 1-inch instead of ⅞-inch.

TRIMMINGS—Seats are trimmed with dark green all wool broadcloth, guaranteed fast color. We will trim with dark blue all wool broadcloth or fine whipcord, if preferred. The ends of the seats are pleated and trimmed to match cushions and backs, and there are fine upholstering springs in both cushions and backs. Seats are very comfortable. We furnish special colors in broadcloth trimmings, if desired, at a small additional charge. Fine genuine leather trimmings in dark green, maroon or russet, $5.00 extra. Full padded patent leather dash. Brussels carpet in bottom of body, or rubber mat if preferred to the carpet. Oil burner lamps.

TOP—Is canopy style with wool cloth to match seat trimmings, and with fringe all around. Rubber side curtains all around and good rubber storm apron for the dash. We furnish full rubber extension top instead of canopy top for $5.00 additional charge. (See small cut above.)

PAINTING—The body is black; gear, Brewster green, correctly striped. We will make any changes in painting desired. Our painting is all fully guaranteed. For system of painting, see page 5.

35

The above cut shows No. 320 without top. Price, $15.00 less than with top.

No. 320—FINE CANOPY TOP, CUT-UNDER TRAP, WITH SIDE DOORS

PRICE
Cash with order, with steel tires and shafts.................................$127.00
C. O. D., with steel tires and shafts... 130.00
Cash with order, with 1-inch guaranteed rubber tires and shafts............... 144.50
C. O. D., with 1-inch guaranteed rubber tires and shafts...................... 147.50

No. 320 is one of the most up-to-date style traps to be found anywhere. It is a very popular seller with us and is a style that gives satisfaction wherever shipped. We are glad to ship No. 320 for full examination and approval, and if it is not found all we claim and as good as usually sells for $40.00 more than our price, it may be returned at our expense. (See small cut in corner of page for appearance of body when used with one seat.)

BODY—Is made from high grade stock throughout. There are heavy steel sill or rocker plates laid in white lead and screwed full length of sills. The front seat is made stationary, and the rear seat folds forward when not in use so that the back of the seat forms a solid deck over the back part of the body, making a neat one seat trap. When used with two seats, access is gained to the rear seat through the side doors in the body. It is one of the best and most up-to-date style trap bodies made.

GEAR—1$\frac{1}{8}$-inch dust proof bell collar long distance axles, with felt oil pads. Axles are fitted with selected straight grain white hickory beds, which are cemented and clipped full length of axles. When these beds are finished up the bed and axles are the same as one piece. Fine oil tempered French pattern open head springs, well graded and very easy riding. Reach is well ironed full length, bolted and properly braced. Fine full circle wrought surrey fifth wheel. Bradley quick shifting shaft couplers, which are the best quick shifting couplers on the market and are used on all high grade work. Roller rub irons. Regulation cut-under surrey shafts made from straight grain selected hickory, full patent leather trimmed with long 36-inch tips. Pole instead of shafts, $1.00 extra. Pole is made from fine selected straight grain hickory, well ironed and properly braced, has nickel pole tip and nickel neck yoke tips. Both pole and shafts, $5.00 extra.

WHEELS—Fine selected straight grain white hickory, 1-inch banded hub style, 40 inches front and 44 inches rear, equipped with 1-inch round edge planished steel tire, which is bolted be-

tween every spoke. Tires are set hot by hand and not by machine. Felloes have screws through them on each side of every spoke, which insures them against checking at the spokes. The wheels we regularly furnish are the correct height for this style gear, but we can lower the height of wheels, if desired. They could not be raised without there being danger of the front wheels striking the wheel house in turning. We also furnish Sarven patent wheels instead of banded hub, if preferred.

TRIMMINGS—Seats are trimmed with fine heavy all wool whipcord, but will trim with dark green or dark blue all wool broadcloth, if preferred. The whipcord and broadcloth used in this trap are guaranteed fast color. Cushions and backs are well tufted and upholstered with hair. Front seat ends are pleated and trimmed to match cushions and backs.. We can furnish any special colors in broadcloths, if desired, at a small additional charge. We trim the seats with fine genuine trimming leather in dark green, maroon or tan for $5.00 additional charge. Velvet carpet in bottom of body, or rubber mat if preferred to carpet. Fine padded dash. Oil burner lamps.

TOP—Fine canopy style lined to match seat trimmings and with fine fringe all around. Standards are finely enameled. There are heavy rubber side curtains all around, also heavy rubber storm apron for the dash.

PAINTING—Body is finely finished in black, correctly striped; gear, New York red, properly striped. We will make any changes in color of painting desired. For system of painting, see page 5.

36

The above cut shows No. 322 without English canopy top. Price, $15.00 less than with top.

No. 322—FINE CUT-UNDER, SIDE DOOR TRAP, WITH BIKE GEAR AND ENGLISH CANOPY TOP

PRICE
- Cash with order, with steel tires and shafts.................................$127.00
- C. O. D., with steel tires and shafts....................................... 130.00
- Cash with order, with 1⅛-inch guaranteed cushion tires and shafts........... 147.00
- C. O. D., with 1⅛-inch guaranteed cushion tires and shafts.................. 150.00

No. 322 is a style that always pleases. We have so much confidence in this trap we are glad to ship it anywhere for full examination and approval, with the understanding that it is to be found highly satisfactory and all we claim or it may be returned at our expense. We know our No. 322 is as good as usually sells for fully $40.00 more than our price. (See small cut in corner of page for appearance of body when used with one seat, also without top.)

BODY—Is made from high grade stock throughout. There are heavy steel sill or rocker plates laid in white lead and screwed full length of sills. The front seat is made stationary and the rear seat folds forward when not in use so that the back of the seat forms a solid deck over the back part of the body, making a neat one seat trap. When used with two seats access is gained to the rear seat through the side doors in the body. It is one of the best and most up-to-date style trap bodies made.

GEAR—True sweep dust proof bell collar long distance bike axles, with felt oil pads. Axles are fitted with light wood beds, which are cemented and clipped to the axles. Fine oil tempered French pattern open head springs, very elastic and easy riding. The reach is ironed full length, bolted and well braced. Full circle wrought fifth wheel with king bolt clipped around axle. It is the style fifth wheel used on all strictly high grade work. Wrought Bailey body loops clipped to springs. Will furnish wood spring bar, if preferred to the Bailey loops. Bradley quick change shaft couplers, which are the most practical quick shifting couplers made. They are usually used on all high grade work. Shafts are regular trap style. They are made from selected hickory, full patent leather trimmed and are well braced. Pole instead of shafts, $1.00 extra. Will furnish pole in addition to shafts for $5.00 extra.

WHEELS—Fine selected straight grain white hickory, ⅞-inch banded hub, 38 inches front and 40 inches rear, with ⅞-inch round edge planished steel tire bolted between each spoke. Tires are ¼-inch thick and are set hot by hand and not by machine. Felloes have screws through them on each side of every spoke, which insures absolutely against checking at the spokes. The height of the wheels we furnish is correct for this style gear, but we can make any change in height desired. We furnish 1-inch wheels instead of ⅞-inch, if preferred. Also Sarven patent style instead of banded hub.

TRIMMINGS—Seats are trimmed with fine heavy all wool whipcord, but will trim with dark green or dark blue all wool broadcloth, if preferred. The whipcord and broadcloth used in this trap are guaranteed fast color. Cushions and backs are well tufted and upholstered with hair. Front seat ends are pleated and trimmed to match cushions and backs. We can furnish any special colors in broadcloths, if desired, at a small additional charge. We trim the seats with fine genuine trimming leather in dark green, maroon or tan for $5.00 additional charge. Velvet carpet in bottom of body, or rubber mat if preferred to carpet. Fine padded dash. Oil burner lamps.

TOP—Is English folding canopy style with lining and fringe to match the trimmings of seats. We can furnish No. 322 with a regular canopy top, same as No. 320, if preferred. We also furnish without top (see small cut above) for $15.00 reduction.

PAINTING—Body is finely finished in black, correctly striped; gear, New York red, properly striped. We will make any changes in color of painting desired. For system of painting, see page 5.

The above cut shows No. 324 with canopy top and back seat ready for use. Price, $15.00 more than without top.

No. 324—FINE TRAP, WITH BIKE GEAR

PRICE
Cash with order, with steel tires and shafts................................$ 93.00
C. O. D., with steel tires and shafts.. 95.00
Cash with order, with 1⅛-inch guaranteed cushion tires and shafts........... 113.00
C. O. D., with 1⅛-inch guaranteed cushion tires and shafts.................. 115.00
If ⅞-inch guaranteed rubber tires are preferred, deduct $5.00 from the price quoted with 1⅛-inch cushion tires.

No. 324 is a trap that gives universal satisfaction. It makes a very neat turnout whether used with one seat or two. The operation of the seats is very simple. We know No. 324 is just as good in style, quality of workmanship and material throughout as usually sells for $30.00 to $40.00 more than our price, and we are glad to ship it for examination and approval.

BODY—Is a very pleasing design. It is made from high grade stock throughout and has good heavy steel sill or rocker plates laid in white lead and screwed full length of sills. The front seat is in two parts, each half tipping forward, allowing access to the back seat from either side. The back seat folds into the body when not in use, forming a solid finished deck and making a neat one seat vehicle.

GEAR—1-inch dust proof bell collar long distance true sweep bike axles, with felt oil pads. Axles are fitted with selected straight grain white hickory beds, which are cemented and clipped full length of axles. When these beds are finished up the bed and axles are the same as one piece. Fine oil tempered French Pattern open head springs, well graded and very easy riding. Reach is well ironed full length, bolted and properly braced. Fine full circle wrought fifth wheel. Bradley quick shifting shaft couplers, which are the best quick shifting couplers on the market and are used on all high grade work. Roller rub irons. Regulation shafts made from straight grain selected hickory, full patent leather trimmed with long 36-inch tips. Pole instead of shafts, $1.00 extra. Pole is made from fine selected straight grain hickory, well ironed and properly braced, has nickel pole tip and nickel neck yoke tips. Both pole and shafts, $5.00 extra.

WHEELS—Fine selected straight grain white hickory, ⅞-inch banded hub style, 38 inches front and 40 inches rear, equipped with ⅞-inch round edge planished steel tire, which is bolted between every spoke. Tires are set hot by hand and not by machine. Felloes have screws through them on each side of every spoke, which insures them against checking at the spokes. The wheels we regularly furnish are the correct height for this style gear, but we can change the height of wheels, if desired. Furnished with fine steel wire wheels and 1⅛-inch guaranteed cushion tires for $25.00 additional charge to price quoted with wood wheels and steel tires. Also furnish Sarven patent wheel instead of banded hub, if preferred.

TRIMMINGS—Seats are trimmed with fine heavy all wool whipcord, but will trim with dark green or dark blue all wool broadcloth, if preferred. The whipcord and broadcloth used in this trap are guaranteed fast color. Cushions and backs are well tufted and upholstered with hair. Front seat ends are pleated and trimmed to match cushions and backs. We can furnish any special colors in broadcloths, if desired, at a small additional charge. We trim the seats with fine genuine trimming leather in dark green, maroon or tan for $5.00 additional charge. Velvet carpet in bottom of body, or rubber mat if preferred to carpet. Fine padded dash. Oil burner lamps.

PAINTING—Body is finely finished in black, correctly striped; gear, New York red, properly striped. We will make any changes in color of painting desired. For system of painting, see page 5.

The above cut shows our No. 325 without top and with back seat folded down. Price, $15.00 less than with top.

No. 325—FINE, LIGHT, CANOPY TOP TRAP

PRICE
- Cash with order, with steel tires and shafts.................................$108.00
- C. O. D., with steel tires and shafts... 110.00
- Cash with order, with ⅞-inch guaranteed rubber tires and shafts.............. 123.00
- C. O. D., with ⅞-inch guaranteed rubber tires and shafts.................... 125.00

If 1-inch guaranteed rubber tires are preferred, add $2.50 to the price quoted with ⅞-inch rubber tires.

No. 325 is a very desirable style canopy top, two or four passenger trap. This trap gives the best of satisfaction and we can unhesitatingly recommend it. We are glad to ship No. 325 anywhere for examination and approval, with the understanding that it is to be found all we claim and you to feel you are saving $25.00 to $35.00, or we will take the shipment back at our expense.

BODY—Is made from high grade stock throughout. There are heavy steel sill or rocker plates laid in white lead and screwed full length of sills. The front seat is in two parts, each half tipping forward and allowing access to back from either side. The rear seat folds forward when not in use and forms a solid deck over the back part of the body, making a neat one seat trap.

GEAR—1⅛-inch dust proof bell collar long distance axles, with felt oil pads. Axles are fitted with selected straight grain white hickory beds, which are cemented and clipped full length of axles. When these beds are finished up the bed and axles are the same as one piece. Fine oil tempered French pattern open head springs, well graded and very easy riding. Reach is well ironed full length, bolted and properly braced. Fine full circle wrought fifth wheel. Bradley quick shifting shaft couplers, which are the best quick shifting couplers on the market and are used on all high grade work. Roller rub irons. Regulation shafts made from straight grain selected hickory, full patent leather trimmed with long 36-inch tips. Pole in place of shafts, $1.00 extra. Pole is made from fine selected straight grain hickory, well ironed and properly braced, has nickel pole tip and nickel neck yoke tips. Both pole and shafts, $5.00 extra.

WHEELS—Fine selected straight grain white hickory, ⅞-inch banded hub style, 40 inches front and 44 inches rear, equipped with 1-inch round edge planished steel tire, which is bolted be-

tween every spoke. Tires are set hot by hand and not by machine. Felloes have screws through them on each side of every spoke, which insures them against checking at the spokes. The wheels we regularly furnish are the correct height for this style gear, but we can change the height of wheels, if desired. We also furnish Sarven patent wheels instead of banded hub, if preferred.

TRIMMINGS—Seats are trimmed with fine heavy all wool whipcord, but will trim with dark green or dark blue all wool broadcloth, if preferred. The whipcord and broadcloth used in this trap are guaranteed fast color. Cushions and backs are well tufted and upholstered with hair. Front seat ends are pleated and trimmed to match cushions and backs. We can furnish any special colors in broadcloths, if desired, at a small additional charge. We trim the seats with fine genuine trimming leather in dark green, maroon or tan for $5.00 additional charge. Velvet carpet in bottom of body, or rubber mat if preferred to carpet. Fine padded dash. Oil burner lamps.

TOP—Fine canopy style lined to match seat trimmings and with fine fringe all around. Standards are finely enameled. There are heavy rubber side curtains all around, also heavy rubber storm apron for the dash.

PAINTING—Body is finely finished in black, correctly striped; gear, New York red, properly striped. We will make any changes in color of painting desired. For system of painting, see page 5.

39

The above cut shows **No. 329** without the top **and** with the back seat removed, thus making **a** neat one seat open buckboard. Of course, the back seat can be taken out and the wagon used with one seat and top, if desired. If top is not wanted, price is **$15.00** less than with top.

No. 329—FINE ENGLISH TOP BUCKBOARD

PRICE
Cash with order, with steel tires and shafts.................................$103.00
C. O. D., with steel tires and shafts.. 105.00
Cash with order, with ⅞-inch guaranteed rubber tires and shafts............. 118.00
C. O. D., with ⅞-inch guaranteed rubber tires and shafts.................... 120.00
If 1-inch guaranteed rubber tires are preferred, add $2.50 to the price quoted with ⅞-inch tires.

No. 329 is one of the best and most popular style buckboards made. The rear seat can be easily removed if only one seat is desired, and the top can be easily taken off, thus making an open, one or two seat buckboard. We are regularly painting our No. 329 body black and gear canary yellow, but finish it in natural wood, if preferred. We know this wagon is as good in quality of workmanship and material throughout as usually sells for $25.00 to $35.00 more than our price. We are glad to ship it for examination and approval.

BODY—Is one of the best buckboard designs made. The seats are very much better style and more comfortable than the ordinary buckboard seat. We use in the construction of body and seats high grade stock throughout. Both seats are made removable and the rear seat can be easily taken out when only one seat is desired.

GEAR—1¼-inch dust proof bell collar long distance axles, with felt oil pads. Axles are equipped with straight grain white hickory beds, which are cemented and clipped full length of axles. Springs are the Shuler patent with roller bearings where attached to front and rear axle. This is undoubtedly the easiest riding vehicle spring made and we expect to use a good many of them on our different styles this season. Reach is ironed full length, bolted and well braced. Full circle wrought fifth wheel. Bradley quick shifting shaft couplers, which are the best quick shifting couplers on the market and are used only on high grade work. Roller rub irons. Regulation buckboard shafts made from straight grain selected white hickory, full patent leather trimmed with long 36-inch tips. Pole in place of shafts, $1.00 extra. Pole in addition to shafts, $5.00 extra.

WHEELS—Fine selected straight grain white hickory, ⅞-inch Sarven patent style, 40 inches front, 44 inches rear, equipped with ⅞ inch round edge planished steel tire, which is bolted between every spoke. Tires are set hot by hand and not by machine.

Felloes have screws through them on each side of every spoke, which insures them against checking at the spokes. The wheels we regularly furnish on this wagon are the correct height, but we can change the height, if desired. We also furnish banded hub instead of Sarven patent, or 1-inch size instead of ⅞-inch.

TRIMMINGS—Seats are trimmed with fine all wool whipcord, guaranteed fast color. We will trim with dark green or dark blue all wool broadcloth, if preferred. Both cushions and backs are upholstered with hair and fine upholstering springs. They are very comfortable and easy riding. We furnish special colors in broadcloth trimmings, if desired, at a small additional charge. Fine genuine leather trimmings in dark green, maroon or russet instead of whipcord, $5.00 extra. Fine full padded patent leather dash. Rubber mat in bottom of body, or velvet carpet if preferred.

TOP—Is English folding canopy style with lining and fringe to match the trimmings of seats. We can furnish No. 329 with **a** regular canopy top, same as No. 320, if preferred. We also furnish without top at $15.00 reduction.

PAINTING—Body is black; gear, canary yellow, correctly striped. We will furnish New York red gear, Brewster green, or make any changes in painting desired. For system of painting, see page 5.

40

The above cut illustrates No. 332 with canopy top and back seat ready for use. Price, $10.00 more than without top.

No. 332—LIGHT, OPEN, TWO OR FOUR PASSENGER TRAP

PRICE
Cash with order, with steel tires and shafts...................................$78.00
C. O. D., with steel tires and shafts... 80.00
Cash with order, with ⅞-inch guaranteed rubber tires and shafts.............. 93.00
C. O. D., with ⅞-inch guaranteed rubber tires and shafts..................... 95.00

No. 332 is one of the lightest weight four passenger traps we have ever made. Although it is compact there is plenty of room for seating four adults comfortably. We know our No. 332 is as good in quality of workmanship and material throughout as usually sells for $25.00 to $30.00 more than our price. We are glad to ship it for full examination and approval, and if it is not found all we claim, it may be returned at our expense.

BODY—Is made from high grade stock throughout and the seats are roomy. There are steel sill or rocker plates laid in white lead and screwed full length of sills. Entrance to the back seat is gained from the front, each half of the front seat tilting to one side as desired. When back of seat is not in use the back of the seat can be folded down and the seat tipped forward, thus forming a solid deck over the back part of the body, making a neat one seat trap.

GEAR—1⅛-inch dust proof bell collar long distance axles, with felt oil pads. Axles are equipped with selected straight grain white hickory beds, which are clipped full length of axles. Fine oil tempered French pattern open head springs, properly graded and very easy riding. Reaches are ironed full length, bolted and well braced. Full circle wrought Brewster fifth wheel, which is one of the best and strongest fifth wheels made. Bradley quick shifting shaft couplers. Regulation trap shafts made from selected straight grain white hickory, full patent leather trimmed, and with heel braces. We will furnish pole in place of shafts for $1.00 additional charge. Pole in addition to shafts, $5.00 additional charge.

WHEELS—Fine selected straight grain white hickory, ⅞-inch Sarven patent, 40 inches front, 44 inches rear, equipped with

⅞-inch round edge planished steel tire, bolted between every spoke. Our tires are set hot by hand and not by machine. Felloes have screws through them on each side of every spoke, which insures them against checking at the spokes. Wheels we furnish are the correct height for this style gear, but we can change height if desired. We will furnish banded hub style wheels, if desired, also 1-inch instead of ⅞-inch.

TRIMMINGS—Seats are trimmed with fine heavy whipcord, but will trim with dark green or dark blue all wool broadcloth, if preferred. The whipcord and broadcloth used in this trap are guaranteed fast color. Cushions and backs are well tufted and upholstered. Front seat ends are pleated and trimmed to match cushion and back. We can furnish any special colors in broadcloths, if desired, at a small additional charge. We trim the seats with fine genuine trimming leather in dark green, maroon or tan for $5.00 additional charge. Velvet carpet in bottom of body, or rubber mat if preferred to carpet. Fine padded dash. Oil burner lamps.

PAINTING—Body is black; gear, New York red, correctly striped. We will furnish Brewster green gear, or make any changes in painting desired. For system of painting, see page 5.

41

The above cut shows No. 334 with canopy top and back seat ready for use. Price, $10.00 more than without top.

No. 334—LIGHT, OPEN, TWO OR FOUR PASSENGER TRAP

PRICE
{
Cash with order, with steel tires and shafts.................................$ 78.00
C. O. D., with steel tires and shafts.. 80.00
Cash with order, with 1⅛-inch guaranteed cushion tires and shafts........... 98.00
C. O. D., with 1⅛-inch guaranteed cushion tires and shafts.................. 100.00
}
If ⅞-inch guaranteed rubber tires are preferred, deduct $5.00 from the price quoted with 1⅛-inch cushion tires.

In our No. 334 we offer a splendid style bike gear trap at a price $25.00 to $30.00 less than traps of this style and grade usually sell for. No. 334 is light running and very comfortable riding. We are glad of an opportunity to ship this trap for examination, with the understanding that it is to be found all we claim, and you to feel you are saving money in buying from us, or we will take the shipment back at our expense.

BODY—Is made from high grade stock throughout and the seats are roomy. There are steel sill or rocker plates laid in white lead and screwed full length of sills. Entrance to the back seat is gained from the front, each half of the front seat tilting to one side as desired. When back seat is not in use the back of the seat can be folded down and the seat tipped forward, thus forming a solid deck over the back part of the body, making a neat one seat trap.

GEAR—Roman bike style dust proof bell collar long distance axles, with felt oil pads. Axles are equipped with short straight grain white hickory beds, which are cemented and clipped to center of axles. Fine oil tempered French pattern open head springs, properly graded and very easy riding. Reaches are ironed full length, bolted and well braced. Full circle wrought Brewster slotted fifth wheel, which is one of the best and strongest fifth wheels made. Bradley quick shifting shaft couplers, the style used on all first class work. Regulation trap shafts made from selected straight grain white hickory, full patent leather trimmed, and with heel braces. We will furnish pole in place of shafts for $1.00 additional charge. Pole in addition to shafts, $5.00 additional charge.

WHEELS—Fine selected straight grain white hickory, ⅞-inch Sarven patent, 38 inches front, 40 inches rear, equipped with ⅞-inch round edge planished steel tires, bolted between every spoke. Our tires are set hot by hand and not by machine. Felloes have screws through them on each side of every spoke, which insures them against checking at the spokes. We will change height of wheels or furnish banded hub style, if desired, also 1-inch instead of ⅞-inch. Furnished with fine steel wire wheels and 1⅛-inch guaranteed cushion tires for $25.00 additional charge to price quoted with wood wheels and steel tires.

TRIMMINGS—Seats are trimmed with f.ne all wool whipcord, guaranteed fast color. We will trim with dark green or dark blue all wool broadcloth, if preferred. The ends of front seat are pleated and trimmed to match the cushions and backs, and both cushions and backs are well upholstered. They are very comfortable and easy riding. We will furnish special colors in broadcloth trimmings, if desired, at a small additional charge. Fine genuine leather trimmings in dark green, maroon or russet instead of whipcord, $5.00 extra. Fine full padded patent leather dash. Velvet carpet, or rubber mat if preferred. Oil burner lamps.

PAINTING—Body is finely finished in black, correctly striped; gear, New York red, properly striped. We will make any changes in color of painting desired. For system of painting, see page 5.

The above cut shows No. 355 as it appears when used with two seats.

No. 355—CANOPY TOP, JUMP SEAT SURREY

PRICE
{ Cash with order, with steel tires and shafts...................................$ 88.00
C. O. D., with steel tires and shafts.. 90.00
Cash with order, with ⅞-inch guaranteed rubber tires and shafts............. 103.00
C. O. D., with ⅞-inch guaranteed rubber tires and shafts.................... 105.00

If 1-inch guaranteed rubber tires are preferred, add $2.50 to prices quoted with ⅞-inch rubber tires.

No. 355 is one of the best style jump seat surreys we have ever made. It is light running, roomy and comfortable riding. It is all right for one horse, or is very suitable for two, if team is desired. We are glad to ship this surrey with the understanding that you are to feel it is equal to similar styles sold by others for $25.00 to $30.00 more than our price, or we will take it back at our expense. (For appearance of surrey when used with two seats, see small cut in corner of page.)

BODY—Is made from high grade stock throughout and there are heavy steel sill or rocker plates laid in white lead and screwed full length of sills. We guarantee the panels not to open at the joints, no matter in what climate used. The shifting arrangement of the seats is so simple that a child can operate them. (See small cut in corner of page showing two seats.)

GEAR—1⅛-inch dust proof bell collar long distance axles, with felt oil pads. Axles are equipped with selected straight grain white hickory beds, which are clipped full length of axles. Fine oil tempered French pattern open head springs, properly graded and very easy riding. Reaches are ironed full length, bolted and well braced. Full circle wrought surrey fifth wheel, which is one of the best and strongest fifth wheels made. Bradley quick shifting shaft couplers. Regulation shafts made from selected straight grain white hickory, full patent leather trimmed, and with heel braces. We will furnish pole in place of shafts for $1.00 additional charge. Pole in addition to shafts, $5.00 additional charge.

WHEELS—Fine selected straight grain white hickory, ⅞-inch Sarven patent, 40 inches front, 44 inches rear, equipped with ⅞-inch round edge planished steel tire, bolted between every spoke. Our tires are set hot by hand and not by machine. Felloes have screws through them on each side of every spoke, which insures them against checking at the spokes. We will change height of

wheels or furnish banded hub style wheels, if desired, also 1-inch instead of ⅞-inch.

TRIMMINGS—Seats are trimmed with fine dark green all wool broadcloth, guaranteed absolutely fast color. Will trim with fine dark blue wool broadcloth, or fine whipcord, if preferred. The ends of large seats are pleated and trimmed to match cushion and back, and both cushions and backs are well upholstered. Large seat has fine upholstering springs in cushion and back, and the seats are very comfortable and easy riding. We can furnish special colors in broadcloth trimmings, if desired, at a small additional charge. Genuine leather trimmings in dark green, maroon or russet instead of broadcloth, $5.00 extra. Fine full padded patent leather dash. Fine Brussels carpet in bottom of body, or if rubber mat is preferred to the carpet we furnish mat. Oil lamps.

TOP—Is canopy style lined with wool cloth to match seat trimmings, and with fringe all around. Rubber side curtains all around and good rubber storm apron for the dash.

PAINTING—The body is black; gear, Brewster green, correctly striped. We will make any changes in painting desired. Our painting is all fully guaranteed. For system of painting, see page 5.

The above cut shows No. 404 hung on three spring full loop gear, and with lamps on loops in front. Price, with this style gear, $5.00 extra.

No. 404—FINE PHAETON, WITH FULL LEATHER TOP AND LEATHER COVERED BOWS

PRICE
{
Cash with order, with steel tires and shafts.................................$117.50
C. O. D., with steel tires and shafts.. 120.00
Cash with order, with ⅞-inch guaranteed rubber tires and shafts............. 132.50
C. O. D., with ⅞-inch guaranteed rubber tires and shafts.................... 135.00
}

No. 404 phaeton is one of the best style phaetons made. It is built in our high grade quality throughout and is equal to phaetons sold by others for fully $35.00 more than our price. The body is correctly proportioned and the seat is very comfortable. We are very glad to ship No. 404 anywhere for full examination and approval, with the understanding that it is to be found just as represented and a highly satisfactory vehicle, or we will take it back at our expense.

BODY—Is made from high grade stock throughout and is constructed in such a manner that it will not come apart at the joints, no matter in what climate used. It is one of the best style phaeton bodies made. The back of the seat is high and the seat is just the right height from the floor to be very comfortable. There are good steel sill or rocker plates laid in white lead and screwed full length of body. Rubber covered steps. Roller rub irons.

GEAR—1⅛-inch dust proof bell collar long distance axles, with felt oil pads. Axles are equipped with selected straight grain hickory beds, which are clipped full length of axles. Reach is ironed full length, bolted and well braced. Fine oil tempered French pattern open head springs, correctly graded and very easy riding. Full circle wrought fifth wheel, with clip king bolt, one of the best and strongest fifth wheels made; it is the style used on all high grade work. Bradley quick shifting shaft couplers, which are the best quick shifting couplers made, and are used on all high grade work. Regulation phaeton style shafts made from select straight grain white hickory, full patent leather trimmed, and with special heel braces. We will furnish pole instead of shafts for $1.00 extra. Pole in addition to shafts, $5.00 extra.

WHEELS—Fine selected straight grain white hickory, ⅞-inch banded hub style, 38 inches front, 44 inches rear, equipped with ⅞-inch round edge planished steel tire, which is bolted between every spoke. Our tires are all set hot by hand and not by machine. Felloes have screws through them on each side of every spoke, which insures them against checking at the spokes. The wheels we furnish are the correct height, but we can change the height of wheels, if desired. We will also furnish Sarven patent style, if preferred.

TRIMMINGS—Seat is trimmed with fine heavy dark green all wool broadcloth, or will trim with dark blue broadcloth or fine all wool whipcord, if preferred. The ends of the seat are pleated and trimmed to match cushion and back, and both cushion and back are upholstered with hair and fine upholstering springs. We furnish special colors in broadcloth trimmings, if desired, at a small additional charge. Fine genuine leather trimmings in dark green, maroon or russet color instead of broadcloth, $3.00 extra. Fine full padded wing style dash with apron flap and storm apron attached. Velvet carpet in bottom of body, or rubber mat if preferred to the carpet. Oil burner lamps.

TOP—Fine full leather with best grade leather covered bows. Heavy rubber side curtains and heavy rubber storm apron. We furnish with leather quarter top and steel bows, if desired, for $10.00 less than with leather top. Top is lined with all wool broadcloth to match seat trimmings.

PAINTING—Body is finely finished in black, correctly striped; gear, Brewster green, properly striped. We will make any changes in color of painting desired. For system of painting, see page 5.

The above cut illustrates our No. 417 fine Goddard phaeton with full leather Victoria top. Description of No. 411 practically covers No. 417, excepting top. Price, cash with order, with steel tires and shafts, $100.00 Price, C. O. D., with steel tires and shafts, $102.00.

No. 411—TWO SPRING, LEATHER QUARTER TOP PHAETON

PRICE		
Cash with order, with steel tires and shafts	$ 85.00	
C. O. D., with steel tires and shafts	87.00	
Cash with order, with 7/8-inch guaranteed rubber tires and shafts	100.00	
C. O. D., with 7/8-inch guaranteed rubber tires and shafts	102.00	

No. 411 is a very desirable style phaeton, and is equal in every particular to similar styles sold for $25.00 to $35.00 more than our price. We are very glad to send No. 411 anywhere for examination and approval, and if not found all we claim and a very satisfactory phaeton we will take it back at our expense.

BODY—Is made from the best of body stock throughout and is constructed in such a manner that we guarantee it not to open at the joints, no matter in what climate used. There are good steel sill or rocker plates laid in white lead and screwed full length of sills. Seat is just the right height to be very comfortable. Fine rubber covered steps. Roller rub irons.

GEAR—1 1/8-inch dust proof bell collar long distance axles, with felt oil pads. Axles are equipped with fine straight grain white hickory beds, which are cemented and clipped full length of axles. Reach is ironed full length, bolted and well braced. Fine oil tempered French pattern open head springs, properly graded and very easy riding. Full circle wrought fifth wheel, with clip king bolt, which is one of the best fifth wheels made. Bradley quick shifting shaft couplers, style that is used on all first class work. Regulation phaeton shafts made from selected straight grain hickory, full patent leather trimmed, and with special heel braces. We will furnish pole instead of shafts for $1.00 extra. Pole in addition to shafts, $5.00 extra.

WHEELS—Fine selected straight grain white hickory, 7/8-inch banded hub style, 38 inches front, 44 inches rear, equipped with 7/8-inch round edge planished steel tire, which is bolted between every spoke. Our tires are all set hot by hand and not by machine. Felloes have screws through them on each side of every spoke, which insures them against checking at the spokes. The wheels we furnish are the correct height, but we can change the height of wheels, if desired. We will also furnish Sarven patent style, if preferred.

TRIMMINGS—Seat is trimmed with fine heavy dark green all wool broadcloth, or will trim with dark blue wool broadcloth or all wool whipcord, if preferred. The ends of the seat are pleated and trimmed to match cushion and back, and both cushion and back are upholstered with hair and fine upholstering springs. We furnish special colors in broadcloth trimmings, if desired, at a small additional charge. Fine genuine leather trimmings in dark green, maroon or russet color instead of broadcloth, $3.00 extra. Fine full padded dash. Velvet carpet in bottom of body, or rubber mat if preferred to the carpet. Oil burner lamps.

TOP—Fine leather quarter with heavy rubber side curtains and storm apron. Bow sockets are the best enamel sockets made, and the joints are the best enamel joints we can buy. Top is lined with dark green all wool broadcloth to match seat trimmings. We will furnish full leather top, with best grade leather covered bow sockets, and with heavy rubber side curtains, for $10.00 extra charge.

PAINTING—The body is black; gear, Brewster green, correctly striped. We will furnish New York red gear or make any changes in painting desired. For system of painting, see page 5.

45

The above cut shows No. 415 with full leather Victoria style top. Price, $20.00 more than with regular style top.

No. 415—FINE FULL LEATHER TOP SPIDER PHAETON

PRICE
{
Cash with order, with steel tires and shafts..................................$150.00
C. O. D., with steel tires and shafts... 153.00
Cash with order, with ⅞-inch guaranteed rubber tires and shafts............. 165.00
C. O. D., with ⅞-inch guaranteed rubber tires and shafts.................... 168.00
}

If 1-inch guaranteed rubber tires are preferred, add $2.50 to the price quoted with ⅞-inch rubber tires.

No. 415 is one of the best style Spider phaetons made. This vehicle is equal in construction, quality of workmanship and material throughout to similar styles sold through city repositories for fully $50.00 more than our price. It is correctly proportioned throughout, is light running and very comfortable riding. We are very glad to ship it for examination and approval, and if it is not found all we claim and a satisfactory vehicle in every way, it may be returned at our expense.

BODY—Is made from high grade stock throughout. It has roomy, comfortable seat which is well proportioned. There are heavy steel sill or rocker plates laid in white lead and screwed full length of sills and rear arms. Roller rub irons. Rubber covered body steps.

GEAR—Is three spring style with 1⅛-inch dust proof bell collar long distance axles, with felt oil pads. Front axle is equipped with straight grain white hickory bed, which is clipped full length of axle. Rear axle is coach pattern. Fine oil tempered French pattern open head springs, correctly graded and very easy riding. Reach is ironed full length on bottom and sides, is bolted and properly braced. Rubber covered steps on axle, and roller rub irons. Full circle wrought fifth wheel, with clipped king bolt, which is the style and grade used on all first class work. Bradley quick shifting shaft couplers, style used on all high grade work. Shafts, regulation style for Spider phaeton, made from fine selected straight grain white hickory, full patent leather trimmed and with heel braces. Pole instead of shafts, $1.00 extra. Pole in addition to shafts, $5.00 extra.

WHEELS—Fine selected straight grain white hickory, ⅞-inch banded hub style, 38 inches front, 44 inches rear, equipped with ⅞-inch round edge planished steel tire, which is bolted between every spoke. Our tires are all set hot by hand and not by machine. Felloes have screws through them on each side of every spoke, which insures them against checking at the spokes. The wheels we furnish are the correct height, but we can change the height of wheels, if desired. We will also furnish Sarven patent style and 1-inch size, if preferred.

TRIMMINGS—Seat is trimmed with fine heavy dark green all wool broadcloth, or will trim with dark blue broadcloth or fine all wool whipcord, if preferred. The ends of the seat are pleated and trimmed to match cushion and back, and both cushion and back are upholstered with hair and fine upholstering springs. We furnish special colors in broadcloth trimmings, if desired, at a small additional charge. Fine genuine leather trimmings in dark green, maroon or russet color instead of broadcloth, $3.00 extra. Fine full padded dash. Velvet carpet in bottom of body, or rubber mat if preferred to the carpet. Oil burner lamps.

TOP—Fine full leather with best grade leather covered bows. Heavy rubber side curtains and heavy rubber storm apron. We furnish with leather quarter top and steel bows, if desired, for $10.00 less than with leather top. Top is lined with all wool broadcloth to match seat trimmings.

PAINTING—Body is finely finished in black, correctly striped; gear, Brewster green, properly striped. We will make any changes in color of painting desired. For system of painting, see page 5.

46

No. 418—FINE ST. LOUIS STORM OR BUSINESS WAGON

PRICE
- Cash with order, with steel tires and shafts.................................$ 93.00
- C. O. D., with steel tires and shafts.. 95.00
- Cash with order, with 1-inch guaranteed rubber tires and shafts.............. 110.50
- C. O. D., with 1-inch guaranteed rubber tires and shafts.................... 112.50

We consider our No. 418 a most desirable style vehicle for either business or pleasure use. It has a very large roomy seat and is light running and most comfortable riding. It is very easy to get into and out of, in fact, is an ideal vehicle in every respect. It is made in our best quality throughout and we know is equal in workmanship and material to similar styles sold by others for fully $50.00 more than our price. We are perfectly willing to ship it anywhere for examination, and if not found all we claim and a highly satisfactory vehicle, it may be returned at our expense.

BODY—Is made from high grade stock throughout and is the regulation St. Louis wagon style. It has a very large, roomy, comfortable seat. The top is made with the body as the rear posts form
part of the rear construction of the body. There are steel sill
or rocker plates laid in white lead and screwed full length of
sills. Rubber covered body steps and roller rub irons.

GEAR—1⅛-inch dust proof bell collar long distance axles, with felt
oil pads. Axles are equipped with selected straight grain hickory
beds, which are clipped full length of axles. Reach is ironed full
length, bolted and well braced. Fine oil tempered French pattern
open head springs, correctly graded and very easy riding. Full circle
wrought fifth wheel, with clip king bolt, one of the best and
strongest fifth wheels made; it is the style used on all high
grade work. Bradley quick shifting shaft couplers, which are
the best quick shifting couplers made, and are used on all high
grade work. Regulation style shafts made from select straight
grain white hickory, full patent leather trimmed and with special
heel braces. We will furnish pole instead of shafts for $1.00
extra. Pole in addition to shafts, $5.00 extra.

WHEELS—Fine selected straight grain white hickory, 1-inch
banded hub style, 40 inches front, 44 inches rear, equipped with

1-inch round edge planished steel tire, which is bolted between
every spoke. Our tires are all set hot by hand and not by machine. Felloes have screws through them on each side of every
spoke, which insures them against checking at the spokes. The
wheels we furnish are the correct height, but we can change the
height of wheels, if desired. We will also furnish Sarven patent
style, if preferred, or 1⅛-inch size.

TRIMMINGS—Seat is trimmed with fine genuine soft trimming
leather. We will trim with all wool broadcloth, if desired, for
$2.00 less than regular price. The ends of seat are pleated and
trimmed to match cushion and back, and the cushion and back are
upholstered with fine upholstering springs and hair. We will
trim with fine all wool whipcord, if preferred, for $2.00 less than
leather. Fine velvet carpet in bottom of body, or rubber mat if
preferred. Extra high full padded dash.

TOP—Is regulation style for storm buggies, with neat leather hood
around the front as shown in picture. Side curtains and rear
curtain are leather. Heavy rubber storm apron for dash.

PAINTING—The body is black; gear, Brewster green, correctly
striped. We will make any changes in painting desired. For
system of painting, see page 5.

47

The above cut shows No. 420 without top. Price, $25.00 less than with top.

No. 420—FINE CUT-UNDER STANHOPE, WITH LEATHER TOP AND LEATHER COVERED BOWS

PRICE
{ Cash with order, complete with steel tires and shafts.........................$125.00
C. O. D., with steel tires and shafts..128.00
Cash with order, with ⅞-inch guaranteed rubber tires and shafts.............140.00
C. O. D., with ⅞-inch guaranteed rubber tires and shafts....................143.00

If 1-inch guaranteed rubber tires are preferred, add $2.50 to the price quoted with ⅞-inch rubber tires.

Our No. 420 is one of the best style cut-under Stanhopes made. It is a light running and very comfortable riding vehicle. We make No. 420 in our high grade quality throughout. We are very glad to ship this Stanhope anywhere for full examination and approval, and if it is not found all we claim and equal to similar styles sold by others and through city repositories for $40.00 to $50.00 more than our price, it may be returned at our expense. We will allow you to be the judge.

BODY—Is made from high grade stock and is constructed in such a manner that we guarantee it not to come apart at the joints, no matter in what climate used. It is correctly proportioned and the seat is roomy and very comfortable. There are good heavy steel sill or rocker plates laid in white lead and screwed full length of sills and over the wheel house. Rubber covered body steps.

GEAR—1-inch dust proof bell collar long distance axles, with felt oil pads. Axles are equipped with selected straight grain hickory beds, which are cemented and clipped full length of axles. Fine oil tempered French pattern open head springs, correctly graded and very easy riding. Reach ironed full length, bolted and well braced. Full circle wrought fifth wheel, with clip king bolt, style used on all high grade work. Bradley quick shifting shaft couplers which are used on all first class work. Roller rub irons. Rubber covered axle steps. Regulation Stanhope shafts made from fine selected straight grain hickory, full patent leather trimmed and with special heel braces. Pole instead of shafts, $1.00 extra. Pole in addition to shafts, $5.00 extra.

WHEELS—Fine selected straight grain white hickory, ⅞-inch banded hub style, 40 inches front, 44 inches rear, equipped with ⅞-inch round edge planished steel tire, which is bolted between spoke. Our tires are all set hot by hand and not by ma-

chine. Felloes have screws through them on each side of every spoke, which insures them against checking at the spokes. The wheels we furnish are the correct height, but we can change the height of wheels, if desired. We will also furnish Sarven patent style, if preferred.

TRIMMINGS—Seat is trimmed with fine heavy dark green all wool broadcloth, or will trim with dark blue wool broadcloth or all wool whipcord, if preferred. The ends of the seat are pleated and trimmed to match cushion and back, and both cushion and back are upholstered with hair and fine upholstering springs. We furnish special colors in broadcloth trimmings, if desired, at a small additional charge. Fine genuine leather trimmings in dark green, maroon or russet color instead of broadcloth, $3.00 extra. Fine full padded dash. Velvet carpet in bottom of body, or rubber mat if preferred to the carpet. Oil burner lamps.

TOP—Fine full leather with best grade leather covered bows. Heavy rubber side curtains and heavy rubber storm apron. We furnish with leather quarter top and steel bows, if desired, for $10.00 less than with leather top. Top is lined with all wool broadcloth to match seat trimmings.

PAINTING—Body is finely finished in black, correctly striped; gear, Brewster green, properly striped. We will make any changes in color of painting desired. For system of painting, see page 5.

No. 422—FINE CUT-UNDER STANHOPE, WITH FULL LEATHER VICTORIA TOP AND HEAVY 1⅛ INCH GEAR

PRICE { Cash with order, with steel tires and shafts..............................$152.50
C. O. D., with steel tires and shafts.. 156.50
Cash with order, with 1⅛-inch guaranteed rubber tires and shafts........... 175.00
C. O. D., with 1⅛-inch guaranteed rubber tires and shafts.................. 179.00

If 1-inch wheels and 1-inch solid rubber tires are preferred, deduct $5.00 from the price with 1⅛-inch rubber tires.

Our No. 422 is one of the best Victoria top cut-under Stanhopes to be found anywhere. It is especially constructed for city use, having extra heavy gear and wheels. This Stanhope is made of our best grade throughout and is equal to similar styles sold through city repositories for fully $50.00 more than our price. We are glad to ship it for full examination and approval, and if it is not found all we claim and highly satisfactory, it may be returned at our expense.

BODY—Is made from high grade stock and is constructed in such a manner that we guarantee it not to come apart at the joints, no matter in what climate used. It is correctly proportioned and the seat is roomy and very comfortable. There are good heavy steel sill or rocker plates laid in white lead and screwed full length of wheels and over the wheel house. Rubber covered body steps.

GEAR—1⅛-inch dust proof bell collar long distance axles, with felt oil pads. Axles are equipped with selected straight grain hickory beds, which are cemented and clipped full length of axles. Fine oil tempered French pattern open head springs, correctly graded and very easy riding. Reach ironed full length, bolted and well braced. Full circle wrought fifth wheel, with clip king bolt, style used on all high grade work. Bradley quick shifting couplers which are used on all first class work. Roller rub irons. Rubber covered axle steps. Regulation Stanhope shafts made from fine selected straight grain hickory, full patent leather trimmed and with special heel braces. Pole instead of shafts, $1.00 extra. Pole in addition to shafts, $5.00 extra.

WHEELS—Fine selected straight grain white hickory, 1⅛-inch banded hub, 40 inches front, 44 inches rear, equipped with round edge planished steel tires, bolted between every spoke. Felloes have screws through them on each side of every spoke, which

insures them against checking at the spokes. Our channel tires for rubber tired wheels, also our round edge planished steel tires, are all set hot by hand and not by machine. We will furnish Sarven patent wheels, if preferred.

TRIMMINGS—Seat is trimmed with fine heavy dark green all wool broadcloth, or will trim with dark blue broadcloth or fine all wool whipcord, if preferred. The ends of the seat are pleated and trimmed to match cushion and back, and both cushion and back are upholstered with hair and fine upholstering springs. We furnish special colors in broadcloth trimmings, if desired, at a small additional charge. Fine genuine leather trimmings in dark green, maroon or russet color instead of broadcloth, $3.00 extra. Fine full padded dash. Velvet carpet in bottom of body, or rubber mat if preferred to the carpet. Oil burner lamps.

TOP—Fine full leather Victoria style with roll up back curtain, beveled plate glass side lights and fine patent leather top wings. Top is lined with all wool broadcloth to match trimmings. This top can be easily let down same as any regular top, if desired. Large rubber storm apron for dash.

PAINTING—Body is finely finished in black, correctly striped; gear, Brewster green, properly striped. We will make any changes in color of painting desired. For system of painting, see page 5.

49

The above cut shows No. 504 without top. Price, $25.00 less than with top.

No. 504—FINE LEATHER TOP STANHOPE, WITH LEATHER COVERED BOWS AND BIKE GEAR

PRICE
{
Cash with order, with steel tires and shafts..................................$110.00
C. O. D., with steel tires and shafts.. 112.00
Cash with order, with 1⅛-inch guaranteed cushion tires and shafts............ 130.00
C. O. D., with 1⅛-inch guaranteed cushion tires and shafts................... 132.00
}

If ⅞-inch guaranteed rubber tires are preferred, deduct $5.00 from the price quoted with 1⅛-inch cushion tires.

No. 504 is one of the most desirable and best selling Stanhopes we are making. It is very light running and comfortable riding. **We** make No. 504 in our high grade quality, and we know it is as good as usually sells for fully $35.00 more than our price. We are glad at any rate to allow you to be the judge by shipping for examination and approval, and if you do not find everything just as represented and are not perfectly satisfied, we will take the shipment back at our expense.

BODY—Is one of our best and most desirable designs. It is made from high grade stock throughout and is so constructed that we guarantee the panels not to come apart at the joints, no matter in what climate used. Side panels are in one piece from the arms to the sills, making it possible for a most beautiful effect in finishing. The back part is decked over solid, but there is a large opening in the front under the seat so that packages can be put in the back part of the body. There are good heavy steel sill or rocker plates laid in white lead and screwed full length of sills. Rubber covered steps and roller rub irons.

GEAR—Roman bike style with dust proof bell collar long distance axles, with felt oil pads. Axles have short wood beds in center which are cemented and clipped to the axles and to these wood beds attach the rear spring in the rear and the fifth wheel in front. Fine full circle wrought Brewster slotted fifth wheel, one of the best and strongest fifth wheels made and is used on all high grade work. Fine oil tempered French pattern open head springs, correctly graded and very easy riding. Reaches are ironed full length with regular channel reach iron, bolted and well braced. Bradley quick shifting shaft couplers, style and grade used on all high grade work. Shafts, regulation high bend bike Stanhope shafts made from selected straight grain white hickory, full patent leather trimmed and with special heel braces. Pole instead of shafts, $1.00 extra. Pole in addition to shafts, $5.00 extra.

WHEELS—Fine selected straight grain white hickory, ⅞-inch banded hub, 38 inches front and 40 inches rear, with ⅞-inch round edge planished steel tire, bolted between each spoke. Tires are ¼-inch thick and are.set hot by hand and not by machine. Felloes have screws through them on each side of every spoke, which insures absolutely against checking at the spokes. The height of wheels we furnish is correct for this style gear, but we can make any change in height desired. We furnish 1-inch wheels instead of ⅞-inch, if preferred. Also Sarven patent style instead of banded hub. Equipped with fine steel wire wheels and 1⅛-inch cushion tires for $25.00 extra charge to price quoted with wood wheels and steel tires.

TRIMMINGS—Seat is trimmed with fine heavy dark green all wool broadcloth, or will trim with dark blue wool broadcloth or all wool whipcord, if preferred. The ends of the seat are pleated and trimmed to match cushion and back, and both cushion and back are upholstered with hair and fine upholstering springs. We furnish special colors in broadcloth trimmings, if desired, at a small additional charge. Fine genuine leather trimmings in dark green, maroon or russet color instead of broadcloth, $3.00 extra. Fine full padded dash. Velvet carpet in bottom of body, or rubber mat if preferred to the carpet. Oil burner lamps.

TOP—Fine full leather with best grade leather covered bows. Heavy rubber side curtains and heavy rubber storm apron. We furnish with leather quarter top and steel bows, if desired, for $10.00 less than with leather top. Top is lined with all wool broadcloth to match seat trimmings.

PAINTING—Body is finely finished in black, correctly striped; gear, New York red, properly striped. We will make any changes in color of painting desired. For system of painting, see page 5.

The above cut shows No. 505 with extra heavy 1⅛-inch gear for hard driving and city use, also fine full leather Victoria style top. Additional charge for the extra heavy gear is $5.00; for the Victoria style top, $25.00.

No. 505—FINE LEATHER TOP STANHOPE, WITH LEATHER COVERED BOWS

PRICE {
Cash with order, with steel tires and shafts.................................$110.00
C. O. D., with steel tires and shafts... 112.00
Cash with order, with ⅞-inch guaranteed rubber tires and shafts............. 125.00
C. O. D., with ⅞-inch guaranteed rubber tires and shafts.................... 127.00

If 1-inch guaranteed rubber tires are preferred, add $2.50 to the price quoted with ⅞-inch rubber tires.

No. 505 is one of the best grade Stanhopes we are making, and is a style that always gives satisfaction. It is what you would call correctness in Stanhope construction throughout. It is built in our high grade quality and is equal to similar styles sold by others for $35.00 to $40.00 more than our price. We are very glad to ship it for full examination and approval, with the distinct understanding that it is to be found all we claim and you to feel you are saving money, or we will take the shipment back at our expense.

BODY—Is one of our best and most desirable designs. It is made from high grade stock throughout and is so constructed that we guarantee the panels not to come apart at the joints, no matter in what climate used. Side panels are in one piece from the arms to the sills, making it possible for a most beautiful effect in finishing. The back part is decked over solid, but there is a large opening in the front under the seat so that packages can be put in the back part of the body. There are good heavy steel sill or rocker plates laid in white lead and screwed full length of sills. Rubber covered steps and roller rub irons.

GEAR—1-inch dust proof bell collar long distance axles, with felt oil pads. Axles are fitted with straight grain white hickory axle beds, which are cemented and clipped full length of axles. Fine full circle wrought Brewster fifth wheel, which is one of the best and strongest fifth wheels made and is used on all high grade work. Fine oil tempered French pattern open head springs, correctly graded and very easy riding. Reaches are ironed full length with regular channel reach iron, bolted and well braced. Bradley quick shifting shaft couplers, style and grade used on all high grade work. Shafts, regulation Stanhope shafts made from selected straight grain white hickory, full patent leather trimmed and with special heel braces. Pole instead of shafts, $1.00 extra. Pole in addition to shafts, $5.00 extra.

WHEELS—Fine selected straight grain white hickory, ⅞-inch banded hub, 40 inches front and 44 inches rear, with ⅞-inch round edge planished steel tire, bolted between each spoke. Tires are ¼-inch thick and are set hot by hand and not by machine. Felloes have screws through them on each side of every spoke, which insures absolutely against checking at the spokes. The height of wheels we furnish is correct for this style gear, but we can make any change in height desired. We furnish 1-inch wheels instead of ⅞-inch, if preferred. Also Sarven patent style instead of banded hub.

TRIMMINGS—Seat is trimmed with fine heavy dark green all wool broadcloth, or will trim with dark blue wool broadcloth or all wool whipcord, if preferred. The ends of seat are pleated and trimmed to match cushion and back, and both cushion and back are upholstered with hair and fine upholstering springs. We furnish special colors in broadcloth trimmings, if desired, at a small additional charge. Fine genuine leather trimmings in dark green, maroon or russet color instead of broadcloth, $3.00 extra. Fine full padded dash. Velvet carpet in bottom of body, or rubber mat if preferred to the carpet. Oil burner lamps.

TOP—Fine full leather with best grade leather covered bows. Heavy rubber side curtains and heavy rubber storm apron. We furnish with leather quarter top and steel bows, if desired, for $10.00 less than with leather top. Top is lined with all wool broadcloth to match seat trimmings.

PAINTING—Body is finely finished in black, correctly striped; gear, Brewster green, properly striped. We will make any changes in color of painting desired. For system of painting, see page 5.

51

No. 508—FINE STANHOPE, WITH LEATHER QUARTER TOP

PRICE
- Cash with order, with steel tires and shafts.................................$ 90.00
- C. O. D., with steel tires and shafts.. 92.00
- Cash with order, with ⅞-inch guaranteed rubber tires and shafts............ 105.00
- C. O. D., with ⅞-inch guaranteed rubber tires and shafts................... 107.00

If 1-inch guaranteed rubber tires are preferred, add $2.50 to the price quoted with ⅞-inch rubber tires.

Our No. 508 is a very desirable style Stanhope. The seat is roomy and just the right height to be comfortable. We know our No. 508 is just as good as usually sells for fully $40.00 more than our price. We are very glad to ship it for examination and approval with the understanding that it is to be found highly satisfactory and all we claim or returned at our expense.

BODY—Is made from the best of stock throughout and is so constructed that we guarantee it not to come apart at the joints, no matter in what climate used. It is a very desirable design, and the seat is roomy and comfortable. There are steel sill or rocker plates laid in white lead and screwed full length of sills. Rubber covered steps. Roller rub irons.

GEAR—1-inch dust proof bell collar long distance axles, with felt oil pads. Axles are fitted with straight grain white hickory axle beds, which are cemented and clipped full length of axles. Fine full circle wrought Brewster fifth wheel, which is one of the best and strongest fifth wheels made and is used on all high grade work. Fine oil tempered French pattern open head springs, correctly graded and very easy riding. Reaches are ironed full length with regular channel reach iron, bolted and well braced. Bradley quick shifting shaft couplers, style and grade used on all high grade work. Shafts, regulation high bend Stanhope shafts, made from selected straight grain white hickory, full patent leather trimmed and with special heel braces. Pole instead of shafts, $1.00 extra. Pole in addition to shafts, $5.00 extra.

WHEELS—Fine selected straight grain white hickory, ⅞-inch banded hub style, 40 inches front, 44 inches rear, equipped with ⅞-inch round edge planished steel tire, which is bolted between every spoke. Our tires are all set hot by hand and not by machine. Felloes have screws through them on each side of every

spoke, which insures them against checking at the spokes. The wheels we furnish are the correct height, but we can change the height of wheels, if desired. We will also furnish Sarven patent style, if preferred.

TRIMMINGS—Seat is trimmed with fine heavy dark green all wool broadcloth, or will trim with dark blue wool broadcloth or all wool whipcord, if preferred. The ends of the seat are pleated and trimmed to match cushion and back, and both cushion and back are upholstered with hair and fine upholstering springs. We furnish special colors in broadcloth trimmings, if desired, at a small additional charge. Fine genuine leather trimmings in dark green, maroon or russet color instead of broadcloth, $3.00 extra. Fine full padded dash. Velvet carpet in bottom of body, or rubber mat if preferred to the carpet. Oil burner lamps.

TOP—Fine leather quarter with heavy rubber side curtains and storm apron. Bow sockets are the best enamel sockets made, and the joints are the best enamel joints we can buy. Top is lined with dark green all wool broadcloth to match seat trimmings. We will furnish full leather top with best grade leather covered bow sockets, and with heavy rubber side curtains, for $10.00 extra charge.

PAINTING—Body is finely finished in black, correctly striped; gear, Brewster green, properly striped. We will make any changes in color of painting desired. For system of painting, see page 5.

The above cut shows No. 510 with fine full leather Victoria top. Price, $35.00 more than with regular style top.

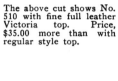

No. 510—FINE STANHOPE, WITH LEATHER QUARTER TOP AND LAMPS

PRICE { Cash with order, with steel tires and shafts.................................$ 88.00
C. O. D., with steel tires and shafts... 90.00
Cash with order, with ⅞-inch guaranteed rubber tires and shafts............. 103.00
C. O. D., with ⅞-inch guaranteed rubber tires and shafts.................... 105.00

If 1-inch guaranteed rubber tires are preferred, add $2.50 to the price quoted for ⅞-inch.

Our No. 510 Stanhope is a very desirable style. It is strictly up-to-date in every particular, and a style that we are very glad to ship anywhere for full examination and approval, and if not found all we claim and a highly satisfactory vehicle, it may be returned at our expense. We know No. 510 is as good as usually sells for $25.00 to $35.00 more than our price.

BODY—Is one of the best designs we are making. It is made from high grade stock throughout. Side panels are in one piece from the arms to the sills. It is open back of the seat and the opening is covered with a boot. Seat is roomy and very comfortable. There are good steel sill or rocker plates laid in white lead and screwed full length of sills. Rubber covered steps. Roller rub irons.

GEAR—1-inch dust proof bell collar long distance axles, with felt oil pads. Axles are fitted with straight grain white hickory beds, which are cemented and clipped full length of axles. Fine full circle wrought Brewster fifth wheel, which is one of the best and strongest fifth wheels made and is used on all high grade work. Fine oil tempered French pattern open head springs, correctly graded and very easy riding. Reaches are ironed full length with regular channel reach iron, bolted and well braced. Bradley quick shifting shaft couplers, style and grade used on all high grade work. Shafts, regulation high bend Stanhope shafts, made from selected straight grain white hickory, full patent leather trimmed and with special heel braces. Pole instead of shafts, $1.00 extra. Pole in addition to shafts, $5.00 extra.

WHEELS—Fine selected straight grain white hickory, ⅞-inch banded hub style, 40 inches front, 44 inches rear, equipped with ⅞-inch round edge planished steel tire, which is bolted between every spoke. Our tires are all set hot by hand and not by machine. Felloes have screws through them on each side of every

spoke, which insures them against checking at the spokes. The wheels we furnish are the correct height, but we can change the height of wheels, if desired. We will also furnish Sarven patent style, if preferred.

TRIMMINGS—Seat is trimmed with fine heavy dark green all wool broadcloth, or will trim with dark blue wool broadcloth or all wool whipcord, if preferred. The ends of the seat are pleated and trimmed to match cushion and back, and both cushion and back are upholstered with hair and fine upholstering springs. We furnish special colors in broadcloth trimmings, if desired, at a small additional charge. Fine genuine leather trimmings in dark green, maroon or russet color instead of broadcloth, $3.00 extra. Fine full padded dash. Velvet carpet in bottom of body, or rubber mat if preferred to the carpet. Oil burner lamps.

TOP—Fine leather quarter with heavy rubber side curtains and storm apron. Bow sockets are the best enamel sockets made, and the joints are the best enamel joints we can buy. Top is lined with dark green all wool broadcloth to match seat trimmings. We will furnish full leather top with best grade leather covered bow sockets and with heavy rubber side curtains, for $10.00 extra charge.

PAINTING—Body is finely finished in black, correctly striped; gear, Brewster green, properly striped. We will make any changes in color of painting desired. For system of painting, see page 5.

The above cut shows No. 512 without top. Price, $15.00 less than with top.

No. 512—FINE STANHOPE, WITH BIKE GEAR AND LEATHER QUARTER TOP

PRICE
Cash with order, with steel tires and shafts.................................$ 88.00
C. O. D., with steel tires and shafts.. 90.00
Cash with order, with 1⅛-inch guaranteed cushion tires and shafts........... 108.00
C. O. D., with 1⅛-inch guaranteed cushion tires and shafts.................. 110.00

If ⅞-inch guaranteed rubber tires are preferred, deduct $5.00 from the price quoted with 1⅛-inch cushion tires.

Our No. 512 is a very popular style Stanhope and one that gives universal satisfaction. It is correctly proportioned throughout, is light running and most comfortable riding. We can freely say that our No. 512 is equal in quality of workmanship and material throughout to similar Stanhopes sold by others for fully $35.00 more than our price. We are very glad of an opportunity to ship it for examination and approval, and if it is not found perfectly satisfactory it may be returned at our expense.

BODY—Is one of the best designs we are making. It is made from high grade stock throughout. Side panels are in one piece from the arms to the sills. It is open back of the seat and the opening is covered with a boot. Seat is roomy and very comfortable. There are good steel sill or rocker plates laid in white lead and screwed full length of sills. Rubber covered steps. Roller rub irons.

GEAR—Roman bike style with dust proof bell collar long distance axles, with felt oil pads. Axles have short wood beds in center which are cemented and clipped to the axles. Fine full circle wrought Brewster fifth wheel, which is one of the best and strongest fifth wheels made and is used on all high grade work. Fine oil tempered French pattern open head springs, correctly graded and very easy riding. Reaches are ironed full length with regular channel reach iron, bolted and well braced. Bradley quick shifting shaft couplers, style and grade used on all high grade work. Shafts, regulation high bend bike Stanhope shafts, made from selected straight grain white hickory, full patent leather trimmed and with special heel braces. Pole instead of shafts, $1.00 extra. Pole in addition to shafts, $5.00 extra.

WHEELS—Fine selected straight grain white hickory, ⅞-inch banded hub style, 38 inches front, 40 inches rear, equipped with ⅞-inch round edge planished steel tire, which is bolted between every spoke. Our tires are all set hot by hand and not by machine. Felloes have screws through them on each side of every

spoke, which insures them against checking at the spokes. The wheels we furnish are the correct height, but we can change the height of wheels, if desired. We will also furnish Sarven patent style, if preferred.

TRIMMINGS—Seat is trimmed with fine heavy dark green all wool broadcloth, or will trim with dark blue wool broadcloth or all wool whipcord, if preferred. The ends of the seat are pleated and trimmed to match cushion and back, and both cushion and back are upholstered with hair and fine upholstering springs. We furnish special colors in broadcloth trimmings, if desired, at a small additional charge. Fine genuine leather trimmings in dark green, maroon or russet color instead of broadcloth, $3.00 extra. Fine full padded dash. Velvet carpet in bottom of body, or rubber mat if preferred to the carpet. Oil burner lamps.

TOP—Fine leather quarter with heavy rubber side curtains and storm apron. Bow sockets are the best enamel sockets made, and the joints are the best enamel joints we can buy. Top is lined with dark green all wool broadcloth to match seat trimmings. We will furnish full leather top with best grade leather covered bow sockets and with heavy rubber side curtains for $10.00 extra charge.

PAINTING—Body is finely finished in black, correctly striped; gear, New York red, properly striped. We will make any changes in color of painting desired. For system of painting, see page 5.

The above cut shows No. 515 without top. Price, $15.00 less than with top.

No. 515—STANHOPE, WITH LEATHER QUARTER TOP AND BIKE GEAR

PRICE
{
Cash with order, with steel tires and shafts..................................$ 83.00
C. O. D., with steel tires and shafts... 85.00
Cash with order, with ⅞-inch guaranteed rubber tires and shafts............ 98.00
C. O. D., with ⅞-inch guaranteed rubber tires and shafts................... 100.00
}

If 1⅛-inch guaranteed cushion tires are preferred, add $5.00 to the price quoted with ⅞-inch solid rubber tires.

Our No. 515 is as fine in style and equal in quality of workmanship and material to similar Stanhopes sold by others for fully $30.00 more than our price. It is light running and very comfortable riding. We are glad to send this Stanhope anywhere for examination and approval, and if not found perfectly satisfactory and all we claim, it may be returned at our expense. We allow you to be the judge.

BODY—Is one of our late designs and a very popular style. It is made from high grade stock throughout and so constructed that we guarantee it not to open at the corners, no matter in what climate used. Back part of the body is decked over solid, but there is a large opening in front under the seat so that packages can be put in the back part of the body. There are good steel sill or rocker plates laid in white lead and screwed full length of sills. Roller rub irons.

GEAR—Roman bike style with dust proof bell collar long distance axles, with felt oil pads. Axles have short wood beds in center which are cemented and clipped to the axles, and to these wood beds attach the rear spring in the rear and the fifth wheel in front. Fine full circle wrought Brewster fifth wheel, which is one of the best and strongest fifth wheels made and is used on all high grade work. Fine oil tempered French pattern open head springs, correctly graded and very easy riding. Reaches are ironed full length with regular channel reach iron, bolted and well braced. Bradley quick shifting shaft couplers, style and grade used on all high grade work. Shafts, regulation high bend bike Stanhope shafts made from selected straight grain white hickory, full patent leather trimmed and with special heel braces. Pole instead of shafts, $1.00 extra. Pole in addition to shafts, $5.00 extra.

WHEELS—Fine selected straight grain white hickory, ⅞-inch Sarven patent, 38 inches front and 40 inches rear, with ⅞-inch round edge planished steel tire, bolted between each spoke. Tires are ¼-inch thick and are set hot by hand and not by machine. Felloes have screws through them on each side of every spoke,

which insures absolutely against checking at the spokes. The height of the wheels we furnish is correct for this style gear, but we can make any change in height desired. We furnish 1-inch wheels instead of ⅞-inch, if preferred. Furnished with fine steel wire wheels and 1⅛-inch cushion tires for $25.00 additional charge to price quoted with wood wheels and steel tires. Also banded hub style, if preferred.

TRIMMINGS—Seat is trimmed with dark green all wool broadcloth, or will trim with dark blue wool broadcloth or all wool whipcord, if preferred. The ends of the seat are pleated and trimmed to match cushion and back, and both cushion and back are upholstered with hair and fine upholstering springs. We furnish special colors in broadcloth trimmings, if desired, at a small additional charge. Fine genuine leather trimmings in dark green, maroon or russet color instead of broadcloth, $3.00 extra. Fine full padded dash. Velvet carpet in bottom of body, or rubber mat if preferred to the carpet. Oil burner lamps.

TOP—Leather quarter with heavy rubber side curtains and storm apron. Bow sockets are the best enamel sockets made, and the joints are the best enamel joints we can buy. Top is lined with dark green all wool broadcloth to match seat trimmings. We will furnish full leather top with best grade leather covered bow sockets and with heavy rubber side curtains for $10.00 extra charge.

PAINTING—Body is finely finished in black, correctly striped; gear, New York red, properly striped. We will make any changes in color of painting desired. For system of painting, see page 5.

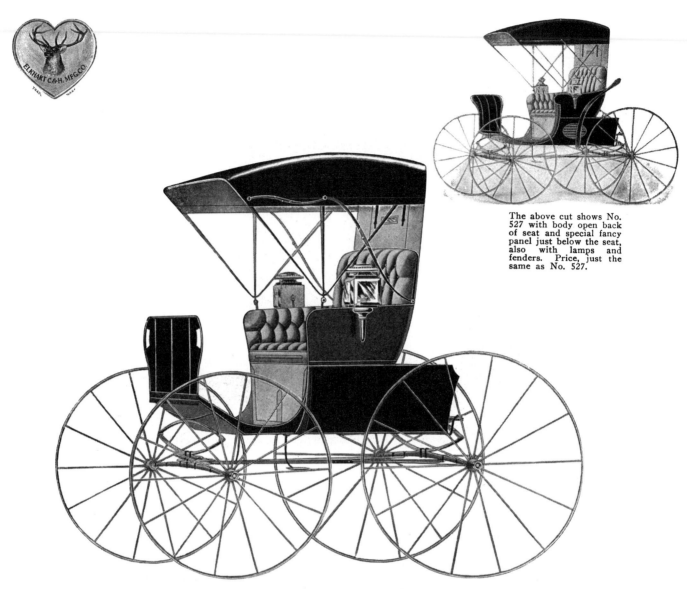

The above cut shows No. 527 with body open back of seat and special fancy panel just below the seat, also with lamps and fenders. Price, just the same as No. 527.

No. 527—LIGHT LEATHER QUARTER TOP STANHOPE

PRICE
- Cash with order, with steel tires and shafts....................................$63.50
- C. O. D., with steel tires and shafts.. 65.00
- Cash with order, with 7/8-inch guaranteed rubber tires and shafts.............. 78.50
- C. O. D., with 7/8-inch guaranteed rubber tires and shafts..................... 80.00

Our No. 527 is a very desirable style light Stanhope. It is well constructed throughout, is well proportioned, roomy and comfortable riding. We can unhesitatingly recommend this Stanhope and are very glad to ship it for full examination and approval, with the distinct understanding that it is to be found all we claim and as good as usually sells for $25.00 to $35.00 more than our price or returned at our expense both ways.

BODY—Is a very popular design and the seat is roomy and comfortable. Back part of the body is decked over solid, but there is an opening under the front seat so packages can be put in the back part of the body. There are good steel sill or rocker plates laid in white lead and screwed on sills. Roller rub irons.

GEAR—1-inch dust proof bell collar long distance axles, with felt oil pads. Axles are fitted with straight grain white hickory axle beds, which are cemented and clipped full length of axles. Fine full circle wrought Brewster fifth wheel, which is one of the best and strongest fifth wheels made and is used on all high grade work. Fine oil tempered French pattern open head springs, correctly graded and very easy riding. Reaches are ironed full length with regular channel reach iron, bolted and well braced. Bradley quick shifting shaft couplers, style and grade used on all high grade work. Shafts, regulation high bend Stanhope shafts, made from selected straight grain white hickory, full patent leather trimmed and with special heel braces. Pole instead of shafts, $1.00 extra. Pole in addition to shafts, $5.00 extra.

WHEELS—Fine selected straight grain white hickory, 7/8-inch Sarven patent, with 7/8-inch round edge planished steel tire, bolted between every spoke. They are 40 inches front and 44 inches rear. This is the regulation height for this style vehicle, but we will change the height of wheels, if desired. Our tires are set hot by hand and not by machine. All felloes have screws through them on each side of every spoke, which insures them against checking at

the spokes. We will furnish banded hub style wheels, if preferred. We also furnish 1-inch tread instead of 7/8-inch, if preferred.

TRIMMINGS—Seat is trimmed with fine dark green heavy all wool broadcloth, or will trim with dark blue wool broadcloth or all wool whipcord, if preferred. The ends of the seat are pleated and trimmed to match cushion and back, and both cushion and back are upholstered with hair and fine upholstering springs. We furnish special colors in broadcloth trimmings, if desired, at a small additional charge. Fine genuine leather trimmings in dark green, maroon or russet color instead of broadcloth, $3.00 extra. Fine full padded dash. Velvet carpet in bottom of body, or rubber mat if preferred to the carpet.

TOP—Fine leather quarter with heavy rubber side curtains and storm apron. Bow sockets are the best enamel sockets made, and the joints are the best enamel joints we can buy. Top is lined with dark green all wool broadcloth trimmings. We will furnish full leather top with best grade leather covered bow sockets and with heavy rubber side curtains for $10.00 extra charge.

PAINTING—Body is finely finished in black, correctly striped; gear, dark Brewster green, properly striped. We will make any changes in color of painting desired. For system of painting, see page 5.

56

No. 528—STANHOPE, WITH LEATHER QUARTER TOP AND LAMPS

PRICE
{ Cash with order, complete with steel tires and shafts.........................$63.50
C. O. D., with steel tires and shafts... 65.00
Cash with order, with ⅞-inch guaranteed rubber tires and shafts.............. 78.50
C. O. D., with ⅞-inch guaranteed rubber tires and shafts.................... 80.00

No. 528 is a roomy, comfortable riding Stanhope. It is a very desirable style and one that we can unhesitatingly recommend. We know this Stanhope is as good in quality of workmanship and material throughout as similar styles sold by others for fully $25.00 more than our price. We are very glad to ship it for examination and approval, with the understanding that it may be returned at our expense if not found perfectly satisfactory.

BODY—Is a very desirable and up-to-date style. The seat is roomy and very comfortable. Both body and seat are made from high grade stock and put together in such a manner that we guarantee the corners not to open at the joints, no matter in what climate used. There are heavy steel sill or rocker plates laid in white lead and screwed full length of sills. Back part of body is open and covered with boot.

GEAR—1-inch dust proof bell collar long distance axles, with felt oil pads. Axles are fitted with straight grain white hickory beds, which are cemented and clipped full length of axles. Fine full circle wrought Brewster fifth wheel, which is one of the best and strongest fifth wheels made and is used on all high grade work. Fine oil tempered French pattern open head springs, correctly graded and very easy riding. Reaches are ironed full length with regular channel reach iron, bolted and well braced. Bradley quick shifting shaft couplers, style and grade used on all high grade work. Shafts, regulation high bend Stanhope shafts, made from selected straight grain white hickory, full patent leather trimmed and with special heel braces. Pole instead of shafts, $1.00 extra. Pole in addition to shafts, $5.00 extra.

WHEELS—Fine selected straight grain white hickory, ⅞-inch Sarven patent, with ⅞-inch round edge planished steel tire, bolted between every spoke. They are 40 inches front and 44 inches rear. This is the regulation height for this style vehicle, but we will change the height of wheels, if desired. Our tires are set hot by hand and not by machine. All felloes have screws through

them on each side of every spoke, which insures them against checking at the spokes. We will furnish banded hub style wheels, if preferred. We also furnish 1-inch tread instead of ⅞-inch, if preferred.

TRIMMINGS—Seat is trimmed with fine dark green heavy all wool broadcloth, or will trim with dark blue wool broadcloth or all wool whipcord, if preferred. The ends of the seat are pleated and trimmed to match cushion and back, and both cushion and back are upholstered with hair and fine upholstering springs. We furnish special colors in broadcloth trimmings, if preferred, at a small additional charge. Fine genuine leather trimmings in dark green, maroon or russet color instead of broadcloth, $3.00 extra. Fine full padded dash. Velvet carpet in bottom of body, or rubber mat if preferred to the carpet. Oil burner lamps.

TOP—Fine leather quarter with heavy rubber side curtains and storm apron. Bow sockets are the best enamel sockets made, and the joints are the best enamel joints we can buy. Top is lined with dark green all wool broadcloth to match seat trimmings. We will furnish full leather top with best grade leather covered bow sockets and with heavy rubber side curtains, for $10.00 extra charge.

PAINTING—Body is finely finished in black, correctly striped; gear, Brewster green, properly striped. We will make any changes in color of painting desired. For system of painting, see page 5.

57

The above cut shows No. 536 equipped with English canopy top. Price, $15.00 more than without top.

No. 536—FINE FULL PANEL COVERT WAGON, WITH BIKE GEAR

PRICE
Cash with order, with steel tires and shafts.................................$ 93.00
C. O. D., with steel tires and shafts.. 95.00
Cash with order, with ⅞-inch guaranteed rubber tires and shafts............. 108.00
C. O. D., with ⅞-inch guaranteed rubber tires and shafts.................... 110.00
If 1⅛-inch guaranteed cushion tires are preferred, add $5.00 to the price quoted with ⅞-inch solid tires.

No. 536 is one of the finest and most up-to-date covert wagons made. It is built in our high quality throughout, and guaranteed equal to similar wagons sold by others for fully $35.00 more than our price. It is well proportioned, light running and very comfortable riding. We are glad of an opportunity to ship No. 536 for full examination and approval, and if it is not found all we claim and a very satisfactory open pleasure vehicle, it may be returned at our expense.

BODY—Is made from high grade stock and has full panels from seat arms to the sills, making it possible for the most beautiful effect in finishing. Seat is roomy and very comfortable. There are steel sill or rocker plates laid in white lead and screwed full length of sills. Rubber covered steps. Roller rub irons.

GEAR—Roman bike style with dust proof bell collar long distance axles, with felt oil pads. Axles have short wood beds in center, which are cemented and clipped to the axles, and to these wood beds attach the rear spring in rear and the fifth wheel in front. Fine full circle wrought Brewster fifth wheel, which is one of the best and strongest fifth wheels made and is used on all high grade work. Fine oil tempered French pattern open head springs, correctly graded and very easy riding. Reaches are ironed full length with regular channel reach iron, bolted and well braced. Bradley quick shifting shaft couplers, style and grade used on all high grade work. Shafts, regulation high bend bike Stanhope shafts, made from selected straight grain white hickory, full patent leather trimmed and with special heel braces. Pole instead of shafts, $1.00 extra. Pole in addition to shafts, $5.00 extra.

WHEELS—Fine selected straight grain white hickory, ⅞-inch banded hub, 38 inches front and 40 inches rear, with ⅞-inch round edge planished steel tire, bolted between each spoke. Tires are ¼-inch thick and are set hot by hand and not by machine. Felloes have screws through them on each side of every spoke, which insures absolutely against checking at the spokes. The height of the wheels we furnish is correct for this style gear, but we can make any change in height desired. We furnish Sarven patent style instead of banded hub, if preferred. Furnished with fine steel wire wheels and 1⅛-inch cushion tires for $25.00 additional charge to price quoted with wood wheels and steel tires.

TRIMMINGS—Seat is trimmed with fine heavy all wool whipcord, but we will trim with fine dark green or blue all wool broadcloth, if preferred. The ends of the seat are pleated and trimmed to match cushion and back, and cushion and back are upholstered with hair and fine upholstering springs. We can furnish special colors in broadcloth trimmings, if desired, at a small additional charge. Fine genuine soft leather trimmings in dark green, maroon or russet instead of broadcloth, $3.00 extra. Fine full oil burner lamps. Velvet carpet or rubber mat in bottom of body.

PAINTING—Body is finely finished in black, correctly striped; gear, New York red, properly striped. We will make any changes in color of painting desired. For system of painting, see page 5.

The above cut shows our special covert seat for No. 538 with full solid panel back. We furnish this seat instead of the regular seat without additional charge, and when it is ordered it is complete with lamps same as No. 538.

No. 538—FINE CUT-UNDER COVERT WAGON, WITH BIKE GEAR

PRICE
Cash with order, with steel tires and shafts................................$ 88.00
C. O. D., with steel tires and shafts... 90.00
Cash with order, with ⅞-inch guaranteed rubber tires and shafts............ 103.00
C. O. D., with ⅞-inch guaranteed rubber tires and shafts................... 105.00
If 1⅛-inch guaranteed cushion tires are preferred, add $5.00 to the price quoted with ⅞-inch solid tires.

No. 538 is one of the best style covert wagons to be found anywhere. It is made in our high grade quality throughout and is just as good as similar wagons sold by others for fully $40.00 more than our price. It is a design that pleases the most critical buyers and we can unhesitatingly recommend it. We are very glad to ship No. 538 for full examination and approval, and it may be returned at our expense both ways if not found highly satisfactory in every way.

BODY—Is made from the best of stock throughout and the seat is roomy and comfortable. We furnish special seat with full panel back, as shown by small cut in corner of page, if preferred to seat with lazy back. There are good steel sill or rocker plates laid in white lead and screwed full length of sills and over the wheel house on body.

GEAR—Roman bike style with dust proof bell collar long distance axles, with felt oil pads. Axles have short wood beds in center, which are cemented and clipped to the axles, and to these wood beds attach the rear spring in rear and the fifth wheel in front. Fine full circle wrought Brewster fifth wheel, which is one of the best and strongest fifth wheels made and is used on all high grade work. Fine oil tempered French pattern open head springs, correctly graded and very easy riding. Reaches are ironed full length with regular channel reach iron, bolted and well braced. Bradley quick shifting shaft couplers, style and grade used on all high grade work. Shafts, regulation high bend bike Stanhope shafts, made from selected straight grain white hickory, full patent leather trimmed and with special heel braces. Pole instead of shafts, $1.00 extra. Pole in addition to shafts, $5.00 extra.

WHEELS—Fine selected straight grain white hickory, ⅞-inch banded hub, 38 inches front and 40 inches rear, with ⅞-inch round edge planished steel tire, bolted between each spoke. Tires

are ¼-inch thick and are set hot by hand and not by machine. Felloes have screws through them on each side of every spoke, which insures absolutely against checking at the spokes. The height of the wheels we furnish is correct for this style gear, but we can make any change in height desired. We furnish 1-inch wheels instead of ⅞-inch, if preferred, also Sarven patent style instead of banded hub. Fine steel wire wheels and 1⅛-inch cushion tires for $25.00 additional charge to price quoted with wood wheels and steel tires.

TRIMMINGS—Seat is trimmed with fine heavy all wool whipcord, but we will trim with fine dark green or blue all wool broadcloth, if preferred. The ends of the seat are pleated and trimmed to match cushion and back, and cushion and back are upholstered ith hair and fine upholstering springs. We can furnish special olors in broadcloth trimmings, if desired, at a small additional charge. Fine genuine soft leather trimmings in dark green, maroon or russet instead of broadcloth, $3.00 extra. Fine full padded dash. Velvet carpet or rubber mat in bottom of body. Oil burner lamps.

PAINTING—Body is finely finished in black, correctly striped; gear, New York red, properly striped. We will make any changes in color of painting desired. For system of painting, see page 5.

The above cut shows No. 552 with basket style seat.
Price, same as with panel seat.

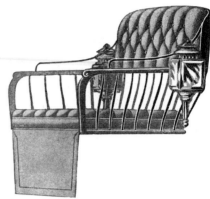

The above cut illustrates fine spindle style seat, which is one of the neatest seats made for a covert wagon of this style. We furnish this seat at the same price as the panel seat.

No. 552—FINE COVERT WAGON, WITH BIKE GEAR

PRICE
Cash with order, with steel tires and shafts................................$78.00
C. O. D., with steel tires and shafts...80.00
Cash with order, with ⅞-inch guaranteed rubber tires and shafts.............93.00
C. O. D., with ⅞-inch guaranteed rubber tires and shafts....................95.00
If 1⅛-inch guaranteed cushion tires are preferred, add $5.00 to the price quoted with ⅞-inch solid tires.

No. 552 is one of the best and most desirable style covert wagons we are making. This wagon is made in our best grade throughout and there is so much style and quality about it for the money that we are very glad to ship it anywhere for full examination. We know No. 552 is as good in general style and construction as similar wagons sold by others for fully $35.00 more than our price.

BODY—Both body and seat are made from high grade stock and are so constructed that we guarantee the panels not to come apart at the joints, no matter in what climate used. Seat is roomy and very comfortable. There are steel sill or rocker plates laid in white lead and screwed full length of sills. Rubber covered steps. Roller rub irons.

GEAR—Roman bike style with dust proof bell collar long distance axles, with felt oil pads. Axles have short wood beds in center, which are cemented and clipped to the axles, and to these wood beds attach the rear spring in rear and the fifth wheel in front. Fine full circle wrought Brewster fifth wheel, which is one of the best and strongest fifth wheels made and is used on all high grade work. Fine oil tempered French pattern open head springs, correctly graded and very easy riding. Reaches are ironed full length with regular channel reach iron, bolted and well braced. Bradley quick shifting shaft couplers, style and grade used on all high grade work. Shafts, regulation high bend bike Stanhope shafts, made from selected straight grain white hickory, full patent leather trimmed and with special heel braces. Pole instead of shafts, $1.00 extra. Pole in addition to shafts, $5.00 extra.

WHEELS—Fine selected straight grain white hickory, ⅞-inch banded hub, 38 inches front and 40 inches rear, with ⅞-inch round edge planished steel tire, bolted between each spoke. Tires are ¼-inch thick and are set hot by hand and not by machine. Felloes have screws through them on each side of every spoke, which insures absolutely against checking at the spokes. The height of the wheels we furnish is correct for this style gear, but we can make any change in height desired. We furnish 1-inch wheels instead of ⅞-inch, if preferred, also Sarven patent style instead of banded hub. Fine steel wire wheels and 1⅛-inch cushion tires $25.00 additional charge to price quoted with wood wheels and steel tires.

TRIMMINGS—Seat is trimmed with fine heavy all wool whipcord, but we will trim with fine dark green or blue all wool broadcloth, if preferred. The ends of the seat are pleated and trimmed to match cushion and back, and cushion and back are upholstered with hair and fine upholstering springs. We can furnish special colors in broadcloth trimmings, if desired, at a small additional charge. Fine genuine soft leather trimmings in dark green, maroon or russet instead of broadcloth, $3.00 extra. Fine full padded dash. Velvet carpet or rubber mat in bottom of body. Oil burner lamps.

PAINTING—Body is finely finished in black, correctly striped; gear, New York red, properly striped. We will make any changes in color of painting desired. For system of painting, see page 5.

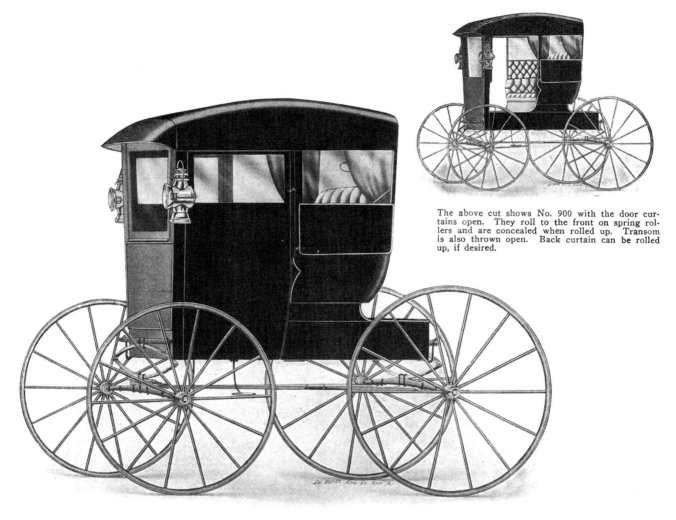

The above cut shows No. 900 with the door curtains open. They roll to the front on spring rollers and are concealed when rolled up. Transom is also thrown open. Back curtain can be rolled up, if desired.

No. 900—FINE EXTRA HEAVY STORM PROOF BUGGY WITH STANHOPE STYLE SEAT

PRICE
Cash with order, with steel tires and shafts.................................$127.50
C. O. D., with steel tires and shafts... 130.00
Cash with order, with 1⅛-inch guaranteed solid rubber tires and shafts.......... 150.00
C. O. D., with 1⅛-inch guaranteed solid rubber tires and shafts.................. 152.50

Our No. 900 is one of the most practicable storm proof buggies made. It is especially constructed for rough roads and city streets, being built with extra heavy piano body and extra heavy 1⅛-inch gear. The top is one of the finest storm proof tops made. It is built under patent of January 16, 1906, No. 810151. Top is practically the same heft as an ordinary buggy top. It can be opened all around, as small cut in corner shows, thus making it as comfortable and pleasant for use in good weather as it is for stormy weather. The front transom can be swung up on the inside where it fastens and the rear curtain rolls up. We guarantee this buggy as fine in quality of workmanship and general finish throughout as similar vehicles sold by others for $50.00 more than our price.

BODY—Piano box style, 26 inches wide and 58 inches long, made extra heavy throughout and put together in such a manner that we guarantee it not to open at the joints, no matter in what climate used. Seat is our half phaeton style which is roomy and very comfortable. Rubber covered steps. Roller rub irons.

GEAR—1⅛-inch dust proof bell collar long distance axles, equipped with felt oil pads. Axles are fitted with straight grain hickory beds, which are cemented and clipped full length. Fine well graded oil tempered French pattern open head springs, which are very easy riding. Reaches have channel reach iron full length and they are bolted and well braced. Extra heavy full circle wrought Brewster fifth wheel, which is one of the best style fifth wheels made. Heavy straight grain hickory spring bars with body loops running full length of body. We will furnish Bailey loops, if preferred. Bradley quick shifting shaft couplers which are the best couplers made and are used on all high grade work. Shafts, regulation buggy style, made from straight grain white hickory, full patent leather trimmed and with special heel braces. We furnish pole instead of shafts for $1.00 extra. Pole in addition to shafts, $5.00 extra.

WHEELS—Fine selected straight grain white hickory, 1-inch Sarven patent, 40 inches front and 44 inches rear, with 1-inch round edge planished steel tire, bolted between each spoke. Our tires are all set hot by hand and not by machine. Felloes have screws through them on each side of every spoke, which insures them against checking at the spokes. Height of wheels we furnish is regulation height, but we can make any changes in height desired. We can also furnish banded hub style, if preferred to

the Sarven patent. If 1⅛-inch wheels are preferred to 1-inch we will furnish them without additional charge.

TRIMMINGS—Seat is trimmed with heavy dark green all wool broadcloth, guaranteed fast color, but will trim with fine dark blue broadcloth or whipcord, if preferred. The ends of the seat are pleated and trimmed to match cushion and back, and both cushion and back are upholstered with hair and upholstering springs, and the seat is very comfortable. We furnish special colors in broadcloth at a small additional charge, or fine genuine leather trimmings in dark green, maroon or russet instead of all wool broadcloth for $3.00 extra. Velvet carpet in bottom of body, or rubber mat, if preferred. Rubber boot over back part of body.

TOP—Best patent storm proof design made. It is full leather and lined throughout to match seat trimmings. Side quarters, roof back stays and back curtain are made of fine top leather. The panels below the side windows and below the front transom are made of genuine patent bow leather. Door curtains are made of heavy top rubber and they roll to the front on spring rollers and work perfectly. They are concealed when rolled up. There is a lookout glass made of flexible transparent fibre as shown in picture. The side windows at the ends of the seat and the front transom are beveled plate glass. Silk tie back curtains at windows as cut shows. Fine Dietz driving lamps.

PAINTING—Body is finely finished in black, correctly striped; gear, Brewster green, properly striped. We will make any changes in color of painting desired. For system of painting in detail, see page 5.

61

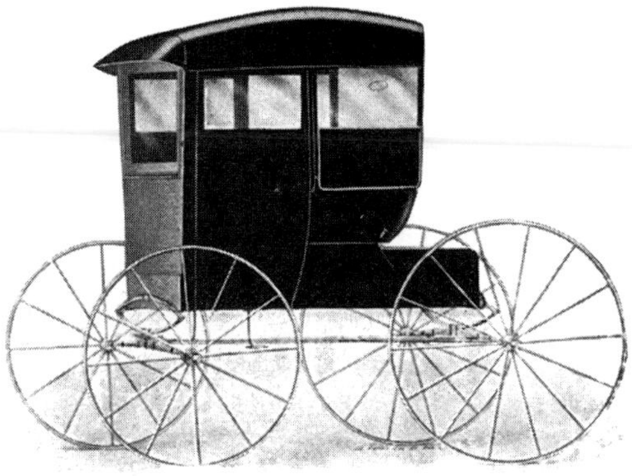

The above cut shows No. 904 with the transom down and the door curtains drawn, which makes it as secure as a closed cab.

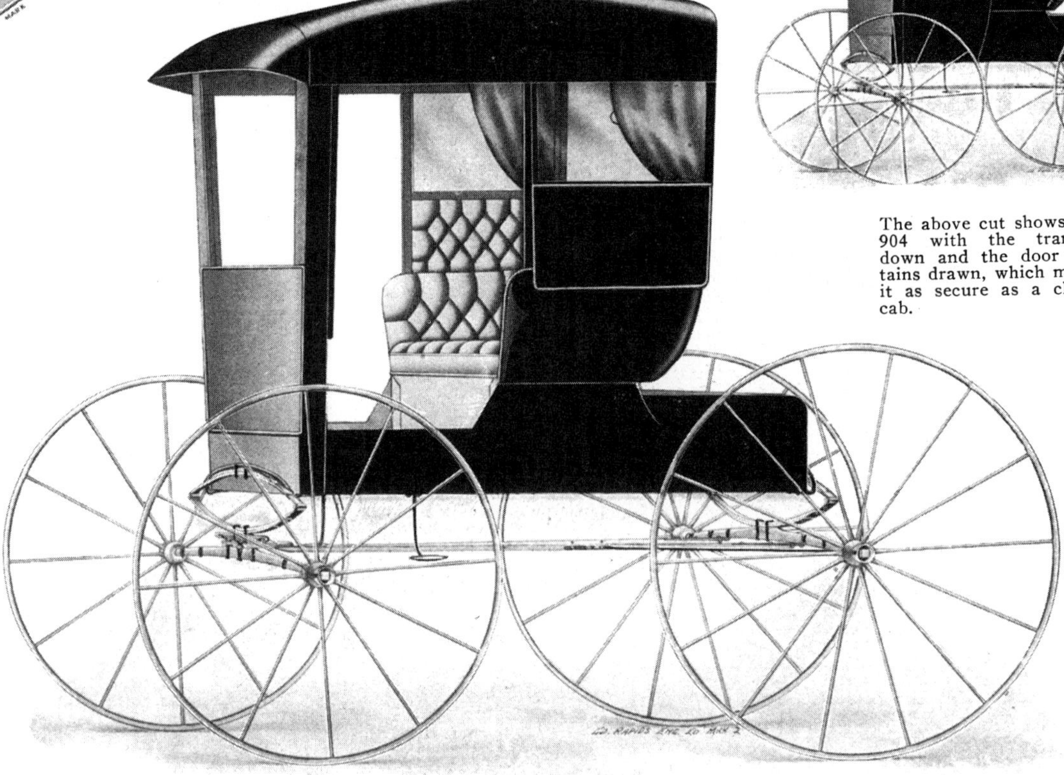

No. 904—FINE STORM PROOF BUGGY WITH SPECIAL PIANO BODY

PRICE		
	Cash with order, with steel tires and shafts	$107.50
	C. O. D., with steel tires and shafts	110.00
	Cash with order, with $\frac{7}{8}$-inch guaranteed rubber tires and shafts	122.50
	C. O. D., with $\frac{7}{8}$-inch guaranteed rubber tires and shafts	125.00

Our No. 904 is one of the best style storm proof and weather proof buggies to be found anywhere. It is equipped with our special piano body which is decked over solid back of seat, making it, with many physicians, a more desirable piano body than the regulation style which is covered with an adjustable rubber boot. There is the usual opening under the seat so that packages can be put in the rear part of the body from the front, same as the regular piano body. Seat is our regular Stanhope style and is a very roomy and comfortable seat. Top is the most practicable storm proof top made. It is built under patent of January 16, 1906, No. 810151. We guarantee No. 904 as fine in quality of workmanship and material throughout as sold by others or through city repositories for $40.00 to $50.00 more than our price. We are glad to ship it for examination and approval.

BODY—Is one of the best style piano bodies made. It is built from the best of body stock throughout, and both body and seat are so constructed that we guarantee them not to open at the corners, no matter in what climate used. The rear part of the body is decked over solid as picture shows, but there is the usual opening underneath the seat so that packages can be put in the rear part of the body from the front. Body is 24 inches wide by 56 inches long. Roller rub irons. Rubber covered steps.

GEAR—$\frac{15}{16}$-inch dust proof bell collar long distance axles, with felt oil pads. Axles are fitted with straight grain hickory beds, which are cemented and clipped full length. Fine oil tempered French pattern open head springs, properly graded and very easy riding. Reaches have channel' irons full length and they are bolted and well braced. Full circle wrought Brewster fifth wheel, which is one of the best fifth wheels made and is used on all high grade work. Bailey body loops clipped to springs. We will furnish wood spring bars, if preferred to Bailey loops. Bradley quick shifting shaft couplers, which are used on all first class work. Shafts, regulation buggy style, made from fine selected straight grain hickory, with full patent leather trimmings and special heel braces. Pole instead of shafts, $1.00 extra. Pole in addition to shafts, $5.00 extra.

WHEELS—Fine selected straight grain white hickory, $\frac{7}{8}$-inch Sarven patent, 40 inches front and 44 inches rear, with $\frac{7}{8}$-inch round edge planished steel tire, bolted between each spoke. Tires are $\frac{1}{4}$-inch thick and are set hot by hand and not by machine. Felloes have screws through them on each side of every spoke, which insures them absolutely against checking at the spokes. The height of wheels we furnish is correct for this style gear, but we can make any change in height desired. We furnish $\frac{3}{4}$-inch wheels instead of $\frac{7}{8}$-inch, if preferred. Also banded hub stylê, if desired, instead of the Sarven patent.

TRIMMINGS—Seat is trimmed with heavy dark green all wool broadcloth, guaranteed fast color, but will trim with fine dark blue broadcloth or whipcord, if preferred. The ends of the seat are pleated and trimmed to match cushion and back, and both cushion and back are upholstered with hair and upholstering springs, and the seat is very comfortable. We furnish special colors in broadcloth at a small additional charge, or fine genuine leather trimmings in dark green, maroon or russet instead of all wool broadcloth, for $3.00 extra. Velvet carpet in bottom of body, or rubber mat if preferred.

TOP—Is fine leather quarter, patent storm proof style, and one of the most practicable storm and waterproof tops made. The side quarters and back stays are of fine top leather; roof and back curtain are made of heavy top rubber. The door curtains are of heavy top rubber and they roll up to the front on spring rollers and are concealed when rolled up. They are equipped with transparent fibre windows and they work perfectly on the rollers. The panels under the side windows and under the front transom are of double faced English moleskin lined to match trimmings. The side windows at ends of seat and front transom are clear No. 1 double strength glass. Silk tie back curtains at windows as cut shows. Extra for fine Dietz driving lamps, as shown on No. 900, $5.00. Extra for full leather top, as described on No. 900, $10.00. Extra for beveled plate glass, as described on No. 900, $4.00.

PAINTING—Body is finely finished in black, correctly striped; gear, Brewster green, properly striped. We will make any changes in color of painting desired. For system of painting in detail, see page 5.

The above cut shows No. 908 with transom open and door curtains rolled up. The back curtain can also be rolled up, if desired, so that the buggy is made perfectly open for pleasant weather.

No. 908—FINE LIGHT STORM PROOF BUGGY

PRICE
{ Cash with order, with steel tires and shafts.....................................$ 98.00
C. O. D., with steel tires and shafts.. 100.00
Cash with order, with ⅞-inch guaranteed rubber tires and shafts.................. 113.00
C. O. D., with ⅞-inch guaranteed rubber tires and shafts........................ 115.00 }

Our No. 908 is a specially desirable storm proof buggy, because it is made as light as possible throughout. We use on this buggy our regular 22-inch piano body, and regular style buggy seat. The top is of the same construction as our other styles. It is built under patent of January 16, 1906, No. 810151, and is one of the most practicable storm proof tops made. We know No. 908 is as good in quality of workmanship and material throughout as usually sells for fully $40.00 more than our price. We are glad at any rate of an opportunity to ship this buggy for full examination and approval, and if it is not found all we claim and a very satisfactory buggy, we will take it back at our expense.

BODY—Regulation piano box style, 22 inches wide and 56 inches long. The seat is our regulation buggy size seat, lighter and smaller than our Stanhope style seat. We use high grade stock in the construction of both body and seat, and they are made in such a manner that we guarantee them not to come apart at the joints, no matter in what climate used. Rubber covered steps and roller rub irons.

GEAR—1⅛-inch dust proof bell collar long distance axles, with felt oil pads. Axles are fitted with straight grain hickory beds, which are cemented and clipped full length. Fine oil tempered French pattern open head springs, properly graded and very easy riding. Reaches have channel irons full length, and they are bolted and well braced. Full circle wrought Brewster fifth wheel, which is one of the best fifth wheels made and is used on all high grade work. Bailey body loops clipped to springs. We will furnish wood spring bars if preferred to the Bailey loops. Bradley quick shifting shaft couplers, which are used on all first class work. Shafts, regulation buggy style made from fine selected straight grain hickory, with full patent leather trimmings and with heel braces. Pole instead of shafts, $1.00 extra. Pole in addition to shafts, $5.00 extra.

WHEELS—Fine selected straight grain white hickory, ⅞-inch Sarven patent, 40 inches front and 44 inches rear, with ⅞-inch round edge planished steel tire, bolted between each spoke. Tires are ¼-inch thick and are set hot by hand and not by machine. Felloes have screws through them on each side of every spoke, which insures them absolutely against checking at the spokes. The height of wheels we furnish is correct for this style gear, but we can make any change in height desired. We furnish ¾-inch

wheels instead of ⅞-inch, if preferred. Also banded hub style, if desired, instead of the Sarven patent.

TRIMMINGS—Seat is trimmed with heavy dark green all wool broadcloth, guaranteed fast color, but will trim with fine dark blue broadcloth or whipcord, if preferred. The ends of the seat are pleated and trimmed to match cushion and back, and both cushion and back are upholstered with hair and upholstering springs, and the seat is very comfortable. We furnish special colors in broadcloth at a small additional charge, or fine genuine leather trimmings in dark green, maroon or russet instead of all wool broadcloth for $3.00 extra. Velvet carpet in bottom of body, or rubber mat, if preferred. Rubber boot over back part of body.

TOP—Is fine leather quarter, patent storm proof style, and one of the most practical storm and waterproof tops made. The side quarters and back stays are of fine top leather; roof and back curtain are made of heavy top rubber. The door curtains are of heavy top rubber and they roll to the front on spring rollers and are concealed when rolled up. They are equipped with transparent fibre windows and they work perfectly on the rollers. The panels under the side windows and under the front transom are of double faced English moleskin, lined to match trimmings. The side windows at ends of seat and front transom are clear No. 1 double strength glass. Extra for fine Dietz driving lamps, as shown on No. 900, $5.00. Extra for full leather top, as described on No. 900, $10.00. Extra for beveled plate glass, as described on No. 900, $4.00.

PAINTING—Body is finely finished in black, correctly striped; gear, Brewster green, properly striped. We will make any changes in color of painting desired. For system of painting in detail, see page 5.

63

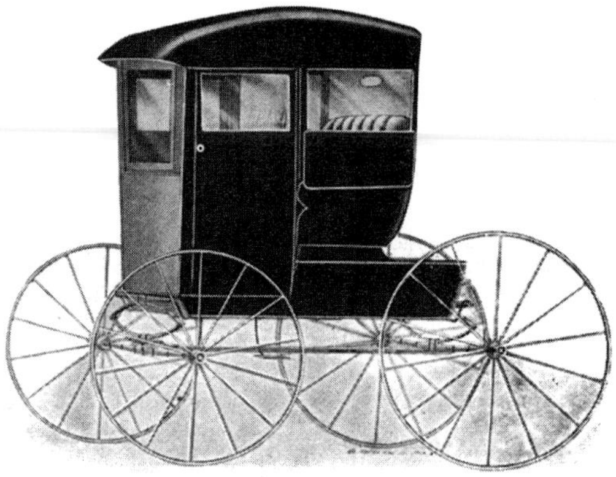

The above cut shows No. 912 with the front transom down and the door curtains closed, making a secure closed carriage for rough, stormy weather.

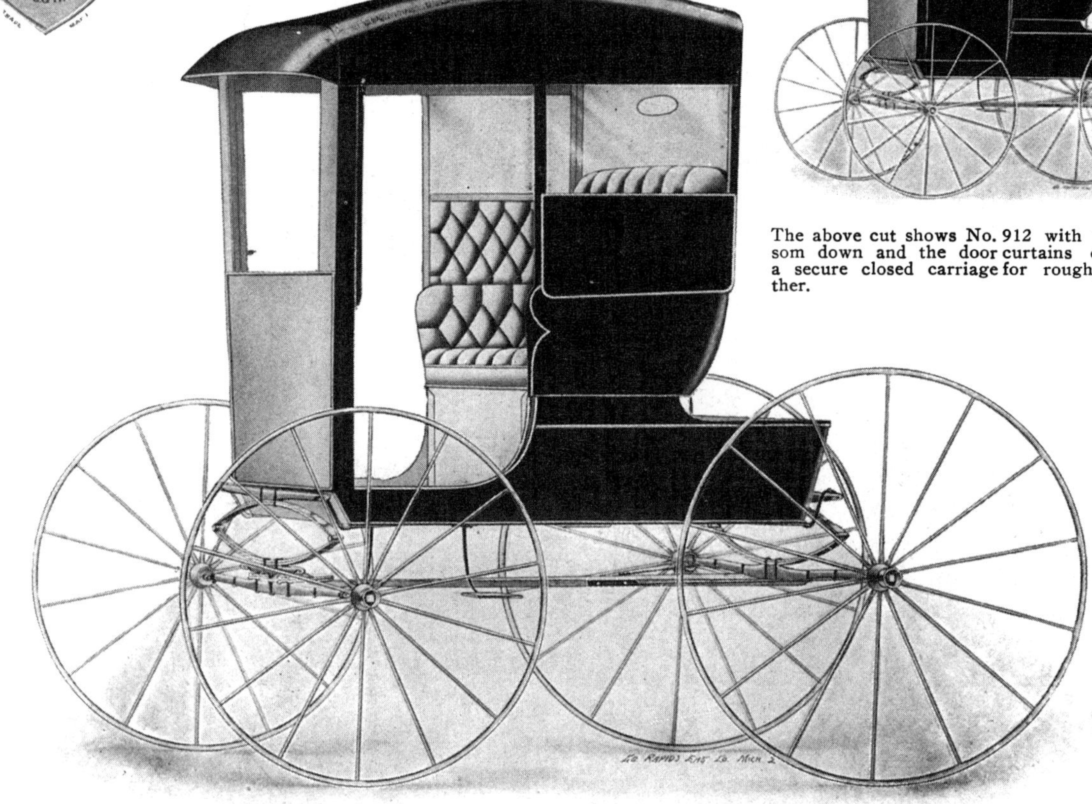

No. 912—FINE STORM PROOF BUGGY WITH CORNING BODY

PRICE	Cash with order, with steel tires and shafts	**$105.00**
	C. O. D., with steel tires and shafts	**107.00**
	Cash with order, with 7/8-inch guaranteed rubber tires and shafts	**120.00**
	C. O. D., with 7/8-inch guaranteed rubber tires and shafts	**122.00**

No. 912 is a very popular seller with us, and is a buggy that gives universal satisfaction. A good many users prefer this particular style on account of the body being cut down in front, making it easy to get into and out of. It is the regulation Corning style buggy. The seat is our Stanhope style which is very comfortable. Although the body is cut down in front there is about 3 inches of panel on each side which is enough to keep in blankets, robes, etc. The top is our regular storm proof top manufactured under patent of January 16, 1906, No. 810151. We know this buggy is as good in quality of workmanship and material throughout as sold by others for fully $40.00 more than our price. We are glad to ship it for examination and approval, and it may be returned at our expense if not found entirely satisfactory.

BODY—Is regulation Corning style with our regular Stanhope style seat, which has high back and is very roomy and comfortable. Both body and seat are made from high grade stock and put together in such a manner that we guarantee them not to open at the corners, no matter in what climate used. Rubber covered steps. Roller rub irons.

GEAR—15/16-inch dust proof bell collar long distance axles, with felt oil pads. Axles are fitted with straight grain hickory beds, which are cemented and clipped full length. Fine oil tempered French pattern open head springs, properly graded and very easy riding. Reaches have channel irons full length, and they are bolted and well braced. Full circle wrought Brewster fifth wheel, which is one of the best fifth wheels made and is used on all high grade work. Bailey body loops clipped to springs. We will furnish wood spring bars if preferred to the Bailey loops. Bradley quick shifting shaft couplers, which are used on all first class work. Shafts, regulation buggy style made from fine selected straight grain hickory, with full patent leather trimmings and with heel braces. Pole instead of shafts, $1.00 extra. Pole in addition to shafts, $5.00 extra.

WHEELS—Fine selected straight grain white hickory, 7/8-inch Sarven patent, 40 inches front and 44 inches rear, with 7/8-inch round edge planished steel tire, bolted between each spoke. Tires are 1/4-inch thick and are set hot by hand and not by machine. Felloes have screws through them on each side of every spoke, which insures them absolutely against checking at the spokes. The height of wheels we furnish is correct for this style gear, but we can make any change in height desired. We furnish 3/4-inch wheels instead of 7/8-inch, if preferred. Also banded hub style, if desired, instead of the Sarven patent.

TRIMMINGS—Seat is trimmed with heavy dark green all wool broadcloth, guaranteed fast color, but will trim with fine dark blue broadcloth or whipcord, if preferred. The ends of the seat are pleated and trimmed to match cushion and back, and both cushion and back are upholstered with hair and upholstering springs, and the seat is very comfortable. We furnish special colors in broadcloth at a small additional charge, or fine genuine leather trimmings in dark green, maroon or russet instead of all wool broadcloth for $3.00 extra. Velvet carpet in bottom of body, or rubber mat, if preferred. Rubber boot over back part of body.

TOP—Is fine leather quarter, patent storm proof style, and one of the most practical storm and waterproof tops made. The side quarters and back stays are of fine top leather; roof and back curtain are made of heavy top rubber. The door curtains are of heavy top rubber and they roll to the front on spring rollers and are concealed when rolled up. They are equipped with transparent fibre windows and they work perfectly on the rollers. The panels under the side windows and under the front transom are of double faced English moleskin, lined to match trimmings. The side windows at ends of seat and front transom are clear No. 1 double strength glass. Extra for silk tie back curtains at windows, as shown on No. 900, $1.00. Extra for fine Dietz driving lamps, as shown on No. 900, $5.00. Extra for full leather top, as described on No. 900, $10.00. Extra for beveled plate glass, as described on No. 900, $4.00.

PAINTING—Body is finely finished in black, correctly striped; gear, Brewster green, properly striped. We will make any changes in color of painting desired. For system of painting in detail, see page 5.

No. 914—HEAVY BUSINESS OR LIVERY WAGON WITH FULL LEATHER TOP AND LEATHER COVERED BOWS

PRICE
{
Cash with order, with steel tires and shafts....................................$ 83.00
C. O. D., with steel tires and shafts... 85.00
Cash with order, with 1-inch guaranteed rubber tires and shafts.................. 100.50
C. O. D., with 1-inch guaranteed rubber tires and shafts........................ 102.50
}

If 1⅛-inch guaranteed rubber tires are preferred, add $5.00 to the price quoted for 1-inch rubber tires.

There is quite a demand for an extra heavy piano body buggy for special livery and business purposes. Our No. 914 is made with extra heavy piano body, 1⅛-inch gear and 1-inch wheels (1⅛-inch wheels, if preferred) and it is suitable for all kinds of hard driving and especially for city streets. This buggy is made in our best grade throughout and is a first class work. We know it is as good as usually sells for fully $35.00 more than our price. We are glad to ship it for full examination and approval.

BODY—Piano box style, 26 inches wide and 58 inches long, made extra heavy throughout and put together in such a manner that we guarantee it not to open at the joints, no matter in what climate used. Seat is our half phaeton style, which is roomy and very comfortable. Rubber covered steps. Roller rub irons.

GEAR—1⅛-inch dust proof bell collar long distance axles, equipped with felt oil pads. Axles are fitted with straight grain hickory beds, which are cemented and clipped full length. Fine well graded oil tempered French pattern open head springs, which are very easy riding. Reaches have channel reach iron full length, and they are bolted and well braced. Extra heavy full circle wrought Brewster fifth wheel, which is one of the best style fifth wheels made. Heavy straight grain hickory spring bars with body loops running full length of body. We will furnish extra heavy Bailey loops, if preferred. Bradley quick shifting shaft couplers, which are the best couplers made and are used on all high grade work. Shafts, regulation buggy style, made from straight grain white hickory, full patent leather trimmed and with special heel braces. We furnish pole instead of shafts for $1.00 extra. Pole in addition to shafts, $5.00 extra.

WHEELS—Fine selected straight grain white hickory, 1-inch Sarven patent, 40 inches front and 44 inches rear, with 1-inch round edge planished steel tire, bolted between each spoke. Our tires are all set hot by hand and not by machine. Felloes have screws through them on each side of every spoke, which insures them against checking at the spokes. Height of wheels we fur-

nish is regulation height, but we can make any changes in height desired. We can also furnish banded hub style, if preferred to the Sarven patent. If 1⅛-inch wheels are preferred to 1-inch we will furnish them without additional charge.

TRIMMINGS—Seat is trimmed with dark green all wool broadcloth, guaranteed fast color, but will trim with dark blue wool broadcloth or all wool whipcord, if preferred. The ends of the seat are trimmed to match the cushion and back, and both cushion and back are upholstered with hair and fine upholstering springs, and the seat is very comfortable. We can furnish any special colors in broadcloth at a small additional charge. Genuine leather trimmings in dark green, maroon or russet instead of broadcloth, $3.00 extra. Fine full padded dash. Velvet carpet in bottom of body, or rubber mat, if preferred. Rubber boot.

TOP—Fine full leather with best grade leather covered bow sockets, heavy rubber side curtains and storm apron for dash. We furnish with leather quarter top and very best grade steel bow sockets, if desired, for $7.00 less than with leather top. We furnish four bows on any of our tops instead of three without additional charge. Top is always lined with broadcloth to match seat trimmings.

PAINTING—The body is black; gear, Brewster green, correctly striped. We will furnish New York red gear or make any changes in painting desired. Our painting is all fully warranted. For system of painting in detail, see page 5.

The above cut shows front view of No. 916 with top removed and you will see that the cushion and back are made the same as on the regular style seat. The top is attached to the seat with shifting rail and can be easily removed, thus giving you a neat open driving wagon if desired.

No. 916—FINE FULL LEATHER TOP BUGGY WITH LEATHER COVERED BOWS

PRICE
{
Cash with order, with steel tires and shafts.....................................$ 83.00
C. O. D., with steel tires and shafts.. 85.00
Cash with order, with ⅞-inch guaranteed rubber tires and shafts.................. 98.00
C. O. D., with ⅞-inch guaranteed rubber tires and shafts........................ 100.00
}

No. 916 is one of the most up-to-date style top buggies we are making. It is equipped with our new twin style auto seat. We make No. 916 in our best grade throughout and it is equal in quality of workmanship and material to similar styles sold by others for fully $30.00 more than our price. We are very glad to ship it for full examination and approval, with the understanding that it may be returned at our expense if not found perfectly satisfactory.

BODY—Is regulation piano box style, 22 inches wide and 56 inches long. We will furnish 24-inch body, if preferred to the 22-inch. The seat is one of the finest auto designs made. It has a good extra high back and is upholstered in such a manner that it is very comfortable. Both body and seat are made from high grade thoroughly seasoned body material and are well ironed and braced and guaranteed not to open at the corners, no matter in what climate they are used. Fine three prong rubber covered steps. Roller rub irons.

GEAR—1⅛-inch true sweep dust proof bell collar long distance axles, with felt oil pads. Axles are fitted with straight grain hickory beds, which are cemented and clipped to the axles. Fine oil tempered French pattern open head springs, very elastic and easy riding. The reaches have channel iron full length, and they are bolted and well braced. Full circle wrought Brewster slotted fifth wheel with king bolt clipped around axle. It is the style Brewster fifth wheel used on all strictly high grade work. Wrought Bailey body loops clipped to springs. Will furnish wood spring bar if preferred to the Bailey loops. Bradley quick change shaft couplers, which are the most practicable quick shifting couplers made and are used on all high grade work. Shafts are regular buggy style, only they are a little higher bend than is commonly used. They are made from selected hickory, full patent leather trimmed and are well braced. Will furnish pole in addition to shafts for $5.00 extra.

WHEELS—Fine selected straight grain white hickory, ⅞-inch banded hub, 40 inches front and 44 inches rear, with ⅞-inch round edge planished steel tire, bolted between each spoke. Tires are ¼-inch thick and are set hot by hand and not by machine. Felloes have screws through them on each side of every spoke,

which insures absolutely against checking at the spokes. The height of wheels we furnish is correct for this style gear, but we can make any change in height desired. We furnish ¾-inch wheels instead of ⅞-inch, if preferred. Also Sarven patent style if desired instead of banded hub.

TRIMMINGS—Seat is trimmed with fine dark green all wool broadcloth, guaranteed fast color. We will trim with fine dark green wool broadcloth or whipcord, if preferred. The ends of the seat are pleated and trimmed to match cushion and back, and cushion and back are upholstered with hair and upholstering springs. The cushion and back are not made with the divided effect as shown in the back of the seat. They are made in one piece as shown by cut in corner. We can furnish any special colors of broadcloth trimmings at a small additional charge. Genuine leather trimmings in dark green, maroon or russet instead of broadcloth, $3.00 extra. Fine full padded leather dash. Velvet carpet in bottom of body, or rubber mat if preferred. Rubber boot to cover back part of body.

TOP—Fine full leather with best grade leather covered bow sockets, heavy rubber side curtains and storm apron for dash. We furnish with leather quarter top and very best grade steel bow sockets, if desired, for $7.00 less than with leather top. We furnish four bows on any of our tops instead of three without additional charge. Top is always lined with broadcloth to match seat trimmings.

PAINTING—Body is finely finished in black, correctly striped; gear, Brewster green, properly striped. We will make any changes in color of painting desired. For system of painting in detail, see page 5.

No 918—FINE FULL LEATHER TOP BUGGY WITH LEATHER COVERED BOWS

PRICE
Cash with order, with steel tires and shafts....................................$82.00
C. O. D., with steel tires and shafts.. 84.00
Cash with order, with ⅞-inch guaranteed rubber tires and shafts.................. 97.00
C. O. D., with ⅞-inch guaranteed rubber tires and shafts........................ 99.00
If ¾-inch rubber tires are preferred, deduct $2.00 from price quoted with ⅞-inch rubber tires.

No. 918 is one of the highest grade top buggies we manufacture. It has the same high grade construction and finish throughout as similar styles sold by others for fully $35.00 more than our price. This buggy has all the latest desirable features used today. It is so well made and so finely finished that we are very glad to ship it with the understanding that it may be compared with anything in the high grade buggy line and if it is not found a superior vehicle and you do not feel you are saving money in ordering from us we will willingly take the buggy back at our expense and you will be nothing out. We know this buggy will please, because every detail is worked out to perfection.

BODY—Is regulation piano box style, 22 inches wide and 56 inches long. We will furnish 24-inch body, if preferred to the 22-inch. The seat is one of the finest auto designs made. It has a good extra high back and is upholstered in such a manner that it is very comfortable. Both body and seat are made from high grade thoroughly seasoned body material and are well ironed and braced and guaranteed not to open at the corners, no matter in what climate they are used. Fine three prong rubber covered steps. Roller rub irons.

GEAR—1⅛-inch true sweep dust proof bell collar long distance axles, with felt oil pads. Axles are fitted with straight grain hickory beds, which are cemented and clipped to the axles. Fine oil tempered French pattern open head springs, very elastic and easy riding. The reaches have channel iron full length, and they are bolted and well braced. Full circle wrought Brewster slotted fifth wheel with king bolt clipped around axle. It is the style Brewster fifth wheel used on all strictly high grade work. Wrought Bailey body loops clipped to springs. Will furnish wood spring bar if preferred to the Bailey loops. Bradley quick change shaft couplers, which are the most practicable quick shifting couplers made and are used on all high grade work. Shafts are regular buggy style only they are a little higher bend than is commonly used. They are made from selected hickory, full patent leather trimmed and well braced. Pole instead of shafts on any of our top buggies, $1.00 extra. Will furnish pole in addition to shafts for $5.00 extra.

WHEELS—Fine selected straight grain white hickory, ⅞-inch banded hub, 40 inches front and 44 inches rear, with ⅞-inch round edge planished steel tire, bolted between each spoke. Tires are ¼-inch thick and are set hot by hand and not by machine.

Felloes have screws through them on each side of every spoke, which insures absolutely against checking at the spokes. The height of wheels we furnish is correct for this style gear, but we can make any change in height desired. We furnish ¾-inch wheels instead of ⅞-inch, if preferred. Also Sarven patent style instead of banded hub.

TRIMMINGS—Seat is trimmed with fine dark green all wool broadcloth, guaranteed absolutely fast color. Will trim with fine dark blue wool broadcloth or fine whipcord, if preferred. Ends of the seat are padded and trimmed to match cushion and back, and both cushion and back are upholstered with hair and up-holstering springs, and the seat is most comfortable. We can furnish any special colors of broadcloth at a small additional charge. Genuine leather trimmings in dark green, maroon or russet instead of all wool broadcloth for $3.00. Fine full padded patent leather dash. Velvet carpet in bottom of body, or rubber mat if preferred to the carpet. Rubber boot to cover back part of body.

TOP—Fine full leather with best grade leather covered bow sock-ets, heavy rubber side curtains and storm apron for dash. We furnish with leather quarter top and very best grade steel bow sockets, if desired, for $7.00 less than with leather top. We furnish four bows on any of our tops instead of three without additional charge. Top is always lined with broadcloth to match seat trimmings.

PAINTING—The body is black; gear, Brewster green, correctly striped. We will furnish New York red gear or make any changes in painting desired. Our painting is all fully guaranteed. For system of painting in detail, see page 5.

The above cut shows No. 920 with cut-under style body with low side panels in front of seat. The additional charge for this style body is $5.00.

No. 920—FINE LIGHT FULL LEATHER TOP BUGGY
WITH LEATHER COVERED BOWS

PRICE
Cash with order, with steel tires and shafts.....................................$80.00
C. O. D., with steel tires and shafts.. 82.00
Cash with order, with ¾-inch guaranteed rubber tires and shafts................... 93.00
C. O. D., with ¾-inch guaranteed rubber tires and shafts.......................... 95.00
If ⅞-inch rubber tires are preferred, add $2.00 to the price quoted with ¾-inch tires.

Our No. 920 is a very popular style top buggy. It is made in our best grade throughout, is finely finished and trimmed, and a buggy equal in every respect to similar styles sold by others for fully $30.00 more than our price. We are glad of an opportunity to ship this buggy for examination and approval, and if it is not found all we claim and perfectly satisfactory it may be returned at our expense.

BODY—Piano box style, 22 inches wide and 56 inches long. We will furnish 24-inch body if preferred to the 22-inch. The seat is one of our most popular style auto seats. It has good high back and is very comfortable. Both body and seat are made from high grade stock and are put together in such a manner and so well ironed and braced that we guarantee them not to open at the corners, no matter in what climate used. Three prong rubber covered steps. Roller rub irons.

GEAR—1⅛-inch dust proof bell collar long distance axles, with felt oil pads. Axles are fitted with straight grain hickory beds, which are cemented and clipped full length. Fine oil tempered French pattern open head springs, properly graded and very easy riding. Reaches have channel irons full length, and they are bolted and well braced. Full circle wrought Brewster fifth wheel, which is one of the best fifth wheels made and is used on all high grade work. Bailey body loops clipped to springs. We furnish wood spring bars, if preferred to the Bailey loops. Bradley quick shifting shaft couplers, which are used on all first class work. Shafts, regulation buggy style made from fine selected straight grain hickory, with full patent leather trimmings and with heel braces. Pole instead of shafts, $1.00 extra. Pole in addition to shafts, $5.00 extra.

WHEELS—Fine selected straight grain white hickory, ¾-inch Sarven patent, 40 inches front and 44 inches rear, with ¾-inch round edge planished steel tire, bolted between each spoke. Tires are ¼-inch thick and are set hot by hand and not by machine. Felloes have screws through them on each side of every spoke, which insures absolutely against checking at the spokes. The height of wheels we furnish is correct for this style gear, but we can make any change in height desired. We furnish ⅞-inch wheels instead of ¾-inch, if preferred. Also banded hub style if desired instead of Sarven patent.

TRIMMINGS—Seat is trimmed with fine dark green all wool broadcloth, guaranteed absolutely fast color. Will trim with fine dark blue wool broadcloth or fine whipcord, if preferred. Ends of the seat are padded and trimmed to match cushion and back, and both cushion and back are upholstered with hair and upholstering springs, and the seat is most comfortable. We can furnish any special colors of broadcloth at a small additional charge. Genuine leather trimmings in dark green, maroon or russet instead of all wool broadcloth for $3.00. Fine full padded patent leather dash. Brussels carpet in bottom of body, or rubber mat if preferred to the carpet. Rubber boot to cover back part of body.

TOP—Fine full leather with best grade leather covered bow sockets, heavy rubber side curtains and storm apron for dash. We furnish with leather quarter top and very best grade steel bow sockets, if desired, for $7.00 less than with leather top. We furnish four bows on any of our tops instead of three without additional charge. Top is always lined with broadcloth to match seat trimmings.

PAINTING—The body is black; gear, Brewster green, correctly striped. We will furnish New York red gear or make any changes in painting desired. Our painting is all fully guaranteed. For system of painting in detail, see page 5.

The above cut shows No. 922 with cut-under style body. Price, $5.00 more than with regular body.

No. 922—FINE FULL LEATHER TOP BUGGY WITH LEATHER COVERED BOWS

PRICE
Cash with order, with steel tires and shafts.....................................$80.00
C. O. D., with steel tires and shafts... 82.00
Cash with order, with ⅞-inch guaranteed rubber tires and shafts................... 95.00
C. O. D., with ⅞-inch guaranteed rubber tires and shafts......................... 97.00
If 1-inch cushion tires are preferred, add $2.50 to price quoted with ⅞-inch rubber tires.

Our No. 922 is one of the most popular and desirable style buggies we are making. It is equipped with what we call our Stanhope style seat, which is a large, roomy, comfortable seat. This buggy is made in our best grade and is as good in quality of workmanship and general finish throughout as similar buggies sold by others for fully $30.00 more than our price. It is well proportioned, light running and very comfortable riding. We are glad to ship this buggy anywhere for examination and approval, and if it is not found all we claim and perfectly satisfactory we will take it back at our expense.

BODY—Piano box style, 24 inches wide and 56 inches long. We will furnish 22-inch body, if preferred. Seat is one of our most popular styles and a design that gives splendid satisfaction. It is roomy, has good high back and is very comfortable. Body and seat are made from high grade stock and are put together in such a way and so well ironed and braced that we guarantee them not to come apart at the joints, no matter in what climate used. Rubber covered steps. Roller rub irons.

GEAR—1⅛-inch dust proof bell collar long distance axles, with felt oil pads. Axles are fitted with light wood beds, which are cemented and clipped to the axles. Fine oil tempered French pattern open head springs, very elastic and easy riding. The reaches have channel iron full length, and they are bolted and well braced. Full circle wrought Brewster slotted fifth wheel with king bolt clipped around axle. It is the style Brewster fifth wheel used on all strictly high grade work. Wrought Bailey body loops clipped to springs. Will furnish wood spring bar if preferred to the Bailey loops. Bradley quick change shaft couplers, which are the most practicable quick shifting couplers made and are used on all high grade work. Shafts are regular buggy style, only they are a little higher bend than is commonly used. They are made from selected hickory, full patent leather trimmed and are well braced. Will furnish pole in addition to shafts for $5.00 extra.

WHEELS—Fine selected straight grain white hickory, ⅞-inch banded hub, 40 inches front and 44 inches rear, with ⅞-inch round edge planished steel tire, bolted between each spoke. Tires are ¼-inch thick and are set hot by hand and not by machine. Felloes have screws through them on each side of every spoke, which insures absolutely against checking at the spokes. The height of wheels we furnish is correct for this style gear, but we can make any change in height desired. We furnish ¾-inch wheels instead of ⅞-inch, if preferred. Also Sarven patent style if desired instead of banded hub.

TRIMMINGS—Seat is trimmed with fine dark green all wool broadcloth, guaranteed absolutely fast color. Will trim with fine dark blue wool broadcloth or fine whipcord, if preferred. Ends of the seat are padded and trimmed to match cushion and back, and both cushion and back are upholstered with hair and upholstering springs, and the seat is most comfortable. We can furnish any special colors of broadcloth at a small additional charge. Genuine leather trimmings in dark green, maroon or russet instead of all wool broadcloth for $3.00. Fine full padded patent leather dash. Velvet carpet in bottom of body, or rubber mat if preferred to the carpet. Rubber boot to cover back part of body.

TOP—Fine full leather with best grade leather covered bow sockets, heavy rubber side curtains and storm apron for dash. We furnish with leather quarter top and very best grade steel bow sockets, if desired, for $7.00 less than with leather top. We furnish four bows on any of our tops instead of three without additional charge. Top is always lined with broadcloth to match seat trimmings.

PAINTING—Body is finely finished in black, correctly striped; gear, Brewster green, properly striped. We will make any change in color of painting desired. For system of painting in detail, see page 5.

69

No. 924—FINE FULL LEATHER TOP BUGGY WITH LEATHER COVERED BOWS

PRICE
- Cash with order, with steel tires and shafts.....................................$80.00
- C. O. D., with steel tires and shafts.. 82.00
- Cash with order, with ⅞-inch guaranteed rubber tires and shafts.................. 95.00
- C. O. D., with ⅞-inch guaranteed rubber tires and shafts........................ 97.00

No. 924 is one of our late styles and is a very desirable design. We use on this buggy our Newport seat which is a new pattern and one of the finest seats made. We know No. 924 is as good in quality of workmanship and material throughout as usually sells by others for $30.00 more than our price. We are glad to ship it for examination and approval, and if not found all we claim and perfectly satisfactory, it may be returned at our expense.

BODY—Piano box style, 24 inches wide and 56 inches long. We will furnish 22-inch body, if preferred. Seat is our Newport style and gives splendid satisfaction. It is roomy, has good high back and is very comfortable. Body and seat are made from high grade stock and are put together in such a way and so well ironed and braced that we guarantee them not to come apart at the joints. no matter in what climate used. Rubber covered steps. Roller rub irons.

GEAR—1⅛-inch dust proof bell collar long distance axles, with felt oil pads. Axles are fitted with light wood beds, which are cemented and clipped to the axles. Fine oil tempered French pattern open head springs, very elastic and easy riding. The reaches have channel iron full length, and they are bolted and well braced. Full circle wrought Brewster slotted fifth wheel with king bolt clipped around axle. It is the style Brewster fifth wheel used on all strictly high grade work. Wrought Bailey body loops clipped to springs. Will furnish wood spring bar if preferred to the Bailey loops. Bradley quick change shaft couplers, which are the most practicable quick shifting couplers made, and are used on all high grade work. Shafts are regular buggy style, only they are a little higher bend than is commonly used. They are made from straight grain selected hickory, full patent leather trimmed and are well braced. Pole instead of shafts on any of our top buggies, $1.00. Will furnish pole in addition to shafts for $5.00 extra.

WHEELS—Fine selected straight grain white hickory, ⅞-inch banded hub, 40 inches front and 44 inches rear, with ⅞-inch round edge planished steel tire, bolted between each spoke. Tires are ¼-inch thick and are set hot by hand and not by machine.

Felloes have screws through them on each side of every spoke, which insures absolutely against checking at the spokes. The height of wheels we furnish is correct for this style gear, but we can make any change in height desired. We furnish ¾-inch wheels instead of ⅞-inch, if preferred. Also Sarven patent style if desired instead of banded hub.

TRIMMINGS—Seat is trimmed with fine dark green all wool broadcloth, guaranteed absolutely fast color. Will trim with fine dark blue wool broadcloth or fine whipcord, if preferred. Ends of the seat are padded and trimmed to match cushion and back, and both cushion and back are upholstered with hair and upholstering springs, and the seat is most comfortable. We can furnish any special colors of broadcloth at a small additional charge. Genuine leather trimmings in dark green, maroon or russet instead of all wool broadcloth for $3.00. Fine full padded patent leather dash. Velvet carpet in bottom of body, or rubber mat if preferred to the carpet. Rubber boot to cover back part of body.

TOP—Fine full leather with best grade leather covered bow sockets, heavy rubber side curtains and storm apron for dash. We furnish with leather quarter top and very best grade steel bow sockets, if desired, for $7.00 less than with leather top. We furnish four bows on any of our tops instead of three without additional charge. Top is always lined with broadcloth to match seat trimmings.

PAINTING—Body is finely finished in black, correctly striped; gear, Brewster green, properly striped. We will make any change in color of painting desired. For system of painting in detail, see page 5.

The above cut shows No. 926 with our regular Stanhope style seat. Price, $2.00 less than with auto seat.

No. 926—FINE FULL LEATHER TOP BUGGY WITH LEATHER COVERED BOWS AND SPECIAL PIANO BODY

PRICE
Cash with order, with steel tires and shafts......................................$ 85.00
C. O. D., with steel tires and shafts... 87.00
Cash with order, with ⅞-inch guaranteed rubber tires and shafts................. 100.00
C. O. D., with ⅞-inch guaranteed rubber tires and shafts........................ 102.00

No. 926 is one of the most up-to-date style buggies we are making. It is equipped with our new special piano body which is decked over solid back of the seat, as picture shows, and our fine late style auto seat. We make this buggy in our best grade throughout and it is as good in quality of workmanship and general finish throughout as sold by others for fully $35.00 more than our price. We are very glad at any rate to ship it for full examination and approval, and if it is not found just as represented and perfectly satisfactory, it may be returned at our expense.

BODY—Is a new and very desirable design, being made a little higher than regular back of seat and decked over as illustration shows. There is the usual opening under the seat so that packages can be put in the rear part of the body from the front. The seat is our fine new auto design and one of the best style seats made. Back is high and very comfortable. We use in the construction of both body and seat high grade stock throughout, and they are well ironed and braced and guaranteed not to open at the joints, no matter in what climate used. Body is 24 inches wide by 56 inches long, but we will furnish body 22 inches wide, if preferred. Three prong rubber covered steps. Roller rub irons.

GEAR—1⅛-inch true sweep dust proof bell collar long distance axles, with felt oil pads. Axles are fitted with straight grain hickory beds, which are cemented and clipped to the axles. Fine oil tempered French pattern open head springs, very elastic and easy riding. The reaches have channel iron full length, and they are bolted and well braced. Full circle wrought Brewster slotted fifth wheel with king bolt clipped around axle. It is the style Brewster fifth wheel used on all strictly high grade work. Wrought Bailey body loops clipped to springs. Will furnish wood spring bar if preferred to the Bailey loops. Bradley quick change shaft couplers, which are the most practicable quick shifting couplers made and are used on all high grade work. Shafts are regular buggy style, only they are a little higher bend than is commonly used. They are made from straight grain selected hickory, full patent leather trimmed and have round shaft straps. They are also well braced. Will furnish pole in addition to shafts for $5.00 extra.

WHEELS—Fine selected straight grain white hickory, ⅞-inch banded hub, 40 inches front and 44 inches rear, with ⅞-inch round edge planished steel tire, bolted between each spoke. Tires are ¼-inch thick and are set hot by hand and not by machine. Felloes have screws through them on each side of every spoke, which insures absolutely against checking at the spokes. The height of wheels we furnish is correct for this style gear, but we can make any change in height desired. We furnish ¾-inch wheels instead of ⅞-inch, if preferred. Also Sarven patent style if desired instead of banded hub.

TRIMMINGS—Seat is trimmed with fine dark green all wool broadcloth, guaranteed absolutely fast color. Will trim with fine dark blue wool broadcloth or fine whipcord, if preferred. Ends of the seat are padded and trimmed to match cushion and back, and both cushion and back are upholstered with hair and upholstering springs, and the seat is most comfortable. We can furnish any special colors of broadcloth at a small additional charge. Genuine leather trimmings in dark green, maroon or russet instead of all wool broadcloth for $3.00. Fine full padded patent leather dash. Velvet carpet in bottom of body, or rubber mat if preferred to the carpet.

TOP—Fine full leather with best grade leather covered bow sockets, heavy rubber side curtains and storm apron for dash. We furnish with leather quarter top and very best grade steel bow sockets, if desired, for $7.00 less than with leather top. We furnish four bows on any of our tops instead of three without additional charge. Top is always lined with broadcloth to match seat trimmings.

PAINTING—Body is finely finished in black, correctly striped; gear, Brewster green, properly striped. We will make any change in color of painting desired. For system of painting in detail, see page 5.

The above cut shows No. 928 with Stanhope style seat, full leather Victoria top and lamps. Price, $25.00 more than with regular style top.

No. 928—FINE FULL LEATHER TOP BUGGY WITH LEATHER COVERED BOWS AND SPECIAL PIANO BODY

PRICE
{
Cash with order, with steel tires and shafts....................................$82.00
C. O. D., with steel tires and shafts.. 84.00
Cash with order, with ⅞-inch guaranteed rubber tires and shafts.................. 97.00
C. O. D., with ⅞-inch guaranteed rubber tires and shafts......................... 99.00
}

No. 928 is one of the best style top buggies made. We build this buggy in our high grade quality throughout and we guarantee it as good in style, quality of workmanship and material and general finish throughout as similar styles sold by others for $25.00 to $35.00 more than our price. We are very glad to ship No. 928 for examination and approval, and if it is not found all we claim and a perfectly satisfactory buggy it may be returned at our expense and you will be out nothing.

BODY—Special piano box style decked over solid back of seat, as illustration shows, 24 inches wide and 56 inches long. The seat is one of our auto designs. The back is extra high and is roomy and luxuriously upholstered. Both body and seat are made from high grade thoroughly seasoned body material and are well ironed and braced and guaranteed not to come apart at the corners, no matter in what climate they are used. Fine three prong rubber covered steps. Roller rub irons.

GEAR—1⅛-inch true sweep dust proof bell collar long distance axles, with felt oil pads. Axles are fitted with light wood beds, which are cemented and clipped to the axles. Fine oil tempered French pattern open head springs, very elastic and easy riding. The reaches have channel iron full length, and they are bolted and well braced. Full circle wrought Brewster slotted fifth wheel with king bolt clipped around axle. It is the style fifth wheel used on all strictly high grade work. Wrought Bailey body loops clipped to springs. Will furnish wood spring bar if preferred to the Bailey loops. Bradley quick change shaft couplers, which are the most practical quick shifting couplers made and are used on all high grade work. Shafts are regular buggy style, only a little higher bend than commonly used. They are made from selected hickory, full patent leather trimmed and are well braced. Will furnish pole in addition to shafts for $5.00 extra.

WHEELS—Fine selected straight grain white hickory, ⅞-inch banded hub, 40 inches front and 44 inches rear, with ⅞-inch round edge planished steel tire, bolted between each spoke. Tires are ¼-inch thick and are set hot by hand and not by machine. Felloes have screws through them on each side of every spoke, which insures absolutely against checking at the spokes. The height of wheels we furnish is correct for this style gear, but we can make any change in height desired. We furnish ¾-inch wheels instead of ⅞-inch, if preferred. Also Sarven patent style if desired instead of banded hub.

TRIMMINGS—Seat is trimmed with fine dark green all wool broadcloth, guaranteed absolutely fast color. Will trim with fine dark blue wool broadcloth or fine whipcord, if preferred. Ends of the seat are pleated and trimmed to match cushion and back, and both cushion and back are upholstered with hair and upholstering springs, and the seat is most comfortable. We can furnish any special colors of broadcloth at a small additional charge. Genuine leather trimmings in dark green, maroon or russet instead of all wool broadcloth for $3.00. Fine full padded patent leather dash. Velvet carpet in bottom of body, or rubber mat if preferred to the carpet.

TOP—Fine full leather with best grade leather covered bow sockets, heavy rubber side curtains and storm apron for dash. We furnish with leather quarter top and very best grade steel bow sockets, if desired, for $7.00 less than with leather top. We furnish four bows on any of our tops instead of three without additional charge. Top is always lined with broadcloth to match seat trimmings.

PAINTING—The body is black; gear, Brewster green, correctly striped. We will furnish New York red gear or make any changes in painting desired. Our painting is all fully guaranteed. For system of painting in detail, see page 5.

The above cut shows No. 930 only it has drop axles and wood spring bars instead of arched axles and Bailey loops. Price, same as No. 930.

No. 930—FINE LIGHT FULL LEATHER TOP BUGGY
WITH LEATHER COVERED BOWS

PRICE
- Cash with order, with steel tires and shafts..$75.00
- C. O. D., with steel tires and shafts.. 77.00
- Cash with order, with ¾-inch guaranteed rubber tires and shafts.................. 88.00
- C. O. D., with ¾-inch guaranteed rubber tires and shafts........................ 90.00

If ⅞-inch guarantee rubber tires are preferred, add $2.50 to the price quoted with ¾-inch rubber tires.

No. 930 is a fine light end spring top buggy. It is a well proportioned, light running, comfortable riding buggy. We know No. 930 is as good in quality of workmanship and material throughout as usually sells for $25.00 more than our price. We are very glad to send it anywhere for examination and approval, and if not found highly satisfactory and all we claim, it may be returned at our expense. We allow you to be the judge.

BODY—Piano box style, 22 inches wide by 56 inches long with regulation style seat which is very comfortable. We furnish 24-inch body instead of 22-inch, if preferred, or if a narrower body is wanted than 22 inches we can furnish 20 inches. We use in the construction of both body and seat high grade stock and they are guaranteed not to open at the joints, no matter in what climate used. Rubber covered steps. Roller rub irons.

GEAR—1⅛-inch dust proof bell collar long distance axles, with felt oil pads. Axles are fitted with straight grain hickory beds, which are cemented and clipped full length. Fine oil tempered French pattern open head springs, properly graded and very easy riding. Reaches have channel irons full length and they are bolted and well braced. Full circle wrought Brewster fifth wheel which is one of the best fifth wheels made and is used on all high grade work. Bailey body loops clipped to springs. We furnish wood spring bars, if preferred to the Bailey loops. Bradley quick shifting shaft couplers, which are used on all first class work. Shafts, regulation buggy style, made from fine selected straight grain hickory, with full patent leather trimmings and with heel braces. Pole instead of shafts, $1.00 extra. Pole in addition to shafts, $5.00 extra.

WHEELS—Fine selected straight grain white hickory, ¾-inch Sarven patent, 40 inches front and 44 inches rear, with ¾-inch round edge planished steel tire, bolted between each spoke. Tires are ¼-inch thick and are set hot by hand and not by machine. Felloes have screws through them on each side of every spoke, which insures absolutely against checking at the spokes. The

height of wheels we furnish is correct for this style gear, but we can make any change in height desired. We furnish ⅞-inch wheels instead of ¾-inch, if preferred. Also banded hub style if desired instead of Sarven patent.

TRIMMINGS—Seat is trimmed with fine dark green all wool broadcloth, guaranteed absolutely fast color. Will trim with fine dark blue wool broadcloth or fine whipcord, if preferred. Ends of the seat are padded and trimmed to match cushion and back, and both cushion and back are upholstered with hair and upholstering springs, and the seat is most comfortable. We can furnish any special colors of broadcloth at a small additional charge. Genuine leather trimmings in dark green, maroon or russet instead of all wool broadcloth for $2.00. Fine full padded patent leather dash. Velvet carpet in bottom of body, or rubber mat if preferred to the carpet. Rubber boot to cover back part of body.

TOP—Fine full leather with best grade leather covered bow sockets, heavy rubber side curtains and storm apron for dash. We furnish with leather quarter top and very best grade steel bow sockets, if desired, for $7.00 less than with leather top. We furnish four bows on any of our tops instead of three without additional charge. Top is always lined with broadcloth to match seat trimmings.

PAINTING—The body is black; gear, Brewster green, correctly striped. We will furnish New York red gear or make any changes in painting desired. Our painting is all fully guaranteed. For system of painting in detail, see page 5.

73

The above cut shows No. 932 seat, only made with twin style back. The upholstering on the back is just the same as on the regular seat. We furnish this twin style seat, when wanted, without additional charge

No. 932—FINE LIGHT THREE-QUARTER FULL LEATHER TOP BUGGY WITH LEATHER COVERED BOWS

PRICE
Cash with order, with steel tires and shafts.......................................$80.00
C. O. D., with steel tires and shafts... 82.00
Cash with order, with ¾-inch guaranteed rubber tires and shafts.................. 93.00
C. O. D., with ¾-inch guaranteed rubber tires and shafts........................ 95.00

We are making No. 932 to meet the demand made by users who want an extra light buggy throughout. Our No. 932 is made in our **high grade** quality and is a strictly three-quarter size buggy, excepting that we are using on it our regulation auto seat instead of **the buggy** seat, style of No. 930. If the small regulation buggy seat, like No. 930, is preferred, we allow a reduction of $3.00 for the difference in seats. We know No. 932 is as good in quality of workmanship and material throughout as similar styles sold by others for $25.00 more than our price. We are glad to ship it for full examination and approval.

BODY—Is regulation piano box style, 22 inches wide by 56 inches long. We furnish 20-inch body, if preferred, but the 22-inch body is more appropriate for the auto style seat. If a wider body than 22 inches is preferred, we furnish 24-inch. We use high grade stock in the construction of both body and seat and they are ironed and braced and guaranteed not to come apart at the joints, no matter in what climate used. If our regulation buggy seat, same as No. 930, if preferred to the auto seat, we allow a reduction of $3.00 for the difference in seats. Three prong rubber covered steps. Roller rub irons.

GEAR—¾-inch true sweep bell collar long distance axles, fitted with light straight grain hickory beds, which are cemented and fully clipped to axles. Fine oil tempered French pattern open head springs, correctly graded and very easy riding. We will furnish the Armstrong single leaf spring if preferred to the regular springs. Reaches have channel irons full length, and they are bolted and well braced. Full circle wrought Brewster fifth wheel, which is one of the best fifth wheels made and is used on all high grade work. Bailey body loops clipped to springs. We furnish wood spring bars if preferred to the Bailey loops. Bradley quick shifting shaft couplers, which are used on all first class work. Shafts, regulation buggy style, made from fine selected straight grain hickory, with full patent leather trimmings and with heel braces. Pole instead of shafts, $1.00 extra. Pole in addition to shafts, $5.00 extra.

WHEELS—Fine selected straight grain white hickory, ¾-inch Sarven patent, 40 inches front and 44 inches rear, with ¾-inch round edge planished steel tire, bolted between each spoke. Tires are ¼-inch thick and are set hot by hand and not by machine.

Felloes have screws through them on each side of every spoke, which insures absolutely against checking at the spokes. The height of wheels we furnish is correct for this style gear, but we can make any change in height desired. We furnish ⅞-inch wheels instead of ¾-inch, if preferred. Also banded hub style if desired instead of Sarven patent.

TRIMMINGS—Seat is trimmed with fine dark green all wool broadcloth, guaranteed absolutely fast color. Will trim with fine dark blue wool broadcloth or fine whipcord, if preferred. Ends of the seat are padded and trimmed to match cushion and back, and both cushion and back are upholstered with hair and upholstering springs, and the seat is most comfortable. We can furnish any special colors of broadcloth at a small additional charge. Genuine leather trimmings in dark green, maroon or russet instead of all wool broadcloth for $3.00. Fine full padded patent leather dash. Velvet carpet in bottom of body, or rubber mat if preferred to the carpet. Rubber boot to cover back part of body.

TOP—Fine full leather with best grade leather covered bow sockets, heavy rubber side curtains and storm apron for dash. We furnish with leather quarter top and very best grade steel bow sockets, if desired, for $7.00 less than with leather top. We furnish four bows on any of our tops instead of three without additional charge. Top is always lined with broadcloth to match seat trimmings.

PAINTING—The body is black; gear, Brewster green, correctly striped. We will furnish New York red gear or make any changes in painting desired. Our painting is all fully guaranteed. For system of painting in detail, see page 5.

The above cut shows No. 934 with our regular half phaeton style seat and plain straight dash. Price $2.00 less than with auto seat and wing dash.

No. 934—FINE FULL LEATHER TOP BUGGY WITH LEATHER COVERED BOWS

PRICE
Cash with order, with steel tires and shafts.....................................$80.00
C. O. D., with steel tires and shafts.. 82.00
Cash with order, with ⅞-inch guaranteed rubber tires and shafts................... 95.00
C. O. D., with ⅞-inch guaranteed rubber tires and shafts......................... 97.00

No. 934 is a very desirable style top buggy. It is hung on drop axle style gear and has wood spring bars with wrought loops running full length on bottom of sills. We know No. 934 is as well made throughout and as finely finished as similar buggies sold by others for fully $25.00 more than our price. We are very glad to ship it for examination and approval, and it may be returned at our expense if not found just as represented.

BODY—Piano box style, 22 inches wide and 56 inches long. We will furnish 24-inch body if preferred to the 22-inch. The seat is one of our most popular style auto seats. It has good high back and is very comfortable. Both body and seat are made from high grade stock and are put together in such a manner and so well ironed and braced that we guarantee them not to open at the corners, no matter in what climate used. Three prong rubber covered steps. Roller rub irons.

GEAR—1⅛-inch dust proof bell collar long distance axles, equipped with felt oil pads. Axles are fitted with straight grain hickory beds, which are cemented and clipped full length. Fine well graded oil tempered French pattern open head springs, which are very easy riding. Reaches have channel reach iron full length and they are bolted and well braced. Extra heavy full circle wrought Brewster fifth wheel, which is one of the best style fifth wheels made. Heavy straight grain hickory spring bars with body loops running full length of body. We will furnish extra heavy Bailey loops, if preferred. Bradley quick shifting shaft couplers, which are the best couplers made and are used on all high grade work. Shafts, regulation buggy style made from straight grain white hickory, full patent leather trimmed and with special heel braces. We furnish pole instead of shafts for $1.00 extra. Pole in addition to shafts, $5.00 extra.

WHEELS—Fine selected straight grain white hickory, ⅞-inch Sarven patent, 40 inches front and 44 inches rear, with ⅞-inch round edge planished steel tire bolted between each spoke. Tires are ¼-inch thick and are set hot by hand and not by machine. Felloes have screws through them on each side of every spoke, which insures absolutely against checking at the spokes. The height of wheels we furnish is correct for this style gear, but we can make any change in height desired. We furnish ¾-inch wheels instead of ⅞-inch, if preferred. Also banded hub style if desired instead of the Sarven patent.

TRIMMINGS—Seat is trimmed with fine dark green all wool broadcloth, guaranteed absolutely fast color. Will trim with fine dark blue wool broadcloth or fine whipcord, if preferred. Ends of seat are pleated and trimmed to match cushion and back, and both cushion and back are upholstered with hair and upholstering springs, and the seat is most comfortable. We can furnish any special colors of broadcloth at a small additional charge. Genuine leather trimmings in dark green, maroon or russet instead of all wool broadcloth for $3.00. Fine full padded patent leather dash. Velvet carpet in bottom of body, or rubber mat if preferred to the carpet. Rubber boot to cover back part of body.

TOP—Fine full leather with best grade leather covered bow sockets, heavy rubber side curtains and storm apron for dash. We furnish with leather quarter top and very best grade steel bow sockets, if desired, for $7.00 less than with leather top. We furnish four bows on any of our tops instead of three without additional charge. Top is always lined with broadcloth to match seat trimmings.

PAINTING—The body is black; gear, Brewster green, correctly striped. We will furnish New York red gear or make any changes in painting desired. Our painting is all fully guaranteed. For system of painting in detail, see page 5.

The above cut shows the rear view of No. 936. The fine large back panel of the seat permits of a most beautiful effect in finishing. This cut shows straight dash which is $1.50 less than wing dash.

No. 936—TOP BUGGY WITH TRUE SWEEP AXLES AND NEW AUTO SEAT

PRICE
Cash with order, with steel tires and shafts.....................................$65.00
C. O. D., with steel tires and shafts.. 67.00
Cash with order, with ⅞-inch guaranteed rubber tires and shafts.................... 80.00
C. O. D., with ⅞-inch guaranteed rubber tires and shafts........................ 82.00

Our No. 936 is one of the best style buggies we are making. It is equipped with the true sweep arched axles, which are very popular and up-to-date. Our No. 936 is well proportioned throughout, light running and very comfortable riding. It has all the latest features and is as good in quality of workmanship and material throughout as buggies sold by others for fully $25.00 more than our price. We are very glad to ship it for full examination and approval.

BODY—Is the regulation piano box style, 22 inches wide and 56 inches long. We will furnish 24-inch body, if preferred to the 22-inch. Seat is one of the best auto designs made, and the back is high and luxuriously upholstered. Both body and seat are made from high grade thoroughly seasoned body material. They are well ironed and braced and guaranteed not to open at the corners, no matter in what climate they are used. Fine three prong steps. Roller rub irons.

GEAR—1⅛-inch true sweep dust proof bell collar long distance axles, with felt oil pads. Axles are fitted with light wood beds, which are cemented and clipped full length. Fine oil tempered French pattern open head springs, very easy riding. Reaches have channel iron full length and they are bolted and well braced. Wrought full circle Brewster slotted fifth wheel, one of the best and strongest fifth wheels made. Bailey body loops clipped to springs. Will furnish wood spring bars, if preferred to the Bailey loop. Bradley quick shifting shaft couplers, the style used on all first class work. Regulation buggy style shafts made from fine selected hickory, full patent leather trimmed and with steel heel braces. We furnish pole in addition to shafts for $5.00 extra.

WHEELS—Fine selected straight grain white hickory, ⅞-inch Sarven patent, 40 inches front and 44 inches rear, with ⅞-inch round edge planished steel tire, bolted between each spoke. Tires are ¼-inch thick and are set hot by hand and not by machine. Felloes have screws through them on each side of every spoke, which insures absolutely against checking at the spokes. The height of wheels we furnish is correct for this style gear, but we can make any change in height desired. We furnish ¾-inch wheels instead of ⅞-inch, if preferred. Also banded hub style, if desired instead of Sarven patent.

TRIMMINGS—Seat is trimmed with dark green all wool broadcloth, guaranteed fast color. Will trim with dark blue broadcloth or fine whipcord, if preferred. The ends of the seat are pleated and trimmed to match cushion and back. There are upholstering springs in both cushion and back, and the seat is very comfortable. We trim the seat with genuine trimming leather in dark green, maroon or russet instead of broadcloth, if desired, for $3.00 extra. We can furnish special colors in broadcloth trimming, if desired, at a small extra charge. Fine full padded wing style dash. Velvet carpet in bottom of body, or rubber mat if preferred to carpet. Boot to cover back part of body.

TOP—Fine leather quarter top with heavy rubber side curtains and storm apron for the dash. The top is lined with broadcloth to match trimmings. It is regular with three bows, but we furnish four bows instead of three bows, if preferred, without extra charge. It has curved top joints, and joints and bow sockets are finely enameled. Furnished with full rubber top instead of leather quarter for $2.00 less. Full leather top with best enameled steel bow sockets and heavy rubber curtains, $5.50 extra. Leather covered bows, $1.50 extra.

PAINTING—Body is plain black; gear, Brewster green, neatly striped. We will paint any color you desire. For system of painting, see page 5.

The above cut shows front view of No. 938 with top removed and you will see that the cushion and back are made the same as on the regular style seat. The top is attached to the seat with shifting rail and can be easily removed, thus giving you a neat open driving wagon, if desired. This cut also shows straight dash which is $1.50 less than wing dash.

No. 938—TOP BUGGY WITH NEW TWIN STYLE AUTO SEAT

PRICE
{
Cash with order, with steel tires and shafts...................................$66.00
C. O. D., with steel tires and shafts.. 68.00
Cash with order, with 1-inch guaranteed cushion tires and shafts.................. 83.50
C. O. D., with 1-inch guaranteed cushion tires and shafts....................... 85.50
}

If ⅞-inch solid rubber tires are preferred, deduct $2.50 from the price quoted with cushion tires.

Our No. 938 is one of the most up-to-date style buggies made. It is equipped with our new twin style auto seat and is a roomy, comfortable riding buggy. Although the back of the seat is divided, the upholstering is made same as shown by small cut in corner of page and is not divided as is the back of the seat. We unhesitatingly recommend No. 938 for it is first class throughout and a style that will please wherever shipped. We know this buggy is as good in quality of workmanship and material throughout as usually sells for $25.00 to $30.00 more than our price. We are glad to ship it for examination and approval.

BODY—Piano box style, 22 inches wide and 56 inches long. We will furnish body 24 inches wide, if preferred. The seat is our new twin pattern auto style and is one of the most popular auto seats made. Body and seat are both made from high grade stock and are so constructed that we guarantee them absolutely not to open at the joints, no matter in what climate used. Fine three prong steps. Roller rub irons.

GEAR—1⅛-inch true sweep dust proof bell collar long distance axles, with felt oil pads. Axles are fitted with light wood beds, which are cemented and clipped full length. Fine oil tempered French pattern open head springs, very easy riding. Reaches have channel iron full length, and they are bolted and well braced. Wrought full circle Brewster slotted fifth wheel, one of the best and strongest fifth wheels made. Bailey body loops clipped to springs. Will furnish wood spring bars, if preferred to the Bailey loop. Bradley quick shifting shaft couplers, the style used on all first class work. Regulation buggy style shafts made from fine selected hickory, full patent leather trimmed and with steel heel braces. We furnish pole in addition to shafts for $5.00 extra.

WHEELS—Fine selected straight grain white hickory, ⅞-inch Sarven patent, 40 inches front and 44 inches rear, with ⅞-inch round edge planished steel tire, bolted between each spoke. Tires are ¼-inch thick and are set hot by hand and not by machine. Felloes have screws through them on each side of every spoke, which insures absolutely against checking at the spokes. The height of wheels we furnish is correct for this style gear, but we

can make any change in height desired. We furnish ¾-inch wheels instead of ⅞-inch, if preferred. Also banded hub style if desired instead of Sarven patent.

TRIMMINGS—Seat is trimmed with dark green all wool broadcloth, guaranteed fast color. Will trim with dark blue broadcloth or fine whipcord, if preferred. The ends of the seat are pleated and trimmed to match cushion and back. There are upholstering springs in both cushion and back, and the seat is very comfortable. We trim the seat with genuine trimming leather in dark green, maroon or russet instead of broadcloth, if desired, for $3.00 extra. We can furnish special colors in broadcloth trimming, if desired, at a small extra charge. Fine full padded wing style dash. Velvet carpet in bottom of body, or rubber mat if preferred to carpet. Boot to cover back part of body.

TOP—Fine leather quarter top with heavy rubber side curtains and storm apron for the dash. The top is lined with broadcloth to match trimmings. It is regular with three bows, but we furnish four bows instead of three bows, if preferred, without extra charge. It has curved top joints, and joints and bow sockets are finely enameled. Furnished with full rubber top instead of leather quarter for $2.00 less. Full leather top with best enameled steel bow sockets and heavy rubber curtains, $5.50 extra. Leather covered bows, $1.50 extra.

PAINTING—Body is plain black; gear, Brewster green, neatly striped. We will furnish New York red gear, correctly striped, or will paint any color you desire. For system of painting in detail, see page 5.

77

No. 940—TOP BUGGY WITH NEWPORT SEAT AND SPECIAL PIANO BODY

PRICE
{ Cash with order, with steel tires and shafts.....................................$66.00
{ C. O. D., with steel tires and shafts... 68.00
{ Cash with order, with ⅞-inch guaranteed rubber tires and shafts.................. 81.00
{ C. O. D., with ⅞-inch guaranteed rubber tires and shafts....................... 83.00

No. 940 is equipped with our special piano body which is decked over back of the seat, giving it a Stanhope effect. It also has our Newport style seat which is one of the best style seats made. We are very glad to ship No. 940 for full examination and approval, with the understanding that it is to be found highly satisfactory and you are to feel you are saving fully $25.00 in dealing with us, or we will take the shipment back at our expense.

BODY—Special piano box style, decked over solid back of seat, giving it a Stanhope effect. It is 24 inches wide by 56 inches long, but we will furnish body 22 inches wide, if preferred. Seat is our new Newport style and is roomy and very comfortable. Both body and seat are made from high grade thoroughly seasoned stock and are well ironed and braced and guaranteed not to come apart at the corners, no matter in what climate used. Fine three prong steps. Roller rub irons.

GEAR—1⅛-inch true sweep dust proof bell collar long distance axles, with felt oil pads. Axles are fitted with light wood beds, which are cemented and clipped full length. Fine oil tempered French pattern open head springs, very easy riding. Reaches have channel iron full length and they are bolted and well braced. Full circle wrought Brewster slotted fifth wheel, one of the best and strongest fifth wheels made. Bailey body loops clipped to springs. Will furnish wood spring bars, if preferred to the Bailey loop. Bradley quick shifting shaft couplers, the style used on all first class work. Regulation buggy style shafts made from fine selected hickory, full patent leather trimmed and with steel heel braces. We furnish pole in addition to shafts for $5.00 extra.

WHEELS—Fine selected straight grain white hickory, ⅞-inch Sarven patent, 40 inches front and 44 inches rear, with ⅞-inch round edge planished steel tire, bolted between each spoke. Tires are ¼-inch thick and are set hot by hand and not by machine. Felloes have screws through them on each side of every spoke, which insures absolutely against checking at the spokes. The

height of wheels we furnish is correct for this style gear, but we can make any change in height desired. We furnish ¾-inch wheels instead of ⅞-inch, if preferred.

TRIMMINGS—Seat is trimmed with dark green all wool broadcloth, guaranteed fast color. Will trim with dark blue broadcloth or fine whipcord, if preferred. The ends of the seat is pleated and trimmed to match cushion and back. There are upholstering springs in both cushion and back, and the seat is very comfortable. We trim the seat with genuine trimming leather in dark green, maroon or russet instead of broadcloth, if desired, for $3.00 extra. We can furnish special colors in broadcloth trimming, if desired, at a small extra charge. Fine full padded wing style dash. Velvet carpet in bottom of body, or rubber mat if preferred to carpet.

TOP—Fine leather quarter top with heavy rubber side curtains and storm apron for the dash. The top is lined with broadcloth to match trimmings. It is regular with three bows, but we furnish four bows instead of three bows, if preferred, without extra charge. It has curved top joints, and joints and bow sockets are finely enameled. Furnished with full rubber top instead of leather quarter for $2.00 less. Full leather top with best enameled steel bow sockets and heavy rubber curtains, $5.50 extra. Leather covered bows, $1.50 extra.

PAINTING—Body is plain black; gear, Brewster green, neatly striped. We will furnish New York red gear, correctly striped, or will paint any color you desire. For system of striping in detail, see page 5.

We make any change in
our vehicles necessary to
suit your ideas, and when
the change represents
only a small extra ex-
pense to us we make no
additional charge.

No. 942—TOP BUGGY WITH SPECIAL PIANO BODY AND TRUE SWEEP AXLES

PRICE
{
Cash with order, with steel tires and shafts.....................................$68.00
C. O. D., with steel tires and shafts.. 70.00
Cash with order, with ⅞-inch guaranteed rubber tires and shafts.................. 83.00
C. O. D., with ⅞-inch guaranteed rubber tires and shafts......................... 85.00
}
If 1-inch guaranteed cushion tires are preferred, add $2.50 to the price quoted with ⅞-inch solid tires.

No. 942 is one of our most up-to-date style top buggies. It has all the desirable features and is as fine in general workmanship and material throughout as similar buggies sold by others for fully $25.00 more than our price. We are very glad of an opportunity to ship No.
942 for examination and approval, and if it is not found all we claim and a very satisfactory buggy in every way, we will take it back at
our expense. We allow you to be the judge.

BODY—Special piano box style decked over solid back of seat, as
illustration shows, 24 inches wide and 56 inches long, 22-inch
body, if preferred. The seat is one of the finest auto seat designs
we have ever made. The back is extra high and is roomy and
luxuriously upholstered. Both body and seat are made from
high grade thoroughly seasoned body material and are well ironed
and braced, and guaranteed not to come apart at the corners, no
matter in what climate they are used. Fine three prong rubber
covered steps. Roller rub irons.

GEAR—1⅛-inch true sweep dust proof bell collar long distance
axles, with felt oil pads. Axles are fitted with light wood beds,
which are cemented and clipped to the axles. Fine oil tempered
French pattern open head springs, very elastic and easy riding. The
reaches have channel iron full length, and they are bolted and
well braced. Full circle wrought Brewster slotted fifth wheel.
Wrought Bailey body loops clipped to springs. Will furnish
wood spring bar, if preferred to the Bailey loops. Bradley quick
change shaft couplers, which are the most practical quick shifting
couplers made and are used on all high grade work. Shafts are
regular buggy style, only a little higher bend than commonly used.
They are made from selected hickory, full patent leather trimmed
and are well braced. Will furnish pole in addition to shafts for
$5.00 extra.

WHEELS—Fine selected straight grain white hickory, ⅞-inch
Sarven patent, 40 inches wide front and 44 inches rear, with ⅞-inch
round edge planished steel tire, bolted between each spoke. Tires
are ¼-inch thick and are set hot by hand and not by machine.
Felloes have screws through them on each side of every spoke,
which insures absolutely against checking at the spokes. The

height of wheels we furnish is correct for this style gear, but we
can make any change in height desired. We furnish ¾-inch
wheels instead of ⅞-inch, if preferred. Also banded hub style,
if desired instead of Sarven patent.

TRIMMINGS—Seat is trimmed with fine dark green all wool broadcloth, guaranteed absolutely fast color. Will trim with fine dark
blue wool broadcloth or fine whipcord, if preferred. Ends of seat
are pleated and trimmed to match cushion and back, and both
cushion and back are upholstered with fine upholstering
springs, and the seat is most comfortable. We can furnish any
special colors of broadcloth at a small additional charge. Genuine
leather trimmings in dark green, maroon or russet instead of all
wool broadcloth for $3.00. Fine full padded patent leather dash.
Velvet carpet in bottom of body, or rubber mat if preferred to
the carpet.

TOP—Fine leather quarter top with heavy rubber side curtains and
storm apron. The top is lined with broadcloth to match trimmings. It is regular with three bows, but we furnish four bows
instead of three, if preferred, without additional charge. It has
curved top joints and the joints and bow sockets are finely enameled. We furnish full rubber top, if preferred to the leather
quarter, and make a reduction of $2.00. If full leather top with
steel bows is preferred to the leather quarter top, our additional
charge is $5.50, including rubber side curtains. If full leather top,
including leather covered bow sockets and rubber side curtains,
is preferred, the additional charge is $7.00.

PAINTING—The body is black; gear, Brewster green, correctly
striped. We will make any changes in painting desired. Our
painting is all fully guaranteed. For system of painting in detail, see page 5.

No. 944—TOP BUGGY WITH STANHOPE STYLE SEAT

PRICE

- Cash with order, with steel tires and shafts.....................................$63.00
- C. O. D., with steel tires and shafts... 65.00
- Cash with order, with ⅞-inch guaranteed rubber tires and shafts................... 78.00
- C. O. D., with ⅞-inch guaranteed rubber tires and shafts.......................... 80.00

If ¾-inch guaranteed rubber tires are preferred, deduct $2.00 from price quoted with ⅞-inch rubber tires.

Our No. 944 is one of the most desirable style piano box top buggies we are making. It is well made and well finished throughout, and we know is as good in every way as usually sells for fully $25.00 more than our price. It has all the up-to-date features. We are glad of an opportunity to ship No. 944 for examination and approval, and if it is not found all we claim and perfectly satisfactory, we will take it back at our expense.

BODY—Piano box style, 24 inches wide and 56 inches long. We will furnish body 22 inches wide, if preferred. Seat is our regular Stanhope style and is roomy and very comfortable. We use high grade stock throughout in the construction of both body and seat, and they are well ironed and braced and guaranteed not to come apart at the corners, no matter in what climate used. Three prong steps. Roller rub irons.

GEAR—1⅛-inch dust proof bell collar long distance axles, with felt oil pads. Axles are fitted with straight grain hickory beds, which are cemented and clipped to the axles. Fine oil tempered French pattern open head springs, very elastic and easy riding. The reaches have channel iron full length, and they are bolted and well braced. Full circle wrought Brewster slotted fifth wheel, one of the best and strongest fifth wheels made. Wrought Bailey body loops clipped to springs. Will furnish wood spring bar, if preferred to the Bailey loops. Bradley quick change shaft couplers, which are the most practicable quick shifting couplers made. They are usually used on all high grade work. Shafts are regular buggy style, only they are a little higher bend than is commonly used. They are made from selected hickory, full patent leather trimmed and well braced. Pole instead of shafts on any of our top buggies, $1.00 extra. Will furnish pole in addition to shafts for $5.00 extra.

WHEELS—Fine selected straight grain white hickory, ⅞-inch Sarven patent, 40 inches front and 44 inches rear, with ⅞-inch round edge planished steel tire, bolted between each spoke. Tires are ¼-inch thick and are set hot by hand and not by machine. Felloes have screws through them on each side of every spoke, which insures absolutely against checking at the spokes. The height of wheels we furnish is correct for this style gear, but we can make any change in height desired. We furnish ¾-inch wheels instead of ⅞-inch, if preferred. Also banded hub style, if desired, instead of the Sarven patent.

TRIMMINGS—Seat is trimmed with fine dark green all wool broadcloth, guaranteed absolutely fast color. Will trim with fine dark blue wool broadcloth or fine whipcord, if preferred. Ends of the seat are pleated and trimmed to match cushion and back, and both cushion and back are upholstered with fine upholstering springs, and the seat is most comfortable. We can furnish any special colors of broadcloth at a small additional charge. Genuine leather trimmings in dark green, maroon or russet instead of all wool broadcloth for $3.00. Fine full padded patent leather dash. Velvet carpet in bottom of body, or rubber mat if preferred to the carpet. Rubber boot to cover back part of body.

TOP—Fine leather quarter top with heavy rubber side curtains and storm apron. The top is lined with broadcloth to match trimmings. It is regular with three bows, but we furnish four bows instead of three, if preferred, without additional charge. It has curved top joints and the joints and bow sockets are very finely enameled. We furnish full rubber top, if preferred to the leather quarter, and make a reduction of $2.00. If full leather top with steel bows is preferred to the leather quarter top, our additional charge is $5.50, including rubber side curtains. If full leather top, including leather covered bow sockets and rubber side curtains, is preferred, the additional charge is $7.00.

PAINTING—The body is black; gear, Brewster green, correctly striped. We will furnish New York red gear or make any changes in painting desired. Our painting is all fully guaranteed. For system of painting in detail, see page 5.

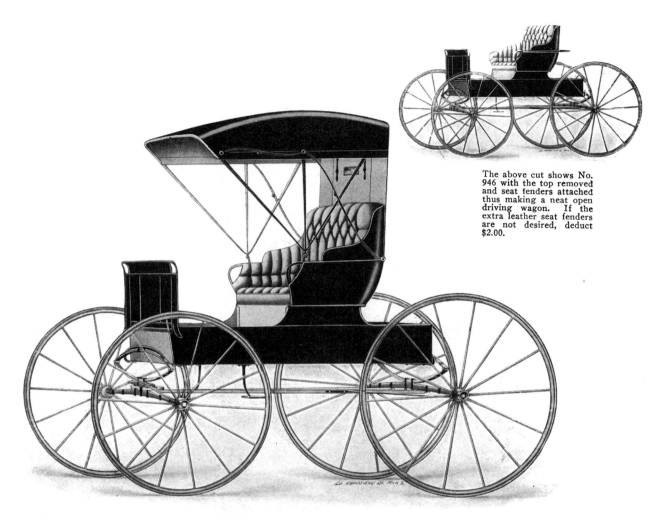

The above cut shows No. 946 with the top removed and seat fenders attached thus making a neat open driving wagon. If the extra leather seat fenders are not desired, deduct $2.00.

No. 946—COMBINATION BUGGY WITH EXTRA LEATHER SEAT FENDERS

PRICE
{
Cash with order, with steel tires and shafts.....................................$65.00
C. O. D., with steel tires and shafts... 67.00
Cash with order, with ⅞-inch guaranteed steel tires and shafts.................... 80.00
C. O. D., with ⅞-inch guaranteed steel tires and shafts.......................... 82.00
}

Our No. 946 is a very desirable style buggy, as it practically combines two buggies in one. The top is attached to the seat with quick shifting top attachments and can be easily removed and the leather seat fenders put on the ends of the seat, thus making a neat open driving wagon. We know No. 946 is as good in quality of workmanship and material throughout as sold by others for fully $25.00 to $35.00 more than our price, and we are glad to ship it for examination and approval, to be returned at our expense if you are not perfectly satisfied.

BODY—Piano box style, 24 inches wide and 56 inches long. We will furnish body 22 inches wide, if preferred. Seat is our regular auto style and is roomy and very comfortable. We use high grade stock throughout in the construction of both body and seat and they are well ironed and braced and guaranteed not to come apart at the corners, no matter in what climate used. Three prong steps. Roller rub irons.

GEAR—1⅛-inch dust proof bell collar long distance axles, with felt oil pads. Axles are fitted with straight grain hickory wood beds, which are cemented and clipped to the axles. Fine oil tempered French pattern open head springs, very elastic and easy riding. The reaches have channel iron full length, and they are bolted and well braced. Full circle wrought Brewster slotted fifth wheel. Wrought Bailey body loops clipped to springs. Will furnish wood spring bar, if preferred to the Bailey loops. Bradley quick change shaft couplers, which are the most practicable quick shifting couplers made. They are used on all high grade work. Shafts are regular buggy style, only they are a little higher bend than is commonly used. They are made from selected hickory, full patent leather trimmed and well braced. Will furnish pole in addition to shafts for $5.00 extra.

WHEELS—Fine selected straight grain white hickory, ⅞-inch Sarven patent, 40 inches front and 44 inches rear, with ⅞-inch round edge planished steel tire, bolted between each spoke. Tires are ¼-inch thick and are set hot by hand and not by machine. Felloes have screws through them on each side of every spoke, which insures absolutely against checking at the spokes. The height of wheels we furnish is correct for this style gear, but we can make any change in height desired. We furnish ¾-inch

wheels instead of ⅞-inch, if preferred. Also banded hub style, if desired.

TRIMMINGS—Seat is trimmed with fine dark green all wool broadcloth, guaranteed absolutely fast color. Will trim with fine dark blue wool broadcloth or fine whipcord, if preferred. Ends of the seat are pleated and trimmed to match cushion and back, and both cushion and back are upholstered with fine upholstering springs, and the seat is most comfortable. We can furnish any special colors of broadcloth at a small additional charge. Genuine leather trimmings in dark green, maroon or russet instead of all wool broadcloth for $3.00. Fine full padded patent leather dash. Velvet carpet in bottom of body, or rubber mat if preferred to the carpet. Rubber boot to cover back part of body. Deduct $2.00 if leather seat fenders are not wanted.

TOP—Fine leather quarter top with heavy rubber side curtains and storm apron. The top is lined with broadcloth to match trimmings. It is regular with three bows, but will furnish four bows instead of three, if preferred, without additional charge. It has curved top joints and the joints and bow sockets are very finely enameled. We furnish full rubber top, if preferred to the leather quarter, and make a reduction of $2.00. If full leather top with steel bows is preferred to the leather quarter top, our additional charge is $5.50, including rubber side curtains. If full leather top, including leather covered bow sockets and rubber side curtains, is preferred, the additional charge is $7.00.

PAINTING—The body is black; gear, Brewster green, correctly striped. We will furnish New York red gear or make any changes in painting desired. Our painting is all fully guaranteed. For system of painting in detail, see page 5.

81

No. 948—TOP BUGGY WITH HALF PHAETON STYLE SEAT

PRICE
{
Cash with order, with steel tires and shafts......................................$62.00
C. O. D., with steel tires and shafts... 64.00
Cash with order, with ⅞-inch guaranteed rubber tires and shafts.................. 77.00
C. O. D., with ⅞-inch guaranteed rubber tires and shafts........................ 79.00
}

Our No. 948 is a very desirable style buggy. It is hung on the regulation drop axle gear and the body hangs lower than on the arched axle gear, thus making it easy to get into and out of. We know our No. 948 is as good in quality of workmanship, material and finish throughout as similar styles sold by others for fully $25.00 more than our price. We are glad, at any rate, to ship it for examination and approval, allowing you to be the judge, and it may be returned at our expense if not found highly satisfactory.

BODY—Is the regulation piano box style, 24 inches wide and 56 inches long. We will furnish 22-inch body, if preferred to the 24-inch. Seat is half phaeton style. The back is high and the seat is roomy and luxuriously upholstered. Both body and seat are made from high grade thoroughly seasoned body material. They are well ironed and braced and guaranteed not to open at the corners, no matter in what climate they are used. Fine three prong steps. Roller rub irons.

GEAR—1⅛-inch dust proof bell collar long distance drop axles, with felt oil pads. Axles are fitted with light wood beds, which are cemented and clipped full length. Fine oil tempered French pattern open head springs, very easy riding. Reaches have channel iron full length and they are bolted and well braced. Wrought full circle Brewster slotted fifth wheel, one of the best and strongest fifth wheels made. Bailey body loops clipped to springs. Will furnish wood spring bars if preferred to the loop. Bradley quick shifting shaft couplers, the style used on first class work. Regulation buggy style shafts made from fine selected hickory, full patent leather trimmed and with steel heel braces. We furnish pole in addition to shafts for $5.00 extra.

WHEELS—Fine selected straight grain white hickory, ⅞-inch Sarven patent, 40 inches front and 44 inches rear, with ⅞-inch round edge planished steel tire, bolted between each spoke. Tires are ¼-inch thick and are set hot by hand and not by machine. Felloes have screws through them on each side of every spoke, which insures absolutely against checking at the spokes. The height of wheels we furnish is correct for this style gear, but we can make any change in height desired. We furnish ¾-inch

wheels instead of ⅞-inch, if preferred. Also banded hub style, if desired instead of Sarven patent.

TRIMMINGS—Seat is trimmed with dark green all wool broadcloth, guaranteed fast color. Will trim with dark blue broadcloth or fine whipcord, if preferred. The ends of the seat are trimmed to match cushion and back. There are upholstering springs in both cushion and back, and the seat is very comfortable. We trim the seat with genuine trimming leather in dark green, maroon or russet instead of broadcloth, if desired, for $3.00 extra. We can furnish special colors in broadcloth trimmings, if desired, at a small additional charge. Fine patent leather dash. Velvet carpet in bottom of body, or rubber mat if preferred to carpet. Boot to cover back part of body.

TOP—Fine leather quarter top with heavy rubber side curtains and storm apron for the dash. The top is lined with broadcloth to match the trimmings. It is regular with three bows, but we furnish with four bows instead of three bows, if preferred, without extra charge. It has straight top joints, and joints and bow sockets are finely enameled. Furnished with full rubber top instead of leather quarter for $2.00 less. Full leather top with the very best leather covered bows and heavy rubber side curtains, $7.00 extra. Full leather top with best enameled steel bow sockets and heavy rubber curtains, $5.50 extra. We can also furnish the handy style top with 2½ or 3½ bows instead of the regular top, if desired.

PAINTING—Body is plain black; gear, Brewster green, neatly striped. We will paint any color you desire. For system of painting in detail, see page 5.

82

No. 950—END SPRING TOP BUGGY

PRICE
Cash with order, with steel tires and shafts.....................................$60.00
C. O. D., with steel tires and shafts.. 62.00
Cash with order, with ⅞-inch guaranteed rubber tires and shafts................... 75.00
C. O. D., with ⅞-inch guaranteed rubber tires and shafts.......................... 77.00
If ¾-inch rubber tires are preferred, deduct $2.00 from the price quoted with ⅞-inch rubber tires.

No. 950 is a neat light weight top buggy with drop axle gear. It is equipped with our regular buggy style seat. The body on this buggy hangs low and it is easy to get into and out of. We know our No. 950 is as well made in every particular and as finely finished as buggies sold by others for fully $25.00 more than our price. We are glad to ship it for examination and approval, with the understanding that it is to be found all we claim and perfectly satisfactory or returned at our expense both ways.

BODY—Is the regulation piano box style, 22 inches wide and 56 inches long. We will furnish 24-inch body, if preferred to the 22-inch. Seat is our regular buggy style. The back is high and the seat is comfortable. Both body and seat are made from high grade thoroughly seasoned body material. They are well ironed and braced and guaranteed not to open at the corners, no matter in what climate they are used. Fine three prong steps. Roller rub irons.

GEAR—1⅛-inch dust proof bell collar long distance drop axles, with felt oil pads. Axles are fitted with light wood beds, which are cemented and clipped full length. Fine oil tempered French pattern open head springs, very easy riding. Reaches have channel iron full length, and they are bolted and well braced. Wrought full circle Brewster slotted fifth wheel, one of the best and strongest fifth wheels made. Bailey body loops clipped to springs. Will furnish wood spring bars if preferred to the loop. Bradley quick shifting shaft couplers, the style used on first class work. Regulation buggy style shafts made from fine selected hickory, full patent leather trimmed and with steel heel braces. We furnish pole in addition to shafts for $5.00 extra.

WHEELS—Fine selected straight grain white hickory, ⅞-inch Sarven patent, 40 inches front and 44 inches rear, with ⅞-inch round edge planished steel tire, bolted between each spoke. Tires are ¼-inch thick and are set hot by hand and not by machine. Felloes have screws through them on each side of every spoke, which insures absolutely against checking at the spokes. The height of wheels we furnish is correct for this style gear, but we

can make any change in height desired. We furnish ¾-inch wheels instead of ⅞-inch, if preferred. Also banded wood hub style, if desired instead of Sarven patent.

TRIMMINGS—Seat is trimmed with dark green all wool broadcloth, guaranteed fast color. Will trim with dark blue broadcloth or fine whipcord, if preferred. The ends of the seat are trimmed to match cushion and back. There are upholstering springs in both cushion and back and the seat is very comfortable. We trim the seat with genuine trimming leather in dark green, maroon or russet instead of broadcloth, if desired, for $3.00 extra. We can furnish special colors in broadcloth trimmings, if desired, at a small extra charge. Fine full padded dash. Velvet carpet in bottom of body, or rubber mat if preferred to carpet. Boot to cover back part of body.

TOP—Fine leather quarter top with heavy rubber side curtains and storm apron for the dash. The top is lined with broadcloth to match the trimmings. It is regular with three bows, but we can furnish four bows instead of three bows, if preferred, without extra charge. The top joints and bow sockets are finely enameled. Furnished with full rubber top instead of leather quarter for $2.00 less. Full leather top with the very best leather covered bows and heavy rubber side curtains, $7.00 extra. Full leather top with best enameled steel bow sockets and heavy rubber curtains, $5.50 extra.

PAINTING—Body is plain black; gear, Brewster green, neatly striped. We will furnish New York red gear, correctly striped, or will paint any color you desire. For system of painting in detail, see page 5.

The above cut shows the extra spindle seat furnished with No. 952 to be used when open wagon is desired.

No. 952—COMBINATION BUGGY AND OPEN DRIVING WAGON

PRICE
Cash with order, with steel tires and shafts.....................................$68.00
C. O. D., with steel tires and shafts... 70.00
Cash with order, with ¾-inch guaranteed rubber tires and shafts.................. 81.00
C. O. D., with ¾-inch guaranteed rubber tires and shafts........................ 83.00
If ⅞-inch guaranteed rubber tires are preferred, add $2.00 to the price quoted for ¾-inch rubber tires.

Our No. 952 is a very popular combination buggy. We furnish with this style one of our regular spindle driving wagon seats extra, and the change from the top seat to the open spindle seat is easily and quickly made. The seats are attached with quick change fasteners. We are glad to ship No. 952 anywhere for examination and approval, and if it is not found all we claim and considered as good as usually sells for fully $25.00 more than our price, we will take it back at our expense. You are to be the judge.

BODY—Regular piano box style, 22 inches wide and 56 inches long. We will furnish body 24 inches wide, if preferred. Regular buggy seat is our Stanhope style and the extra driving wagon seat is our regular spindle seat used on open driving wagons. Body and seat are made from high grade stock and guaranteed absolutely not to open at the joints.

GEAR—1⅛-inch dust proof bell collar long distance axles, with felt oil pads. Axles are fitted with light wood beds, which are cemented and clipped full length. Fine oil tempered French pattern open head springs, very easy riding. Reaches have channel iron full length, and they are bolted and well braced. Wrought full circle Brewster slotted fifth wheel, one of the best and strongest fifth wheels made. Bailey body loops clipped to springs. Will furnish wood spring bars if preferred to the loop. Bradley quick shifting shaft couplers, the style used on first class work. Regulation buggy style shafts made from fine selected hickory, full patent leather trimmed and with steel heel braces. Will furnish pole in addition to shafts for $5.00 extra.

WHEELS—Fine selected straight grain white hickory, ⅞-inch Sarven patent, 40 inches front and 44 inches rear, with ⅞-inch round edge planished steel tire, bolted between each spoke. Tires are ¼-inch thick and are set hot by hand and not by machine. Felloes have screws through them on each side of every spoke, which insures absolutely against checking at the spokes. The height of wheels we furnish is correct for this style gear, but we can make any change in height desired. We furnish ¾-inch wheels instead of ⅞-inch, if preferred. Also banded hub style, if desired instead of Sarven patent.

TRIMMINGS—Regular buggy seat is trimmed with dark green all wool broadcloth, guaranteed fast color. We will trim with dark blue broadcloth or whipcord, if preferred. The ends of the seat are pleated and trimmed to match cushion and back. There are upholstering springs in both cushion and back, and the seat is very comfortable. The extra spindle seat is regularly trimmed with whipcord, but we will trim with dark green or blue broadcloth, if preferred. There are springs in cushion. We trim the regular buggy seat with genuine leather in dark green, maroon or russet for $3.00 extra, and the spindle seat, $1.50 extra. Velvet carpet or rubber mat in bottom of body. Padded dash. Rubber boot over back part of body.

TOP—Fine leather quarter top with heavy rubber side curtains and storm apron for the dash. The top is lined with broadcloth to match the trimmings. It is regular with three bows, but we furnish four bows instead of three bows, if preferred, without extra charge. It has curved top joints, and joints and bow sockets are finely enameled. Furnished with full rubber top instead of leather quarter for $2.00 less. Full leather top with the very best leather covered bows and heavy rubber side curtains, $7.00 extra. Full leather top with best enameled steel bow sockets and heavy rubber curtains, $5.50 extra.

PAINTING—Body is plain black; gear, Brewster green, neatly striped. We will furnish New York red gear, correctly striped, or will paint any color you desire. For system of painting in detail, see page 5.

84

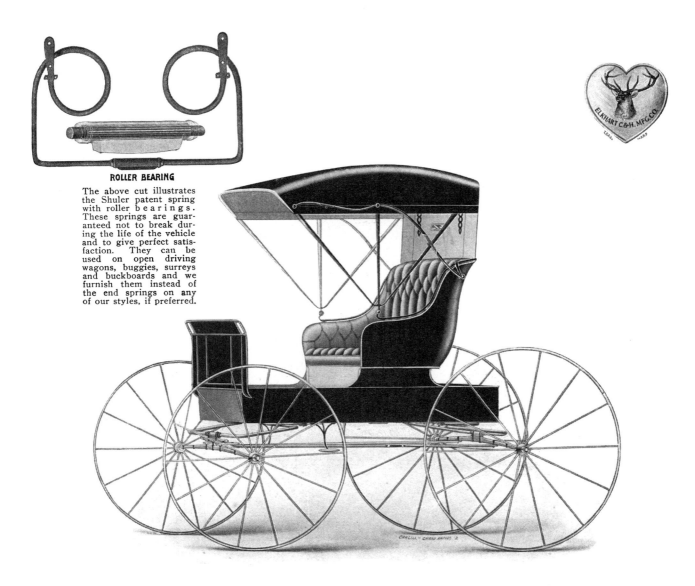

ROLLER BEARING

The above cut illustrates the Shuler patent spring with roller bearings. These springs are guaranteed not to break during the life of the vehicle and to give perfect satisfaction. They can be used on open driving wagons, buggies, surreys and buckboards and we furnish them instead of the end springs on any of our styles, if preferred.

No. 953—TOP BUGGY WITH SHULER PATENT ROLLER BEARING SPRINGS

PRICE
Cash with order, with steel tires and shafts....................................$65.00
C. O. D., with steel tires and shafts.. 67.00
Cash with order, with ⅞-inch guaranteed rubber tires and shafts.................. 80.00
C. O. D., with ⅞-inch guaranteed rubber tires and shafts........................ 82.00

No. 953 is a very desirable style top buggy. We are using on this buggy the Shuler Improved Patent Spring with roller bearings and it is unquestionably one of the easiest riding springs made. It makes a very neat light appearing gear and we can unhesitatingly recommend it. These springs are being made for all styles of pleasure vehicles and they must be used in order to be thoroughly appreciated. We guarantee our No. 953 as good in quality of workmanship and material throughout as similar styles sold by others for fully $25.00 more than our price. We are glad to ship it for full examination and approval.

BODY—Is the regulation piano box style, 24 inches wide and 56 inches long. We will furnish 22-inch body, if preferred to the 24-inch. Seat is one of the best auto designs made. The back is high and the seat is roomy and luxuriously upholstered. Both body and seat are made from high grade thoroughly seasoned body material. They are well ironed and braced and guaranteed not to open at the corners, no matter in what climate they are used. Fine three prong steps. Roller rub irons.

GEAR—1⅛-inch dust proof bell collar long distance axles, with felt oil pads. Axles are fitted with light straight grain hickory beds, which are cemented and clipped full length. Best grade Shuler Improved Patent Roller Bearing Springs, which are guaranteed not to break during the life of the vehicle and to give perfect satisfaction. Reaches have channel iron full length and they are bolted and well braced. Full circle wrought Brewster slotted fifth wheel, one of the best and strongest fifth wheels made. Bradley quick shifting shaft couplers, which are the most practicable quick shifting couplers made, and are used on all first class work. Regulation buggy shafts made from fine straight grain white hickory, full patent leather trimmed and with heel braces. Pole in addition to shafts, $5.00 extra.

WHEELS—Fine selected straight grain white hickory, ⅞-inch Sarven patent, 40 inches front and 44 inches rear, with ⅞-inch round edge planished steel tire, bolted between each spoke. Tires are ¼-inch thick and are set hot by hand and not by machine. Felloes have screws through them on each side of every spoke, which insures absolutely against checking at the spokes. The height of wheels we furnish is correct for this style gear, but we

can make any change in height desired. We furnish ¾-inch wheels instead of ⅞-inch, if preferred. Also banded hub style, if desired instead of Sarven patent.

TRIMMINGS—Seat is trimmed with dark green all wool broadcloth, guaranteed fast color. Will trim with dark blue broadcloth or fine whipcord, if preferred. The ends of the seat are pleated and trimmed to match cushion and back. There are upholstering springs in both cushion and back, and the seat is very comfortable. We trim the seat with genuine trimming leather in dark green, maroon or russet instead of broadcloth, if desired, for $3.00 extra. We can furnish special colors in broadcloth trimming, if desired, at a small extra charge. Fine full padded wing style dash. Velvet carpet in bottom of body, or rubber mat if preferred to carpet. Boot to cover back part of body.

TOP—Fine leather quarter top with heavy rubber side curtains and storm apron for the dash. The top is lined with broadcloth to match trimmings. It is regular with three bows, but we furnish four bows instead of three bows, if preferred, without extra charge. It has curved top joints, and joints and bow sockets are finely enameled. Furnished with full rubber top instead of leather quarter for $2.00 less. Full leather top with best enameled steel bow sockets and heavy rubber curtains, $5.50 extra. Leather covered bows, $1.50 extra.

PAINTING—Body is plain black; gear, Brewster green, neatly striped. We will furnish New York red gear, correctly striped, or will paint any color you desire. For system of painting in detail, see page 5.

Brass top prop nuts furnished on any buggy if desired without extra charge

No. 954—FANCY PAINTED AND TRIMMED TOP BUGGY WITH AUTO SEAT

PRICE
{
Cash with order, with steel tires and shafts......................................$69.00
C. O. D., with steel tires and shafts... 71.00
Cash with order, with ⅞-inch guaranteed rubber tires and shafts.................... 84.00
C. O. D., with ⅞-inch guaranteed rubber tires and shafts......................... 86.00
}

No. 954 is one of the best style high wheeled fancy painted and trimmed buggies we are making. It is hung on the regulation arched axle buggy gear and is light and very comfortable riding. We know our No. 954 is as good in quality of workmanship and material throughout as similar buggies sold by others for fully $25.00 more than our price. It is well trimmed and finely finished. We are glad to ship it for examination and approval, and it may be returned at our expense if not found perfectly satisfactory.

BODY—Piano box style, 24 inches wide and 56 inches long. We will furnish body 22 inches wide, if preferred. Seat is our regular auto style and is roomy and very comfortable. We use high grade stock throughout in the construction of both body and seat and they are well ironed and braced and guaranteed not to come apart at the corners, no matter in what climate used. Three prong steps. Roller rub irons.

GEAR—1⅛ inch dust proof bell collar long distance axles, with felt oil pads. Axles are fitted with straight grain hickory beds, which are cemented and clipped to the axles. Fine oil tempered French pattern open head springs, very elastic and easy riding. The reaches have channel iron full length, and they are bolted and well braced. Full circle wrought Brewster slotted fifth wheel. Wrought Bailey body loops clipped to springs. Will furnish wood spring bar, if preferred to the Bailey loops. Bradley quick change shaft couplers, which are the most practicable quick shifting couplers made and are used on all high grade work. Shafts are regular buggy style, only they are a little higher bend than is commonly used. They are made from selected hickory, full patent leather trimmed and well braced. Will furnish pole in in addition to shafts for $5.00 extra.

WHEELS—Fine selected straight grain white hickory, ⅞-inch Sarven patent, 40 inches front and 44 inches rear, with ⅞-inch round edge planished steel tires bolted between each spoke. Tires are ¼-inch thick and are set hot by hand and not by machine. Felloes have screws through them on each side of every spoke, which insures absolutely against checking at the spokes. The

height of wheels we furnish is correct for this style gear, but we can make any change in height desired. We furnish ¾-inch wheels instead of ⅞-inch, if preferred.

TRIMMINGS—Seat is trimmed in a combination of red plush, dark green wool broadcloth and maroon trimming leather. The center part of the back and the cushion are dark green wool broadcloth; the smooth part of the back is red plush, and the roll around the back of the seat and the facing on the cushion are maroon leather. We will trim the seat entirely with leather in maroon or tan color or dark green, if preferred, for $3.00 additional charge. Cushion and back are both upholstered with fine upholstering springs. The ends of the seat are pleated and trimmed to match cushion and back. There are nickel top prop nuts on top and nickel point bands on the hubs of the wheels. Dash is fine padded wing style. Good rubber boot over back part of body. Velvet carpet in bottom of body, or rubber mat if preferred.

TOP—Four bow leather quarter top with good rubber side curtains and storm apron. We will furnish full leather top with leather covered bows, if preferred, for $7.00 additional charge. We also furnish three bow top, if preferred to the four bow. There are arm straps attached to the top, as shown in picture; also small neat mirrors in the back stays, and the back stays are fancy stitched, as picture shows. Nickel top prop nuts.

PAINTING—The body is painted black, neatly striped and decorated; gear, New York red, correctly striped. We will furnish Brewster green gear or make any changes in painting desired. For system of painting in detail, see page 5.

No. 956—TOP BUGGY WITH DROP AXLES AND AUTO SEAT

PRICE
{
Cash with order, with steel tires and shafts.....................................$65.00
C. O. D., with steel tires and shafts... 67.00
Cash with order, with ⅞-inch guaranteed rubber tires and shafts.................. 80.00
C. O. D., with ⅞-inch guaranteed rubber tires and shafts........................ 82.00
}

If 1 inch guaranteed cushion tires are preferred to ⅞-inch solid rubber, add $2.50 to price quoted with ⅞-inch rubber tires.

No. 956 is a style that always appeals to those who prefer a buggy hung a little lower than the ordinary arched axle buggy. This buggy has the regulation drop style axle and the body hangs low, making it easy to get into and out of. No. 956 has all the most desirable features to be found on good work and we know quality of workmanship and material taken into consideration that it is as good as usually sells by others for $25.00 to $30.00 more than our price. We are glad to ship it for examination and approval, and if not found entirely satisfactory it may be returned at our expense.

BODY—Is the regulation piano box style, 24 inches wide and 56 inches long. We will furnish 22-inch body, if preferred to the 24 inch. Seat is one of the best auto designs made. The back is high and the seat is roomy and luxuriously upholstered. Both body and seat are made from high grade thoroughly seasoned body material. They are well ironed and braced and guaranteed not to open at the corners, no matter in what climate they are used. Fine three prong steps. Roller rub irons.

GEAR—1⅛ inch dust proof bell collar long distance drop axles, with felt oil pads. Axles are fitted with light wood beds, which are cemented and clipped full length. Fine oil tempered French pattern open head springs, very easy riding. Reaches have channel iron full length and they are bolted and well braced. Wrought full circle Brewster slotted fifth wheel, one of the best and strongest fifth wheels made. Bailey body loops clipped to springs. Will furnish wood spring bars if preferred to the loop. Bradley quick shifting shaft couplers, style used on all first class work. Regulation buggy style shafts made from fine selected hickory, full patent leather trimmed and with steel heel braces. We furnish pole in addition to shafts for $5.00 extra.

WHEELS—Fine selected straight grain white hickory, ⅞-inch Sarven patent, 40 inches front and 44 inches rear, with ⅞-inch round edge planished steel tire, bolted between each spoke. Tires are ¼-inch thick and are set hot by hand and not by machine. Felloes have screws through them on each side of every spoke, which insures absolutely against checking at the spokes. The height of wheels we furnish is correct for this style gear, but we can make any change in height desired. We furnish ¾-inch

wheels instead of ⅞-inch, if preferred. Also banded hub style, if desired instead of Sarven patent.

TRIMMINGS—Seat is trimmed with dark green all wool broadcloth, guaranteed fast color. Will trim with dark blue broadcloth or fine whipcord, if preferred. The ends of the seat are pleated and trimmed to match cushion and back. There are upholstering springs in both cushion and back and the seat is very comfortable. We trim the seat with genuine trimming leather in dark green, maroon or russet instead of broadcloth, if desired, for $3.00 extra. We can furnish special colors in broadcloth trimmings, if desired, at a small extra charge. Fine full padded wing style dash. Velvet carpet in bottom of body, or rubber mat if preferred to carpet. Boot to cover back part of body.

TOP—Fine leather quarter top with heavy rubber side curtains and storm apron for the dash. The top is lined with broadcloth to match the trimmings. It is regular with three bows, but we furnish four bows instead of three bows, if preferred, without extra charge. It has curved top joints, and joints and bow sockets are finely enameled. Furnished with full rubber top instead of leather quarter for $2.00 less. Full leather top with the very best leather covered bows and heavy rubber side curtains, $7.00 extra. Full leather top with best enameled steel bow sockets and heavy rubber curtains, $5.50 extra.

PAINTING—Body is plain black; gear, Brewster green, neatly striped. We will furnish New York red gear, correctly striped, or will paint any color you desire. For system of painting in detail, see page 5.

87

No. 958—TOP BUGGY WITH STANHOPE STYLE SEAT

PRICE
{
Cash with order, with steel tires and shafts.....................................$63.00
C. O. D., with steel tires and shafts.. 65.00
Cash with order, with ⅞-inch guaranteed rubber tires and shafts.................. 78.00
C. O. D., with ⅞-inch guaranteed rubber tires and shafts........................ 80.00
}

No. 958 is a very desirable style top buggy. It is up-to-date in every respect and as good in quality of workmanship and material as usually sells for $25.00 to $30.00 more than our price. It is equipped with our Stanhope style seat, which is roomy and very comfortable. Axles are the drop style and they allow the body to hang low, thus making it easier to get into and out of than the ordinary arched axle buggy. We are glad to ship this buggy for examination and approval, and it may be returned at our expense if not found perfectly satisfactory.

BODY—Piano box style, 24 inches wide and 56 inches long. We will furnish body 22 inches wide, if preferred. Seat is our regular Stanhope style and is roomy and very comfortable. We use high grade stock throughout in the construction of both body and seat and they are well ironed and braced and guaranteed not to come apart at the corners, no matter in what climate used. Three prong steps. Roller rub irons.

GEAR—1⅛ inch dust proof bell collar long distance drop axles, with felt oil pads. Axles are fitted with light wood beds, which are cemented and clipped full length. Fine oil tempered French pattern open head springs, very easy riding. Reaches have channel iron full length and they are bolted and well braced. Wrought full circle Brewster slotted fifth wheel, one of the best and strongest fifth wheels made. Bailey body loops clipped to springs. Will furnish wood spring bars if preferred to the Bailey loops. Bradley quick shifting shaft couplers, style used on all first class work. Regulation buggy style shafts made from fine selected hickory, full patent leather trimmed and with steel heel braces. We furnish pole in addition to shafts for $5.00 extra.

WHEELS—Fine selected straight grain white hickory, ⅞-inch Sarven patent, 40 inches front and 44 inches rear, with ⅞-inch round edge planished steel tire, bolted between each spoke. Tires are ¼-inch thick and are set hot by hand and not by machine. Felloes have screws through them on each side of every spoke, which insures absolutely against checking at the spokes. The height of wheels we furnish is correct for this style gear, but we can make any change in height desired. We furnish ¾-inch

wheels instead of ⅞-inch, if preferred. Also banded hub style, if desired instead of Sarven patent.

TRIMMINGS—Seat is trimmed with dark green all wool broadcloth, guaranteed fast color. Will trim with dark blue broadcloth or fine whipcord, if preferred. The ends of the seat are pleated and trimmed to match cushion and back. There are upholstering springs in both cushion and back and the seat is very comfortable. We trim the seat with genuine trimming leather in dark green, maroon or russet instead of broadcloth, if desired, for $3.00 extra. We can furnish special colors in broadcloth trimmings, if desired, at a small extra charge. Fine full padded wing style dash. Velvet carpet in bottom of body, or rubber mat if preferred to carpet. Boot to cover back part of body.

TOP—Fine leather quarter top with heavy rubber side curtains and storm apron for the dash. The top is lined with broadcloth to match the trimmings. It is regular with three bows, but we furnish four bows instead of three bows, if preferred, without extra charge. It has curved top joints, and joints and bow sockets are finely enameled. Furnished with full rubber top instead of leather quarter for $2.00 less. Full leather top with the very best leather covered bows and heavy rubber side curtains, $7.00 extra. Full leather top with best enameled steel bow sockets and heavy rubber curtains, $5.50 extra.

PAINTING—Body is plain black; gear, Brewster green, neatly striped. We will furnish New York red gear, correctly striped, or will paint any color you desire. For system of painting in detail, see page 5.

The above cut shows No. 960 with special fancy trimmings, painting and top. Trimmings, top and painting same as No. 954. Price, $3.00 more than No. 960.

No. 960—TOP BUGGY WITH AUTO SEAT

PRICE
Cash with order, with steel tires and shafts.....................................$63.00
C. O. D., with steel tires and shafts.. 65.00
Cash with order, with ⅞-inch guaranteed rubber tires and shafts................... 78.00
C .O. D., with ⅞-inch guaranteed rubber tires and shafts........... .... 80.00

No. 960 is one of our best style end spring top buggies. It is up-to-date in every respect and as good in workmanship and material throughout as usually sells for fully $25.00 more than our price. We are glad of an opportunity to snip No. 960 for examination and approval, if it is not found all we claim it may be returned at our expense.

BODY—Is the regulation piano box style, 24 inches wide and 56 inches long. We will furnish 22-inch body if preferred to the 24-inch. Seat is one of our best auto designs. The back is high and the seat is roomy and luxuriously upholstered. Both body and seat are made from high grade thoroughly seasoned body material. They are well ironed and braced and guaranteed not to open at the corners, no matter in what climate they are used. Fine three prong steps. Roller rub irons.

GEAR—1⅛ inch dust proof bell collar long distance drop axles, with felt oil pads. Axles are fitted with light wood beds, which are cemented and clipped full length. Fine oil tempered French pattern open head springs, very easy riding. Reaches have channel iron full length and they are bolted and well braced. Wrought full circle Brewster slotted fifth wheel, one of the best and strongest fifth wheels made. Bailey body loops clipped to springs. Will furnish wood spring bars if preferred to the loop. Bradley quick shifting shaft couplers, style used on all first class work. Regulation buggy style shafts made from fine selected hickory, full patent leather trimmed and with steel heel braces. We furnish pole in addition to shafts for $5.00 extra.

WHEELS—Fine selected straight grain white hickory, ⅞-inch Sarven patent, 40 inches front and 44 inches rear, with ⅞-inch round edge planished steel tire, bolted between each spoke. Tires are ¼-inch thick and are set hot by hand and not by machine. Felloes have screws through them on each side of every spoke, which insures absolutely against checking at the spokes. The height of wheels we furnish is correct for this style gear, but we can make any change in height desired. We furnish ¾-inch

wheels instead of ⅞-inch, if preferred. Also banded hub style, if desired instead of Sarven patent.

TRIMMINGS—Seat is trimmed with dark green all wool broadcloth, guaranteed fast color. Will trim with dark blue broadcloth or fine whipcord, if preferred. The ends of the seat are pleated and trimmed to match cushion and back. There are upholstering springs in both cushion and back and the seat is very comfortable. We trim the seat with genuine trimming leather in dark green, maroon or russet instead of broadcloth, if desired, for $3.00 extra. We can furnish special colors in broadcloth trimmings, if desired, at a small extra charge. Fine full padded wing style dash. Velvet carpet in bottom of body, or rubber mat if preferred to carpet. Boot to cover back part of body.

TOP—Fine leather quarter top with heavy rubber side curtains and storm apron for the dash. The top is lined with broadcloth to match the trimmings. It is regular with three bows, but we furnish four bows instead of three bows, if preferred, without extra charge. It has curved top joints, and joints and bow sockets are finely enameled. Furnished with full rubber top instead of leather quarter for $2.00 less. Full leather top with the very best leather covered bows and heavy rubber side curtains, $7.00 extra. Full leather top with best enameled steel bow sockets and heavy rubber curtains, $5.50 extra.

PAINTING—Body is plain black; gear, Brewster green, neatly striped. We will furnish New York red gear, correctly striped, or will paint any color you desire. For system of painting in detail, see page 5.

No. 962—TOP BUGGY WITH LONGITUDINAL CENTER SPRINGS

PRICE
Cash with order, with steel tires and shafts.....................................$60.00
C. O. D., with steel tires and shafts.. 62.00
Cash with order, with ⅞-inch guaranteed rubber tires and shafts................. 75.00
C. O. D., with ⅞-inch guaranteed rubber tires and sha.ts....................... 77.00

No. 962 is a style that gives the best of satisfaction. It is equipped with our regular half phaeton style seat which is roomy and **very** comfortable. We know No. 962 is as good in quality of workmanship and material as usually sells for $25.00 more than our price. **We** are very glad to ship it anywhere for examination and approval, with the understanding that it may be returned at our expense if not found highly satisfactory.

BODY—Is the regulation piano box style, 24 inches wide and 56 inches long. We will furnish 22-inch body if preferred to the 24-inch. Seat is our half phaeton style. The back is high and seat is roomy and luxuriously upholstered. Both body and seat are made from high grade thoroughly seasoned body material. They are well ironed and braced and guaranteed not to open at the corners, no matter in what climate they are used. Fine three prong steps. Roller rub irons.

GEAR—1⅛ inch dust proof bell collar long distance drop axles, with felt oil pads. Axles are fitted with light wood beds, which are cemented and clipped full length. Fine oil tempered French pattern open head springs, very easy riding. Reaches have channel iron full length and they are bolted and well braced. Wrought full circle Brewster slotted fifth wheel, one of the best and strongest fifth wheels made. Bailey body loops clipped to springs. Will furnish wood spring bars if preferred to the loop. Bradley quick shifting shaft couplers, style used on all first class work. Regulation buggy style shafts made from fine selected hickory, full patent leather trimmed and with steel heel braces. We furnish pole in addition to shafts for $5.00 extra.

WHEELS—Fine selected straight grain white hickory, ⅞-inch Sarven patent, 40 inches front and 44 inches rear, with ⅞-inch round edge planished steel tire, bolted between each spoke. Tires are ¼-inch thick and are set hot by hand and not by machine. Felloes have screws through them on each side of every spoke, which insures absolutely against checking at the spokes. The height of wheels we furnish is correct for this style gear, but we can make any change in height desired. We furnish ¾-inch wheels instead of ⅞-inch, if preferred. Also banded hub style, if desired instead of Sarven patent.

TRIMMINGS—Seat is trimmed with whipcord in fancy pattern, as picture shows, but we will trim with dark green or dark blue wool broadcloth, if preferred. Both cushion and back are upholstered with fine upholstering springs and the ends of the seat are trimmed to match cushion and back. We will trim the seat with fine genuine trimming leather in dark green, maroon or tan color for $2.00 additional charge. There are nickel top prop nuts on the top, nickel line rail on the dash, nickel hub bands on wheels and nickel rail around the back of the seat. Velvet carpet in bottom of body, or rubber mat if preferred. Rubber boot over back part of body. Padded dash.

TOP—Full rubber with good rubber side curtains and storm apron. We will furnish leather quarter top instead of rubber, if desired, for $2.00 additional charge. We also furnish four bows instead of three, if preferred, without extra charge. Top is lined to match seat trimmings, and the back stays are fancy stitched, as picture shows.

PAINTING—The body is black; gear, Brewster green, correctly striped. We will furnish New York red gear or make any changes in painting desired. For system of painting, see page 5.

The above cut shows No. 964 with full leather Victoria style top and lamps for physicians and business men. Additional charge for this style top and lamps, $25.00.

No. 964—FINE CORNING BODY BUGGY WITH FULL LEATHER TOP AND LEATHER COVERED BOWS

PRICE
{ Cash with order, with steel tires and shafts.....................................$80.00
C. O. D., with steel tires and shafts.. 82.00
Cash with order, with ⅞-inch guaranteed rubber tires and shafts.................. 95.00
C. O. D., with ⅞-inch guaranteed rubber tires and shafts........................ 97.00

No. 964 is one of the best corning body buggies made. It is well proportioned, light running and most comfortable riding. The body on this buggy hangs low and it is very easy to get into and out of. We know No. 964 is as good in quality of workmanship and material throughout as usually sells for $25.00 to $30.00 more than our price. We are glad to ship it for examination and approval, with the understanding that it is to be found all we claim or it may be returned at our expense both ways.

BODY—Regulation Corning style, equipped with our Stanhope buggy seat. Both body and seat are made from high grade stock and are so constructed that we guarantee them not to open at the joints, no matter in what climate used. The panels being cut down in front makes it very easy to get into and out of. Roller rub irons and three prong steps.

GEAR—1⅛-inch dust proof bell collar long distance axles, equipped with felt oil pads. Axles are fitted with straight grain hickory beds, which are cemented and clipped full length. Fine well graded oil tempered French pattern open head springs which are very easy riding. Reaches have channel reach iron full length, and they are bolted and well braced. Full circle wrought Brewster fifth wheel, which is one of the best style fifth wheels made. Straight grain hickory spring bars with body loops running full length of body. We will furnish wrought Bailey loops, if preferred. Bradley quick shifting shaft couplers, which are the best couplers made and are used on all high grade work. Shafts, regulation buggy style made from straight grain white hickory, full patent leather trimmed and with special heel braces. We furnish pole instead of shafts for $1.00 extra. Pole in addition to shafts, $5.00 extra.

WHEELS—Selected straight grain white hickory, ⅞-inch Sarven patent, 40 inches front and 44 inches rear, with ⅞-inch round edge planished steel tire, bolted between each spoke. Tires are ¼-inch thick and are set hot by hand and not by machine. Felloes have screws through them on each side of every spoke, which insures absolutely against checking at the spokes. The height of wheels

we furnish is correct for this style gear, but we can make any change in height desired. We furnish ¾-inch wheels instead of ⅞-inch, if preferred. Also banded hub style, if desired instead of the Sarven patent.

TRIMMINGS—Seat is trimmed with fine dark green all wool broadcloth, guaranteed absolutely fast color. Will trim with fine dark blue wool broadcloth or fine whipcord, if preferred. Ends of the seat are pleated and trimmed to match cushion and back, and both cushion and back are upholstered with hair and upholstering springs, and the seat is most comfortable. We can furnish any special colors of broadcloth at a small additional charge. Genuine leather trimmings in dark green, maroon or russet instead of all wool broadcloth for $3.00. Fine full padded patent leather dash. Velvet carpet in bottom of body, or rubber mat if preferred to the carpet. Rubber boot to cover back part of body.

TOP—Fine full leather with best grade leather covered bow sockets, heavy rubber side curtains and storm apron for dash. We furnish with leather quarter top and very best grade steel bow sockets, if desired, for $7.00 less than with leather top. We furnish four bows on any of our tops instead of three without additional charge. Top is always lined with broadcloth to match seat trimmings.

PAINTING—The body is black; gear, Brewster green, correctly striped. We will make any changes in painting desired. Our painting is all fully guaranteed. For system of painting, see page 5.

91

The above cut shows No. 966 equipped with lamps and fenders. Additional charge for lamps and fenders, $5.00.

No. 966—CORNING BODY BUGGY WITH HALF PHAETON STYLE SEAT

PRICE
{ Cash with order, with steel tires and shafts......................................$62.00
{ C. O. D., with steel tires and shafts.. 64.00
{ Cash with order, with ⅞-inch guaranteed rubber tires and shafts.................... 77.00
{ C. O. D., with ⅞-inch guaranteed rubber tires and shafts........................ 79.00

Our No. 966 is a very popular seller with us and a buggy that gives the best of satisfaction everywhere. It has the regulation corning body, drop axle gear and is very easy to get into and out of. It is light running and most comfortable riding. We guarantee this buggy as good as usually sells for fully $25.00 more than our price, and are glad to ship it for examination and approval.

BODY—Regulation Corning style, equipped with our half phaeton seat. Both body and seat are made from high grade stock and are so constructed that we guarantee them not to open at the joints, no matter in what climate used. The panels being cut down in front makes it very easy to get into and out of. Roller rub irons and three prong steps.

GEAR—1⅛-inch dust proof bell collar long distance axles, equipped with felt oil pads. Axles are fitted with straight grain hickory beds, which are cemented and clipped full length. Fine well graded oil tempered French pattern open head springs, which are very easy riding. Reaches have channel reach iron full length, and they are bolted and well braced. Wrought full circle Brewster slotted fifth wheel, which is one of the best style fifth wheels made. Heavy straight grain hickory spring bars with body loops running full length of body. We will furnish Bailey loops, if preferred. Bradley quick shifting couplers, which are the best couplers made and are used on all high grade work. Shafts, regulation buggy style made from straight grain white hickory, full patent leather trimmed and with special heel braces. We furnish pole instead of shafts for $1.00 extra. Pole in addition to shafts, $5.00 extra.

WHEELS—Selected straight grain white hickory, ⅞-inch Sarven patent, 40 inches front and 44 inches rear, with ⅞-inch round edge planished steel tire, bolted between each spoke. Tires are ¼-inch thick and are set hot by hand and not by machine. Felloes have screws through them on each side of every spoke, which insures absolutely against checking at the spokes. The height of wheels we furnish is correct for this style gear, but we can make any change in height desired. We furnish ¾-inch wheels instead of ⅞-inch, if preferred. Also banded hub style, if desired instead of Sarven patent.

TRIMMINGS—Seat is trimmed with dark green all wool broadcloth, guaranteed absolutely fast color. Will trim with dark blue wool broadcloth or whipcord, if preferred. Ends of the seat are trimmed to match cushion and back, and both cushion and back are upholstered with fine upholstering springs, and the seat is most comfortable. We can furnish any special colors of broadcloth at a small additional charge. Genuine leather trimmings in dark green, maroon or russet instead of all wool broadcloth for $3.00. Fine full padded patent leather dash. Velvet carpet in bottom of body, or rubber mat, if preferred to the carpet. Rubber boot to cover back part of body.

TOP—Leather quarter top with heavy rubber side curtains and storm apron. The seat is lined with broadcloth to match trimmings. It is regular with three bows, but we furnish four bows instead of three, if preferred, without additional charge. The joints and bow sockets are very finely enameled. We furnish full rubber top, if preferred to the leather quarter, and make a reduction of $2.00. If full leather top with steel bows is preferred to the leather quarter top our additional charge is $5.50, including rubber side curtains. If full leather top, including leather covered bow sockets and rubber side curtains, is preferred, the additional charge is $7.00. We can furnish handy style top with 2½ or 3½ bows instead of the regular top, if desired.

PAINTING—The body is black; gear, Brewster green, correctly striped. We will make any changes in painting desired. Our painting is all fully guaranteed. For system of painting, see page 5.

92

The above cut shows No. 968 with auto style seat. Price, just the same as with Stanhope seat.

No. 968—CORNING BODY BUGGY WITH STANHOPE STYLE SEAT

PRICE
Cash with order, with steel tires and shafts.....................................$65.00
C. O. D., with steel tires and shafts.. 67.00
Cash with order, with ⅞-inch guaranteed rubber tires and shafts................... 80.00
C. O. D., with ⅞-inch guaranteed rubber tires and shafts......................... 82.00

Our No. 968 is one of the most desirable style corning body buggies made. Body is regulation style corning and the gear has drop axle, allowing the body to hang low, making it very easy to get into and out of. We know No. 968 is as good in quality of workmanship and material throughout as usually sells for $25.00 to $30.00 more than our price. We are glad to ship it for examination and approval.

BODY—Regulation Corning style, equipped with our Stanhope buggy seat. Both body and seat are made from high grade stock and are so constructed that we guarantee them not to open at the joints, no matter in what climate used. The panels being cut down in front on a Corning body makes it very easy to get into and out of. Roller rub irons and three prong steps.

GEAR—1⅛-inch dust proof bell collar long distance axles, equipped with felt oil pads. Axles are fitted with straight grain hickory beds, which are cemented and clipped full length. Fine well graded oil tempered French pattern open head springs, which are very easy riding. Reaches have channel reach iron full length, and they are bolted and well braced. Full circle wrought Brewster slotted fifth wheel, which is one of the best fifth wheels made. Straight grain hickory spring bars with body loops running full length of body. We will furnish Bailey loops, if preferred. Bradley quick shifting couplers, which are the best couplers made and are used on all high grade work. Shafts, regulation buggy style made from straight grain white hickory, full patent leather trimmed and with special heel braces. We furnish pole instead of shafts for $1.00 extra. Pole in addition to shafts, $5.00 extra.

WHEELS—Selected straight grain white hickory, ⅞-inch Sarven patent, 40 inches front and 44 inches rear, with ⅞-inch round edge planished steel tire, bolted between each spoke. Tires are ¼-inch thick and are set hot by hand and not by machine. Felloes have screws through them on each side of every spoke, which insures absolutely against checking at the spokes. The height of wheels we furnish is correct for this style gear, but we can make any change in height desired. We furnish ¾-inch wheels instead

of ⅞-inch, if preferred. Also banded hub style, if desired instead of Sarven patent.

TRIMMINGS—Seat is trimmed with dark green all wool broadcloth, guaranteed fast color. Will trim with dark blue broadcloth or whipcord, if preferred. The ends of the seat are pleated and trimmed to match cushion and back. There are upholstering springs in both cushion and back, and the seat is very comfortable. We trim the seat with genuine trimming leather in dark green, maroon or russet instead of broadcloth, if desired, for $3.00 extra. We can furnish special colors in broadcloth trimming, if desired, at a small extra charge. Fine full padded dash. Velvet carpet in bottom of body, or rubber mat if preferred to carpet. Boot to cover back part of body.

TOP—Leather quarter top with heavy rubber side curtains and storm apron. The top is lined with broadcloth to match trimmings. It is regular with three bows, but we furnish four bows instead of three, if preferred, without additional charge. It has curved top joints and the joints and bow sockets are very finely enameled. We furnish full rubber top, if preferred to the leather quarter, and make a reduction of $2.00. If full leather top with steel bows is preferred to the leather quarter top, our additional charge is $5.50, including rubber side curtains. If full leather top, including leather covered bow sockets and rubber side curtains, is preferred, the additional charge is $7.00.

PAINTING—The body is black; gear, Brewster green, correctly striped. We will make any changes in painting desired. Our painting is all fully guaranteed. For system of painting, see page 5.

93

The above cut shows No. 969 as an open driving wagon with spindle seat. Price, without top and with spindle seat, $15.00 less than with top.

No. 969—BRACKET FRONT BUGGY WITH STANHOPE STYLE SEAT

PRICE
⎧ Cash with order, with steel tires and shafts.....................................$65.00
⎪ C. O. D., with steel tires and shafts... 67.00
⎨ Cash with order, with ⅞-inch guaranteed rubber tires and shafts.................. 80.00
⎩ C. O. D., with ⅞-inch guaranteed rubber tires and shafts........................ 82.00

No. 969 is one of our most up-to-date style buggies. It is equipped with the regulation bracket front body which is cut down to the sill in front of seat, thus making it very easy to get into and out of. We know No. 969 is as good in quality of workmanship and material throughout as usually sells for $25.00 to $30.00 more than our price. We are glad, at any rate, to allow you to be the judge by shipping for full examination and approval.

BODY—Is regulation bracket front style. Both body and seat are made from high grade thoroughly seasoned stock and put together in such a manner that we guarantee them not to come apart at the joints, no matter in what climate used. Seat is our regular Stanhope style and is roomy and comfortable. Roller rub irons and three prong steps.

GEAR—1⅛-inch dust proof bell collar long distance axles, equipped with felt oil pads. Axles are fitted with straight grain hickory beds, which are cemented and clipped full length. Fine well graded oil tempered French pattern open head springs, which are very easy riding. Reaches have channel reach iron full length, and they are bolted and well braced. Full circle wrought Brewster slotted fifth wheel, which is one of the best fifth wheels made. Straight grain hickory spring bars with body loops running full length of body. We will furnish Bailey loops, if preferred. Bradley quick shifting couplers, which are the best couplers made and are used on all high grade work. Shafts, regulation buggy style made from straight grain white hickory, full patent leather trimmed and with special heel braces. We furnish pole instead of shafts for $1.00 extra. Pole in addition to shafts, $5.00 extra.

WHEELS—Selected straight grain white hickory, ⅞-inch Sarven patent, 40 inches front and 44 inches rear, with ⅞-inch round edge planished steel tire, bolted between each spoke. Tires are ¼-inch thick and are set hot by hand and not by machine. Felloes have screws through them on each side of every spoke, which insures absolutely against checking at the spokes. The height of wheels we furnish is correct for this style gear, but we can make any change in height desired. We furnish ¾-inch wheels instead

of ⅞-inch, if preferred. Also banded hub style, if desired instead of the Sarven patent.

TRIMMINGS—Seat is trimmed with dark green all wool broadcloth, guaranteed absolutely fast color. Will trim with dark blue wool broadcloth or whipcord, if preferred. Ends of seat are padded and trimmed to match cushion and back, and both cushion and back are upholstered with fine upholstering springs, and the seat is most comfortable. We can furnish any special colors of broadcloth at a small additional charge. Genuine leather trimmings in dark green, maroon or russet instead of all wool broadcloth for $3.00. Fine full padded patent leather dash. Velvet carpet in bottom of body, or rubber mat if preferred to the carpet. Rubber boot to cover back part of body.

TOP—Leather quarter top with heavy rubber side curtains and storm apron. The top is lined with broadcloth to match trimmings. It is regular with three bows, but we furnish four bows instead of three, if preferred, without additional charge. It has curved top joints and the joints and bow sockets are very finely enameled. We furnish full rubber top, if preferred to the leather quarter, and make a reduction of $2.00. If full leather top with steel bows is preferred to the leather quarter top our additional charge is $5.50, including rubber side curtains. If full leather top, including leather covered bow sockets and rubber side curtains, is preferred, the additional charge is $7.00.

PAINTING—The body is black; gear, Brewster green, correctly striped. We will make any changes in painting desired. Our painting is all fully guaranteed. For system of painting, see page 5.

The Following Description Covers Nos. 970 and 975, also Nos. 971, 972, 973, 974, 976, 977, 978 and 979, Excepting Seats, which are Extra as Shown on Pages 96 and 97:

PRICE
Cash with order, with steel tires and shafts for either Nos. 970 or 975..........$50.00
C. O. D., with steel tires and shafts for either Nos. 970 or 975.................. 51.50
Cash with order, with ⅞-inch guaranteed rubber tires and shafts, for
 either Nos. 970 or 975.. 65.00
C. O. D., with ⅞-inch guaranteed rubber tires and shafts, for either
 Nos. 970 or 975.. 66.50

Our Nos. 970 and 975 are made in our regular grade and finish throughout and are up-to-date style in every particular. They are equipped with more expensive and better style seats than the regulation buggy seat. These buggies have all the late desirable features, as you will see from the detailed description below. They are all fully warranted for two years the same as the highest priced work we make, and we can unhesitatingly recommend them. We are very glad to ship any of these styles with the distinct understanding that you are to be perfectly satisfied in every way and to feel that you are saving $20.00 to $35.00 or we will take the shipment back at our expense and you will be nothing out.

BODY—Is the regulation piano body style, 24 inches wide and 56 inches long. We will furnish 22-inch body if preferred to the 24-inch. We have a large body factory of our own and do not have to buy bodies and seats from other manufacturers. We use none but high grade, thoroughly seasoned stock in the construction of our bodies and seats and they are well glued, screwed, plugged and ironed, and guaranteed not to open at the joints. We think our bodies and seats are much better made throughout than those manufactured by many exclusive body and seat manufacturers. No. 970 is equipped with our half phaeton style seat and No. 975 with our fine deep panel concave seat. Roller rub irons on bodies, also fine three prong steps.

GEARS—No. 970 has dust proof bell collar long distance axles, with felt oil pads. These axles are slightly arched and are fitted with selected straight grain hickory beds, securely cemented and clipped to axles. No. 975 has true sweep bike style axles with dust proof bell collar long distance spindles, with felt oil pads. They are fitted with fine selected straight grain hickory beds which are securely cemented and clipped to axles. When these beds are smoothed up for painting, the axle and the bed are the same as one piece. Fine oil tempered French pattern open head springs, which are specially graded and are very easy riding. Reaches have channel iron full length and they are bolted and well braced. Full circle fifth wheel, one of the best and strongest fifth wheels made. Wrought Bailey body loops clipped to springs. We will furnish wood spring bars instead of Bailey loops if they are preferred. Fernald quick shifting shaft couplers.

SHAFTS—Our shafts are all made from thoroughly seasoned straight grain white hickory. They are full patent leather trimmed with long tips and are well braced at the heels. We furnish pole in addition to shafts for $5.00 extra.

WHEELS—Fine selected straight grain white hickory, ⅞ inch Sarven patent, 40 inches front, 44 inches rear for No. 970 style gear, and 38 inches front and 40 inches rear for No. 975 bike style gear. Our wheels are equipped with round edge planished steel tire, bolted between each spoke. Tires are ¼-inch thick and are set hot by hand and not by machine. Felloes have screws through them on each side of every spoke, which insures them against checking at the spokes. We furnish the banded hub style wheel instead of the Sarven patent, if preferred. The Sarven wheel is considered by many users the most substantial wheel. It has sixteen spokes, while the banded hub has fourteen spokes. We consider the tiring of the wheels one of the most important features of wheel construction. In tiring our wheels, we pay special attention to the "dish," as it is very important that the wheels be properly "dished." The height wheels specified are regulation height for the different style gears, but we will make any change in height desired. We also furnish ¾-inch instead of ⅞-inch, if preferred. We equip wheels with ⅞-inch high grade guaranteed rubber tires for $15.00 additional charge over steel tires. Every wheel that leaves our factory is fully warranted for two years.

TRIMMINGS AND UPHOLSTERING—We regularly trim the seats of these buggies with fine all wool dark green broadcloth, guaranteed fast color. We will trim with dark blue broadcloth or whipcord, if preferred. The ends of the seat are pleated and trimmed to match the cushion and back. There are upholstering springs in both cushion and back, and the seats are very comfortable. When leather is ordered instead of broadcloth for the seat trimmings we make an additional charge of $3.00. We can furnish special colors in broadcloth, if desired, at a small extra charge. Dashes are full padded and made from fine patent dash leather. Brussels carpet in bottom of body, or rubber mat if preferred. Good boot to cover back part of body.

TOP—Full rubber top with heavy rubber side curtains and storm apron. Top is lined with broadcloth to match seat trimmings. It is regular with three bows, but we furnish four instead of three, if preferred, without extra charge. Our top joints and sockets are the best we can buy and are finely enameled. We furnish leather quarter top instead of full rubber at an additional charge of $2.00. Full leather top, complete with heavy rubber side curtains and with best grade leather covered bows, $9.00 extra. We furnish handy style top with 2½ or 3½ bows instead of regular top, if desired.

PAINTING—We employ in our paint shop none but skilled painters. We use the best and most durable system of painting known. We have ample capacity in our large factories to enable us to carry the work in our paint department the length of time it should be carried. Each coat is treated properly and given the required length of time to season before another coat is applied. Filler coats are all properly rubbed down so that all surfaces are perfectly smooth before the different color varnish coats are applied. The different color varnish coats are rubbed down with powdered pumice and each coat of color varnish is made perfectly smooth before another coat is applied. Finally the last rubbing varnish coat is rubbed down and all surfaces are polished and made perfectly smooth before the last coats of finishing varnish are applied. We use high grade material from the foundation coats to the last finishing coat and our painting is fully guaranteed. Bodies on all these styles are painted jet black; gears on Nos. 970, 971, 972, 973 and 974 are painted Brewster green. On Nos. 975, 976, 977, 978 and 979, New York red. We will make any changes in color of painting desired.

The above cut shows No. 971, which is the same as No. 970, only with our regular auto seat and drop axles.
(See description on page 95.)

PRICE {
For No. 971, as shown above, cash with order.$53.00
C. O. D............ 54.50
⅞-inch guaranteed rubber tires, extra 15.00
}

The above cut shows No. 972, which is the same as No. 970, only with our new auto seat.
(See description on page 95.)

PRICE {
For No. 972, as shown above, cash with order.$55.00
C. O D........ 56.50
⅞-inch guaranteed rubber tires, extra 15.00
}

The above cut shows our No. 970 which is equipped with our fine half phaeton style seat. This is one of the best $50.00 buggies ever made. (See description page 95.)

PRICE {
For No. 970, as shown above, cash with order... $50.00
For No. 970, as shown above, C. O. D... 51.50
}

The above cut shows No. 973, which is the same as No. 970, only with our regular auto seat, fancy painting, trimmings and top and special padded dash with rail attached. (See description on page 95.) Furnished with bike gear, if preferred.

PRICE {
For No. 973, as shown above, cash with order....$54.50
C. O. D... 56.00
Deduct $1.50 if ordered with plain dash.
⅞-inch guaranteed rubber tires, extra.............. 15.00
}

The above cut shows No. 974, which is the same as No. 970, only with new Stanhope style seat and wing dash. (See description on page 95.)

PRICE {
For No. 974, as shown above, cash with order......$54.50
C. O. D.. 56.00
Deduct $1.50 if ordered with plain dash.
⅞-inch guaranteed rubber tires, extra 15.00
}

The above cut shows No. 976, which is the same as No. 975, only with our new twin auto seat.

(See description on page 95.)

PRICE { For No. 976, as shown above, cash with order. $56.00
C. O. D......... 57.50
⅞-inch guaranteed rubber tires, extra 15.00

The above cut shows No. 977, which is the same as No. 975, only with our new auto seat and wing style dash.

(See description on page 95.)

PRICE { For No. 977, as shown above, cash with order. $56.50
C. O. D......... 58.00
⅞-inch guaranteed rubber tires, extra 15.00
Deduct $1.50 if ordered with plain dash.

The above cut shows No. 975, equipped with our fine concave style seat and true sweep bike axles, guaranteed one of the best $50.00 buggies ever made. See description on page 95.

PRICE { For No. 975, as shown above, cash with order..$50.00
For No. 975, as shown above, C. O. D... 51.50
We furnish any of the styles shown on this page with fine steel wire wheels and 1⅛-inch cushion tires for $25.00 extra.

The above cut shows our No. 978, which is the same as our No. 975, only with our regular auto style seat and wing dash. (See description on page 95.)

PRICE { For No. 978, as shown above, cash with order......$54.50
C. O. D... 56.00
⅞-inch guaranteed rubber tires, extra............. 15.00
Deduct $1.50 if ordered with plain dash.

The above cut illustrates our No. 979, which is the same as No. 975, only with our fine Newport style seat. (See description on page 95.)

PRICE { For No. 979, as shown above, cash with order......$53.00
C. O. D... 54.50
⅞-inch guaranteed rubber tires, extra 15.00

The above cut shows No. 980 with cut-under body with side panels cut down in front of seat and with our regular style auto seat. Price, with this style body, $5.00 more than with regular piano body.

No. 980—FINE FULL LEATHER TOP BUGGY WITH LEATHER COVERED BOWS AND 1⅛-INCH CUSHION TIRES

PRICE { Cash with order, with 1⅛-inch guaranteed cushion tires and shafts................$105.00
C. O. D., with 1⅛-inch guaranteed cushion tires and shafts......................107.00

No. 980 is one of our most up-to-date style bike gear top buggies. It is equipped with one of the best wire wheel gears made and is a style that gives universal satisfaction. It is well proportioned, light running and very comfortable riding. We know No. 980 is as high grade in every respect as similar buggies sold by others for fully $35.00 more than our price. We are very glad to ship it for examination and approval, with the distinct understanding that if it is not found perfectly satisfactory and all we claim it may be returned at our expense.

BODY—Is regulation piano box style, 22 inches wide and 56 inches long. We will furnish 24-inch body, if preferred to the 22-inch. The seat is one of the finest auto designs made. It has a good extra high back and is upholstered in such a manner that it is very comfortable. Both body and seat are made from high grade thoroughly seasoned body material and are well ironed and braced and guaranteed not to open at the corners, no matter in what climate they are used. Fine three prong rubber covered steps. Roller rub irons.

GEAR—Is Roman bike style with dust proof bell collar long distance axles, with felt oil pads. These axles are what are generally known as naked axles as they have wood beds only in the center where the fifth wheel attaches on the front axle and the rear spring on the rear axle. These beds are cemented and clipped to the axles so that when they are smoothed up ready for finishing the axle and the bed are the same as one piece. Oil tempered French pattern open head springs, correctly graded and very easy riding. Full circle wrought Brewster slotted fifth wheel, the style used on all high grade work. Reaches have channel reach iron full length, and they are bolted and well braced. Wrought Bailey body loops clipped to springs. Will furnish with wood bars, if preferred. Bradley quick shifting shaft couplers, which are used on all first class work. Shafts are the regulation high bend bike style made from selected straight grain white hickory. They are full patent leather trimmed and have special heel braces. Pole instead of shafts, $1.00 extra. Pole in addition to shafts, $5.00 extra.

WHEELS—We use the finest grade wire wheels manufactured. They are equipped with 1⅛-inch channel for 1⅛-inch cushion tires. The regular axle nut is covered by an outside nickel axle cap which screws into the hub of the wheel. Wheels are equipped with 1⅛-inch high grade guaranteed cushion tires.

TRIMMINGS—Seat is trimmed with fine dark green all wool broadcloth, guaranteed absolutely fast color. Will trim with fine dark blue wool broadcloth or fine whipcord, if preferred. Ends of the seat are pleated and trimmed to match cushion and back, and both cushion and back are upholstered with hair and upholstering springs, and the seat is most comfortable. We can furnish any special colors of broadcloth at a small additional charge. Genuine leather trimmings in dark green, maroon or russet instead of all wool broadcloth for $3.00. Fine full padded patent leather dash. Velvet carpet in bottom of body, or rubber mat if preferred to the carpet. Good rubber boot.

TOP—Fine full leather with best grade leather covered bow sockets, heavy rubber side curtains and storm apron for dash. We furnish with leather quarter top and very best grade steel bow sockets, if desired, for $7.00 less than with leather top. We furnish four bows on any of our tops instead of three without additional charge. Top is always lined with broadcloth to match seat trimmings.

PAINTING—The body is black; gear, New York red, correctly striped. We will furnish Brewster green gear or make any changes in painting desired. Our painting is all fully guaranteed For system of painting, see page 5.

The above cut illustrates No. 981 with the top removed, thus making a neat open driving wagon.

No. 981—FINE FULL LEATHER TOP BUGGY WITH LEATHER COVERED BOWS AND BIKE GEAR

PRICE
{
Cash with order, with steel tires and shafts.....................................$82.00
C. O. D., with steel tires and shafts...84.00
Cash with order, with ⅞-inch guaranteed rubber tires and shafts...................97.00
C. O. D., with ⅞-inch guaranteed rubber tires and shafts.........................99.00
}

If 1⅛-inch guaranteed cushion tires are preferred, add $5.00 to the price quoted with ⅞-inch solid rubber tires.

No. 981 is one of our best and most desirable style bike gear buggies. It has the true sweep bike style axles with wood beds full length. This buggy is well proportioned throughout, light running and most comfortable riding. We know No. 981 is just as good as usually sells for fully $25.00 to $35.00 more than our price. We are glad of an opportunity to ship it for examination and approval, allowing you to judge for yourself.

BODY—Is regulation piano box style, 22 inches wide and 56 inches long. We will furnish 24-inch body, if preferred to the 22-inch. The seat is one of the finest auto designs made. It has a good extra high back and is upholstered in such a manner that it is very comfortable. Both body and seat are made from high grade thoroughly seasoned body material and are well ironed and braced and guaranteed not to open at the corners, no matter in what climate they are used. Fine three prong rubber covered steps. Roller rub irons.

GEAR—1⅛-inch true sweep dust proof long distance bell collar bike axles, with felt oil pads. Axles are fitted with light straight grain hickory beds, which are cemented and clipped full length. Fine oil tempered French pattern open head springs, properly graded and very easy riding. Reaches have channel reach iron full length, and they are bolted and well braced. Full circle wrought Brewster slotted fifth wheel, one of the best style fifth wheels made. Wrought Bailey body loops clipped to axles. Will furnish wood spring bars, if preferred. Bradley quick shifting shaft couplers, which are the style couplers used on all high grade work. Regulation high bend bike style shafts made from straight grain selected hickory, full patent leather trimmed and with special heel braces. We furnish pole instead of shafts for $1.00 extra. Pole in addition to shafts, $5.00 extra.

WHEELS—Fine selected straight grain white hickory, ⅞-inch banded hub, 38 inches front and 40 inches rear, with ⅞-inch round edge planished steel tire, bolted between each spoke. Tires are ¼-inch thick and are set hot by hand and not by machine. Felloes have screws through them on each side of every spoke,

which insures absolutely against checking at the spokes. The height of wheels we furnish is correct for this style gear, but we can make any change in height desired. We furnish ¾-inch wheels instead of ⅞-inch, if preferred. Also Sarven patent style, if desired instead of banded hub.

TRIMMINGS—Seat is trimmed with fine dark green all wool broadcloth, guaranteed absolutely fast color. Will trim with fine dark blue wool broadcloth or fine whipcord, if preferred. Ends of the seat are pleated and trimmed to match cushion and back, and both cushion and back are upholstered with hair and upholstering springs, and the seat is most comfortable. We can furnish any special colors of broadcloth at a small additional charge. Genuine leather trimmings in dark green, maroon or russet instead of all wool broadcloth for $3.00. Fine full padded patent leather dash. Velvet carpet in bottom of body, or rubber mat if preferred to the carpet. Good rubber boot.

TOP—Fine full leather with best grade leather covered bow sockets, heavy rubber side curtains and storm apron for dash. We furnish with leather quarter top and very best grade steel bow sockets, if desired, for $7.00 less than with leather top. We furnish four bows on any of our tops instead of three without additional charge. Top is always lined with broadcloth to match seat trimmings.

PAINTING—The body is black; gear, New York red, correctly striped. We will furnish Brewster green gear or make any changes in painting desired. Our painting is all fully guaranteed. For system of painting, see page 5.

The above cut shows No. 982 with the top removed and leather seat fenders attached to the top irons, thus making a neat open driving wagon. If seat fenders are not desired, deduct $2.00 from price quoted.

No. 982—FINE COMBINATION FULL LEATHER TOP BUGGY WITH LEATHER COVERED BOWS AND ROMAN BIKE AXLES

PRICE
{ Cash with order, with steel tires and shafts.......................................$82.00
{ C. O. D., with steel tires and shafts... 84.00
{ Cash with order, with ⅞-inch guaranteed rubber tires and shafts................... 97.00
{ C. O. D., with ⅞-inch guaranteed rubber tires and shafts.......................... 99.00
If 1⅛-inch guaranteed cushion tires are preferred, add $5.00 to the price quoted with ⅞-inch solid rubber tires.

Our No. 982 is one of the most popular style top buggies we are making. It is a combination buggy, or in other words, two buggies in one, as the top is attached to the seat with quick shifting attachments and can be easily removed. When the top is removed there are leather seat fenders for attaching to the irons on the ends of the seat, thus making a neat open driving wagon with regular leather seat fenders. We guarantee our No. 982 to be as good in quality of workmanship and material throughout as usually sells for $25.00 more than our price. We are glad to ship it for examination and approval.

BODY—Is regulation piano box style, 22 inches wide and 56 inches long. We will furnish 24 inch body, if preferred to the 22-inch. The seat is one of the finest auto designs made. It has a good extra high back and is upholstered in such a manner that it is very comfortable. Both body and seat are made from high grade thoroughly seasoned body material and are well ironed and braced and guaranteed not to open at the corners, no matter in what climate they are used. Fine three prong rubber covered steps. Roller rub irons.

GEAR—Is Roman bike style with dust proof bell collar long distance axles, with felt oil pads. They are what are generally known as naked axles, as they have wood beds only in the center where the fifth wheel attaches to the front axle and the rear spring to the rear axle. These beds are cemented and clipped to the axles so that when they are smoothed up ready for finishing the axle and the bed are the same as one piece. Oil tempered French pattern open head springs, correctly graded and very easy riding. Full circle wrought Brewster slotted fifth wheel, the style used on all high grade work. Reaches have channel reach irons full length, and they are bolted and well braced. Wrought Bailey body loops clipped to springs. Will furnish with wood bars, if preferred. Bradley quick shifting shaft couplings, which are used on all first class work. Shafts are the regulation high bend bike style made from selected straight grain white hickory. They are full patent leather trimmed and have special heel braces. Pole instead of shafts, $1.00 extra. Pole in addition to shafts, $5.00 extra.

WHEELS—Fine selected straight grain white hickory, ⅞-inch banded hub, 38 inches front and 40 inches rear, with ⅞-inch round edge planished steel tire, bolted between each spoke. Tires are ¼-inch thick and are set hot by hand and not by machine. Felloes have screws through them on each side of every spoke, which insures absolutely against checking at the spokes. The height of wheels we furnish is correct for this style gear, but we can make any change in height desired. We furnish ¾-inch wheels instead of ⅞-inch, if preferred. Also Sarven patent, if desired instead of banded hub.

TRIMMINGS—Seat is trimmed with dark green all wool broadcloth, guaranteed fast color. Will trim with dark blue broadcloth or fine whipcord, if preferred. The ends of the seat are pleated and trimmed to match the cushion and back. There are upholstering springs in both cushion and back and the seat is very comfortable. We trim the seat with genuine trimming leather in dark green, maroon or russet instead of broadcloth, if desired, for $3.00 extra. We can furnish special colors in broadcloth trimmings, if desired, at a small additional charge. Fine full padded wing style dash. Velvet carpet in bottom of body, or rubber mat if preferred. Boot to cover back part of body.

TOP—Fine full leather with best grade leather covered bow sockets, heavy rubber side curtains and storm apron for dash. We furnish with leather quarter top and very best grade steel bow sockets, if desired, for $7.00 less than with leather top. We furnish four bows on any of our tops instead of three without additional charge. Top is always lined with broadcloth to match seat trimmings. If the extra leather seat fenders are not wanted with this buggy, deduct $2.00.

PAINTING—Body is plain black; gear, New York red, neatly striped. We will furnish Brewster green gear, correctly striped, or will paint any color you desire. For system of painting, see page 5.

100

The above cut shows No. 984 with the top removed and leather seat fenders attached to the top irons, thus making a neat open driving wagon. If seat fenders are not desired, deduct $2.00 from price quoted. Cut also shows wing dash which is $1.50 more than straight dash.

No. 984—FINE COMBINATION FULL LEATHER TOP BUGGY WITH LEATHER COVERED BOWS AND BIKE AXLES

PRICE
Cash with order, with steel tires and shafts.....................................$81.00
C. O. D., with steel tires and shafts.. 83.00
Cash with order, with ⅞-inch guaranteed rubber tires and shafts................... 96.00
C. O. D., with ⅞-inch guaranteed rubber tires and shafts......................... 98.00
If 1⅛-inch guaranteed cushion tires are preferred, add $5.00 to the price quoted with ⅞-inch solid rubber tires.

Our No. 984 is a very desirable style top buggy. The top attaches to seat with shifting rail, which fastens to the seat irons with quick shifting attachments, enabling the top to be removed easily, thus making a neat open driving wagon. We furnish leather seat fenders to be attached to the irons on the ends of the seat when the top is removed. We know our No. 984 is as good in quality of workmanship and material throughout as usually sells for $25.00 more than our price, and we are glad to ship it for examination and approval.

BODY—Is regulation piano box style, 24 inches wide and 56 inches long. We will furnish 22-inch body, if preferred to the 24-inch. The seat is Stanhope style, it has a good extra high back and is upholstered in such a manner that it is very comfortable. Both body and seat are made from high grade thoroughly seasoned body material and are well ironed and braced and guaranteed not to open at the corners, no matter in what climate they are used. Fine three prong rubber covered steps. Roller rub irons.

GEAR—1⅛-inch true sweep dust proof long distance bell collar bike axles, with felt oil pads. Axles are fitted with light straight grain hickory beds, which are cemented and clipped full length, fine oil tempered French pattern open head springs, properly graded and very easy riding. Reaches have channel reach iron full length and are bolted and well braced. Full circle wrought Brewster slotted fifth wheel, one of the best style fifth wheels made. Wrought Bailey body loops clipped to axles. Will furnish wood spring bars, if preferred. Bradley quick shifting shaft couplers, which are the style couplers used on all high grade work. Regulation high bend bike style shafts made from straight grain selected hickory, full patent leather trimmed and with special heel braces. We furnish pole instead of shafts for $1.00 extra. Pole in addition to shafts, $5.00 extra.

WHEELS—Fine selected straight grain white hickory, ⅞-inch banded hub, 38 inches front and 40 inches rear, with ⅞-inch round edge planished steel tire, bolted between each spoke. Tires are ¼-inch thick and are set hot by hand and not by machine. Felloes have screws through them on each side of every spoke,

which insures absolutely against checking at the spokes. The height of wheels we furnish is correct for this style gear, but we can make any change in height desired. We furnish ¾-inch wheels instead of ⅞-inch, if preferred. Also Sarven patent style, if desired.

TRIMMINGS—Seat is trimmed with fine dark green all wool broadcloth, guaranteed absolutely fast color. Will trim with fine dark blue wool broadcloth or fine whipcord, if preferred. Ends of the seat are pleated and trimmed to match cushion and back, and both cushion and back are upholstered with hair and upholstering springs, and the seat is most comfortable. We can furnish any special colors of broadcloth at a small additional charge. Genuine leather trimmings in dark green, maroon or russet instead of all wool broadcloth for $3.00. Fine full padded patent leather dash. Velvet carpet in bottom of body, or rubber mat if preferred to the carpet. Good rubber boot.

TOP—Fine full leather with best grade leather covered bow sockets, heavy rubber side curtains and storm apron for dash. We furnish with leather quarter top and very best grade steel bow sockets, if desired, for $7.00 less than with leather top. We furnish four bows on any of our tops instead of three without additional charge. Top is always lined with broadcloth to match seat trimmings.

PAINTING—The body is black; gear, New York red, correctly striped. We will furnish Brewster green gear or make any changes in painting desired. Our painting is all fully guaranteed. For system of painting, see page 5.

101

The above cut shows front view of No. 986 showing that the cushion and back are upholstered just the same as regular seat and not made divided as the back of the seat shows. Top on No. 986 can be easily removed if an open vehicle is desired, as cut shows.

No. 986—FINE FULL LEATHER TOP BUGGY WITH LEATHER COVERED BOWS AND BIKE AXLES

PRICE
{
Cash with order, with steel tires and shafts....................................$ 83.00
C. O. D., with steel tires and shafts... 85.00
Cash with order, with 1⅛-inch guaranteed cushion tires and shafts............... 103.00
C. O. D., with 1⅛-inch guaranteed cushion tires and shafts...................... 105.00
}

If ⅞-inch guaranteed rubber tires are preferred, deduct $5.00 from the price quoted with cushion tires.

Our No. 986 is one of the most up-to-date style auto seat buggies we are making. It is equipped with our new twin style auto seat. Although the back of this seat is made divided, the front part of the seat is trimmed up the same as the regular style seat and is not made divided. We know our No. 986 is as fine in quality of workmanship and general finish throughout as similar buggies sold by others for fully $30.00 more than our price. We are glad of an opportunity to ship it for examination and approval, with the understanding that it may be returned at our expense if not found perfectly satisfactory.

BODY—Regulation piano box style. The seat is our fine new twin auto design and one of the best style seats made. Back is high and is very comfortable. We use in the construction of both body and seat high grade stock throughout and they are well ironed and braced and guaranteed not to open at the joints, no matter in what climate used. Body is 24 inches wide by 56 inches long, but we will furnish body 22 inches wide, if preferred.

GEAR—1⅛-inch true sweep dust proof long distance bell collar bike axles, with felt oil pads. Axles are fitted with light straight grain hickory beds, which are cemented and clipped full length. Fine oil tempered French pattern open head springs, properly graded and very easy riding. Reaches have channel reach irons full length and they are bolted and well braced. Full circle wrought Brewster slotted fifth wheel, one of the best style fifth wheels made. Wrought Bailey body loops clipped to axles. Will furnish wood spring bars, if preferred. Bradley quick shifting shaft couplers, which are the style couplers used on all high grade work. Regulation high bend bike style shafts made from straight grain selected hickory, full patent leather trimmed and with special heel braces. We furnish pole instead of shafts for $1.00 extra. Pole in addition to shafts, $5.00 extra.

WHEELS—Fine selected straight grain white hickory, ⅞-inch banded hub, 38 inches front and 40 inches rear, with ⅞-inch round edge planished steel tire, bolted between each spoke. Tires are ¼-inch thick and are set hot by hand and not by machine. Felloes have screws through them on each side of every spoke, which insures absolutely against checking at the spokes. The height of wheels we furnish is correct for this style gear, but we

can make any change in height desired. We furnish ¾-inch wheels instead of ⅞-inch, if preferred. Also Sarven patent style if preferred to banded hub.

TRIMMINGS—Seat is trimmed with fine dark green all wool broadcloth, guaranteed fast color. We will trim with fine dark blue wool broadcloth or whipcord, if preferred. The ends of the seat are pleated and trimmed to match cushion and back, and cushion and back are upholstered with hair and upholstering springs. The cushion and back are not made with the divided effect as shown in the back of the seat. They are made in one piece as shown by small cut in corner. We can furnish any special colors of broadcloth trimmings at a small additional charge. Genuine leather trimmings in dark green, maroon or russet instead of broadcloth, $3.00 extra. Fine full padded leather dash. Velvet carpet in bottom of body, or rubber mat if preferred. Rubber boot to cover back part of body.

TOP—Fine full leather with best grade leather covered bow sockets, heavy rubber side curtains and storm apron for dash. We furnish with leather quarter top and very best grade steel bow sockets, if desired, for $7.00 less than with leather top. We furnish four bows on any of our tops instead of three without additional charge. Top is always lined with broadcloth to match seat trimmings.

PAINTING—The body is black; gear, New York red, correctly striped. We will furnish Brewster green gear or make any changes in painting desired. Our painting is all fully guaranteed. For system of painting, see page 5.

The above cut shows No. 988 with fine wire wheels with 1⅛-inch guaranteed cushion tires. Price, cash with order, $100.00. Price, C. O. D., $102.00.

No. 988—FINE LIGHT FULL LEATHER TOP BUGGY
WITH LEATHER COVERED BOWS AND ROMAN BIKE AXLES

PRICE
{
Cash with order, with steel tires and shafts...................................$75.00
C. O. D., with steel tires and shafts.. 77.00
Cash with order, with ⅞-inch guaranteed rubber tires and shafts................... 90.00
C. O. D., with ⅞-inch guaranteed rubber tires and shafts....................... 92.00
}

Our No. 988 is a fine light top buggy made in our best grade throughout and guaranteed as good in quality of workmanship and material as usually sells for $25.00 to $35.00 more than our price. We are glad of an opportunity to ship No. 988 for full examination and approval, and if it is not found all we claim and perfectly satisfactory, it may be returned at our expense.

BODY—Piano box style, 22 inches wide by 56 inches long, with regulation style seat, which is very comfortable. We furnish 24-inch body instead of 22-inch, if preferred, or if a narrower body is wanted than 22-inch we can furnish 20-inch. We use in the construction of both body and seat high grade stock and they are guaranteed not to open at the joints, no matter in what climate used.

GEAR—Is Roman bike style with dust proof bell collar long distance axles, with felt oil pads. They are what are generally known as naked axles as they have wood beds only in the center where the fifth wheel attaches on the front axle and the rear spring on the rear axle. These beds are cemented and clipped to the axles so that when they are smoothed up ready for finishing the axle and the bed are the same as one piece. Oil tempered French pattern open head springs, correctly graded and very easy riding. Full circle wrought Brewster slotted fifth wheel, the style used on all high grade work. Reaches have channel reach iron full length, and they are bolted and well braced. Wrought Bailey body loops clipped to springs. Will furnish with wood bars, if preferred. Bradley quick shifting shaft couplers, which are used on all first class work. Shafts are the regulation high bend bike style made from selected straight grain white hickory. They are full patent leather trimmed and have special heel braces. Pole instead of shafts, $1.00 extra. Pole in addition to shafts, $5.00 extra.

WHEELS—Fine selected straight grain white hickory, ⅞-inch banded hub, 38 inches front and 40 inches rear, with ⅞-inch round edge planished steel tire, bolted between each spoke. Tires are ¼-inch thick and are set hot by hand and not by machine. Felloes have screws through them on each side of every spoke, which insures absolutely against checking at the spokes. The height of wheels we furnish is correct for this style gear, but we can make any change in height desired. We furnish ¾-inch wheels instead of ⅞-inch, if preferred. Also Sarven patent style if desired instead of the banded hub.

TRIMMING—Seat is trimmed with fine dark green all wool broadcloth, guaranteed absolutely fast color. Will trim with fine dark blue wool broadcloth or fine whipcord, if preferred. Ends of the seat are padded and trimmed to match cushion and back, and both cushion and back are upholstered with hair and upholstering springs, and the seat is most comfortable. We can furnish any special colors of broadcloth at a small additional charge. Genuine leather trimmings in dark green, maroon or russet instead of all wool broadcloth for $3.00. Fine full padded patent leather dash. Velvet carpet in bottom of body, or rubber mat if preferred to the carpet. Rubber boot to cover back part of body.

TOP—Fine full leather with best grade leather covered bow sockets, heavy rubber side curtains and storm apron for dash. We furnish with leather quarter top and very best grade steel bow sockets, if desired, for $7.00 less than with leather top. We furnish four bows on any of our top instead of three without additional charge. Top is always lined with broadcloth to match seat trimmings.

PAINTING—The body is black; gear, New York red, correctly striped. We will furnish Brewster green gear or make any changes in painting desired. Our painting is all fully guaranteed. For system of painting, see page 5.

103

The above cut shows No. 990 with our new pattern auto seat and body with full panels in front of seat. Price for this style seat, $2.00 more than with the Stanhope style seat.

No. 990—CUT-UNDER TOP BUGGY WITH ROMAN BIKE GEAR

PRICE
Cash with order, with steel tires and shafts.....................................$68.00
C. O. D., with steel tires and shafts... 70.00
Cash with order, with 7/8-inch guaranteed rubber tires and shafts................... 83.00
C. O. D., with 7/8-inch guaranteed rubber tires and shafts......................... 85.00

If 1 1/8-inch guaranteed cushion tires are preferred, add $5.00 to the price quoted with 7/8-inch solid rubber tires.

Our No. 990 is a very desirable style cut-under top buggy. The body is cut down in front, making it somewhat easier to get into and out of than the full panel front, yet there is enough panel to keep in blankets, etc. We know our No. 990 is as good style and quality of workmanship and material as usually sells for $25.00 more than our price, and we are glad to ship it for examination and approval with the understanding that it may be returned at our expense if not found all that we claim.

BODY—Is one of the best cut-under piano box styles made. The side panels in front of seat are cut down, but there is enough panel left to keep in robes and blankets. Seat is our regular Stanhope style which has good high back and is very comfortable. Both body and seat are made from high grade stock and put together in such a manner that we guarantee them not to open at the joints, no matter in what climate used. There are good heavy steel sill or rocker plates laid in white lead and screwed full length of sills. Body is 23 inches wide and 56 inches long.

GEAR—Axles are Roman bike style with dust proof bell collar long distance spindles, with felt oil pads. These axles are what are known as the naked style axle with only short wood center pieces for attaching fifth wheel in front and the rear spring in the rear. Fine oil tempered French pattern open head springs, very easy riding. Reaches have channel iron full length and they are bolted and well braced. Wrought full circle Brewster slotted fifth wheel, one of the best and strongest fifth wheels made. Bailey body loops clipped to springs. Will furnish wood spring bars if preferred to the Bailey loop. Bradley quick shifting shaft couplers, which is the coupler used on first class work. Regulation bike style shafts made from fine selected hickory, full patent leather trimmed and with steel heel braces. Pole in addition to shafts for $5.00 extra.

WHEELS—Selected straight grain white hickory, 7/8-inch Sarven patent, 38 inches front and 40 inches rear, with 7/8-inch round edge planished steel tire, bolted between each spoke. Tires are 1/4-inch thick and are set hot by hand and not by machine. Felloes have screws through them on each side of every spoke, which insures absolutely against checking at the spokes. The height of

wheels we furnish is correct for this style gear, but we can make any change in height desired. We furnish 3/4-inch wheels instead of 7/8-inch, if preferred. Also banded hub style, if desired, instead of Sarven patent.

TRIMMINGS—Seat is trimmed with dark green all wool broadcloth, guaranteed fast color. Will trim with dark blue broadcloth or fine whipcord, if preferred. The ends of the seat are pleated and trimmed to match cushion and back. There are upholstering springs in both cushion and back, and the seat is very comfortable. We trim the seat with genuine trimming leather in dark green, maroon or russet instead of broadcloth, if desired, for $3.00 extra. We can furnish special colors in broadcloth trimming, if desired, at a small extra charge. Fine full padded wing style dash. Velvet carpet in bottom of body, or rubber mat if preferred to the carpet. Boot to cover back part of body.

TOP—Leather quarter top with heavy rubber side curtains and storm apron for the dash. The top is lined with broadcloth to match trimmings. It is regular with three bows, but we furnish four bows instead of three bows, if preferred, without extra charge. It has curved top joints, and joints and bow sockets are finely enameled. Furnished with full rubber top instead of leather quarter for $2.00 less. Full leather top with the very best leather covered bows and heavy rubber side curtains, $7.00 extra. Full leather top with best enameled steel bow sockets and heavy rubber curtains, $5.50 extra.

PAINTING—Body is plain black; gear, New York red, neatly striped. We will furnish Brewster green gear, correctly striped, or will paint any color you desire. For system of painting, see page 5.

104

The above cut shows No. 992 with fine steel wire wheels and 1⅛-inch guaranteed cushion tires. Price, $25.00 more than with wood wheels and steel tires.

No. 992—TOP BUGGY WITH ROMAN BIKE AXLES AND AUTO SEAT

PRICE
{
Cash with order, with steel tires and shafts.....................................$65.00
C. O. D., with steel tires and shafts.. 67.00
Cash with order, with ⅞-inch guaranteed rubber tires and shafts.................. 80.00
C. O. D., with ⅞-inch guaranteed rubber tires and shafts........................ 82.00
}

If 1⅛-inch guaranteed cushion tires are preferred, add $5.00 to the price quoted with ⅞-inch solid tire.

No. 992 is a light up-to-date top buggy. It is one of the most desirable styles we think we have ever made. It has all the desirable features. The seat is one of the latest pattern auto designs and is roomy and comfortable. Read fully our description of this buggy and compare it with anything similar on the market and you will find our price very low for the high grade quality of our work. We are very glad to send this buggy anywhere for full examination and to be compared with anything sold by other companies at anywhere near our price, and if you do not find our buggy the best value for the money we will take it back at our expense and you will be nothing out. We guarantee, quality of work considered, to save you fully $25.00.

BODY—Is the regulation piano box style, 22 inches wide and 56 inches long. We will furnish 24-inch body, if preferred to the 22-inch. Seat is one of the best auto designs made, and the back is high and the seat is roomy and luxuriously upholstered. Both body and seat are made from high grade thoroughly seasoned body material. They are well ironed and braced and guaranteed not to open at the corners, no matter in what climate they are used. Fine three prong steps. Roller rub irons.

GEAR—Axles are Roman bike style with dust proof bell collar long distance spindles, with felt oil pads. These axles are what are known as the naked style axle with only short wood center pieces for attaching fifth wheel in front and the rear spring in the rear. Fine oil tempered French pattern open head springs, very easy riding. Reaches have channel iron full length and they are bolted and well braced. Wrought full circle Brewster slotted fifth wheel, one of the best and strongest fifth wheels made. Bailey body loops clipped to springs. Will furnish wood spring bars, if preferred to the Bailey loop. Bradley quick shifting shaft couplers, the style used on first class work. Regulation bike style shafts made from fine selected hickory, full patent leather trimmed and with steel heel braces. Pole in addition to shafts for $5.00 extra.

WHEELS—Selected straight grain white hickory, ⅞-inch Sarven patent, 38 inches front and 40 inches rear, with ⅞-inch round edge planished steel tire, bolted between each spoke. Tires are ¼-inch thick and are set hot by hand and not by machine. Felloes have screws through them on each side of every spoke, which insures absolutely against checking at the spokes. The height of wheels we furnish is correct for this style gear, but we can make

any change in height desired. We furnish ¾-inch wheels instead of ⅞-inch, if preferred. Also banded hub style, if desired, instead of Sarven patent.

TRIMMINGS—Seat is trimmed with dark green all wool broadcloth, guaranteed fast color. Will trim with dark blue broadcloth or fine whipcord, if preferred. The ends of the seat are pleated and trimmed to match cushion and back. There are upholstering springs in both cushion and back, and the seat is very comfortable. We trim the seat with genuine trimming leather in dark green, maroon or russet instead of broadcloth, if desired, for $3.00 extra. We can furnish special colors in broadcloth trimming, if desired, at a small extra charge. Fine full padded wing style dash. Velvet carpet in bottom of body, or rubber mat if preferred to the carpet. Boot to cover back part of body.

TOP—Leather quarter top with heavy rubber side curtains and storm apron for dash. The top is lined with broadcloth to match trimmings. It is regular with three bows, but we furnish four bows instead of three, if preferred, without extra charge. It has curved top joints, and joints and bow sockets are finely enameled. Furnished with full rubber top instead of leather quarter for $2.00 less. Full leather top with the very best leather covered bows and heavy rubber side curtains, $7.00 extra. Full leather top with best enameled steel bow sockets and heavy rubber curtains, $5.50 extra.

PAINTING—Body is plain black; gear, New York red, neatly striped. We will furnish Brewster green gear, correctly striped, or will paint any color you desire. For system of painting, see page 5.

105

The above cut shows No. 994 with fine steel wire wheels and 1⅛-inch guaranteed cushion tires. Price, $25.00 more than with wood wheels and steel tires.

No. 994—TOP BUGGY WITH AUTO SEAT AND ROMAN BIKE GEAR

PRICE
{ Cash with order, with steel tires and shafts....................................$62.00
{ C. O. D., with steel tires and shafts.. 64.00
{ Cash with order, with ⅞-inch guaranteed rubber tires and shafts.................. 77.00
{ C. O. D., with ⅞-inch guaranteed rubber tires and shafts........................ 79.00
If 1⅛-inch guaranteed cushion tires are preferred, add $5.00 to the price quoted with ⅞-inch solid rubber tires.

No. 994 is a very desirable style light bike gear buggy. It is equipped with the Roman bike style gear and has one of our best style auto seats. We will gladly ship No. 994 for examination and approval with the understanding that it is to be found highly satisfactory and to be considered as good as usually sells for $25.00 more than our price or we will take it back at our expense. We allow you to be the judge.

BODY—Is regular piano box style, made from high grade stock throughout. Both body and seat are put together in such a manner that we guarantee them not to come apart at the corners, no matter in what climate used. Seat is one of our most popular auto designs. It has good high back and is very comfortable. Body is 22 inches wide and 56 inches long, but we will furnish 24-inch body, if preferred. Three prong steps. Roller rub irons.

GEAR—Axles are Roman bike style with dust proof bell collar long distance spindles, with felt oil pads. These axles are what are known as the naked style axle with only short wood center pieces for attaching fifth wheel in front and the rear spring in the rear. Fine oil tempered French pattern open head springs, very easy riding. Reaches have channel iron full length and they are bolted and well braced. Wrought full circle Brewster slotted fifth wheel, one of the best and strongest fifth wheels made. Bailey body loops clipped to springs. Will furnish wood spring bars, if preferred to the Bailey loop. Bradley quick shifting shaft couplers, the style used on first class work. Regulation bike style shafts made from fine selected hickory, full patent leather trimmed and with steel heel braces. Pole in addition to shafts for $5.00 extra.

WHEELS—Selected straight grain white hickory, ⅞-inch Sarven patent, 38 inches front and 40 inches rear, with ⅞-inch round edge planished steel tire, bolted between each spoke. Tires are ¼-inch thick and are set hot by hand and not by machine. Felloes have screws through them on each side of every spoke, which insures absolutely against checking at the spokes. The height of wheels we furnish is correct for this style gear, but we can make any change in height desired. We furnish ¾-inch wheels instead of ⅞-inch, if preferred. Also banded hub style, if desired, instead of Sarven patent.

TRIMMINGS—Seat is trimmed with dark green all wool broadcloth, guaranteed fast color. Will trim with dark blue broadcloth or fine whipcord, if preferred. The ends of the seat are pleated and trimmed to match cushion and back. There are upholstering springs in both cushion and back, and the seat is very comfortable. We trim the seat with genuine trimming leather in dark green, maroon or russet instead of broadcloth, if desired, for $3.00 extra. We can furnish special colors in broadcloth trimming, if desired, at a small additional charge. Fine patent leather padded dash. Velvet carpet in bottom of body, or rubber mat if preferred to the carpet. Boot to cover back part of body.

TOP—Leather quarter top with heavy rubber side curtains and storm apron for the dash. The top is lined with broadcloth to match trimmings. It is regular with three bows, but we furnish four bows instead of three bows, if preferred, without extra charge. It has curved top joints, and joints and bow sockets are finely enameled. Furnished with full rubber top instead of leather quarter for $2.00 less. Full leather top with the very best leather covered bows and heavy rubber side curtains, $7.00 extra. Full leather top with best enameled steel bow sockets and heavy rubber curtains, $5.50 extra.

PAINTING—Body is plain black; gear, New York red, neatly striped. We will furnish Brewster green gear, correctly striped, or will paint any color you desire. For system of painting, see page 5.

106

The above cut shows No. 996 without top. Top on this buggy is attached to seat with shifting rail and can be easily removed if open vehicle is desired.

No. 996—TOP BUGGY WITH AUTO SEAT AND TRUE SWEEP BIKE GEAR

PRICE {
Cash with order, with steel tires and shafts.....................................$65.00
C. O. D., with steel tires and shafts.. 67.00
Cash with order, with ⅞-inch guaranteed rubber tires and shafts.................. 80.00
C. O. D., with ⅞-inch guaranteed rubber tires and shafts........................ 82.00
}

If 1⅛-inch guaranteed cushion tires are preferred, add $5.00 to the price quoted with ⅞-inch rubber tires.

Our No. 996 is up-to-date in every respect and has all the latest and most desirable features. The seat is one of the latest auto designs and is roomy and comfortable. Read carefully our description of this buggy and compare it with other buggies sold for many dollars more than our price. We are glad to send this buggy anywhere for full examination and to be compared with anything in this line sold by other companies at anywhere near our price, and if you do not find our buggy to be superior in all respects, we will willingly take it back at our expense and you will be nothing out. We guarantee No. 996 to be as good as usually sells for $25.00 to $35.00 more than our price, you to be judge.

BODY—Is regulation piano box style, 24 inches wide and 56 inches long, but we furnish 22-inch body, if preferred to the 24-inch. The seat is one of the finest auto designs made. It has a good extra high back and is roomy and luxuriously upholstered. Both body and seat are made from high grade thoroughly seasoned body materials and are well ironed and braced, and guaranteed not to open at the corners in any climate. Three prong steps. Roller rub irons.

GEAR—1⅛-inch true sweep dust proof bell collar long distance bike style axles, with felt oil pads. Axles are fitted with light wood beds which are cemented and fully clipped to axles. Fine oil tempered French pattern open head springs, very easy riding. Reaches have channel iron full length, and they are bolted and well braced. Wrought full circle Brewster slotted fifth wheel, and one of the best and strongest fifth wheels made. Bailey body loops clipped to springs. Will furnish wood spring bars if preferred to the loop. Bradley quick shifting shaft couplers, the style used on first class work. Regulation bike style shafts made from fine selected hickory, full patent leather trimmed and with steel heel braces. We furnish pole in addition to shafts for $5.00 extra.

WHEELS—Selected straight grain white hickory, ⅞-inch Sarven patent, 33 inches front and 40 inches rear, with ⅞-inch round edge planished steel tire, bolted between each spoke. Tires are ¼-inch thick and are set hot by hand and not by machine. Felloes have screws through them on each side of every spoke, which insures absolutely against checking at the spokes. The height of wheels we furnish is correct for this style gear, but we can make

any change in height desired. We furnish ¾-inch wheels instead of ⅞-inch, if preferred. Also banded hub style, if desired instead of Sarven patent.

TRIMMINGS—Seat is trimmed with dark green all wool broadcloth, guaranteed fast color. Will trim with dark blue broadcloth or fine whipcord, if preferred. The ends of the seat are pleated and trimmed to match cushion and back. There are upholstering springs in both cushion and back, and the seat is very comfortable. We trim the seat with genuine trimming leather in dark green, maroon or russet instead of broadcloth, if desired, for $3.00 extra. We can furnish special colors in broadcloth trimming, if desired, at a small extra charge. Fine full padded wing style dash. Velvet carpet in bottom of body, or rubber mat if preferred. Boot to cover back part of body.

TOP—Leather quarter top with heavy rubber side curtains and storm apron for the dash. The top is lined with broadcloth to match trimmings. It is regular with three bows, but we furnish four bows instead of three, if preferred, without extra charge. It has curved top joints, and joints and bow sockets are finely enameled. Furnished with full rubber top instead of leather quarter for $2.00 less. Full leather top with the very best leather covered bows and heavy rubber side curtains, $7.00 extra. Full leather top with best enameled steel bow sockets and heavy rubber curtains, $5.50 extra.

PAINTING—Body is plain black; gear, New York red, neatly striped. We will furnish Brewster green gear, correctly striped, or will paint any color you desire. For system of painting, see page 5.

The above cut shows No. 998 without the top. Top on No. 998 is attached to the seat with shifting rail and can be easily removed if an open vehicle is desired.

No. 998—TOP BUGGY WITH TRUE SWEEP BIKE AXLES, AUTO SEAT AND SPECIAL PIANO BODY

PRICE
{ Cash with order, with steel tires and shafts.....................................$68.00
C. O. D., with steel tires and shafts... 70.00
Cash with order, with 1⅛-inch guaranteed cushion tires and shafts................. 88.00
C. O. D., with 1⅛-inch guaranteed cushion tires and shafts. .'..................... 90.00

If ⅞-inch guaranteed solid rubber tires are preferred, deduct $5.00 from the price quoted with cushion tires.

Our No. 998 is one of the most desirable style bike gear piano box buggies we are making. It has our new style piano body which is decked over back of the seat as the picture shows, giving it somewhat the appearance of a Stanhope body. The seat is our new pattern auto seat. This buggy has all the latest and most desirable features and is equal in every particular to buggies sold by others for fully $30.00 more than our price. We are glad to ship it for examination and approval with. the distinct understanding that it is to be found all we claim and highly satisfactory or returned at our expense.

BODY—Special piano box style decked over solid back of seat, as illustration shows, 24 inches wide and 56 inches long. 22-inch body, if preferred. The seat is one of the finest auto seat designs we have ever made. The back is extra high and is roomy and luxuriously upholstered. Both body and seat are made from high grade thoroughly seasoned body material and are well ironed and braced and guaranteed not to come apart at the corners, no matter in what climate they are used. Fine three prong steps. Roller rub irons.

GEAR—1⅛-inch true sweep dust proof bell collar long distance bike style axles, with felt oil pads. Axles are fitted with light wood beds, which are cemented and fully clipped to axles. Fine oil tempered French pattern open head springs, very easy riding. Reaches have channel iron full length, and they are bolted and well braced. Wrought circle Brewster slotted fifth wheel, one of the best and strongest fifth wheels made. Bailey body loops clipped to springs. Will furnish wood spring bars, if preferred to the loop. Bradley quick shifting shaft couplers, the style used on first class work. Regulation bike style shafts made from fine selected hickory, full patent leather trimmed and with steel heel braces. We furnish pole in addition to shafts for $5.00 extra.

WHEELS—Selected straight grain white hickory, ⅞-inch Sarven patent, 38 inches front and 40 inches rear, with ⅞-inch round edge planished steel tire, bolted between each spoke. Tires are ¼-inch thick and are set hot by hand and not by machine. Felloes have screws through them on each side of every spoke, which insures absolutely against checking at the spokes. The height of wheels we furnish is correct for this style gear, but we can make

any change in height desired. We furnish ¾-inch wheels instead of ⅞-inch, if preferred. Also banded hub style, if desired instead of the Sarven patent.

TRIMMINGS—Seat is trimmed with dark green all wool broadcloth, guaranteed fast color. Will trim with dark blue broadcloth or fine whipcord, if preferred. The ends of the seat are pleated and trimmed to match the cushion and back. There are upholstering springs in both cushion and back, and the seat is very comfortable. We trim the seat with genuine trimming leather in dark green, maroon or russet instead of broadcloth, if desired, for $3.00 extra. We can furnish special colors in broadcloth trimming, if desired, at a small extra charge. Fine full padded wing style dash. Velvet carpet in bottom of body, or rubber mat if preferred.

TOP—Leather quarter top, with heavy rubber side curtains and storm apron for the dash. The top is lined with broadcloth to match trimmings. It is regular with three bows, but we furnish four bows instead of three, if preferred, without extra charge. It has curved top joints, and joints and bow sockets are finely enameled. Furnished with full rubber top instead of leather quarter for $2.00 less. Full leather top with the very best leather covered bows and heavy rubber side curtains, $7.00 extra. Full leather top with best enameled steel bow sockets and heavy rubber curtains, $5.50 extra.

PAINTING—Body is plain black; gear, New York red, neatly striped. We will furnish Brewster green gear, correctly striped, or will paint any color you desire. For system of painting, see page 5.

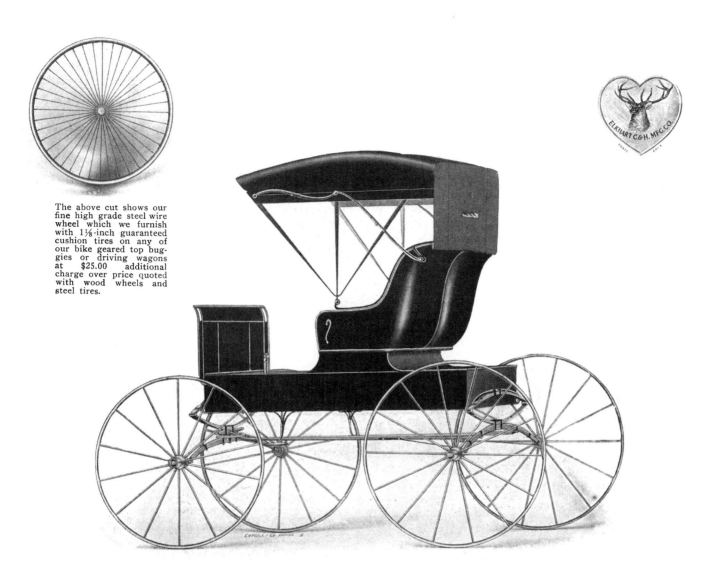

The above cut shows our fine high grade steel wire wheel which we furnish with 1⅛-inch guaranteed cushion tires on any of our bike geared top buggies or driving wagons at $25.00 additional charge over price quoted with wood wheels and steel tires.

No. 1000—TOP BUGGY WITH TWIN AUTO SEAT AND TRUE SWEEP BIKE AXLES

PRICE
- Cash with order, with steel tires and shafts.....................................$66.00
- C. O. D., with steel tires and shafts.. 68.00
- Cash with order, with ⅞-inch guaranteed rubber tires and shafts................... 81.00
- C. O. D., with ⅞-inch guaranteed rubber tires and shafts......................... 83.00

If 1⅛-inch guaranteed cushion tires are preferred, add $5.00 to the price quoted with ⅞-inch solid rubber tires.

No. 1000 is equipped with our twin or divided auto style seat which is one of the latest auto buggy seats made. Although the back is divided as the picture shows the upholstering is made just the same as on the ordinary seat and is not made in two parts. We are very glad to ship our No. 1000 anywhere for examination and approval and if it is not found a highly satisfactory buggy in every way, and does not seem to be as good in quality of workmanship, material and general finish throughout as buggies sold by others for fully $25.00 more than our price, we will take shipment back at our expense.

BODY—Is the regulation piano box style, 22 inches wide and 56 inches long. We will furnish 24-inch body, if preferred to the 22-inch. Seat is one of the best auto designs made. The back is high and the seat is roomy and luxuriously upholstered. Both body and seat are made from high grade thoroughly seasoned body material. They are well ironed and braced and guaranteed not to open at the corners, no matter in what climate they are used. Fine three prong steps. Roller rub irons.

GEAR—1⅛-inch true sweep dust proof bell collar long distance bike axles, with felt oil pads. Axles are fitted with light wood beds, which are cemented and fully clipped to axles. Fine oil tempered French pattern open head springs, very easy riding. Reaches have channel iron full length and they are bolted and well braced. Wrought full circle Brewster slotted fifth wheel, one of the best and strongest fifth wheels made. Bailey body loops clipped to springs. Will furnish wood spring bars, if preferred to the loop. Bradley quick shifting shaft couplers, the style used on first class work. Regulation bike style shafts made from fine selected hickory, full patent leather trimmed and with steel heel braces. We furnish pole in addition to shafts for $5.00 extra.

WHEELS—Selected straight grain white hickory, ⅞-inch Sarven patent, 38 inches front and 40 inches rear, with ⅞-inch round edge planished steel tire, bolted between each spoke. Tires are ¼-inch thick and are set hot by hand and not by machine. Felloes have screws through them on each side of every spoke, which insures absolutely against checking at the spokes. The height of wheels we furnish is correct for this style gear, but we can make any change in height desired. We furnish ¾-inch wheels instead

of ⅞-inch, if preferred. Also banded hub style, if desired, instead of the Sarven patent.

TRIMMINGS—Seat is trimmed with dark green all wool broadcloth, guaranteed fast color. Will trim with dark blue broadcloth or fine whipcord, if preferred. The ends of the seat are pleated and trimmed to match the cushion and back. There are upholstering springs in both cushion and back, and the seat is very comfortable. We trim the seat with genuine trimming leather in dark green, maroon or russet instead of broadcloth, if desired, for $3.00 extra. We can furnish special colors in broadcloth trimming, if desired, at a small extra charge. Fine full padded wing style dash. Velvet carpet in bottom of body, or rubber mat if preferred. Boot to cover back part of body.

TOP—Leather quarter top, with heavy rubber side curtains and storm apron for the dash. The top is lined with broadcloth to match trimmings. It is regular with three bows, but we furnish four bows instead of three, if preferred, without extra charge. It has curved top joints, and joints and bow sockets are finely enameled. Furnished with full rubber top instead of leather quarter for $2.00 less. Full leather top with the very best leather covered bows and heavy rubber side curtains, $7.00 extra. Full leather top with best enameled steel bow sockets and heavy rubber curtains, $5.50 extra.

PAINTING—Body is plain black; gear, New York red, neatly striped. We will furnish Brewster green gear, correctly striped, or will paint any color you desire. For system of painting, see page 5.

The above cut shows No. 1002 without top and with leather seat fenders attached to the top irons on ends of seat thus making a neat open driving wagon. If these seat fenders are not wanted, deduct $2.00 from price quoted.

No. 1002—COMBINATION BUGGY WITH BIKE GEAR AND AUTO SEAT

PRICE
- Cash with order, with steel tires and shafts.....................................$66.00
- C. O. D., with steel tires and shafts... 68.00
- Cash with order, with ⅞-inch guaranteed rubber tires and shafts................... 81.00
- C. O. D., with ⅞-inch guaranteed rubber tires and shafts......................... 83.00

If 1⅛-inch guaranteed cushion tires are preferred, add $5.00 to the price quoted with ⅞-inch solid rubber tires.

Our No. 1002 is one of the most practicable top buggies made. A great many users desire a buggy that can be used without top. When the top is removed there are neat leather seat fenders to attach to the irons on the end of the seat, thus making a neat open driving wagon with patent leather seat fenders. Top is attached to the seat with reliable quick shifters, thus enabling the top to be removed easily and quickly. We know No. 1002 is as good in quality of workmanship and material as usually sells for $25.00 to $35.00 more than our price. We are glad to ship it for examination and approval.

BODY—Is regulation piano box style, 24 inches wide and 56 inches long, but we furnish 22-inch body, if preferred to the 24-inch. The seat is one of the finest auto designs made. It has a good extra high back and is roomy and luxuriously upholstered. Both body and seat are made from high grade thoroughly seasoned body materials and are well ironed and braced, and guaranteed not to open at the corners in any climate. Three prong steps. Roller rub irons.

GEAR—1⅛-inch true sweep dust proof bell collar long distance bike style axles, with felt oil pads. Axles are fitted with light wood beds, which are cemented and full clipped to axles. Fine oil tempered French pattern open head springs, very easy riding. Reaches have channel iron full length and they are bolted and well braced. Wrought full circle Brewster slotted fifth wheel, one of the best and strongest fifth wheels made. Bailey body loops clipped to springs. Will furnish wood spring bars, if preferred to the loop. Bradley quick shifting shaft couplers, the style used on all first class work. Regulation bike style shafts made from fine selected hickory, full patent leather trimmed and with steel heel braces. We furnish pole in addition to shafts for $5.00 extra.

WHEELS—Selected straight grain white hickory, ⅞-inch Sarven patent, 38 inches front and 40 inches rear, with ⅞-inch round edge planished steel tire, bolted between each spoke. Tires are ¼-inch thick and are set hot by hand and not by machine. Felloes have screws through them on each side of every spoke, which insures absolutely against checking at the spokes. The height of wheels we furnish is correct for this style gear, but we can make any change in height desired. We furnish ¾-inch wheels instead of ⅞-inch, if preferred. Also banded hub style, if desired, instead of the Sarven patent.

TRIMMINGS—Seat is trimmed with dark green all wool broadcloth, guaranteed fast color. Will trim with dark blue broadcloth or fine whipcord, if preferred. The ends of the seat are pleated and trimmed to match the cushion and back. There are upholstering springs in both cushion and back, and the seat is very comfortable. We trim the seat with genuine trimming leather in dark green, maroon or russet instead of broadcloth, if desired, for $3.00 extra. We can furnish special colors in broadcloth trimming, if desired, at a small extra charge. Fine full padded wing style dash. Velvet carpet in bottom of body, or rubber mat if preferred. Boot to cover back part of body.

TOP—Leather quarter top, with heavy rubber side curtains and storm apron for the dash. The top is lined with broadcloth to match trimmings. It is regular with three bows, but we furnish four bows instead of three, if preferred, without extra charge. It has curved top joints, and joints and bow sockets are finely enameled. Furnished with full rubber top instead of leather quarter for $2.00 less. Full leather top with the very best leather covered bows and heavy rubber side curtains, $7.00 extra. Full leather top with best enameled steel bow sockets and heavy rubber curtains, $5.50 extra.

PAINTING—Body is plain black; gear, New York red, neatly striped. We will furnish Brewster green gear, correctly striped, or will paint any color you desire. For system of painting, see page 5.

No. 1004—TOP BUGGY WITH NEWPORT SEAT AND BIKE GEAR

PRICE
{
Cash with order, with steel tires and shafts....................................$64.00
C. O. D., with steel tires and shafts... 66.00
Cash with order, with ⅞-inch guaranteed rubber tires and shafts............... 79.00
C. O. D., with ⅞-inch guaranteed rubber tires and shafts...................... 81.00
}

If 1⅛-inch guaranteed cushion tires are preferred, add $5.00 to the price quoted with ⅞-inch solid tires.

No. 1004 is one of the most up-to-date styles we are making. It is equipped with our late Newport style seat which is one of the finest buggy seats on the market. We know No. 1004 is as good in quality of workmanship and general finish throughout as buggies sold by others for $25.00 more than our price. We are glad, at any rate, of an opportunity to ship this buggy for full examination and approval and to be compared with anything sold elsewhere, and if you do not feel you are saving money in buying from us, we will take the shipment back at our expense.

BODY—Regulation piano box style, equipped with our new New-port style seat. Both body and seat are made from high grade stock and put together in such a manner that we guarantee them absolutely not to open at the joints, no matter in what climate used. Body is 24 inches wide by 56 inches long. Will furnish 22-inch body if preferred to the 24-inch.

GEAR—1⅛-inch true sweep dust proof bell collar long distance bike style axles, with felt oil pads. Axles are fitted with light wood beds, which are cemented and fully clipped to axles. Fine oil tempered French pattern open head springs, very easy riding. Reaches have channel iron full length and they are bolted and well braced. Wrought full circle Brewster slotted fifth wheel, one of the best and strongest fifth wheels made. Bailey body loops clipped to springs. Will furnish wood spring bars, if preferred to the loop. Bradley quick shifting shaft couplers, the style used on all first class work. Regulation bike style shafts made from fine selected hickory, full patent leather trimmed and with steel heel braces. We furnish pole in addition to shafts for $5.00 extra.

WHEELS—Selected straight grain white hickory, ⅞-inch Sarven patent, 38 inches front and 40 inches rear, with ⅞-inch round edge planished steel tire, bolted between each spoke. Tires are ¼ inch thick and are set hot by hand and not by machine. Felloes have screws through them on each side of every spoke, which insures absolutely against checking at the spokes. The height of wheels we furnish is correct for this style gear, but we can make any change in height desired. We furnish ¾-inch wheels instead of ⅞-inch, if preferred. Also banded hub style, if desired, instead of the Sarven patent.

TRIMMINGS—Seat is trimmed with dark green all wool broad-cloth, guaranteed fast color. Will trim with dark blue broadcloth or fine whipcord, if preferred. The ends of the seat are pleated and trimmed to match cushion and back. There are upholstering springs in both cushion and back, and the seat is very comfortable. We trim the seat with genuine trimming leather in dark green, maroon or russet instead of broadcloth, if desired, for $3.00 extra. We can furnish special colors in broadcloth trimming, if desired, at a small extra charge. Fine full padded dash. Velvet carpet in bottom of body, or rubber mat if preferred. Boot to cover back part of body.

TOP—Leather quarter top, with heavy rubber side curtains and storm apron for the dash. The top is lined with broadcloth to match trimmings. It is regular with three bows, but we furnish four bows instead of three, if preferred, without extra charge. It has curved top joints, and joints and bow sockets are finely enameled. Furnished with full rubber top instead of leather quarter for $2.00 less. Full leather top with the very best leather covered bows and heavy rubber side curtains, $7.00 extra. Full leather top with best enameled steel bow sockets and heavy rubber curtains, $5.50 extra.

PAINTING—Body is plain black; gear, New York red, neatly striped. We will furnish Brewster green gear, correctly striped, or will paint any color you desire. For system of painting, see page 5.

111

The above cut shows the extra spindle seat we furnish with No. 1006 to be used when the regular buggy seat and top are taken off.

No. 1006—COMBINATION BUGGY WITH STANHOPE SEAT, BIKE GEAR AND EXTRA SPINDLE SEAT

PRICE {
Cash with order, with steel tires and shafts.....................................$70.00
C. O. D., with steel tires and shafts... 72.00
Cash with order, with ⅞-inch guaranteed rubber tires and shafts.................. 85.00
C. O. D., with ⅞-inch guaranteed rubber tires and shafts......................... 87.00
}

No. 1006 is a very popular combination buggy with us, and it is a style that gives the best of satisfaction everywhere. It is equipped with extra stick seat to be used when the Stanhope seat with top is removed. The change in seats is easily and quickly made, as we equip them with patent quick change fasteners. We know No. 1006 is as good in quality of workmanship and material throughout as usually sells for $25.00 to $30.00 more than our price. We are glad to ship it for examination and approval, and if not found very satisfactory and all we claim, it may be returned at our expense.

BODY—Regular piano box style, 22 inches wide and 56 inches long. We will furnish body 24 inches wide, if preferred. Regular buggy seat is our Stanhope style, and the extra driving wagon seat is our regular spindle seat used on open driving wagons. Body and seats are made from high grade stock and guaranteed absolutely not to open at the joints.

GEAR—1⅛-inch true sweep dust proof bell collar long distance bike style axles, with felt oil pads. Axles are fitted with light wood beds, which are cemented and fully clipped to axles. Fine oil tempered French pattern open head springs, very easy riding. Reaches have channel iron full length and they are bolted and well braced. Wrought full circle Brewster slotted fifth wheel, one of the best and strongest fifth wheels made. Bailey body loops clipped to springs. Will furnish wood spring bars, if preferred to the loop. Bradley quick shifting shaft couplers, the style used on all first class work. Regulation bike style shafts made from fine selected hickory, full patent leather trimmed and with steel heel braces. We furnish pole in addition to shafts for $5.00 extra.

WHEELS—Selected straight grain white hickory, ⅞-inch Sarven patent, 38 inches front and 40 inches rear, with ⅞-inch round edge planished steel tire, bolted between each spoke. Tires are ¼-inch thick and are set hot by hand and not by machine. Felloes have screws through them on each side of every spoke, which insures absolutely against checking at the spokes. The height of wheels we furnish is correct for this style gear, but we can make any change in height desired. We furnish ¾-inch wheels instead of ⅞ inch, if preferred. Also banded hub style, if desired, instead of the Sarven patent.

TRIMMINGS—Regular buggy seat is trimmed with dark green all wool broadcloth, guaranteed fast color. We will trim with dark blue broadcloth or whipcord, if preferred. The ends of the seat are pleated and trimmed to match cushion and back. There are upholstering springs in both cushion and back, and the seat is very comfortable. The extra spindle seat is regularly trimmed with whipcord, but we will trim with dark green or blue broadcloth, if preferred. There are springs in cushion. We trim the regular buggy seat with genuine leather in dark green, maroon or russet for $3.00 extra, and the spindle seat, $1.50 extra. Velvet carpet or rubber mat in bottom of body. Padded dash. Rubber boot over back part of body.

TOP—Leather quarter top, with heavy rubber side curtains and storm apron for the dash. The top is lined with broadcloth to match trimmings. It is regular with three bows, but we furnish four bows instead of three, if preferred, without extra charge. It has curved top joints, and joints and bow sockets are finely enameled. Furnished with full rubber top instead of leather quarter for $2.00 less. Full leather top with the very best leather covered bows and heavy rubber side curtains, $7.00 extra. Full leather top with best enameled steel bow sockets and heavy rubber curtains, $5.50 extra.

PAINTING—Body is plain black; gear, New York red, neatly striped. We will furnish Brewster green gear, correctly striped, or will paint any color you desire. For system of painting, see page 5.

112

The above cut shows No. 1008 with top removed and fenders attached to ends of seat thus making a neat open driving wagon. If these fenders are not wanted, deduct $2.00.

No. 1008—TOP BUGGY WITH QUICK SHIFTING TOP, BIKE GEAR AND EXTRA SEAT FENDERS

PRICE
{
Cash with order, with steel tires and shafts......................................$66.00
C. O. D., with steel tires and shafts.. 68.00
Cash with order, with ⅞-inch guaranteed rubber tires and shafts.................... 81.00
C. O. D., with ⅞-inch guaranteed rubber tires and shafts........................ 83.00
}

No. 1008 is a very desirable top buggy, because it practically combines two buggies in one. The top on No. 1008 is attached to the seat by shifting rail and has quick shifting fasteners, and when removed there are extra seat fenders to attach to the irons on the ends of the seat, thus making a very neat open driving wagon. No. 1008 is one of our most popular style buggies and we guarantee it equal in quality of workmanship and material, also general finish throughout, to similar buggies sold by others for $25.00 to $30.00 more than our price. We are glad to ship it for examination and approval, and allow you to be the judge.

BODY—Is regulation piano box style, 24 inches wide and 56 inches long, but we furnish 22-inch body if preferred to the 24-inch. The seat is Stanhope style. It has a good extra high back and is roomy and luxuriously upholstered. Both body and seat are made from high grade thoroughly seasoned body materials and are well ironed and braced, and guaranteed not to open at the corners in any climate. Three prong steps. Roller rub irons.

GEAR—1⅛-inch true sweep dust proof bell collar long distance bike style axles, with felt oil pads. Axles are fitted with light wood beds, which are cemented and fully clipped to axles. Fine oil tempered French pattern open head springs, very easy riding. Reaches have channel iron full length and they are bolted and well braced. Full circle wrought Brewster slotted fifth wheel, one of the best and strongest fifth wheels made. Bradley body loops clipped to springs. Will furnish wood spring bars, if preferred to the loop. Bradley quick shifting shaft couplers, the style used on all first class work. Regulation bike style shafts made from fine selected hickory, full patent leather trimmed and with steel heel braces. We furnish pole in addition to shafts for $5.00 extra.

WHEELS—Selected straight grain white hickory, ⅞-inch Sarven patent, 38 inches front and 40 inches rear, with ⅞ inch round edge planished steel tire, bolted between each spoke. Tires are ¼-inch thick and are set hot by hand and not by machine. Felloes have screws through them on each side of every spoke, which insures absolutely against checking at the spokes. The height of wheels we furnish is correct for this style gear, but we can make any change in height desired. We furnish ¾-inch wheels instead

of ⅞-inch, if preferred. Also banded hub style, if desired, instead of the Sarven patent.

TRIMMINGS—Seat is trimmed with dark green all wool broadcloth, guaranteed fast color. Will trim with dark blue broadcloth or fine whipcord, if preferred. The ends of the seat are pleated and trimmed to match cushion and back. There are upholstering springs in both cushion and back, and the seat is very comfortable. We trim the seat with genuine trimming leather in dark green, maroon or russet instead of broadcloth, if desired, for $3.00 extra. We will furnish special colors in broadcloth trimming, if desired, at a small extra charge. Fine full padded wing style dash. Velvet carpet in bottom of body, or rubber mat if preferred. Boot to cover back part of body.

TOP—Leather quarter top, with heavy rubber side curtains and storm apron for the dash. The top is lined with broadcloth to match trimmings. It is regular with three bows, but we furnish four bows instead of three, if preferred, without extra charge. It has curved top joints, and joints and bow sockets are finely enameled. Furnished with full rubber top instead of leather quarter for $2.00 less. Full leather top with the very best leather covered bows and heavy rubber side curtains, $7.00 extra. Full leather top with best enameled steel bow sockets and heavy rubber curtains, $5.50 extra.

PAINTING—Body is plain black; gear, New York red, neatly striped. We will furnish Brewster green gear, correctly striped, or will paint any color you desire. For system of painting, see page 5.

113

The above cut shows No. 110 seat, only made with twin style back. The upholstering on the back is just the same as on the regular seat. We furnish this twin style seat when wanted without additional charge.

No. 1010—TOP BUGGY WITH FANCY TRIMMINGS AND PAINTING AND ROMAN BIKE AXLES

PRICE {
Cash with order, with steel tires and shafts...............................$68.00
C. O. D., with steel tires and shafts.. 70.00
Cash with order, with ⅞-inch guaranteed rubber tires and shafts.............. 83.00
C. O. D., with ⅞-inch guaranteed rubber tires and shafts.................... 85.00
}

Our No. 1010 is one of the best fancy painted and trimmed top buggies made. The seat is neatly upholstered and the top is lined to match seat trimmings. This buggy is light running and very comfortable riding. It is as good in quality of workmanship and material throughout as similar styles sold by others for fully $25.00 more than our price. We are glad to ship it for full examination and approval.

BODY—Is regulation piano box style, 22 inches wide and 56 inches long. We will furnish 24-inch body if preferred to the 22-inch. The seat is one of the finest auto designs made. It has a good extra high back and is upholstered in such a manner that it is very comfortable. Both body and seat are made from high grade thoroughly seasoned body material and are well ironed and braced and are guaranteed not to open at the corners, no matter in what climate they are used. Fine three prong steps. Roller rub irons.

GEAR—Axles are Roman bike style with dust proof bell collar long distance spindles, with felt oil pads. These axles are what is known as the naked style axle with only short wood center pieces for attaching fifth wheel in front and the rear spring in the rear. Fine oil tempered French pattern open head springs, very easy riding. Reaches have channel iron full length and they are bolted and well braced. Wrought full circle Brewster slotted fifth wheel, one of the best and strongest fifth wheels made. Bailey body loops clipped to springs. Will furnish wood spring bars, if preferred to the Bailey loop. Bradley quick shifting shaft couplers, the style used on all first class work. Regulation bike style shafts made from fine selected hickory, full patent leather trimmed and with steel heel braces. Pole in addition to shafts, $5.00 extra.

WHEELS—Selected straight grain white hickory, ⅞-inch Sarven patent, 38 inches front and 40 inches rear, with ⅞ inch round edge planished steel tire, bolted between each spoke. Tires are ¼-inch thick and are set hot by hand and not by machine. Felloes have screws through them on each side of every spoke, which insures absolutely against checking at the spokes. The height of

wheels we furnish is correct for this style gear, but we can make any change in height desired. We furnish ¾-inch wheels instead of ⅞-inch, if preferred. Also banded hub style, if desired instead of Sarven patent.

TRIMMINGS—Seat is trimmed in a combination of red plush, dark green wool broadcloth and maroon trimming leather. The center part of the back and the cushion are dark green wool broadcloth, the smooth part of the back is red plush, and the roll around the back of the seat and the facing on the cushion are maroon leather. We will trim the seat entirely with leather in maroon or tan color or dark green, if preferred, for $3.00 additional charge. Cushion and back are both upholstered with fine upholstering springs. The ends of the seat are pleated and trimmed to match cushion and back. There are nickel top prop nuts on top and nickel point bands on the hubs of the wheels. Dash is fine padded wing style. Good rubber boot over back part of body. Velvet carpet in bottom of body, or rubber mat if preferred.

TOP—Leather quarter top, with good rubber side curtains and storm apron. We will furnish full leather top with leather covered bows, if preferred, for $7.00 additional charge. We also furnish four bow top, if preferred to the three bow. There are arm straps attached to the top, as shown in picture, also small, neat mirrors in the back stays, and the back stays are fancy stitched, as picture shows.

PAINTING—The body is black, finely striped; gear, New York red, correctly striped. We will furnish Brewster green gear or make any changes in painting desired. Our painting is all fully guaranteed. For system of painting, see page 5.

114

The above cut shows our fine high grade steel wire wheel which we furnish with 1⅛-inch guaranteed cushion tires on any of our bike gear top buggies or driving wagons for $25.00 additional charge over prices quoted with wood wheels and steel tires.

No. 1012—FANCY PAINTED AND TRIMMED TOP BUGGY
WITH TRUE SWEEP BIKE AXLES

PRICE
{ Cash with order, with steel tires and shafts.....................................$70.00
{ C. O. D., with steel tires and shafts.. 72.00
{ Cash with order, with ⅞-inch guaranteed rubber tires and shafts.................. 85.00
{ C. O. D., with ⅞-inch guaranteed rubber tires and shafts........................ 87.00

If 1⅛-inch cushion tires are preferred, add $5.00 to the price quoted with ⅞-inch solid rubber tires.

No. 1012 is a very desirable style fancy painted and trimmed buggy. The combination of colors used in painting and trimming this buggy are good, and the buggy is very neat and attractive in appearance. It is light running and most comfortable riding. We are glad to ship No. 1012 for examination and approval with the understanding that it is to be found all we claim and a very satisfactory vehicle or it may be returned at our expense both ways. We guarantee it as good as usually sells for $25.00 more than our price.

BODY—Is regulation piano box style, 22 inches wide and 56 inches long, but we furnish 24-inch body if preferred to the 22 inch. The seat is one of the finest auto designs made. It has a good extra high back and is roomy and luxuriously upholstered. Both body and seat are made from high grade thoroughly seasoned body materials and are well ironed and braced, and guaranteed not to open at the corners in any climate. Three prong steps. Roller rub irons.

GEAR—1⅛-inch true sweep dust proof bell collar long distance bike style axles, with felt oil pads. Axles are fitted with light wood beds, which are cemented and fully clipped to axles. Fine oil tempered French pattern open head springs, very easy riding. Reaches have channel iron full length and they are bolted and well braced. Wrought full circle Brewster slotted fifth wheel, one of the best and strongest fifth wheels made. Bailey body loops clipped to springs. Will furnish wood spring bars if preferred to the loop. Bradley quick shifting shaft couplers, the style used on first class work. Regulation bike style shafts made from fine selected hickory, full patent leather trimmed and with steel heel braces. We furnish pole in addition to shafts for $5.00 extra.

WHEELS—Selected straight grain white hickory, ⅞-inch Sarven patent, 38 inches front and 40 inches rear, with ⅞-inch round edge planished steel tire, bolted between each spoke. Tires are ¼-inch thick and are set hot by hand and not by machine. Felloes have screws through them on each side of every spoke, which insures absolutely against checking at the spokes. The height of wheels we furnish is correct for this style gear, but we can make

any change in height desired. We furnish ¾ inch wheels instead of ⅞-inch, if preferred. Also banded hub style, if desired, instead of the Sarven patent.

TRIMMINGS—Seat is trimmed in a combination of red plush, dark green wool broadcloth and maroon trimming leather. The center part of the back and the cushion are dark green wool broadcloth, the smooth part of the back is red plush and the roll around the back of the seat and the facing on the cushion are maroon leather. We will trim the seat entirely with leather in maroon or tan color or dark green, if preferred, for $3.00 additional charge. Cushion and back are both upholstered with fine upholstering springs. The ends of the seat are pleated and trimmed to match cushion and back. There are nickel top prop nuts on top and nickel point bands on the hubs of the wheels. Dash is fine padded wing style. Good rubber boot over back part of body. Velvet carpet in bottom of body, or rubber mat if preferred.

TOP—Leather quarter top, with good rubber side curtains and storm apron. We will furnish full leather top with leather covered bows, if preferred, for $7.00 additional charge. We also furnish four bow top if preferred to the three bow. There are arm straps attached to the top, as shown in picture, also small, neat mirrors in the back stays, and the back stays are fancy stitched, as picture shows.

PAINTING—Body is black, finely striped; gear, New York red, neatly striped. We will furnish Brewster green gear, correctly striped, or will paint any color you desire. For system of painting, see page 5.

The above cut shows No. 1014 with end spring gear. Price, same as with Concord gear.

No. 1014—FINE CONCORD BUSINESS OR PLEASURE BUGGY

PRICE
{
Cash with order, with steel tires and shafts.....................................$ 90.00
C. O. D., with steel tires and shafts... 92.00
Cash with order, with ⅞-inch guaranteed rubber tires and shafts.................. 105.00
C. O. D., with ⅞-inch guaranteed rubber tires and shafts....................... 107.00
}
If 1-inch guaranteed rubber tires are preferred, add $2.50 to the price quoted for ⅞-inch.

Our No. 1014 is one of the most desirable style Concord buggies we have ever made. It is a light running, comfortable riding vehicle, and the body hangs low, making it easy to get into and out of. We know this buggy is as good as usually sells for $25.00 to $30.00 more than our price. We are glad to ship it for full examination and approval, with the understanding that it may be returned at our expense if not found highly satisfactory and all we claim.

BODY—Is one of the best style bodies for a business buggy that is made. The seat is roomy and very comfortable. We use in the construction of body and seat high grade stock throughout. There are steel sill or rocker plates laid in white lead and screwed full length of sills.

GEAR—Regulation triple reach Concord style with 1⅛-inch dust proof bell collar long distance axles, with felt oil pads. Axles are equipped with straight grain hickory beds, which are cemented and clipped full length of axles. Oil tempered regulation Concord springs, which are hung on equalizers front and rear. Reaches are straight grain white hickory, well ironed and braced. Regulation Concord style fifth wheel. Bradley quick change shaft couplers, which are always used on high grade work. Regular Concord style shafts made from fine selected straight grain hickory, full patent leather trimmed and with special heel braces. Pole instead of shafts, $1.00 extra. Pole in addition to shafts, $5.00 extra. We furnish this wagon with 1⅛ inch axles and wheels, if extra heavy gear is desired, for $5.00 additional charge.

WHEELS—Selected straight grain white hickory, ⅞-inch Sarven patent, with ⅞-inch round edge planished steel tire, bolted between each spoke. They are 40 inches front and 44 inches rear. This is the regulation height for this style vehicle, but we will change the height of wheels, if desired. Our tires are set hot by hand and not by machine. All felloes have screws through them

on each side of every spoke, which insures them against checking at the spokes. We will furnish banded hub style wheels, if preferred. We also furnish 1-inch tread instead of ⅞-inch, if preferred.

TRIMMINGS—Seat is trimmed with fine dark green heavy all wool broadcloth, or will trim with dark blue wool broadcloth or all wool whipcord, if preferred. The ends of the seat are pleated and trimmed to match cushion and back, and both cushion and back are upholstered with hair and fine upholstering springs. We furnish special colors in broadcloth trimmings, if desired, at a small additional charge. Fine genuine leather trimmings in dark green, maroon or russet color instead of broadcloth, $3.00 extra. Fine full padded dash. Velvet carpet in bottom of body, or rubber mat if preferred to the carpet.

TOP—Fine leather quarter, with heavy rubber side curtains and storm apron. Bow sockets are the best enamel sockets made, and the joints are the best enamel joints we can buy. Top is lined with dark green all wool broadcloth to match seat trimmings. We will furnish full leather top with best grade leather covered bow sockets and with heavy rubber side curtains for $10.00 extra charge. Deduct $15.00 if ordered without top.

PAINTING—Body is finely finished in black, correctly striped; gear, New York red, properly striped. We will make any changes in color of painting desired. For system of painting, see page 5.

The above cut shows No. 1018 with top and boot. Additional charge for leather quarter top, $15.00. Special Concord boot, as shown, $1.50.

No. 1018—FINE OPEN CONCORD WAGON

PRICE
- Cash with order, with steel tires and shafts......................................$60.00
- C. O. D., with steel tires and shafts.. 62.00
- Cash with order, with ⅞-inch guaranteed rubber tires and shafts.................. 75.00
- C. O. D., with ⅞-inch guaranteed rubber tires and shafts......................... 77.00

No. 1018 is a very desirable style Concord wagon. It is hung on regulation triple reach Concord gear which is a very popular gear. We know our No. 1018 is as good in quality of workmanship and material throughout as usually sells for $25.00 to $35.00 more than our price. We are glad to ship it for examination and approval.

BODY—Is regulation Concord style and one of the most popular Concord bodies made. Seat is our half phaeton style, and both body and seat are made from high grade thoroughly seasoned stock.

GEAR—Axles, 1⅛-inch, dust proof bell collar long distance, with felt oil pads. It is the regulation Concord equipment, with triple reaches which are well ironed and braced. Axles have light straight grain hickory beds, which are cemented and clipped full length. Fine oil tempered regulation Concord springs, hung on equalizers front and rear. Regulation Concord fifth wheel. Bradley quick shifting shaft couplers, style used on all high grade work. Shafts are regulation Concord style, made from select straight grain hickory, full patent leather trimmed and with heel braces. We furnish pole instead of shafts for $1.00 extra. Pole in addition to shafts, $5.00 extra.

WHEELS—Selected straight grain white hickory, ⅞-inch Sarven patent, 40 inches front and 44 inches rear, with ⅞ inch round edge planished steel tire, bolted between each spoke. Tires are ¼-inch thick and are set hot by hand and not by machine. Felloes have screws through them on each side of every spoke, which insures absolutely against checking at the spokes. The height of wheels we furnish is correct for this style gear, but we can make any change in height desired. We furnish banded hub style, if desired, instead of the Sarven patent.

TRIMMINGS—Seat is trimmed with good, soft genuine trimming leather, and both cushion and back are upholstered with hair and fine upholstering springs. We will trim the seat with dark green or blue all wool broadcloth or fine whipcord for $2.00 less than regular price. The ends of the seat are trimmed to match cushion and back. Full padded dash. Velvet carpet in bottom, or rubber mat. We equip No. 1018 with fine leather quarter top for $15.00 additional charge.

PAINTING—The body is black; gear, New York red, correctly striped. We will furnish Brewster green gear, or make any changes in painting desired. Our painting is all fully guaranteed. For system of painting, see page 5.

The above cut shows No. 1020 with what is known as the California Punt style body. Price, same as No. 1020.

No. 1020—FINE CONCORD WAGON

PRICE
Cash with order, with steel tires and shafts......................................$60.00
C. O. D., with steel tires and shafts.. 62.00
Cash with order, with ⅞-inch guaranteed rubber tires and shafts.................. 75.00
C. O. D., with ⅞-inch guaranteed rubber tires and shafts........................ 77.00

No. 1020 is one of the best Concord wagons made. It has the regulation style body with Concord seat risers as picture shows. It is the same in style and as good in quality of workmanship and material throughout as regulation Concords sold by others for fully $30.00 more than our price. We are glad to ship No. 1020 for examination and approval, and if it is not found all we claim and highly satisfactory, it may be returned at our expense both ways.

BODY—Is regulation Concord style and one of the most popular Concord bodies made. Seat is our half phaeton style and both body and seat are made from high grade thoroughly seasoned stock.

GEAR—Axles, 1¹⁄₁₆-inch, dust proof bell collar long distance, with felt oil pads. It is the regulation Concord equipment, with triple reaches which are well ironed and braced. Axles have light straight grain hickory beds, which are cemented and clipped full length. Fine oil tempered regulation Concord springs, hung on equalizers front and rear. Regulation Concord fifth wheel. Bradley quick shifting shaft couplers, style used on all high grade work. Shafts are regulation Concord style, made from select straight grain hickory, full patent leather trimmed and with heel braces. We furnish pole instead of shafts for $1.00 extra. Pole in addition to shafts, $5.00 extra.

WHEELS—Selected straight grain white hickory, ⅞-inch Sarven patent, 40 inches front and 44 inches rear, with ⅞ inch round edge planished steel tire, bolted between each spoke. Tires are ¼-inch

thick and are set hot by hand and not by machine. Felloes have screws through them on each side of every spoke, which insures absolutely against checking at the spokes. The height of wheels we furnish is correct for this style gear, but we can make any change in height desired. We furnish banded hub style, if desired, instead of Sarven patent.

TRIMMINGS—Seat is trimmed with good, soft genuine trimming leather, and both cushion and back are upholstered with hair and fine upholstering springs. We will trim the seat with dark green or blue all wool broadcloth or fine whipcord for $2.00 less than regular price. The ends of seat are trimmed to match cushion and back. Full padded dash. Velvet carpet in bottom, or rubber mat. We equip No. 1020 with fine leather quarter top for $15.00 additional charge.

PAINTING—The body is black; gear, New York red, correctly striped. We will make any changes in painting desired. Our painting is all fully guaranteed. For system of painting, see page 5.

The above cut shows No. 1022 with cut-under body with full side panels in front of seat and with spindle seat with leather seat fenders. Price with this style body and seat, same as below.

No. 1022—FINE CUT-UNDER DRIVING WAGON WITH BIKE GEAR, WIRE WHEELS AND 1⅛-INCH CUSHION TIRES

PRICE
{ Cash with order, with 1⅛-inch guaranteed cushion tires and shafts.................$95.00
C. O. D., with 1⅛-inch guaranteed cushion tires and sha.ts....................... 97.00
Ball bearing axles instead of long distance axles, extra......................... 10.00 }

Our No. 1022 is one of the finest and most up-to-date driving wagons made. It is high grade in quality of workmanship and material, and guaranteed as good as usually sells for $30.00 to $35.00 more than our price. We are very glad to ship this wagon for full examination and approval with the understanding that it is to be found all we claim and perfectly satisfactory or returned at our expense.

BODY—Is one of the best cut-under styles made. Seat is our Newport design and very roomy and comfortable. Both body and seat are made of high grade stock and put together in such a manner that we guarantee them not to come apart, no matter in what climate used. There are steel sill or rocker plates laid in white lead and screwed full length of sills and over wheel house. Body is 23 inches wide and 56 inches long. Rubber covered steps. Roller rub irons.

GEAR—Axles are Roman bike style with dust proof bell collar long distance spindles, with felt oil pads. These axles are what is known as the naked style axle with only short wood center pieces for attaching fifth wheel in front and the rear spring in the rear. Fine oil tempered French pattern open head springs, very easy riding. Reaches have channel iron full length and they are bolted and well braced. Full circle wrought Brewster slotted fifth wheel, the style used on all high grade work. Bailey body loops clipped to springs. Will furnish wood spring bars if preferred to the Bailey loop. Bradley quick shifting shaft couplers, style used on all first class work. Regulation bike style shafts made from fine selected hickory, full patent leather trimmed and with steel heel braces. Pole in addition to shafts for $5.00 extra.

WHEELS—We use the finest grade wire wheels manufactured. They are equipped with 1⅛-inch channel for 1⅛-inch cushion

tires. The regular axle nut is covered by an outside nickel axle cap which screws into the hub of the wheel. Wheels are equipped with 1⅛ inch high grade guaranteed cushion tires.

TRIMMINGS—Seat is trimmed with fine all wool whipcord, and cushion and back are upholstered with hair and fine upholstering springs. We will trim the seat with fine dark green or dark blue all wool broadcloth, if preferred. We will trim with dark green, maroon or tan colored genuine trimming leather for $3.00 extra. The ends of seat are pleated and trimmed to match cushion and back. Fine full padded wing dash. Velvet carpet in bottom of body, or rubber mat if preferred.

PAINTING—The best and most durable system known. Each coat is treated properly and given the required length of time to season before another coat is put on. The filler coats are properly rubbed down and color varnish coats and rubbing varnish coats are rubbed down and all surfaces polished so that they are perfectly smooth before the finishing varnish is applied. We use high grade material from the foundation coats to the finishing coat, and we guarantee the painting high grade. The body is black; gear, New York red, correctly striped. We will furnish Brewster green gear or make any changes in painting desired. Our painting is all fully guaranteed.

119

The above cut shows No. 1024 with regular style piano body and Newport seat. Price, $3.00 less than with body decked over back of seat.

The above cut shows No. 1024 with regular style piano body, straight padded dash and spindle seat with leather seat fenders. Price, $3.00 less than No. 1024.

No. 1024—FINE DRIVING WAGON WITH BIKE GEAR, WIRE WHEELS AND 1⅛-INCH CUSHION TIRES

PRICE
{
Cash with order, with 1⅛-inch guaranteed cushion tires and shafts................$93.00
C. O. D., with 1⅛-inch guaranteed cushion tires and shafts....................... 95.00
Ball bearing axles instead of long distance axles, extra.......................... 10.00
}

No. 1024 is one of the best style wire wheel wagons we have ever made. The body is our special piano box style with the back part decked over solid, giving it a Stanhope effect. We know this wagon is as good in quality of workmanship and material throughout as usually sells for fully $30.00 more than our price. We are very glad to send it anywhere for full examination and approval, and if it is not found all we claim and perfectly satisfactory it may be returned at our expense.

BODY—Is our special piano box style, 24 inches wide and 56 inches long. Back part is decked over solid giving it a Stanhope effect. We will furnish 22-inch body if preferred to the 24-inch. The seat is one of the finest auto designs made. It has good extra high back and is upholstered in such a manner that it is very comfortable. Both body and seat are made from high grade thoroughly seasoned body material and are well ironed and braced and guaranteed not to open at the corners, no matter in what climate they are used. Fine three prong rubber covered steps. Roller rub irons.

GEAR—Axles are Roman bike style with dust proof bell collar long distance spindles, with felt oil pads. These axles are what is know as the naked style axle with only short wood center pieces for attaching fifth wheel in front and rear spring in the rear. Fine oil tempered French pattern open head springs, very easy riding. Reaches have channel iron full length and they are bolted and well braced. Full circle wrought Brewster slotted fifth wheel, style used on all high grade work, one of the best and strongest fifth wheels made. Bailey body loops clipped to springs. Will furnish wood spring bars if preferred to the Bailey loop. Bradley quick shifting shaft couplers, style used on all first class work. Regulation bike style shafts made from fine selected hickory, full patent leather trimmed and with steel heel braces. Pole in addition to shafts for $5.00 extra.

WHEELS—We use the finest grade wire wheels manufactured. They are equipped with 1⅛-inch channel for 1⅛-inch cushion tires. The regular axle nut is covered by an outside nickel axle cap which screws into the hub of the wheel. Wheels are equipped with 1⅛ inch high grade guaranteed cushion tires.

TRIMMINGS—Seat is trimmed with fine all wool whipcord, and cushion and back are upholstered with hair and fine upholstering springs. We will trim the seat with fine dark green or dark blue all wool broadcloth, if preferred. We will trim with dark green, maroon or tan colored genuine trimming leather for $3.00 extra. The ends of the seat are pleated and trimmed to match cushion and back. Fine full padded wing dash. Velvet carpet in bottom of body, or rubber mat if preferred.

PAINTING—The best and most durable system. Each coat is treated properly and given the required length of time to season before another coat is put on. The filler coats are properly rubbed down and color varnish coats and rubbing varnish coats are rubbed down and all surfaces polished so that they are perfectly smooth before the finishing varnish is applied. We use high grade material from the foundation coats to the finishing coat, and we guarantee the painting high grade. The body is black; gear, New York red, correctly striped. We will furnish Brewster green gear or make any changes in painting desired. Our painting is all fully guaranteed.

The above cut shows No. 1026 with cut-under style body. Price, complete with lamps and with cut-under body, $5.00 more than with regular body.

No. 1026—FINE BIKE GEAR DRIVING WAGON WITH STANHOPE SEAT AND LAMPS

PRICE
{
Cash with order, with steel tires and shafts.....................................$66.00
C. O. D., with steel tires and shafts... 68.00
Cash with order, with 1⅛-inch guaranteed cushion tires and shafts................ 86.00
C. O. D., with 1⅛-inch guaranteed cushion tires and shafts....................... 88.00
}
If ⅞-inch solid rubber tires are preferred, deduct $5.00 from the price quoted with cushion tires.

No. 1026 is one of our most desirable style bike gear driving wagons. It is made in our high grade quality throughout and we guarantee it is good as usually sells for fully $30.00 more than our price. We are perfectly willing to ship this wagon for full examination and approval, and if it is not found all we claim and satisfactory in every way, it may be returned at our expense.

BODY—Is regulation piano box style, 24 inches wide and 56 inches long. We will furnish 22-inch body if preferred to the 24-inch. The seat is Stanhope style, has extra high back and is upholstered in such a manner that it is very comfortable. Both body and seat are made from high grade thoroughly seasoned body material and are well ironed and braced and guaranteed not to open at the corners, no matter in what climate they are used. Fine three prong rubber covered steps. Roller rub irons.

GEAR—1⅛-inch dust proof bell collar long distance Roman bike style axles, with felt oil pads. Axles are fitted with light wood beds, which are cemented and fully clipped to axles. Fine oil tempered French pattern open head springs, very easy riding. Reaches have channel iron full length and they are bolted and well braced. Full circle wrought Brewster slotted fifth wheel, style used on all high grade work. Bailey body loops clipped to springs. Will furnish wood spring bars if preferred to the loop. Bradley quick shifting shaft couplers, style used on all high grade work. Regulation bike style shafts made from fine selected hickory, full patent leather trimmed and with steel heel braces. We furnish pole in addition to shafts for $5.00 extra.

WHEELS—Fine selected straight grain white hickory, ⅞-inch banded hub, 38 inches front and 40 inches rear, with ⅞-inch round edge planished steel tire, bolted between each spoke. Tires are ¼ inch thick and are set hot by hand and not by machine.

Felloes have screws through them on each side of every spoke, which insures absolutely against checking at the spokes. The height of wheels we furnish is correct for this style gear, but we can make any change in height desired. We furnish ¾-inch wheels instead of ⅞-inch, if preferred. Also Sarven patent style if desired.

TRIMMINGS—Seat is trimmed with fine all wool whipcord, and cushion and back are upholstered with hair and fine upholstering springs. We will trim the seat with fine dark green or dark blue all wool broadcloth, if preferred. We will trim with dark green, maroon or tan colored genuine trimming leather for $3.00 extra. The ends of seat are pleated and trimmed to match cushion and back. Fine full padded wing dash. Velvet carpet in bottom of body, or rubber mat if preferred.

PAINTING—The best and most durable system known. Each coat is treated properly and given the required length of time to season before another coat is put on. The filler coats are properly rubbed down and all surfaces polished so that they are perfectly smooth before the finishing varnish is applied. We use high grade material from the foundation coats to the finishing coat, and we guarantee the painting high grade. The body is black; gear, New York red, correctly striped. We will furnish Brewster green gear or make any changes in painting desired. Our painting is all fully guaranteed.

No. 1028—FINE BIKE GEAR DRIVING WAGON WITH AUTO SEAT

PRICE
{ Cash with order, with steel tires and shafts.....................................**$68.00**
C. O. D., with steel tires and shafts..**70.00**
Cash with order, with 1⅛-inch guaranteed cushion tires and shafts.................**88.00**
C. O. D., with 1⅛-inch guaranteed cushion tires and shafts.......................**90.00**

If ⅞-inch guaranteed solid rubber tires are preferred, deduct $5.00 from the price quoted with cushion tires.

No. 1028 is one of our new designs and one of the best style open driving wagons made. It is made in our high grade quality throughout and is equal in every respect to similar styles sold by others for $25.00 to $35.00 more than our price. We are very glad to ship it for full examination and approval, with the understanding that it is to be found all we claim and perfectly satisfactory or returned at our expense.

BODY—Is regulation piano box style, 24 inches wide and 56 inches long, but we furnish 22-inch body if preferred to the 24-inch. The seat is one of the finest auto designs made. It has good extra high back and is roomy and luxuriously upholstered. Both body and seat are made from high grade thoroughly seasoned body materials and are well ironed and braced, and guaranteed not to open at the corners in any climate. Three prong rubber covered steps. Roller rub irons.

GEAR—1⅛-inch true sweep dust proof bell collar long distance bike style axles, with felt oil pads. Axles are fitted with light wood beds, which are cemented and fully clipped to axles. Fine oil tempered French pattern open head springs, very easy riding. Reaches have channel iron full length and they are bolted and well braced. Full circle wrought Brewster slotted fifth wheel, and one of the best fifth wheels made. Bailey body loops clipped to springs. Will furnish wood spring bars if preferred to the loop. Bradley quick shifting shaft couplers, the style used on all first class work. Regulation bike style shafts made from fine selected hickory, full patent leather trimmed and with steel heel braces. We furnish pole in addition to shafts for $5.00 extra.

WHEELS—Fine selected straight grain white hickory, ⅞-inch banded hub, 38 inches front and 40 inches rear, with ⅞ inch round edge planished steel tire, bolted between each spoke. Tires are ¼-inch thick and are set hot by hand and not by machine.

Felloes have screws through them on each side of every spoke, which insures absolutely against checking at the spokes. The height of wheels we furnish is correct for this style gear, but we can make any change in height desired. We furnish ¾-inch wheels instead of ⅞-inch, if preferred. Also Sarven patent style if desired.

TRIMMINGS—Seat is trimmed with fine all wool whipcord, and cushion and back are upholstered with hair and fine upholstering springs. We will trim the seat with fine dark green or dark blue all wool broadcloth, if preferred. We will trim with dark green, maroon or tan colored genuine trimming leather for $3.00 extra. The ends of seat are pleated and trimmed to match cushion and back. Fine full padded wing dash. Velvet carpet in bottom of body, or rubber mat if preferred. Fine oil burner lamps.

PAINTING—Regular lead and oil system. Each coat of filler, color varnish, etc., is given the necessary length of time to thoroughly dry before tne next coat is applied. The filler coats are rubbed down before the color varnish and rubbing varnish coats are put on. All surfaces are finely polished and are perfectly smooth before the last coats of finishing varnish are put on. We use first class material from the priming coat to the last finishing coat of varnish, and the painting is guaranteed. Body is plain black; gear, New York red, neatly striped. We will furnish Brewster green gear, correctly striped, or will paint any color you desire.

The above cut shows No. 1030 with special piano body with Newport seat, wing style dash and with wire wheels, with 1⅛-inch guaranteed cushion tires. Price, $15.00 more than with ⅞-inch solid rubber tires as listed below.

No. 1030—FINE ROMAN BIKE GEAR SPINDLE SEAT DRIVING WAGON

PRICE
{
Cash with order, with steel tires and shafts.................................$56.00
C. O. D., with steel tires and shafts... 58.00
Cash with order, with ⅞-inch guaranteed rubber tires and shafts...`........... 71.00
C. O. D., with ⅞-inch guaranteed rubber tires and shafts...................... 73.00
}
If 1⅛-inch guaranteed cushion tires are preferred, add $5.00 to the price quoted with ⅞-inch rubber tires.

No. 1030 is our regulation spindle seat driving wagon. It is a very light running wagon and is most comfortable riding. We guarantee it as good in quality of workmanship and general finish throughout as similar wagons sold by others for fully $30.00 more than our price. We are glad of an opportunity to ship this wagon for examination and approval, and if it is not found all we claim and satisfactory in every way, we will take it back at our expense.

BODY—Regular piano box style, 22 inches wide and 56 inches long. We furnish body 20 inches wide or 24 inches, if preferred. Seat is our regular spindle driving wagon seat. It has well shaped high back and is very comfortable. It is equipped with leather seat fenders. Both body and seat are made from high grade stock throughout. Rubber covered steps. Roller rub irons.

GEAR—1⅛-inch dust proof bell collar long distance bike style axles, with felt oil pads. Axles are fitted with light wood beds, which are cemented and fully clipped to axles. Fine oil tempered French pattern open head springs, very easy riding. Reaches have channel iron full length and they are bolted and well braced. Full circle wrought Brewster slotted fifth wheel, style used on all high grade work. Bailey body loops clipped to springs. Will furnish wood springs bars if preferred to the loops. Bradley quick shifting shaft couplers, style used on all first class work. Regulation bike style shafts made from fine selected hickory, full patent leather trimmed and with steel heel braces. We furnish pole in addition to shafts for $5.00 extra.

WHEELS—Fine selected straight grain white hickory, ⅞-inch banded hub, 38 inches front and 40 inches rear, with ⅞ inch round edge planished steel tire, bolted between each spoke. Tires are ¼-inch thick and are set hot by hand and not by machine. Felloes have screws through them on each side of every spoke,

which insures absolutely against checking at the spokes. The height of wheels we furnish is correct for this style gear, but we can make any change in height desired. We furnish ¾-inch wheels instead of ⅞-inch, if preferred. Also Sarven patent style if desired.

TRIMMINGS—Seat is trimmed with fine all wool whipcord, and cushion and back are upholstered with hair and fine upholstering springs. We will trim the seat with fine dark green or dark blue all wool broadcloth, if preferred. We will trim with dark green, maroon or tan colored genuine trimming leather for $3.00 extra. Fine full padded dash. Velvet carpet in bottom of body, or rubber mat if preferred. Fine leather seat fenders.

PAINTING—Regular lead and oil system. Each coat of filler, color varnish, etc., is given the necessary length of time to thoroughly dry before the next coat is applied. The filler coats are rubbed down before the color varnish and rubbing varnish coats are put on. All surfaces are finely polished and are perfectly smooth before the last coats of finishing varnish are put on. We use first class material from the priming coat to the last finishing coat of varnish, and the painting is guaranteed. Body is plain black; gear, New York red, neatly striped. We will furnish Brewster green gear, correctly striped, or will paint any color you desire.

The above cut shows No. 1032 with full spindle seat, with leather seat fenders. Price, same as below.

The above cut shows No. 1032 with straight dash and half spindle seat with leather seat fenders. Price, $1.50 less than below.

No. 1032—CUT-UNDER DRIVING WAGON WITH BIKE GEAR AND AUTO SEAT

PRICE
{
Cash with order, with steel tires and shafts.....................................$53.50
C. O. D., with steel tires and shafts... 55.00
Cash with order, with 1⅛-inch guaranteed cushion tires and shafts................ 73.50
C. O. D., with 1⅛-inch guaranteed cushion tires and shafts...................... 75.00
}

If ⅞-inch guaranteed solid rubber tires are preferred, deduct $5.00 from the price quoted with cushion tires.

No. 1032 is an up-to-date style driving wagon. It has our full panel cut-under piano body and our late style auto seat. We know No. 1032 is as good in quality of workmanship and material as similar wagons sold by others for fully $30.00 more than our price. We are very glad to ship No. 1032 for full examination and approval and it may be returned at our expense if not found highly satisfactory and all we claim.

BODY—Regular cut-under piano box style, 23 inches wide and 56 inches long. Seat is one of our best auto styles. The back is high and it is very comfortable. Both body and seat are made from high grade stock and are put together in such a manner that we guarantee them not to come apart at the joints, no matter in what climate they are used. There are steel sill or rocker plates laid in white lead and screwed full length of sills and over the wheel house. Three prong steps. Roller rub irons.

GEAR—Axles are Roman bike style with dust proof bell collar long distance spindles, with felt oil pads. These axles are what is known as the naked style axle with only short wood center pieces for attaching fifth wheel in front and the rear spring in the rear. Fine oil tempered French pattern open head springs, very easy riding. Reaches have channel iron full length and they are bolted and well braced. Full circle wrought Brewster slotted fifth wheel, one of the best and strongest fifth wheels made. Bailey body loops clipped to springs. Will furnish wood spring bars if preferred to the Bailey loop. Bradley quick shifting shaft couplers, style used on all high grade work. Regulation bike style shafts made from fine selected hickory, full patent leather trimmed and with steel heel braces. Pole in addition to shafts for $5.00 extra.

WHEELS—Fine selected straight grain white hickory, ⅞-inch Sarven patent, 38 inches front and 40 inches rear, with ⅞-inch round edge planished steel tire, bolted between each spoke. Tires are ¼-inch thick and are set hot by hand and not by machine. Felloes have screws through them on each side of every spoke, which insures absolutely against checking at the spokes. The height of wheels we furnish is correct for this style gear, but we can make any change in height desired. We furnish ¾-inch wheels instead of ⅞-inch, if preferred. Also banded hub style if desired instead of Sarven patent.

TRIMMINGS—Seat is trimmed with fine whipcord, but we will trim with dark green or dark blue broadcloth, if all wool broadcloth is preferred to the whipcord. We will trim with any special colors of broadcloth at a small additional charge. The ends of the seat are pleated and trimmed to match cushion and back. There are upholstering springs in both cushion and back and the seat is very comfortable. We will cover cushion, back, seat ends and cushion fall with fine genuine trimming leather for $3.00 additional charge. Fine full padded wing style dash. Velvet carpet in bottom of body, or rubber mat if preferred to the carpet.

PAINTING—The best and most durable system known. Each coat is treated properly and given the required length of time to season before another coat is put on. The filler coats, color varnish and rubbing varnish coats are properly rubbed down and all surfaces polished so that they are perfectly smooth before the finishing varnish is applied. We use high grade material from the foundation coats to the finishing coat, and we guarantee the painting high grade. The body is black; gear, New York red, correctly striped. We will furnish Brewster green gear or make any changes in painting desired. Our painting is all fully guaranteed.

124

The above cut shows No. 1034 with our new auto style seat and wing dash. Price, $3.50 extra for difference in seat and dash.

No. 1034—CUT-UNDER DRIVING WAGON WITH BIKE GEAR AND STANHOPE STYLE SEAT

PRICE
Cash with order, with steel tires and shafts.................................$55.00
C. O. D., with steel tires and shafts.. 56.50
Cash with order, with ⅞-inch guaranteed rubber tires and shafts.............. 70.00
C. O. D., with ⅞-inch guaranteed rubber tires and shafts..................... 71.50
If 1⅛-inch cushion tires are preferred, add $5.00 to the price quoted with ⅞-inch solid rubber tires.

No. 1034 is one of our leaders and a wagon that pleases wherever shipped. It is strictly up-to-date and first class in quality of workmanship and material throughout. We are glad to ship this wagon anywhere for examination and approval with the understanding that it is to be found all we claim and perfectly satisfactory or returned at our expense. We guarantee it as good as usually sells for $25.00 more than our price.

BODY—Is the regulation piano box style, 24 inches wide and 56 inches long, but we furnish 22-inch body if preferred to the 24-inch. The seat is regular Stanhope style. It has a good extra high back and is roomy and luxuriously upholstered. Both body and seat are made from high grade thoroughly seasoned body materials and are well ironed and braced, and guaranteed not to open at the corners in any climate. Three prong steps. Roller rub irons.

GEAR—Axles are Roman bike style with dust proof bell collar long distance spindles, with felt oil pads. These axles are what is known as the naked style axle with only short wood center pieces for attaching fifth wheel in front and the rear spring in the rear. Fine oil tempered French pattern open head springs, very easy riding. Reaches have channel iron full length and they are bolted and well braced. Full circle wrought Brewster slotted fifth wheel, one of the best and strongest fifth wheels made. Bailey body loops clipped to springs. Will furnish wood spring bars if preferred to the Bailey loop. Bradley quick shifting shaft couplers, style used on all first class work. Regulation bike style shafts made from fine selected hickory, full patent leather trimmed and with steel heel braces. Pole in addition to shafts for $5.00 extra.

WHEELS—Fine selected straight grain white hickory, ⅞-inch Sarven patent, 38 inches front and 40 inches rear, with ⅞-inch round edge planished steel tire, bolted between each spoke. Tires are ¼ inch thick and are set hot by hand and not by machine. Felloes have screws through them on each side of every spoke,

which insures absolutely against checking at the spokes. The height of wheels we furnish is correct for this style gear, but we can make any change in height desired. We furnish ¾-inch wheels instead of ⅞-inch, if preferred. Also banded hub style, if desired, instead of the Sarven patent.

TRIMMINGS—Seat is trimmed with fine whipcord, but we will trim with dark green or dark blue broadcloth, if all wool broadcloth is preferred to the whipcord. We will trim with any special colors of broadcloth at a small additional charge. The ends of the seat are pleated and trimmed to match cushion and back. There are upholstering springs in both cushion and back and the seat is very comfortable. We will cover cushion, back, seat ends and cushion fall with fine genuine trimming leather for $3.00 additional charge. Fine full padded dash. Velvet carpet in bottom of body, or rubber mat if preferred to the carpet.

PAINTING—The best and most durable system known. Each coat is treated properly and given the required length of time to season before another coat is put on. The filler coats, color varnish and rubbing varnish coats are properly rubbed down and all surfaces polished so that they are perfectly smooth before the finishing varnish is applied. We use high grade material from the foundation coats to the finishing coat, and we guarantee the painting high grade. The body is black; gear, New York red, correctly striped. We will furnish Brewster green gear or make any changes in painting desired. Our painting is all fully guaranteed.

125

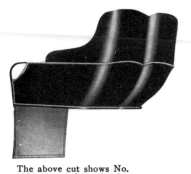

The above cut shows No. 1036 seat, only made with twin style back. The upholstering on the back is just the same as on the regular seat. We furnish this twin style seat when wanted without additional charge.

The above cut shows No. 1036 equipped with basket style seat with seat fenders and straight dash. Price, same as with auto seat.

No. 1036—BIKE WAGON WITH AUTO STYLE SEAT

PRICE
{ Cash with order, with steel tires and shafts.....................................$48.50
C. O. D., with steel tires and shafts.. 50.00
Cash with order, with ⅞-inch guaranteed rubber tires and shafts................. 63.50
C. O. D., with ⅞-inch guaranteed rubber tires and shafts........................ 65.00

If 1⅛-inch guaranteed cushion tires are preferred, add $5.00 to the price quoted with ⅞-inch solid rubber tires.

No. 1036 is one of our best style open driving wagons. This wagon is in every way up-to-date in style, and we guarantee it as good in quality of workmanship and material as usually sells for fully $25.00 more than our price. It is well proportioned, light running and very comfortable riding. We are glad to ship it anywhere for examination and approval, and it may be returned at our expense if not found perfectly satisfactory.

BODY—Is the regulation piano box style, 24 inches wide and 56 inches long, but we furnish 22-inch body if preferred to the 24-inch. The seat is one of the finest auto designs made. It has a good extra high back and is roomy and luxuriously upholstered. Both body and seat are made from high grade thoroughly seasoned body materials and are well ironed and braced, and guaranteed not to open at the corners in any climate. Three prong steps. Roller rub irons.

GEAR—Axles are Roman bike style with dust proof bell collar long distance spindles, with felt oil pads. These axles are what is known as the naked style axle with only short wood center pieces for attaching fifth wheel in front and the rear spring in the rear. Fine oil tempered French pattern open head springs, very easy riding. Reaches have channel iron full length and they are bolted and well braced. Full circle wrought Brewster slotted fifth wheel, one of the best and strongest fifth wheels made. Bailey body loops clipped to springs. Will furnish wood spring bars if preferred to the Bailey loop. Bradley quick shifting shaft couplers, style used on all first class work. Regulation bike style shafts made from fine selected hickory, full patent leather trimmed and with steel heel braces. Pole in addition to shafts for $5.00 extra.

WHEELS—Fine selected straight grain white hickory, ⅞ inch Sarven patent, 38 inches front and 40 inches rear, with ⅞-inch round edge planished steel tire, bolted between each spoke. Tires are ¼-inch thick and are set hot by hand and not by machine. Felloes have screws through them on each side of every spoke, which insures absolutely against checking at the spokes. The height of wheels we furnish is correct for this style gear, but we can make any change in height desired. We furnish ¾-inch wheels instead of ⅞-inch, if preferred. Also banded hub style, if desired, instead of Sarven patent.

TRIMMINGS—Seat is trimmed with fine whipcord, but we will trim with dark green or dark blue broadcloth, if all wool broadcloth is preferred to the whipcord. We will trim with any special colors of broadcloth at a small additional charge. The ends of the seat are pleated and trimmed to match cushion and back. There are upholstering springs in both cushion and back and the seat is very comfortable. We will cover cushion, back, seat ends and cushion fall with fine genuine trimming leather for $3.00 additional charge. Fine full padded wing style dash. Velvet carpet in bottom of body, or rubber mat if preferred to the carpet.

PAINTING—The best and most durable system known. Each coat is treated properly and given the required length of time to season before another coat is put on. The filler coats, color varnish and rubbing varnish coats are properly rubbed down and all surfaces polished so that they are perfectly smooth before the finishing varnish is applied. We use high grade material from the foundation coats to the finishing coat, and we guarantee the painting high grade. The body is black; gear, New York red, correctly striped. We will furnish Brewster green gear or make any changes in painting desired. Our painting is all fully guaranteed.

126

The above cut shows No.
1038 with Stanhope style
seat. Price $2.00 less
than with auto seat.

No. 1038—FINE OPEN DRIVING WAGON WITH TRUE SWEEP BIKE AXLES AND TULIP PATTERN AUTO SEAT

PRICE
{
Cash with order, with steel tires and shafts.....................................$50.50
C. O. D., with steel tires and shafts..52.00
Cash with order, with ⅞-inch guaranteed rubber tires and shafts...................65.50
C. O. D., with ⅞-inch guaranteed rubber tires and shafts.........................67.00
}

If 1⅛-inch guaranteed cushion tires are preferred, add $5.00 to the price quoted with ⅞-inch solid rubber tires.

Our No. 1038 open driving wagon is a style that has all the most desirable features. The seat is one of the latest and best made auto designs on the market. It is roomy and comfortable. We know our No. 1038 is as good style and as fine in quality of workmanship and material throughout as wagons sold by others for fully $25.00 more than our price. If you are in the market for a driving wagon and will read carefully our description of this wagon you will decide that it will be very much to your advantage to order our No. 1038. Remember, we ship for full examination and approval.

BODY—Is the regulation piano box style, 24 inches wide and 56 inches long, but we furnish 22-inch body if preferred to the 24-inch. The seat is one of the finest auto designs made. It has a good extra high back and is roomy and luxuriously upholstered. Both body and seat are made from high grade thoroughly seasoned body materials and are well ironed and braced, and guaranteed not to open at the corners in any climate. Three prong steps. Roller rub irons.

GEAR—1⅛-inch true sweep dust proof bell collar long distance bike style axles, with felt oil pads. Axles are fitted with light wood beds, which are cemented and fully clipped to axles. Fine oil tempered French pattern open head springs, very easy riding. Reaches have channel iron full length and they are bolted and well braced. Full circle wrought Brewster slotted fifth wheel, one of the best and strongest fifth wheels made. Bailey body loops clipped to springs. Will furnish wood spring bars if preferred to the loops. Bradley quick shifting shaft couplers, the style used on all first class work. Regulation bike style shafts made from fine selected hickory, full patent leather trimmed and with steel heel braces. We furnish pole in addition to shafts for $5.00 extra.

WHEELS—Fine selected straight grain white hickory, ⅞-inch Sarven patent, 38 inches front and 40 inches rear, with ⅞-inch round edge planished steel tire, bolted between each spoke. Tires are ¼-inch thick and are set hot by hand and not by machine. Felloes have screws through them on each side of every spoke,

which insures absolutely against checking at the spokes. The height of wheels we furnish is correct for this style gear, but we can make any change in height desired. We furnish ¾ inch wheels instead of ⅞-inch, if preferred. Also banded hub style, if desired, instead of the Sarven patent.

TRIMMINGS—Seat is trimmed with fine whipcord, but we will trim with dark green or dark blue broadcloth, if all wool broadcloth is preferred to the whipcord. We will trim with any special colors of broadcloth at a small additional charge. The ends of the seat are pleated and trimmed to match cushion and back. There are upholstering springs in both cushion and back and the seat is very comfortable. We will cover cushion, back, seat ends and cushion fall with fine genuine trimming leather for $3.00 additional charge. Fine full padded wing style dash. Velvet carpet in bottom of body, or rubber mat if preferred to the carpet.

PAINTING—The best and most durable system known. Each coat is treated properly and given the required length of time to season before another coat is put on. The filler coats, color varnish and rubbing varnish coats are properly rubbed down and all surfaces polished so that they are perfectly smooth before the finishing varnish is applied. We use high grade material from the foundation coats to the finishing coat, and we guarantee the painting high grade. The body is black; gear, New York red, correctly striped. We will furnish Brewster green gear or make any changes in painting desired. Our painting is all fully guaranteed.

127

The above cut shows No. 1040 with fine steel wire w h e e l g e a r and 1⅛-inch guaranteed cushion tires. Extra charge for cushion tires and wire wheels on any of our bike gear driving wagons over the price quoted with steel tires and wood wheels, $25.00.

No. 1040—DRIVING WAGON WITH BIKE GEAR AND TWIN AUTO SEAT

PRICE
Cash with order, with steel tires and shafts...................................$51.50
C. O. D., with steel tires and shafts.. 53.00
Cash with order, with ⅞-inch guaranteed rubber tires and shafts.............. 66.50
C. O. D., with ⅞-inch guaranteed rubber tires and shafts...................... 68.00
If 1⅛-inch guaranteed cushion tires are preferred, add $5.00 to the price quoted with ⅞-inch rubber tires.

No. 1040 is one of our latest style open driving wagons. It is equipped with our new twin style auto seat. We know this wagon is as good in quality of workmanship and material throughout as usually sells for $25.00 to $30.00 more than our price. We are perfectly willing to ship it anywhere for examination and approval, and if it is not found all we claim and highly satisfactory it may be returned at our expense.

BODY—Regulation piano box style, 24 inches wide and 56 inches long. We furnish body 22 inches wide if preferred. Seat is our new twin auto style and is roomy and comfortable. Both body and seat are made from high grade thoroughly seasoned stock and are well ironed and braced and guaranteed not to open at the corners, no matter in what climate used. Three prong steps. Roller rub irons.

GEAR—1⅛-inch true sweep dust proof bell collar long distance bike style axles, with felt oil pads. Axles are fitted with light wood beds, which are cemented and fully clipped to axles. Fine oil tempered French pattern open head springs, very easy riding. Reaches have channel iron full length and they are bolted and well braced. Full circle wrought Brewster slotted fifth wheel, one of the best and strongest fifth wheels made. Bailey body loops clipped to springs. Will furnish wood spring bars if preferred to the loops. Bradley quick shifting shaft couplers, style used on all high grade work. Regulation bike style shafts made from fine selected hickory, full patent leather trimmed and with steel heel braces. We furnish pole in addition to shafts for $5.00 extra.

WHEELS—Fine selected straight grain white hickory, ⅞-inch Sarven patent, 38 inches front and 40 inches rear, with ⅞-inch round edge planished steel tire, bolted between each spoke. Tires are ¼ inch thick and are set hot by hand and not by machine. Felloes have screws through them on each side of every spoke, which insures absolutely against checking at the spokes. The height of wheels we furnish is correct for this style gear, but we can make any change in height desired. We furnish ¾-inch wheels instead of ⅞-inch, if preferred. Also banded hub style, if desired, instead of the Sarven patent.

TRIMMINGS—Seat is trimmed with fine whipcord, but we will trim with dark green or dark blue broadcloth, if all wool broadcloth is preferred to the whipcord. We will trim with any special colors of broadcloth at a small additional charge. The ends of the seat are pleated and trimmed to match cushion and back. There are upholstering springs in both cushion and back and the seat is very comfortable. We will cover cushion, back, seat ends and cushion fall with fine genuine trimming leather for $3.00 additional charge. Fine full padded wing style dash. Velvet carpet in bottom of body, or rubber mat if preferred to the carpet.

PAINTING—The best and most durable system known. Each coat is treated properly and given the required length of time to season before another coat is put on. The filler coats, color varnish and rubbing varnish coats are properly rubbed down and all surfaces polished so that they are perfectly smooth before the finishing varnish is applied. We use high grade material from the foundation coats to the finishing coat, and we guarantee the painting high grade. The body is black; gear, New York red, correctly striped. We will furnish Brewster green gear or make any changes in painting desired. Our painting is all fully guaranteed.

128

The above cut shows No. 1042 equipped with English canopy top. Additional charge for this style top, $10.00.

No. 1042—BIKE WAGON WITH SPINDLE SEAT AND LEATHER SEAT FENDERS

PRICE
{
Cash with order, with steel tires and shafts....................................$47.00
C. O. D., with steel tires and shafts... 48.50
Cash with order, with ⅞-inch guaranteed rubber tires and shafts.............. 62.00
C. O. D., with ⅞-inch guaranteed rubber tires and shafts...................... 63.50
}

If 1⅛-inch guaranteed cushion tires are preferred, add $5.00 to the price quoted with ⅞-inch solid rubber tires.

No. 1042 is a very popular wagon with our customers. It is what might be called the regulation open driving wagon. It is correctly proportioned, light running and comfortable riding. We know this wagon is as good in quality of workmanship and material throughout as usually sells for $25.00 to $30.00 more than our price. We are glad to ship it for full examination and approval, allowing you to be the judge, and if it is not, in your estimation, all we claim it may be returned at our expense.

BODY—Is regulation piano box style, 22 inches wide and 56 inches long. We will furnish body 20 inches wide or 24 inches wide, if desired. Seat is our regular spindle driving wagon seat, equipped with leather seat fenders. Both body and seat are made from high grade stock throughout, and guaranteed not to open at the corners, no matter in what climate used. Three prong steps. Roller rub irons.

GEAR—Axles are Roman bike style with dust proof bell collar long distance spindles, with felt oil pads. These axles are what is known as the naked style axle with only short wood center pieces for attaching fifth wheel in front and the rear spring in the rear. Fine oil tempered French pattern open head springs, very easy riding. Reaches have channel iron full length and they are bolted and well braced. Full circle wrought Brewster slotted fifth wheel, one of the best and strongest fifth wheels made. Bailey body loops clipped to springs. Will furnish wood spring bars if preferred to the Bailey loop. Bradley quick shifting shaft couplers, style used on all first class work. Regulation bike style shafts made from fine selected hickory, full patent leather trimmed and with steel heel braces. Pole in addition to shafts for $5.00 extra.

WHEELS—Fine selected straight grain white hickory, ⅞-inch Sarven patent, 38 inches front and 40 inches rear, with ⅞ inch round edge planished steel tire, bolted between each spoke. Tires are ¼-inch thick and are set hot by hand and not by machine. Felloes have screws through them on each side of every spoke,

which insures absolutely against checking at the spokes. The height of wheels we furnish is correct for this style gear, but we can make any change in height desired. We furnish ¾-inch wheels instead of ⅞-inch, if preferred. Also banded hub style, if desired, instead of Sarven patent.

TRIMMING—Seat is trimmed with fine whipcord, but we will trim with dark green or dark blue broadcloth, if all wool broadcloth is preferred to the whipcord. We will trim with any special colors of broadcloth at a small additional charge. There are upholstering springs in cushion, and the seat is very comfortable. We will cover cushion, back and cushion fall with genuine trimming leather for $1.50 additional charge. Fine full padded dash. Velvet carpet in bottom of body, or rubber mat if preferred to the carpet.

PAINTING—The best and most durable system known. Each coat is treated properly and given the required length of time to season before another coat is put on. The filler coats, color varnish and rubbing varnish coats are properly rubbed down and all surfaces polished so that they are perfectly smooth before the finishing varnish is applied. We use high grade material from the foundation coats to the finishing coat, and we guarantee the painting high grade. The body is black; gear, New York red, correctly striped. We will furnish Brewster green gear or make any changes in painting desired. Our painting is all fully guaranteed.

129

The above cut shows No. 1044 with our new auto style seat and cut-under piano body. Price, $5.00 more than with regular body and seat as listed below.

No. 1044—FINE DRIVING WAGON WITH AUTO STYLE SEAT

PRICE
- Cash with order, with steel tires and shafts...................................$60.00
- C. O. D., with steel tires and shafts.. 62.00
- Cash with order, with ⅞-inch guaranteed rubber tires and shafts............... 75.00
- C. O. D., with ⅞-inch guaranteed rubber tires and shafts...................... 77.00

If 1-inch guaranteed cushion tires are preferred, add $2.50 to price quoted with ⅞-inch rubber tires.

This is one of our most up-to-date high wheel driving wagons. It is made in our best grade throughout, is well proportioned and very comfortable riding. We are glad of an opportunity to ship No. 1044 for full examination and approval, and if it is not found all we claim and a highly satisfactory wagon it may be returned at our expense. We know this wagon is as good as usually sells for $25.00 more than our price.

BODY—Piano box style, 22 inches wide and 56 inches long. We will furnish 24 inch body if preferred to the 22-inch. The seat is one of our most popular style auto seats. It has good high back and is very comfortable. Both body and seat are made from high grade stock and are put together in such a manner and so well ironed and braced that we guarantee them not to open at the corners, no matter in what climate used. Three prong rubber covered steps. Roller rub irons.

GEAR—1⅛-inch dust proof bell collar long distance axles, with felt oil pads. Axles are fitted with light wood beds, which are cemented and clipped full length. Fine oil tempered French pattern open head springs, very easy riding. Reaches have channel iron full length and they are bolted and well braced. Full circle wrought Brewster slotted fifth wheel, one of the best fifth wheels made. Bailey body loops clipped to springs. Will furnish wood spring bars if preferred to the Bailey loop. Bradley quick shifting shaft couplers, style used on all first class work. Regulation style shafts made from fine selected hickory, full patent leather trimmed and with steel heel braces. We furnish pole in addition to shafts for $5.00 extra.

WHEELS—Fine selected straight grain white hickory, ⅞-inch banded hub, 40 inches front and 44 inches rear, with ⅞-inch round edge planished steel tire, bolted between each spoke. Tires are ¼-inch thick and are set hot by hand and not by machine. Felloes have screws through them on each side of every spoke, which insures absolutely against checking at the spokes. The

height of wheels we furnish is correct for this style gear, but we can make any change in height desired. We furnish ¾-inch wheels instead of ⅞-inch, if preferred. Also Sarven patent style, if desired, instead of banded hub.

TRIMMINGS—Seat is trimmed with fine whipcord, but we will trim with dark green or dark blue broadcloth, if all wool broadcloth is preferred to the whipcord. We will trim with any special colors of broadcloth at a small additional charge. The ends of the seat are pleated and trimmed to match cushion and back. There are upholstering springs in both cushion and back and the seat is very comfortable. We will cover cushion, back, seat ends and cushion fall with fine genuine trimming leather for $3.00 additional charge. Fine full padded wing style dash. Velvet carpet in bottom of body, or rubber mat if preferred to the carpet.

PAINTING—The best and most durable system. Each coat is treated properly and given the required length of time to season before another coat is put on. The filler coats are properly rubbed down and color varnish coats and rubbing varnish coats are rubbed down and all surfaces polished so that they are perfectly smooth before the finishing varnish is applied. We use high grade material from the foundation coats to the finishing coat, and we guarantee the painting high grade. The body is black; gear, New York red, correctly striped. We will furnish Brewster green gear or make any changes in painting desired. Our painting is all fully guaranteed.

130

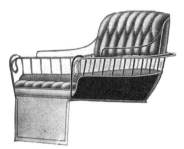

The above cut shows our half spindle style seat which we can furnish including leather seat fenders instead of regular seat on No. 1046, without additional charge.

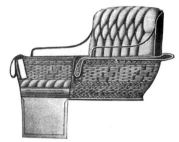

The above cut shows basket style seat which we furnish on No. 1046 with leather seat fenders for $2.00 additional charge.

No. 1046—FINE LIGHT DRIVING WAGON WITH SPINDLE SEAT AND LEATHER SEAT FENDERS

PRICE
{
Cash with order, with steel tires and shafts.....................................$57.00
C. O. D., with steel tires and shafts.. 59.00
Cash with order, with ¾-inch guaranteed rubber tires and shafts................... 70.00
C. O. D., with ¾-inch guaranteed rubber tires and shafts......................... 72.00
}

If ⅞-inch rubber tires are preferred, add $2.00 to the price quoted with ¾-inch rubber tires.

No. 1046 is a very desirable style light wagon. It has the regulation spindle seat with leather seat fenders. This wagon is correctly proportioned throughout, is light running and very comfortable riding. We know No. 1046 is as good as usually sells for $25.00 to $30.00 more than our price. We are glad to ship it for examination and approval, allowing you to be the judge.

BODY—Regular piano box style, 22 inches wide and 56 inches long. We furnish body 20 inches wide or 24 inches wide, if preferred. Seat is our regular spindle driving wagon seat. It has well shaped high back and is very comfortable. It is equipped with leather seat fenders. Both body and seat are made from high grade stock throughout. Rubber covered steps. Roller rub irons.

GEAR—1⅛-inch dust proof bell collar long distance axles, with felt oil pads. Axles are fitted with light wood beds, which are cemented and clipped to axles. Fine oil tempered French pattern open head springs, very elastic and easy riding. The reaches have channel iron full length and they are bolted and well braced. Full circle wrought Brewster slotted fifth wheel with king bolt clipped around axle. It is the style fifth wheel used on all strictly high grade work. Wrought Bailey body loops clipped to springs. Will furnish wood spring bar if preferred to the Bailey loops. Bradley quick shifting shaft couplers, which are the most practical quick shifting couplers made. They are used on all high grade work. Shafts are regular buggy style, only a little higher bend than commonly used. They are made from selected hickory, full patent leather trimmed and well braced. Will furnish pole in addition to shafts for $5.00 extra.

WHEELS—Fine selected straight grain white hickory, ¾-inch Sarven patent, 40 inches front and 44 inches rear, with ¾-inch round edge planished steel tire. bolted between each spoke. Tires are ¼-inch thick and are set hot by hand and not by machine.

Felloes have screws through them on each side of every spoke, which insures absolutely against checking at the spokes. The height of wheels we furnish is correct for this style gear, but we can make any change in height desired. We furnish ⅞-inch wheels instead of ¾ inch, if preferred. Also banded hub style, if desired, instead of the Sarven patent.

TRIMMINGS—Seat is trimmed with fine whipcord, but we will trim with dark green or dark blue broadcloth, if all wool broadcloth is preferred to the whipcord. We will trim with any special colors of broadcloth at a small additional charge. There are upholstering springs in cushion, and the seat is very comfortable. We will cover cushion, back and cushion fall with fine genuine trimming leather for $1.50 additional charge. Fine full padded dash. Velvet carpet in bottom of body, or rubber mat if preferred to the carpet.

PAINTING—The best and most durable system known. Each coat is treated properly and given the required length of time to season before another coat is put on. The filler coats, color varnish and rubbing varnish coats are properly rubbed down and all surfaces polished so that they are perfectly smooth before the finishing varnish is applied. We use high grade material from the foundation coats to the finishing coat, and we guarantee the painting high grade. The body is black; gear, New York red, correctly striped. We will furnish Brewster green gear or make any changes in painting desired. Our painting is all fully guaranteed.

131

The above cut shows No. 1048 with Stanhope style seat and drop style axles. Price, $2.00 less than with auto seat.

No. 1048—DRIVING WAGON WITH FINE AUTO SEAT AND TRUE SWEEP AXLES

PRICE
{
Cash with order, with steel tires and shafts...............................$ 50.50
C. O. D., with steel tires and shafts...................................... 52.00
Cash with order, with ¾-inch guaranteed rubber tires and shafts.................. 63.50
C. O. D., with ¾-inch guaranteed rubber tires and shafts........................ 65.00
If ⅞-inch rubber tires are preferred, add $2.00 to the price quoted with ¾-inch rubber tires.
}

No. 1048 is one of the most up-to-date style high wheel driving wagons we are making. It is equipped with our new style auto seat which has good high back and is very roomy and comfortable. It is correctly proportioned throughout, light running and comfortable riding. We know No. 1048 is as good in every particular as usually sells for $25.00 more than our price. We are glad to ship it anywhere for examination and approval, allowing you to be the judge.

BODY—Regular piano box style, 22 inches wide and 56 inches long. We furnish body 24 inches wide, if preferred. Seat is our fine new automobile style seat. It has well shaped high back and is very comfortable. Both body and seat are made from high grade stock throughout. Three prong steps. Roller rub irons.

GEAR—1⅛-inch true sweep dust proof bell collar long distance axles, with felt oil pads. Axles are fitted with light wood beds, which are cemented and clipped full length. Fine oil tempered French pattern open head springs, very easy riding. Reaches have channel iron full length and they are bolted and well braced. Full circle wrought Brewster slotted fifth wheel, one of the best and strongest fifth wheels made. Bailey body loops clipped to springs. Will furnish wood spring bars if preferred to the Bailey loop. Bradley quick shifting shaft couplers, the style used on all first class work. Regulation buggy style shafts made from fine selected hickory, full patent leather trimmed and with steel heel braces. Will furnish pole in addition to shafts for $5.00 extra.

WHEELS—Fine selected straight grain white hickory, ⅞-inch Sarven patent, 40 inches front and 44 inches rear, with ⅞-inch round edge planished steel tire, bolted between each spoke. Tires are ¼-inch thick and are set hot by hand and not by machine. Felloes have screws through them on each side of every spoke, which insures absolutely against checking at the spokes. The height of wheels we furnish is correct for this style gear, but we

can make any change in height desired. We furnish ¾ inch wheels instead of ⅞-inch, if preferred. Also banded hub style, if desired, instead of Sarven patent.

TRIMMINGS—Seat is trimmed with fine whipcord, but we will trim with dark green or dark blue broadcloth, if all wool broadcloth is preferred to the whipcord. We will trim with any special colors of broadcloth at a small additional charge. The ends of the seat are pleated and trimmed to match cushion and back. There are upholstering springs in both cushion and back and the seat is very comfortable. We will cover cushion, back, seat ends and cushion fall with fine genuine trimming leather for $3.00 additional charge. Fine full padded wing style dash. Velvet carpet in bottom of body, or rubber mat if preferred to the carpet.

PAINTING—The best and most durable system known. Each coat is treated properly and given the required length of time to season before another coat is put on. The filler coats, color varnish and rubbing varnish coats are properly rubbed down and all surfaces polished so that they are perfectly smooth before the finishing varnish is applied. We use high grade material from the foundation coats to the finishing coat, and we guarantee the painting high grade. The body is black; gear, New York red, correctly striped. We will furnish Brewster green gear or make any changes in painting desired. Our painting is all fully guaranteed.

The above cut shows No. 1050 with cut-under style body. Price, $5.00 more than with the regular body.

The above cut shows No. 1050 with straight dash instead of wing dash and half spindle style seat. Price, $3.50 less than with auto seat and wing dash. The difference in the seats is $2.00, and in the dash, $1.50.

No. 1050—DRIVING WAGON WITH AUTO SEAT AND PADDED WING DASH

PRICE
Cash with order, with steel tires and shafts.....................................$48.50
C. O. D., with steel tires and shafts.. 50.00
Cash with order, with ⅞-inch guaranteed rubber tires and shafts.................. 63.50
C. O. D., with ⅞-inch guaranteed rubber tires and shafts......................... 65.00

No. 1050 is one of our best style high wheel driving wagons. It is correctly proportioned, light running and very comfortable riding. We are glad to ship this wagon for full examination and approval with the understanding that it is to be found as good as usually sells for $25.00 more than our price or it may be returned at our expense. You are out nothing if not perfectly satisfied.

BODY—Is the regulation piano box style, 24 inches wide and 56 inches long, but we furnish 22-inch body if preferred to the 24-inch. The seat is one of the finest auto designs made. It has a good extra high back and is roomy and luxuriously upholstered. Both body and seat are made from high grade thoroughly seasoned body materials and are well ironed and braced, and guaranteed not to open at the corners in any climate. Three prong steps. Roller rub irons.

GEAR—1⅛-inch dust proof bell collar long distance style axles, with felt oil pads. Axles are fitted with light wood beds, which are cemented and fully clipped to axles. Fine oil tempered French pattern open head springs, very easy riding. Reaches have channel iron full length and they are bolted and well braced. Full circle wrought Brewster slotted fifth wheel, one of the best and strongest fifth wheels made. Bailey body loops clipped to springs. Will furnish wood spring bars if preferred to the loops. Bradley quick shifting shaft couplers, style used on all first class work. Regulation buggy style shafts made from fine selected hickory, full patent leather trimmed and with steel heel braces. We furnish pole in addition to shafts for $5.00 extra.

WHEELS—Fine selected straight grain white hickory, ⅞-inch Sarven patent, 38 inches front and 40 inches rear, with ⅞-inch round edge planished steel tire, bolted between each spoke. Tires are ¼-inch thick and are set hot by hand and not by machine. Felloes have screws through them on each side of every spoke, which insures absolutely against checking at the spokes. The height of wheels we furnish is correct for this style gear, but we can make any change in height desired. We furnish ¾-inch wheels instead of ⅞-inch, if preferred. Also banded hub style, if desired.

TRIMMINGS—Seat is trimmed with fine whipcord, but we will trim with dark green or dark blue broadcloth, if all wool broadcloth is preferred to the whipcord. We will trim with any special colors of broadcloth at a small additional charge. The ends of the seat are pleated and trimmed to match cushion and back. There are upholstering springs in both cushion and back and the seat is very comfortable. We will cover cushion, back, seat ends and cushion fall with fine genuine trimming leather for $3.00 additional charge. Fine full padded wing style dash. Velvet carpet in bottom of body, or rubber mat if preferred to the carpet.

PAINTING—The best and most durable system known. Each coat is treated properly and given the required length of time to season before another coat is put on. The filler coats, color varnish and rubbing varnish coats are properly rubbed down and all surfaces polished so that they are perfectly smooth before the finishing varnish is applied. We use high grade material from the foundation coats to the finishing coat, and we guarantee the painting high grade. The body is black; gear, New York red, correctly striped. We will furnish Brewster green gear or make any changes in painting desired. Our painting is all fully guaranteed.

The above cut shows No. 1052 without top. Price, $10.00 less than with top.

No. 1052—CANOPY TOP DUPLEX SPRING WAGON

PRICE { Cash with order, complete with pole or shafts...................................$57.50
{ C. O. D., complete with pole or shafts.. 59.00

Our No. 1052 is a very desirable style canopy top spring wagon. It is one of our leading sellers and a wagon that always gives satisfaction. We know this wagon is as good as usually sells for $20.00 to $25.00 more than our price, and we are glad to ship it anywhere
for full examination and approval, with the understanding that it may be returned at our expense if not found entirely satisfactory.

BODY—Is made from the best of body stock throughout. It is 33 inches wide and 6 feet 6 inches long and 8 inches deep. The seats are wide and roomy and have good high backs. The rear end of body is made to drop. Upper edges of body are ironed. Both seats are removable.

GEAR—Is the latest improved, short turn Duplex style, with 1⅛-inch double collar steel axles. There are four springs, one on each side and running parallel with the axles. The bearings of the axles being near the hubs of the wheels this wagon will carry fully 1000 pounds with perfect safety. The reach is ironed and well braced. We furnish both pole and shafts for $5.00.

WHEELS—1-inch Sarven patent, with 1-inch round edge steel tire, bolted between every spoke. Felloes have screws through them on each side of every spoke. We will furnish 1⅛-inch Sarven patent wheels instead of 1-inch, if desired.

TRIMMINGS—Seats are trimmed with good imitation leather, and there are springs in both cushions and backs. We trim with genuine leather instead of imitation leather for $4.00 additional charge.

TOP—Regular canopy style, complete with fringe all around and with good heavy rubber side curtains and good storm apron for the dash.

PAINTING—Body is painted in black, neatly striped; gear, dark Brewster green, correctly striped. Will change color of painting, if desired.

134

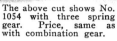
The above cut shows No. 1054 with three spring gear. Price, same as with combination gear.

No. 1054—TWO-SEAT COMBINATION SPRING WAGON

PRICE { Cash with order, complete with pole or shafts.................................$49.50
{ C. O. D., complete with pole or shafts...51.00

The Combination Spring wagon with elliptic spring in front and platform springs back is one of the most popular style wagons made. Our No. 1054 is a splendid seller with us and a wagon that gives our customers the best of satisfaction everywhere. We know this wagon is as good as usually sells for $20.00 to $25.00 more than our price. We are glad to ship for examination and approval, and if not found all we claim and perfectly satisfactory it may be returned at our expense.

BODY—Is made from the best of body stock throughout. It is 33 inches wide, 7 feet 6 inches long and 8 inches deep. The upper edges of body are ironed all around and corners are well ironed. The seats are full width and have good high panel backs. Both seats are removable. There is a drop end gate in rear of body.

GEAR—Is the regulation combination style with elliptic spring in front and four platform springs behind. Axles are 1⅛-inch double collar steel and there is a wood axle bed cemented and fully clipped to front axle. Reaches are well braced. The capacity of this wagon is fully 1000 pounds. We equip it with 1¼-inch axles and wheels for $5.00 additional. Good foot or hand lever brake, $4.00 additional charge. Both pole and shafts, $5.00 additional charge.

WHEELS—1⅛-inch Sarven patent, with 1⅛-inch round edge steel tires, fully bolted between every spoke. Felloes have screws through them on each side of every spoke.

TRIMMINGS—Seats are trimmed with good imitation leather and there are upholstering springs in both cushions and backs. We trim seats with good genuine trimming leather instead of imitation for $4.00 extra. If canopy top is desired on this wagon style of No. 1052 top, our additional charge for same is $12.00.

PAINTING—Body, black, neatly striped; gear, dark Brewster green, nicely striped. Will paint gear New York red or make any change in painting desired.

The above cut shows No. 1056 with full rubber extension top which is complete with rubber curtains and storm apron. Price, $20.00 more than without top. We furnish this extension top on any of our two seated spring wagons for $20.00 more than without top.

The above cut shows No. 1056 with canopy top, which is complete with curtains all around attached to top, and storm apron. Price, $15.00 more than without top.

No. 1056—TWO-SEAT FULL PLATFORM WAGON

PRICE { Cash with order, complete with pole or shafts.....................................$54.50
{ C. O. D., complete with pole or shafts... 56.00

No. 1056 is hung on the regulation full platform gear which is considered by many the most practicable spring wagon gear made. This is a well constructed wagon throughout; is light running and easy riding. We guarantee it as good as usually sells for fully $25.00 more than our price, and we are glad to ship it for examination and approval, with the understanding that it may be returned at our expense if not found perfectly satisfactory.

BODY—Is made from the best of body stock throughout. It is 3 feet wide by 8 feet 6 inches long and 8 inches deep. The upper edge of body is well ironed and corners are well ironed. Drop end gate in rear. Seats have full panel backs which are high and comfortable. Both seats are removable.

GEAR—Full platform style, with well built, well braced truss over front axle and a large full circle fifth wheel. This front gearing will not settle and bind in fifth wheel. Axles are coach pattern, 1⅛-inch double collar steel. Capacity of wagon, 1000 to 1200 pounds. We furnish 1¼-inch axles and wheels with carrying capacity of 1500 pounds for $5.00 additional charge. Good foot or hand lever brake, $4.00 additional charge. Both pole and shafts, $5.00 additional charge.

WHEELS—1⅛-inch Sarven patent with 1⅛-inch round edge steel tires, bolted between every spoke. Felloes have screws through them on each side of every spoke.

TRIMMINGS—Seats are trimmed in good imitation leather and there are upholstering springs in both cushions and backs. We trim seats with good genuine trimming leather instead of imitation for $4.00 extra. If canopy top is desired on this wagon same as shown by small cut above, our additional charge for same is $15.00; with full rubber extension top same as shown in corner of page, $20.00 extra.

PAINTING—Body, black, neatly striped; gear, dark Brewster green, nicely striped. Will paint gear New York red or make any change in painting desired.

The above cut shows No. 1058 with combination style gear. Price, same as with platform gear.

No. 1058—DRUMMERS' OR SUMMER RESORT WAGON, HUNG ON FULL PLATFORM GEAR

PRICE { Cash with order, complete with pole or shafts....................................$80.00
{ C. O. D., complete with pole or shafts...82.00

No. 1058 is one of the best selling three-seated wagons we have ever made. It is equipped with six standard standing top, with good rubber side curtains to roll up all around. This wagon is used a great deal by liverymen as drummers' wagon and for transfer purposes. It is also a desirable style for summer resorts. All three seats can be removed if desired, or when used for transfer purposes in going from town to town with drummers, the two rear seats can be removed. This gives plenty of room for trunks and valises. We know this wagon is as good as usually sells for $25.00 more than our price, and are glad to ship for examination and approval, with the understanding that it may be returned at our expense if not found perfectly satisfactory.

BODY—Is made from the best of body stock throughout. It is 3 feet wide by 8 feet 6 inches long and 8 inches deep. Upper edges of body are ironed all around and corners are well ironed and protected. Drop rear end gate. Seats are full panel back style and backs are high and comfortable.

GEAR—Regulation full platform style, with well made, well braced truss over front axle. This front gearing will not settle and bind in fifth wheel. Axles are 1¼-inch double collar steel. Large full circle fifth wheel. Carrying capacity of this gear is full 1500 pounds. We furnish both pole and shafts at $5.00 additional charge. Good foot or hand lever brake, $4.00 additional charge.

WHEELS—1¼-inch Sarven patent, with 1¼-inch round edge steel tires, bolted between every spoke. Felloes have screws through them on each side of every spoke.

TRIMMINGS—Seats are trimmed with good imitation leather and the cushions and backs are upholstered with springs. We will trim the seats with genuine leather instead of imitation for $6.00 additional charge.

TOP—Six standard canopy top with head lining and fringe. Good heavy roll-up curtains all around, also good storm apron for the dash. We can furnish the curtains so they will knob on and can be removed entirely if that style curtain is preferred to curtains attached to top made to roll up. If ordered without top, deduct $15.00 from price.

PAINTING—Body, black, neatly striped; gear, dark Brewster green, nicely striped. Will paint gear New York red or make any change in painting desired.

137

The above cut shows No. 1053 delivery wagon, which has the same size body and same gear as No. 1054, page 135, only it is made up with foot board and seat with high seat risers without back and flaring side boards back of seat as picture shows. Price, same as No. 1054.

The above cut shows No. 1060 equipped with panel style body instead of plain body. Price, same as with regular plain body.

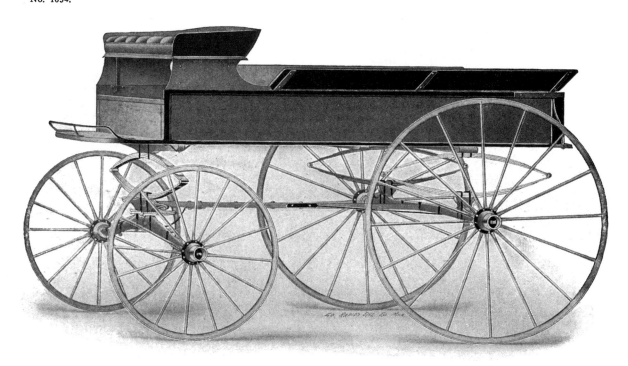

No. 1060—DELIVERY WAGON WITH CUT-UNDER FRONT WHEELS

PRICE { Cash with order, complete with pole or shafts....................................$63.00
{ C. O. D., complete with pole or shafts... 65.00

Our No. 1060 is a good, strong, desirable style delivery wagon. It is suitable for almost any kind of work. The front axle arched enough so that front wheels turn under to reach. We know this wagon is as good in quality of workmanship and material as usually sells for $25.00 more than our price. We are glad to ship for examination and approval.

BODY—Is made from the best of body stock throughout and is strongly constructed and well braced. It is 37 inches wide, 7 feet 6 inches long and 9½ inches deep outside. Has drop end gate full width. The upper edges of panel are well protected with irons and corners are well braced and stayed. The seat and side boards are easily removed.

GEAR—Regulation three spring style with 1⅛-inch double collar steel axles, with axle beds clipped to axles. Good heavy full circle wrought fifth wheel. Reach ironed full length, bolted and well braced. Carrying capacity 1000 to 1200 pounds. We furnish 1¼-inch axles and wheels with carrying capacity of 1500 to 1700

pounds for $5.00 additional charge. Both pole and shafts, $5.00 additional charge.

WHEELS—1⅛-inch Sarven patent with 1⅛-inch round edge steel tires, bolted between every spoke. Felloes have screws through them on each side of every spoke.

TRIMMINGS—Seat is trimmed with good imitation leather cushion. We will furnish genuine leather cushion for $1.00 additional charge.

PAINTING—Body, black, neatly striped; gear, New York red, correctly striped. Will make change in painting, if desired. We letter name of firm and business on each side of body and number on end gate for $2.00 additional charge.

The above cut shows our No. 1062 with panel style body instead of plain body. Price, same as with plain body.

No. 1062—THREE-SPRING LOW DOWN SHORT TURN DELIVERY WAGON

PRICE { Cash with order, complete with pole or shafts....................................$63.00
{ C. O. D., complete with pole or shafts.. 65.00

On No. 1062 the front axle is dropped, as the picture shows, and the rear axle is cranked so that the body hangs low. We know that our No. 1062 is as good in every particular as similar style wagons selling for fully $25.00 more than our price. We are glad to ship it anywhere for examination and approval. It may be returned at our expense if not found satisfactory and all we claim.

BODY—Is made from the best body stock throughout and is strongly constructed and well braced. It is 37 inches wide, 7 feet 6 inches long and 9½ inches deep outside. Has drop end gate full width. The upper edges of panels are well protected with irons and corners are well braced and stayed. The seat and side boards are easily removed.

GEAR—Three spring style with 1⅛-inch double collar steel axles, both of which are dropped, making the body hang very low. Short turn fifth wheel. Carrying capacity is fully 1000 pounds. We furnish 1¼-inch axles and wheels with carrying capacity of 1500 lbs. for $5.00 additional charge. Both pole and shafts, $5.00 additional charge.

WHEELS—1⅛-inch Sarven patent, with 1⅛-inch round edge steel tires, bolted between every spoke. Felloes have screws through them on each side of every spoke.

TRIMMINGS—Seat is equipped with good imitation leather cushion. We will furnish genuine leather cushion for $1.00 additional charge.

PAINTING—Body, black, neatly striped; gear, New York red, correctly striped. Will make change in painting, if desired. We letter name of firm and business on each side of body and number on end gate for $2.00 additional charge.

139

The above cut shows No. 1064 with straight sill body instead of cut-under. Price, $5.00 less than with cut-under body.

No. 1064—CUT-UNDER SHORT TURN DELIVERY WAGON

PRICE { Cash with order, complete with pole or shafts...................................$83.00
C. O. D., complete with pole or shafts.. 85.00

Our No. 1064 is an up-to-date light delivery wagon. We know this wagon is as good in quality of workmanship and material throughout as usually sells for fully $25.00 more than our price. It is especially suitable for delivery work where short turns are necessary, as front wheels cut under to reach. We unhesitatingly recommend No. 1064, and are glad to ship it anywhere for examination and approval.

BODY—Is made from the best of body stock throughout. It is 37 inches wide and 6 feet 10 inches long outside. Has drop end gate full width. Top is so made that it can be removed in shipping, thus enabling us to crate the wagon in the smallest space possible which reduces the freight classification and makes the rate low. The sides of top are heavy canvas which is sized with glue and well painted. Roof is covered with good heavy canvas sized with glue and well painted, making it thoroughly water proof. There is a rubber roll up curtain at the rear end. There are double strength glass windows at ends of driver's seat, as shown in picture.

GEAR—Low down three spring style, with drop axles. Axles are 1⅛-inch double collar steel. Front axle is fitted with wood axle bed, which is cemented and fully clipped to axle. Reach is ironed full length, bolted and well braced. Short turn fifth wheel. Springs are regulation height for this style wagon and carrying capacity of wagon is 1000 pounds. We can furnish with extra heavy 1¼-inch axles and wheels, if desired, for $5.00 additional charge. We furnish with both pole and shafts for $5.00 additional charge.

WHEELS—1⅛-inch Sarven patent, 1⅛-inch round edge steel tires, bolted between every spoke. Felloes have screws through them on each side of every spoke.

TRIMMINGS—Seat is equipped with good imitation leather cushion. We will furnish genuine leather cushion for $1.00 additional charge.

TOP—Is substantially constructed throughout and well ironed and braced. Sides are heavy canvas, sized with glue and well painted. Roof is covered with canvas, which is sized with glue and well painted so that it is perfectly water proof. There is a roll up curtain for the rear end which comes down to end gate.

PAINTING—Main part of body is painted black, with panel between body and canvas part of top carmine color, and sides of top, primrose. Body and top are neatly striped. Gear, New York red, neatly striped. Will change color of painting if desired. We letter sides of top with name of business and address for $2.00 additional charge.

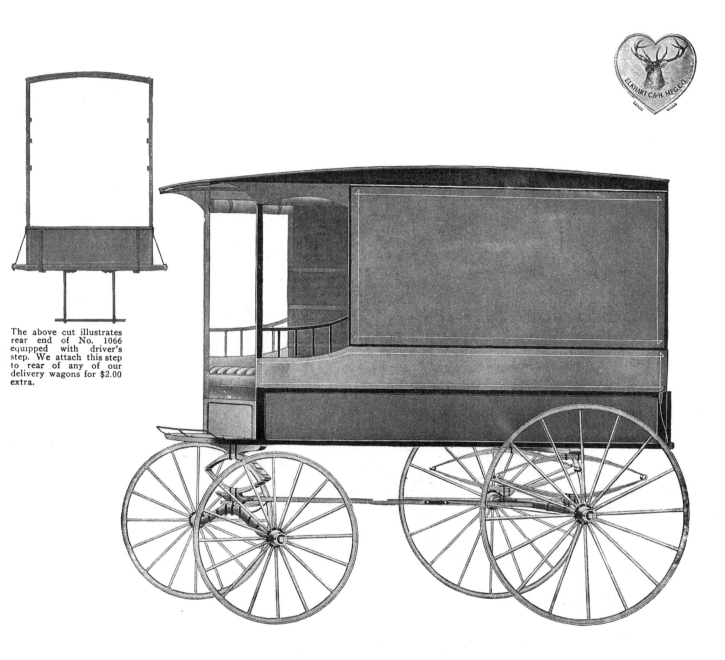

The above cut illustrates rear end of No. 1066 equipped with driver's step. We attach this step to rear of any of our delivery wagons for $2.00 extra.

No. 1066—TOP DELIVERY WAGON WITH THREE-SPRING GEAR AND CUT-UNDER FRONT WHEELS

PRICE { Cash with order, complete with pole or shafts...................................$78.00
C. O. D., complete with pole or shafts.. 80.00

On No. 1066 the front axle arches and the wheels are low so that they turn under the body to the reach. This wagon is adapted to almost any line of business and is well made and nicely finished. We are glad to ship No. 1066 for examination and approval, with the understanding that it is to be considered as good as usually sells for $25.00 to $35.00 more than our price or returned at our expense.

BODY—Is made from best of body stock throughout, is 37 inches wide by 7 feet 5 inches long. Top is well framed, braced and ironed. It is made so that it can be removed if desired, thus giving you an open wagon. This enables us to knock down in shipping so that we can crate in the smallest space possible, which secures a low freight classification. The upper sides of top are covered with heavy canvas, which is sized with glue and painted. Roof is covered with canvas, which is sized with glue and well painted. Rear end has drop end gate.

GEAR—Regulation delivery wagon three spring style with arched front axle and cut-under wheels. Axles are 1⅛-inch double collar steel, fitted with heavy wood axle beds, which are cemented and fully clipped to axles. Reach is ironed full length, bolted and well braced. Heavy full circle wrought fifth wheel. Regulation delivery wagon springs. This gear has carrying capacity of 1000 to 1200 pounds. We equip No. 1066 with 1¼-inch axles and

wheels having carrying capacity of 1500 pounds for $5.00 additional charge. Both pole and shafts add $5.00 to price.

WHEELS—1⅛-inch Sarven patent, 1⅛-inch round edge steel tires, bolted between every spoke. Felloes have screws through them on each side of every spoke.

TRIMMINGS—Seat is equipped with good imitation leather cushion. We will furnish genuine leather cushion for $1.00 additional charge. There are good heavy rubber side curtains at ends of the seat and a good rubber roll up curtain at the rear end from top to end gate.

PAINTING—Main part of body is painted black with panel between body and canvas part of top carmine color, and sides of top, primrose. Body and top are neatly striped. Gear, New York red, neatly striped. Will change color of painting if desired. We letter sides of top with name of business and address for $2.00 additional charge.

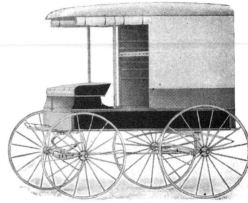

The above cut shows No. 1067 which has same style and size body and gear as No. 1068, the only difference being in style of top. Price, same as No. 1068.

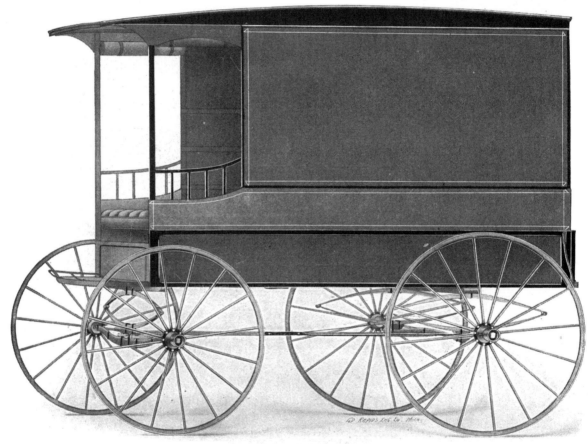

No. 1068—LOW DOWN SHORT TURN THREE-SPRING TOP DELIVERY WAGON

PRICE { Cash with order, complete with pole or shafts.....................................$78.00
C. O. D., complete with pole or shafts.. 80.00

No. 1068 is one of the most desirable top delivery wagons we are making and is a wagon that we guarantee to give entire satisfaction. It is hung on our low down short turn three-spring gear, which makes the body very convenient to load and unload and get into and out of. We know this wagon is as good as usually sells for $25.00 to $35.00 more than our price. We are glad to ship it for examination and approval, and if not found all we claim it may be returned at our expense.

BODY—Is made from best of body stock throughout. Is 37 inches wide by 7 feet 5 inches long. Top is well framed, braced and ironed. It is made so that it can be removed if desired, thus giving you an open wagon. This enables us to knock top down in shipping so that we can crate in the smallest space possible, which secures a low freight classification. The upper sides of top are covered with heavy canvas which is sized with glue and painted. Roof is covered with canvas which is sized with glue and well painted. Rear end has drop end gate.

GEAR—Low down three spring style with drop axles. Axles are 1⅛-inch double collar steel. Front axle is fitted with wood axle bed, which is cemented and fully clipped to axle. Short turn fifth wheel. Reach is ironed full length, bolted and well braced. Springs are regulation heft for this style wagon and carrying capacity of wagon is 1000 pounds. We can furnish with extra heavy 1¼-inch axles and wheels having capacity of 1500 pounds

if desired for $5.00 additional charge. We furnish with both pole and shafts for $5.00 additional charge.

WHEELS—1⅛-inch Sarven patent, 1⅛-inch round edge steel tires, bolted between every spoke. Felloes have screws through them on each side of every spoke.

TRIMMINGS—Seat is equipped with good imitation leather cushion. We will furnish genuine leather cushion for $1.00 additional charge. There are good heavy rubber side curtains at ends of the seat and a good rubber roll up curtain at the rear end from top to end gate.

PAINTING—Main part of body is painted black with panel between body and canvas part of top, carmine color, and sides of top, primrose. Body and top are neatly striped. Gear, New York red, neatly striped. Will change color of painting if desired. We letter sides of top with name of business and address for $2.00 additional charge.

The above cut shows our No. 1075 duplex gear top delivery wagon. Gear same as No. 1070. Body 3 feet wide, 6 feet 6 inches long and 10 inches deep. Top is made light and can be removed if desired. Roll up back curtain, and curtains at sides in front. Price, $17.00 less than No. 1070.

No. 1070—LOW DOWN DUPLEX SHORT TURN MILK OR BAKER'S WAGON

PRICE { Cash with order, complete with pole or shafts.................................$83.00
{ C. O. D., complete with pole or shafts.. 85.00

Our No. 1070 is a most desirable style wagon for either milk delivery or baker's wagon. Body hangs low and is easy to get into and out of. It has regular short turn, low down, duplex gear. It is short coupled, light draught, and a wagon as good in quality of workmanship and material throughout as usually sells for $25.00 to $35.00 more than our price. Step is about 17 inches from the ground. We are glad to ship No. 1070 for examination and approval.

BODY—Is made from the best of body stock throughout. It is 36 inches wide and 7 feet long. Front transom swings to roof inside when desired. Side doors slide back on iron track on inside and work freely. Doors are paneled up to the glass and there are windows in front quarters, as picture shows. Sides of top above body panels are covered with heavy canvas sized with glue and well painted. Roof is covered with heavy canvas sized with glue and well painted. Rear end is made with full width panel doors, 38 inches high. Front end is paneled up to transom as cut shows, and there are holes for lines. Front of body inside is arranged with platform for cans and there are three drawers underneath this platform. When it is desired to use this wagon for baker's delivery wagon we make body up with drawers in front up to the bottom of front window and with shelves back of seat, sealing up sides and top back of seat with galvanized iron so that it makes a splendid wagon for baked goods. Price when made up for baker's use, $25.00 more than regular price.

GEAR—Regular short turn Duplex style with 1⅛-inch double collar steel axles. Duplex gear consists of four springs, one on each side of and running parallel with the axles. It is a very popular gear and one that gives the best of satisfaction everywhere. This gear will carry 1000 pounds with perfect safety. We equip with 1¼-inch axles and wheels having carrying capacity of 1500 pounds for $5.00 additional charge. Both pole and shafts add $5.00.

WHEELS—1⅛-inch Sarven patent, 1⅛-inch round edge steel tires, bolted between every spoke. Felloes have screws through them on each side of every spoke.

TRIMMINGS—Seat is equipped with good imitation leather cushion. We will furnish genuine leather cushion for $1.00 additional charge.

PAINTING—The body is nicely painted and striped, the lower part of body being painted chocolate brown, and top of sides light primrose, neatly striped. Gear, New York red, correctly striped. We will change color of painting if desired. We letter sides with name of business or firm and street number for $2.00 additional charge.

The small cut shows rear end of No. 1100 body.

No. 1100—FINE ONE OR TWO-HORSE WAGONETTE WITH DROP SASH WINDOWS

PRICE
{
Cash with order, complete with pole or shafts.....................................$195.00
C. O. D., complete with pole or shafts... 200.00
1⅜-inch guaranteed rubber tires... 35.00
}

There is quite a demand for a medium weight six passenger wagonette for hotel use and transfer purposes. Our No. 1100 is a splendid design of this character and is as good in quality of workmanship and material throughout as usually sells for $50.00 to $75.00 more than our price. We ship for full examination and approval, with the understanding that the wagonette is to be found just as represented or we will take the shipment back at our expense.

BODY—Is made from the best of body stock, and is thoroughly well constructed. It is a very neat design; has drop side windows and the middle window in front and in the rear door also drop. The inside seating capacity is six passengers and one can ride with driver. The rear door works perfectly, same as a regular cab door. We furnish beveled plate glass in the windows instead of regular double strength glass for $8.00 additional charge.

GEAR—Three spring style with 1¼-inch dust proof bell collar long distance axles. The front axle has wood bed cemented and clipped full length of axle. Rear axle is coach pattern. Regulation heft pole and shafts made from fine select hickory. Carrying capacity 1500 to 1800 pounds.

WHEELS—1¼-inch Sarven patent with round edge steel tire,

bolted between every spoke. Felloes have screws through them on each side of every spoke. We equip the wheels with 1⅜-inch guaranteed rubber tires for $35.00 additional.

TRIMMINGS—Inside seats, as well as outside driver's seat, are trimmed with good genuine trimming leather and there are springs in cushions. We regularly furnish carpet in the bottom of body on the inside and rubber mat in front at the driver's seat, but we will furnish carpet in front, or we will furnish rubber mat inside if preferred. Large oil burner lamps. Top is lined on inside with imitation leather.

PAINTING—Body is finely finished in black, appropriately striped. Gear, New York red, neatly striped. We will change color of painting if desired. We letter wagonettes when desired.

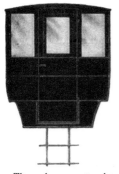

The above cut shows rear end of No. 1200 body.

The above cut shows foot board with dash which we furnish if desired.

No. 1200—FINE FULL PLATFORM WAGONETTE WITH DROP SASH

PRICE
{ Cash with order, complete with pole..$247.50
C. O. D., complete with pole.. 255.00
1½-inch guaranteed rubber tires... 40.00 }

We know our No. 1200 wagonette is made as good grade throughout as similar styles sold by other companies for fully $100.00 more than our price. We ship for full examination and approval, with the understanding that it is to be found just as represented or we will take it back at our expense.

BODY—Is made from the very best of body stock throughout and is thoroughly well constructed. It is one of the best designs we have ever made in this line. Inside seating capacity is eight passengers. (Ten are often carried.) Front seat is wide enough for two with driver. There are windows all around and side windows and center windows in front and rear door drop. The sash can be taken out if desired. The rear door is made to work perfectly, the same as cab door. We furnish beveled edge plate glass in windows instead of double strength glass for $10.00 additional charge.

GEAR—Full platform style with 1⅜-inch dust proof bell collar long distance front axle and 1½-inch dust proof bell collar long distance back axle. Stiff pole and regular coach style whiffletrees. Springs are regulation heft for this style wagon.

WHEELS—Sarven patent, 1⅜-inch front, 1½-inch back, with round edge steel tires, bolted between every spoke. Felloes have screws through them on each side of every spoke. 1½-inch guaranteed rubber tires, $40.00 additional charge.

TRIMMINGS—Inside seats as well as outside seat are trimmed with good trimming leather and there are springs in cushions. There is carpet in bottom of body, or we will furnish rubber mat if preferred to carpet. We furnish rubber mat in front of front seat. Large oil burner lamps. Top is lined with imitation leather.

PAINTING—Body is finely finished in black and correctly striped. Gear, New York red, nicely striped. We will change color of painting if desired. We letter wagonette when desired.

145

PONY VEHICLES AND HARNESS

If you are thinking of buying anything in the pony vehicle or harness line, drop us a card at once for our special pony vehicle and harness catalog. For the past two years we have been selling this line of pony vehicles and harness and while we do not make them, they are manufactured by a company who make a specialty of this class of work, and the pony vehicles and harness we have shipped during the past two years have given the best of satisfaction everywhere.

These pony vehicles and harness are the only styles we do not manufacture here in our own factory, but we stand back of each and every pony vehicle and harness we ship, and guarantee them to give the best of satisfaction.

If you are in the market for anything in this line, send for our special pony vehicle and harness catalogs.

We give in pony catalog a list of men and firms raising ponies.

No. 85—PONY DRIVING WAGON

Made in three sizes for ponies from 33 inches to over 50 inches in height.

PRICE
Cash with order, complete with shafts, without canopy $40.00
C. O. D., complete with shafts, with canopy 42.00
Extra for English canopy as shown in picture 8.00
Extra for rubber tires 10.00

No. 165—CUT-UNDER TWO AND FOUR PASSENGER PONY TRAP

Made in three sizes for ponies from 33 inches to over 50 inches in height.

PRICE
Cash with order, complete with shafts, without lamps and without canopy $69.00
C. O. D., complete with shafts, with lamps and without canopy........ 71.00
Extra for lamps as shown in picture 2.50
Extra for canopy as shown in picture 12.00
Extra for rubber tires 10.00

FREIGHT CHARGES TO PRINCIPAL POINTS IN EVERY STATE

We give below the total amount of freight charges on a single top buggy crated in 50 to 54 inch crate, and on an open single seat driving wagon crated in 30 to 34-inch crate to many important points in every state. If your shipping point is not given you can easily approximate the charges to your station. If you are thinking of buying any other style, write us and we will be glad to tell you just what the freight will be to your station. If at all in doubt about the freight let us give you a guaranteed freight charge on any style vehicle you are thinking of buying.

THE USER ALWAYS PAYS THE FREIGHT

Remember, it is the last buyer or user who pays the freight, and whether you buy from us or from a local dealer you pay the freight charges. The local dealer's price naturally covers the freight charges, and also all his other expenses, besides a net profit of $20.00 to $35.00. We deliver everything on board cars here at our factory carefully crated, and all vehicles are covered with heavy paper covers. We not only guarantee our vehicles to reach you safely and in perfect condition, but agree positively to save you from $20.00 to $35.00 on your purchase after you have added the freight charges to our price.
A harness shipped with a vehicle adds but very little to the freight. For freight estimates on harness shipped alone, see page 148.

	Top Buggy	Open Driving Wagon
ALABAMA		
Birmingham	$ 8.80	$ 5.25
Decatur	8.80	5.25
Mobile	8.25	4.95
Montgomery	10.45	6.05
Tuscaloosa	11.00	6.60
ARIZONA		
Flagstaff	$31.35	$27.50
Phoenix	30.80	26.40
Prescott	30.80	26.40
Tucson	29.15	25.30
ARKANSAS		
Arkansas City	$13.20	$12.10
Fort Smith	10.75	9.35
Helena	8.25	4.95
Hot Springs	11.55	10.20
Little Rock	9.90	8.80
Pine Bluff	9.90	8.80
Texarkana	10.75	9.35
CALIFORNIA		
Bakersfield	$27.50	$24.50.
Fresno	26.40	23.10
Los Angeles	22.30	19.80
Sacramento	22.30	19.80
San Diego	22.30	19.80
San Francisco	22.30	19.80
San Jose	22.30	19.80
Stockton	22.30	19.80
COLORADO		
Denver	$18.15	$15.70
Grand Junction	30.25	26.70
Greeley	18.15	15.70
Pueblo	18.15	15.70
CONNECTICUT		
Danbury	$ 8.00	$ 4.40
Hartford	8.00	4.40
New Haven	8.00	4.40
DIST. OF COLUMBIA		
Washington	$ 7.15	$ 3.85
DELAWARE		
Dover	$ 7.15	$ 4.00
Wilmington	6.95	3.85
FLORIDA		
Gainesville	$14.30	$ 9.90
Jacksonville	10.45	7.15
Key West	14.85	9.90
Pensacola	11.00	6.60
St. Augustine	12.10	8.25
Tampa	14.30	9.35
Tallahasse	15.95	11.00
GEORGIA		
Atlanta	$11.00	$ 6.60
Augusta	11.00	6.60
Brunswick	10.20	6.35
Macon	11.00	6.60
Savannah	10.20	6.35
IDAHO		
Boise	$27.50	$24.20
Moscow	29.70	26.40
Pocatello	27.50	24.20
INDIANA		
Evansville	$ 4.00	$ 2.20
Fort Wayne	2.05	1.20
Indianapolis	3.15	1.70
LaFayette	2.75	1.65
Marion	2.40	1.35
Muncie	3.10	1.70
New Albany	4.00	2.20
Terre Haute	3.15	1.70
Vincennes	3.70	2.05
ILLINOIS		
Cairo	$ 4.50	$ 2.50
Chicago	2.50	1.40
Danville	3.15	1.70
E. St. Louis	4.15	2.35
Freeport	5.25	2.90
Joliet	2.50	1.40
Peoria	4.00	2.20
Quincy	4.70	2.60
Springfield	4.15	2.35

	Top Buggy	Open Driving Wagon
IOWA		
Burlington	$ 5.25	$ 3.05
Cedar Rapids	6.90	5.25
Council Bluffs	8.55	6.60
Davenport	5.25	2.90
Des Moines	7.45	6.05
Dubuque	5.25	2.90
Keokuk	5.25	2.90
Ottumwa	7.15	5.50
Sioux City	8.55	6.60
KANSAS		
Atchison	$ 8.55	$ 6.60
Dodge City	1.85	12.65
Fort Scott	9.65	7.70
Leavenworth	8.55	6.60
Norton	13.75	11.55
Topeka	10.75	8.55
Wichita	12.95	10.75
Winfield	12.95	10.75
KENTUCKY		
Frankfort	$ 5.80	$ 3.30
Hopkinsville	7.70	5.50
Louisville	4.15	2.50
Paducah	4.70	2.75
Paris	6.05	3.60
LOUISIANA		
Baton Rouge	$ 8.25	$ 4.95
New Orleans	8.25	4.95
Shreveport	11.00	8.25
MAINE		
Augusta	$ 9.10	$ 4.95
Bangor	9.35	5.25
Dover	9.90	5.50
Portland	8.00	4.40
MARYLAND		
Annapolis	$ 7.70	$ 5.50
Baltimore	6.90	3.85
Hagerstown	6.90	3.85
MASSACHUSETTS		
Barnstable	$ 8.00	$ 4.40
Boston	8.00	4.40
Springfield	8.00	4.40
Worcester	8.00	4.40
MICHIGAN		
Adrian	$ 2.50	$ 1.40
Alpena	5.10	2.80
Bay City	3.15	1.80
Benton Harbor	1.85	1.00
Detroit	3.05	1.65
Grand Rapids	2.50	1.40
Kalamazoo	1.85	1.00
Lansing	2.75	1.55
Manistee	4.05	2.50
Petoskey	4.70	2.60
Sault Ste. Marie	6.05	3.30
MINNESOTA		
Albert Lea	$ 7.40	$ 4.40
Crookston	12.10	9.90
Duluth	7.45	4.40
Minneapolis	7.45	4.40
St. Paul	7.45	4.40
Winona	7.45	4.40
MISSISSIPPI		
Holly Springs	$10.45	$ 6.60
Jackson	10.45	6.60
Meridian	10.45	6.60
Natchez	8.25	4.85
Vicksburg	8.25	4.85
West Point	11.55	7.15
MISSOURI		
Chillicothe	$ 8.55	$ 6.60
Hannibal	5.50	3.30
Jefferson City	7.70	6.05
Kansas City	8.55	6.60
Poplar Bluff	9.90	7.45
Springfield	9.35	7.45
St. Joseph	8.55	6.60
St. Louis	4.40	2.75
MONTANA		
Billings	$23.65	$20.35
Butte	25.85	22.00
Dillon	25.85	22.00
Glendive	18.70	15.95

	Top Buggy	Open Driving Wagon
MONTANA—Continued		
Great Falls	24.75	19.80
Helena	25.85	22.00
Kalispell	26.95	23.10
Missoula	26.95	23.10
NEBRASKA		
Beatrice	$ 9.35	$ 7.70
Hastings	12.10	9.90
Hemingford	16.50	14.30
Lincoln	8.80	7.15
Omaha	8.55	6.60
O'Neil	12.10	9.90
Valentine	14.85	12.65
NEVADA		
Carson City	$34.10	$30.25
Elko	37.15	33.00
Reno	31.90	28.60
NEW HAMPSHIRE		
Concord	$ 8.00	$ 4.40
Keene	8.00	4.40
Portsmouth	8.00	4.40
NEW JERSEY		
Newark	$ 7.15	$ 4.00
Trenton	7.15	4.00
NEW MEXICO		
Albuquerque	$19.80	$17.60
Las Vegas	19.80	17.60
Sante Fe	19.80	17.60
NEW YORK		
Albany	$ 6.90	$ 3.80
Brooklyn	7.15	4.00
Buffalo	4.40	2.45
Elmira	5.80	3.30
Gloversville	7.70	4.20
Jamestown	4.40	2.45
New York	7.15	4.00
Oswego	5.80	3.30
Poughkeepsie	7.15	4.00
Rochester	5.50	3.05
Syracuse	5.80	3.30
Utica	6.60	3.60
Watertown	8.00	4.40
NORTH CAROLINA		
Charlotte	$10.45	$ 6.35
Raleigh	9.90	6.05
Salisbury	10.45	6.35
Wilkesboro	10.45	6.35
Wilmington	9.35	6.05
NORTH DAKOTA		
Bismarck	$14.30	$12.10
Fargo	12.10	9.90
Grand Forks	12.10	9.90
Jamestown	13.20	11.00
Minot	15.40	13.20
OHIO		
Canton	$ 4.10	$ 2.20
Cincinnati	4.10	2.20
Cleveland	4.10	2.20
Columbus	4.10	2.20
Mansfield	3.85	2.20
Sandusky	3.50	1.95
Springfield	4.10	2.20
Steubenville	4.40	2.45
Toledo	2.90	1.60
Youngstown	4.20	2.35
OKLAHOMA		
Enid	$13.75	$11.55
Oklahoma City	13.75	11.55
Ardmore	13.75	12.10
Atoka	13.75	12.10
OREGON		
Baker City	$29.70	$25.85
Grant's Pass	30.25	26.95
Portland	22.30	19.80
Salem	24.20	21.45
PENNSYLVANIA		
Allentown	$ 6.95	$ 3.85
Emporium	5.50	3.05
Erie	4.40	2.45
Harrisburg	6.95	3.85
Johnstown	5.50	3.00
Oil City	4.40	2.45
Philadelphia	6.95	3.85

	Top Buggy	Open Driving Wagon
PENNSYLVANIA—Continued		
Pittsburg	4.40	2.45
Reading	6.95	3.85
Scranton	6.95	3.85
RHODE ISLAND		
Bristol	$ 8.00	$ 4.40
Newport	8.00	4.40
Providence	8.00	4.40
SOUTH CAROLINA		
Charlestown	$10.20	$ 6.05
Columbia	11.00	6.60
Florence	11.55	7.15
Greenville	11.85	7.15
Sumter	11.85	7.15
SOUTH DAKOTA		
Aberdeen	$11.00	$ 9.35
Huron	11.00	9.35
Mitchell	10.45	8.55
Pierre	11.55	9.90
Yankton	9.10	7.70
TENNESSEE		
Bristol	$ 8.25	$ 4.70
Chattanooga	8.80	5.25
Jackson	9.35	6.60
Knoxville	8.80	5.25
Memphis	6.35	3.85
Nashville	5.80	3.60
TEXAS		
Austin	$12.65	$11.30
Beaumont	13.20	11.85
Dallas	12.65	11.30
Eagle Pass	13.20	11.85
El Paso	13.20	11.85
Fort Worth	12.65	11.30
Galveston	12.65	11.30
Houston	12.65	11.30
Laredo	13.20	11.85
San Antonio	12.65	11.30
Waco	12.65	11.30
UTAH		
Logan	$26.95	$23.65
Ogden	25.85	22.55
Provo City	25.85	22.55
Salt Lake City	25.85	22.55
VERMONT		
Bennington	$ 8.00	$ 4.40
Burlington	8.00	4.40
Rutland	8.00	4.40
White River Jct.	8.00	4.40
VIRGINIA		
Alexandria	$ 6.90	$ 3.80
Harrisonburg	6.90	3.80
Lexington	6.90	3.80
Norfolk	6.90	3.80
Petersburg	6.90	3.80
Richmond	6.90	3.80
Suffolk	6.90	3.80
WASHINGTON		
Colfax	$29.70	$28.60
Kalama	22.30	19.80
New Whatcom	22.30	19.80
Olympia	22.30	19.80
Seattle	22.30	19.80
Spokane	29.70	28.60
Tacoma	22.30	19.80
WEST VIRGINIA		
Charleston	$ 4.70	$ 2.50
Grafton	5.50	3.30
Huntington	4.70	2.50
Wheeling	4.40	2.45
WISCONSIN		
Ashland	$ 7.45	$ 4.40
Green Bay	7.45	4.40
Janesville	7.45	4.40
Madison	7.45	4.40
Milwaukee	3.05	2.20
Prairie du Chien	7.45	4.40
Superior	7.45	4.40
WYOMING		
Cheyenne	$17.60	$15.40
Evanston	25.85	22.55
Green Bay	25.85	22.55
Laramie	21.45	19.25
Rawlins	25.30	23.10

HARNESS DEPARTMENT

We are large manufacturers of harness, and are in a position to buy all classes of material necessary for the manufacture of harness at the lowest possible prices. We have one of the best and most modern equipped harness plants in the country, and employ in this department of our business none but skilled workmen, just as we do in our vehicle departments. It requires a combination of these essentials to produce good harness at the lowest possible cost, and to the item of first cost we add only a small profit to make our wholesale selling prices to you. You do not, however, have to buy a dozen or a hundred sets of harness, as a dealer or wholesaler usually does, in order to get these low prices, for we sell our harness just the same as we do our vehicles. The price to you is just as low per set for one set of harness as it would be for a dozen or a hundred sets. It would require practically as much labor and expense to ship a hundred sets of harness to one person as it would to a hundred persons, and a hundred sets to a hundred users means about a hundred times more advertising for us than the same number of sets to one person.

We have always bought good solid leather stock, also the best grades of trimmings, etc., and we know our harness are better in quality of material and workmanship throughout than the average harness sold by others. At any rate, we have so much confidence in the style and general quality of our harness that we are perfectly willing to ship for examination and approval the same as we do our vehicles, and if you are not perfectly satisfied with the style, quality and finish, and do not feel you are saving enough to pay you well for ordering from us, we gladly take the harness back at our expense. We do not feel that we are taking any risk in shipping in this way, for we think our harness are even better than we claim. We are continually receiving letters from our customers, who actually claim more for our harness than we do.

The reason we can afford to sell harness on a very small margin of profit is because we manufacture and sell so many.

We give two prices, as you will see—one price when ordered C. O. D., another price when cash is sent in advance. Whether the order is paid for in advance or not, we ship for full examination and approval, with the distinct understanding that if the harness is not just as described and perfectly satisfactory we take the shipment back at our expense, and if paid for in advance every cent of your money will be refunded.

Size of Collars

Do not hesitate to send us your order thinking we will not be able to fit your horses with collars. We have no trouble in that respect. If you will give us the size of your collars measuring from top to bottom on inside, as per illustration herewith, we will send the right size. Or, if you will tell us the weight of your horse we can send you the correct size. Horses weighing from 900 to 1000 pounds usually take an 18-inch collar; 1000 to 1100 pounds, 19-inch; 1100 to 1200 pounds, 20-inch. 19-inch is the size used most.

Measure the Collar
The Above Measures
19½ Inches

Halters and Halter Straps

No. 1 Five Ring Sewed Halter without Tie, 1 inch ....$ .65
No. 2. Five Ring Sewed Halter, without Tie, 1 inch .... .75
No. 3. Neck Halter, 1½ inch neck, 1¼ inch, 7 foot Tie............ .85
Good 1 inch Halter Straps..... .30
Good 1¼ inch Halter Straps..... .35

The Above Cut Shows
Style of our Sewed
Halter

Harness for Large Horses

Horses weighing over 1250 pounds usually require extra large harness. We quote an additional charge for extra large harness below each style that we can furnish large enough to fit horses weighing from 1250 to 1500 pounds.

Freight Charges

The freight charges on a harness shipped alone is a very small item indeed, as compared with the dealer's profit. The freight on a harness shipped with a vehicle is much smaller than when shipped alone. The freight on a set of harness shipped alone to points anywhere in Illinois, Indiana, Michigan or Ohio is from 25 to 50c. Anywhere in the New England States, New York, New Jersey, Pennsylvania, Delaware, Maryland, Virginia, West Virginia, Kentucky, Tennessee, Missouri, Iowa or Wisconsin is 50c to $1.00. To most points in the Southern States, Minnesota, Kansas, Nebraska, North and South Dakota, $1.00 to $1.50. Pacific Coast points and Rocky Mountain States, $3.00 to $3.90. As we say, when shipped with vehicles the charges for harness are very much less. If in doubt about the freight charges, write us and we will guarantee a rate.

No. 4—SINGLE STRAP HARNESS WITH CURVED BREAST COLLAR

PRICE { Cash with order, with nickel or imitation rubber trimmings.................$11.25
C. O. D., with nickel or imitation rubber trimmings....................... 11.50

No. 4 is one of our best selling single strap harness and is a style that compares favorably with harness that sells for $5.00 to $6.00 more than our price. It is well made and nicely trimmed. We are glad to ship it anywhere for examination and approval, and it may be returned at our expense if not found perfectly satisfactory.

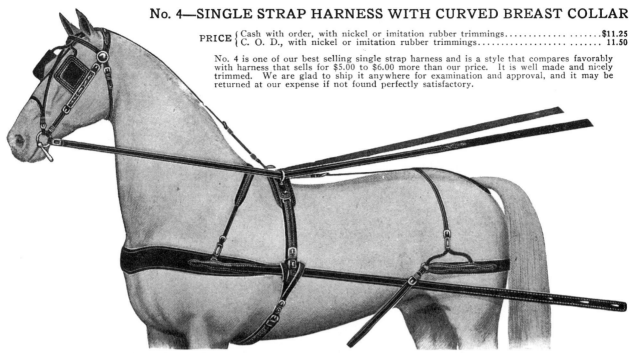

BRIDLE—⅝-inch, overcheck, with nose band, box loops, round winker stays.
BREAST COLLAR—2⅞-inch curved.
TRACES—1⅛-inch, stitched to breast collar.
BREECHING—1½-inch.
HIP STRAP—⅝-inch.

TURNBACK—¾-inch, round crupper.
SADDLE—2¾-inch, "strap" patent leather jockey, harness leather skirts, leather bottom, swinging bearers, Urbana check hook.
BELLY BAND—"Griffith" with long straps to wrap around shafts.
LINES—Black flat. Hitch strap. Will furnish flat russet lines for 50c extra.

No. 8—SINGLE STRAP HARNESS

PRICE { Cash with order, with nickel or imitation rubber trimmings..............$11.25
C. O. D., with nickel or imitation rubber trimmings.................... 11.50

No. 8 harness is cut from good solid stock throughout and is one of our best selling single strap harness. It is made smooth without any creasing. We know this harness is as good as usually sells for $5.00 to $6.00 more than our price. We are glad to ship it for examination and approval, and if not found all we claim it may be returned at our expense.

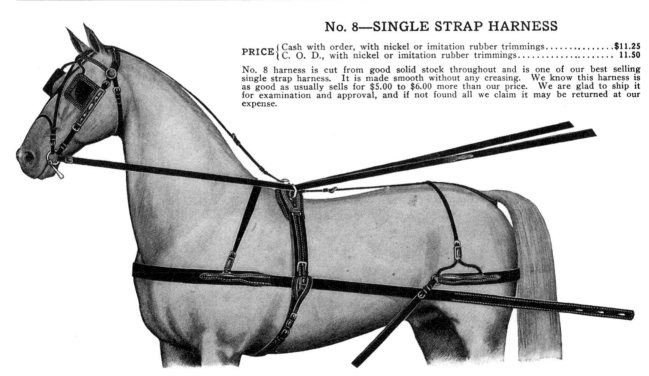

BRIDLE—⅝-inch, overcheck, with nose band, box loops, round winker stays.
BREAST COLLAR—1⅞-inch. We will furnish wide curved breast collar like shown on No. 4 harness for 50c extra.
TRACES—1¼-inch, stitched to breast collar.
BREECHING—1⅝-inch.
SIDE STRAPS—⅞-inch.

HIP STRAP—¾-inch.
TURNBACK—⅞-inch, scalloped, round crupper.
SADDLE—3-inch, "strap," patent leather jockey, harness leather skirts, leather bottom, swinging bearers; Urbana check hook.
BELLYBAND—"Griffith," with long straps to wrap around shafts.
LINES—Black flat, 1-inch. Hitch strap. Will furnish flat russet lines for 50c extra.

No. 8½—SINGLE STRAP HARNESS WITH CURVED BREAST COLLAR

PRICE

Cash with order, with nickel or imitation rubber trimmings.....................$11.25
C. O. D., with nickel or imitation rubber trimmings...........................11.50

No. 8½ harness is cut from good stock throughout and is one of the latest style single strap harness on the market. We know this harness is as good as usually sells for $5.00 to $6.00 more than our price. We are glad to ship it for examination and approval, and if not found all we claim it may be returned at our expense. We allow you to be the judge.

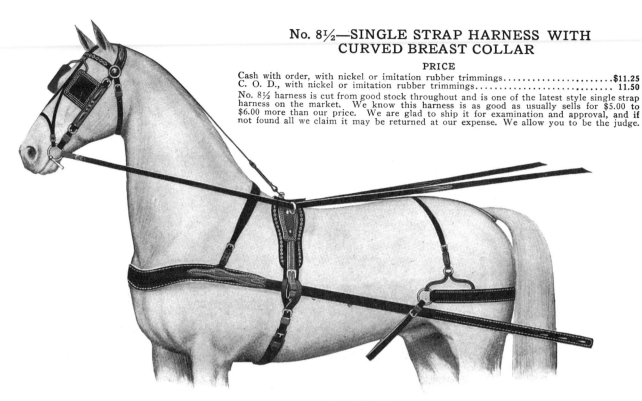

BRIDLE—⅝-inch, overcheck, with nose band, box loops, round winker stays.
BREAST COLLAR—Fine curved breast collar with wide layer.
TRACES—1¼-inch, stitched to breast collar.
BREECHING—1⅝-inch, with wide layer.
SIDE STRAPS—⅞-inch.
HIP STRAP—¾-inch.

TURNBACK—⅞-inch, scalloped, round crupper.
SADDLE—3½-inch "strap," patent leather jockey with one row of spots around edge of housing, harness leather skirts, leather bottom, swinging bearers; Urbana check hook.
BELLYBAND—"Griffith," with long straps to wrap around shafts. Double belly band if preferred.
LINES—Black flat, 1-inch. Hitch strap. Will furnish flat russet lines for 50c extra.

No. 9—LIGHT SINGLE COLLAR AND HAME HARNESS WITH SINGLE STRAP TRACES

PRICE { Cash with order, complete with collar, nickel or imitation rubber trimmings.......$13.65
{ C. O. D., complete with collar, nickel or imitation rubber trimmings.............14.00

There is a large demand for a medium priced collar and hame buggy harness. No. 9 is a very desirable collar harness and is all right for buggy or light surrey use. We know this harness is as good as usually sells for $18.00 to $20.00. It is made smooth, without any creasing to catch the dirt. We are glad to ship No. 9 for examination and approval, and if not found a splendid harness and all we claim, it may be returned at our expense.

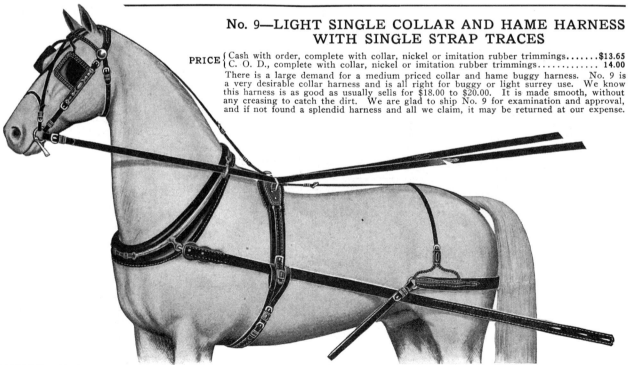

BRIDLE—⅝-inch, overcheck, with nose band, box loops, round winker stays; side check if preferred.
COLLAR—Kip.
HAMES—Iron, japan finished.
TRACES—1¼-inch, single strap to hames.
BREECHING—1⅝-inch.
SIDE STRAPS—⅞-inch.
HIP STRAP—¾-inch.

SADDLE—3-inch, "strap," patent leather jockey, harness leather skirts, leather bottom, swinging bearers; Urbana check hook.
TURNBACK—⅞-inch, scalloped, round cruppers.
BELLYBAND—"Griffith," with long straps to wrap around shafts; double belly bands with billet shaft tugs if preferred.
LINES—1-inch, black flat. Flat russet lines if preferred. Hitch strap.

150

No. 10—SINGLE COLLAR AND HAME HARNESS

PRICE { Cash with order, complete with collar, with nickel or imitation rubber trimmings..$15.60
{ C. O. D., complete with collar, with nickel or imitation rubber trimmings........ 16.00

Our No. 10 is a very desirable style light collar and hame harness. It is suitable for single buggy, stanhope, phaeton or light surrey. Traces are double and stitched, and they buckle to hame tugs, as picture shows. We know No. 10 is as good as usually sells for $5.00 to $6.00 more than our price, and are glad to ship harness for examination and approval. We allow you to be the judge.

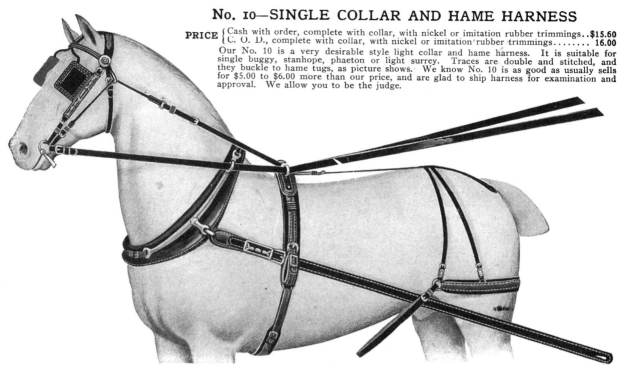

BRIDLE—⅝ inch with side check and round winker stays; will furnish overcheck if preferred to side check.
COLLAR—Black kip.
HAMES—Full iron hames, japan finished. Hame tugs with box loops.
TRACES—1⅛ inch, raised double and stitched to buckle to hames.
BREECHING—Folded with raised layer.
SIDE STRAPS—⅞ inch.

TURNBACK—⅞ inch, round crupper to buckle.
HIP STRAPS—⅝ inch double.
SADDLE—3 inch enameled leather pad; Urbana check hook.
BELLYBAND—Double, with billet shaft tugs. Will furnish "Griffith" style bellyband with long straps to wrap around shafts, if preferred.
LINES—Black flat lines to buckle. Will furnish flat russet lines, if preferred. Hitch strap.

No. 11—SINGLE STRAP HARNESS WITH LIGHT OPEN BRIDLE

PRICE { Cash with order, with nickel or imitation rubber trimmings................$12.70
{ C. O. D., with nickel or imitation rubber trimmings........................ 13.00

No. 11 single harness is made up from as good stock and in as good style as usually sells through dealers for full $18.00. This harness is well finished and trimmed and all straps are made smooth without creasing. We are glad to ship this harness for full examination and approval, and if not found all we claim it may be returned at our expense.

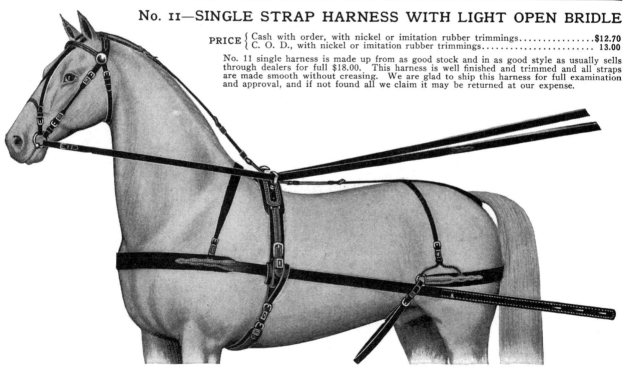

BRIDLE—Fine open bridle with round cheek pieces, five-buckle overcheck, with nose band, layer on crown. Bridle with blinds, if preferred.
BREAST COLLAR—1¾ inch.
TRACES—1⅛ inch, stitched to breast collar.
BREECHING—1⅝ inch, side straps, ⅞ inch.
HIP STRAPS—⅝ inch.

TURNBACK—¾ inch, scalloped round crupper.
SADDLE—3 inch "strap," patent leather jockey, patent leather skirts, leather bottom, swinging bearers; Urbana check hook.
BELLYBAND—"Griffith," with long straps to wrap around shafts.
LINES—1 inch, flat russet with steel spring billet. Black lines, if preferred. Hitch strap.

No. 12—LIGHT SWISS BREAST COLLAR HARNESS

PRICE { Cash with order, with nickel, brass or imitation rubber trimmings..................$16.10
C. O. D., with nickel, brass or imitation rubber trimmings......................... 16.50
Genuine rubber trimmings, if preferred to the regular trimmings, add.............. **3.00**

As the cut shows, No. 12 is a very desirable style single harness. It is suitable for buggy, road wagon, Stanhope or light surrey. We unhesitatingly recommend it and we are glad to ship for examination and approval, with the understanding that you are to feel you are saving fully $5.00 over what you would pay for the same style and grade elsewhere or shipment may be returned at our expense.

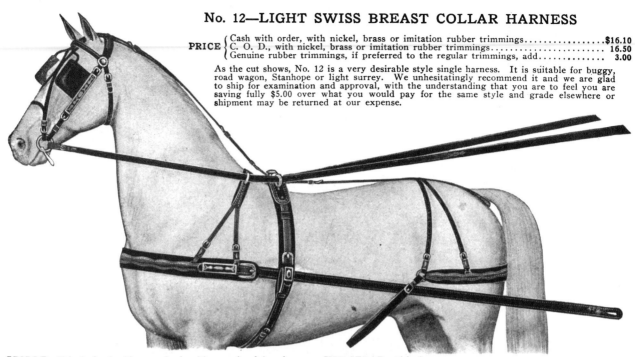

BRIDLE—⅝-inch, five-buckle, overcheck with nose band, box loops, extended billets; round winker stays, layer on crown. Side check, if preferred.
BREAST COLLAR—Wide single leather, folded, open bottom, Swiss style, box loops; neck strap has swivel terrets.
TRACES—1⅛-inch, raised, double and stitched, round edge.
BREECHING—Folded, with scalloped raised layer, side strap ⅞-inch.

HIP STRAP—⅝-inch.
TURNBACK—⅞-inch, scalloped, round crupper.
SADDLE—3-inch, leather covered seat, enamel leather pad; Urbana check hook.
BELLYBANDS—Double bellybands with billet shaft tugs, "Griffith," with long strap to wrap around shafts, if preferred.
LINES—⅞-inch, steel spring billets, 1⅛-inch hand parts; flat russet lines, if preferred. Hitch straps.

No. 13—SINGLE HARNESS WITH DOUBLE AND STITCHED BREAST COLLAR AND TRACES

PRICE { Cash with order, with nickel, brass or imitation rubber trimmings..................$12.70
C. O. D., with nickel, brass or imitation rubber trimmings......................... 13.00

Our No. 13 harness is nicely made up throughout. It is well finished and trimmed. We know this harness is as good as usually sells for $5.00 to $7.00 more than our price, and we are glad to ship it for examination and approval, with the understanding it may be returned at our expense if not found all we claim.

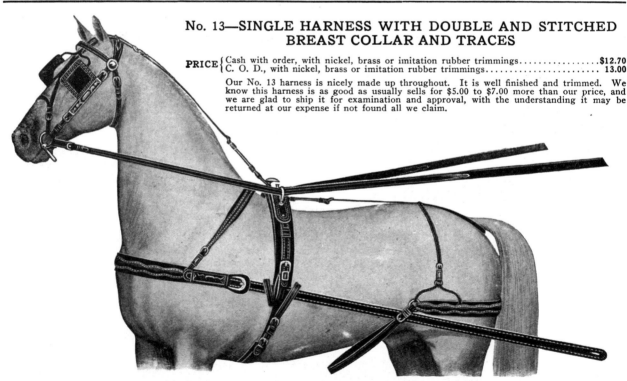

BRIDLE—⅝-inch, five-buckle overcheck, with nose band, box loops, extended billets, round winker stays, layer on crown. Will furnish light open bridle instead of bridle with blinds, if preferred.
BREAST COLLAR—Folded, with scalloped raised layer, box loops, safe underbuckles. We furnish No. 13 with good collar and hames instead of breast collar for $1.50 additional charge.
TRACES—1⅛-inch, raised, double and stitched, round edge.
BREECHING—Folded, with scalloped raised layer, side straps, ⅞-inch.

HIP STRAP—¾-inch.
TURNBACK—⅞-inch, scalloped, round crupper.
SADDLE—3-inch, leather covered seat, enamel leather pad; Urbana check hook.
BELLYBAND—"Griffith," folded, with long straps to wrap around shafts. Double bellybands and billet shaft tugs, if preferred.
LINES—⅞-inch, steel spring billets, 1⅛-inch hand parts; flat russet lines, if preferred. Hitch strap.

We make an additional charge of $1.50 for harness large enough to fit horses weighing 1250 to 1500 pounds.

No. 13½—SINGLE HARNESS WITH SWISS NECK PIECE

PRICE
Cash with order, with nickel, brass or imitation rubber trimmings................$14.00
C. O. D., with nickel, brass or imitation rubber trimmings...................... 15.00
Genuine rubber trimmings, if preferred to the regular trimmings, add........... 2.50

Our No. 13½ is an up-to-date harness and a style that always pleases. It is cut from first class stock throughout, is nicely finished and well trimmed. We know this harness is as good as usually sells for $5.00 to $6.00 more than our price. We are glad to ship it for full examination and approval, and it may be returned at our expense if not found perfectly satisfactory.

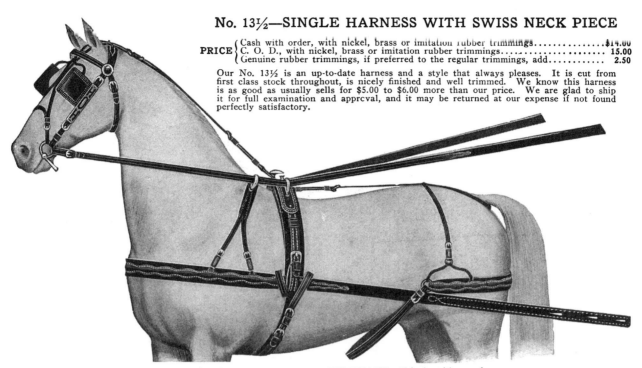

BRIDLE—⅝-inch, five-buckle overcheck, with nose band, box loops, extended billets, round winker stays, and layer on crown.
BREAST COLLAR—Folded, with waved layer on top, and has Swiss style neck piece.
TRACES—1⅛-inch, single strap, stitched to breast collar.
BREECHING—Folded, with wave layer on top and ⅞-inch side straps.
HIP STRAPS—¾-inch.

TURNBACK—⅞-inch, with round crupper.
SADDLE—3-inch, leather covered seat and enamel leather pad; Urbana check hook.
BELLYBAND—Double, with billet shaft tugs. Will furnish "Griffith" style bellyband with long straps to wrap around shafts, if preferred.
LINES—⅞-inch, steel spring billets; 1⅛-inch hand parts; flat russet lines, if preferred. Hitch strap.

No. 14—FINE SINGLE STRAP HARNESS WITH CURVED BREAST COLLAR

PRICE
Cash with order, with nickel, brass or imitation rubber trimmings...............$14.10
C. O. D., with nickel, brass or imitation rubber trimmings...................... 14.50
Genuine rubber trimmings, if preferred to the regular trimmings, add........... 2.00

No. 14 is one of the best selling single strap harness we are manufacturing. It has a good wide curved breast collar which many users prefer, because they feel that when the breast collar curves down away from throat of horse it affords better breathing powers and relieves a nervous horse of much annoyance. We know our No. 14 is as good as usually sells for $7.00 to $8.00 more than our price and we are glad to ship it for examination and approval, and if it is not considered all we claim and a splendid harness for the money, it may be returned at our expense.

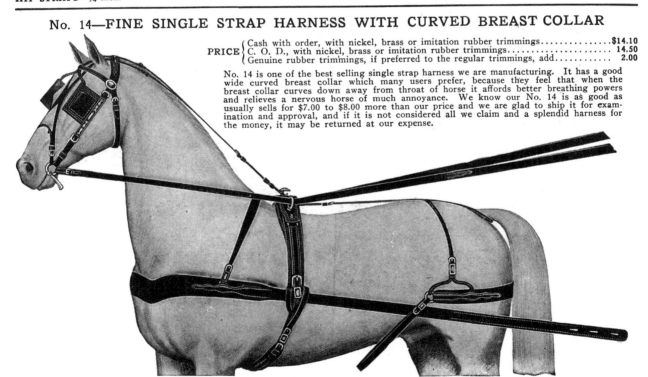

BRIDLE—⅝-inch, five-buckle overcheck, with nose band, box loops, extended billets, round winker stays, layer on crown.
BREAST COLLAR—3-inch curved. We will furnish No. 14 with Swiss style neck piece same as No. 16¾ for 50c additional charge.
TRACES—1¼-inch, stitched to breast collar.
BREECHING—1¾-inch, side straps ⅞-inch.
HIP STRAP—¾-inch. We will furnish double hip straps instead of single hip strap, if preferred, for 50c additional charge.

TURNBACK—⅞-inch, scalloped, round crupper.
SADDLE—3-inch, "strap," swell underhousing, patent leather jockey, patent leather skirts, leather bottom, swinging bearers; shaft tugs, 1-inch, with creased box loops. Urbana check hook.
BELLYBAND—"Griffith," with long straps to wrap around shafts. Double bellybands and billet shaft tugs, if preferred.
LINES—1-inch, buckle and steel spring billets; made smooth; no creasing; flat russet lines, if preferred. Hitch strap.

No. 14½—SINGLE HARNESS WITH CURVED BREAST COLLAR AND DOUBLE HIP STRAPS

PRICE { Cash with order, with nickel, brass or imitation rubber trimmings..............$14.60
C. O. D., with nickel, brass or imitation rubber trimmings.....................15.00
Genuine rubber trimmings, if preferred to the regular trimmings, add............2.00

We make No. 14½ harness to meet the demand for a neat style buggy harness with double hip strap breeching. We know No. 14½ is cut from as good stock and made up in as good style and quality throughout as usually sells at retail for many dollars more than our price. It has the wide curved breast collar, which a good many buyers prefer to the straight breast collar. We are glad to ship this harness for examination and approval, and it may be returned at our expense if not found perfectly satisfactory and all we claim.

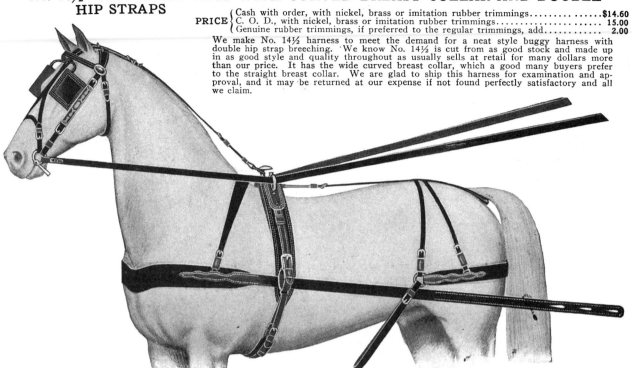

BRIDLE—⅝-inch, five-buckle overcheck with nose band, box loops, extended billets, round winker stays and layer on crown.
BREAST COLLAR—3 inches wide, curved.
TRACES—1¼-inch, stitched to breast collar.
BREECHING—1¾-inch, with ⅞-inch side straps.
HIP STRAPS—⅝-inch, double.
TURNBACK—⅞-inch, scalloped round crupper.

SADDLE—3-inch, leather covered seat, enamel leather pad. Urbana check hook.
BELLYBAND—Double, with billet shafts tugs. "Griffith" bellyband with long strap to wrap around shafts, if preferred.
LINES—1-inch, buckle with steel spring billets; flat russet lines, if preferred. Hitch strap.

We make an additional charge of $1.50 for harness large enough to fit horse weighing 1250 to 1500 pounds.

No. 15—SINGLE STRAP HARNESS WITH HALF TRACK SADDLE

PRICE { Cash with order, with nickel or brass trimmings.............................$14.60
C. O. D., with nickel or brass trimmings......................................15.00
Genuine rubber trimmings, if preferred to the regular trimmings, add............2.00

Our No. 15 is made up from A number one stock throughout. It is well finished and nicely trimmed and a harness that usually retails for $5.00 to $8.00 more than our price. We are glad to ship No. 15 for examination and approval, and if not found all we claim and a very satisfactory harness it may be returned at our expense.

BRIDLE—⅝-inch, five-buckle overcheck, with nose band, box loops, extended billets, round winker stays, layer on crown. Will furnish open bridle with round cheek pieces if preferred.
BREAST COLLAR—1¾-inch.
TRACES—1⅛-inch, stitched to breast collar.
BREECHING—1⅝-inch.
HIP STRAP—⅝-inch.
SIDE STRAPS—⅞-inch, with creased box loops.

TURNBACK—¾-inch, scalloped, round crupper.
SADDLE—3-inch, half track, leather covered seat and ring back band, enameled leather pad. Urbana check hook.
SHAFT TUGS—1-inch, with creased box loops.
BELLYBAND—Inside folded with layer, outside single attached, with long straps to wrap around shafts.
LINES—⅞-inch, steel spring billets, 1⅛-inch hand parts; flat russet lines, if preferred. Hitch strap. Will furnish lines with beaded fronts, if preferred, for $1.50 extra.

We make an additional charge of $1.50 for harness large enough to fit horse weighing 1250 to 1500 pounds.

No. 16—FINE SINGLE STRAP HARNESS WITH HALF TRACK FLEXIBLE SADDLE

PRICE
{ Cash with order, with nickel, imitation rubber or brass trimmings...............$15.10
{ C. O. D., with nickel, imitation rubber or brass trimmings....................... 15.50
{ Genuine rubber trimmings, if preferred to the regular trimmings, add........... 2.00

Our No. 16 is a well made single strap harness and equal in quality of workmanship and material throughout to similar harness sold at retail for $8.00 to $10.00 more than our price. It is made in single strap work throughout, except saddle, and stitching is all nicely done. We are glad to ship this harness anywhere for examination and approval, and it may be returned at our expense if not found highly satisfactory.

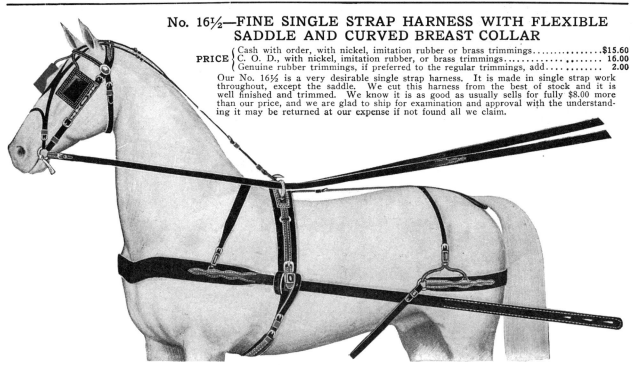

BRIDLE—⅝-inch; overcheck has five buckles, and nose band, box loops, round winker stays, layer on crown.
BREAST COLLAR—1⅞-inch.
BREECHING—1¾-inch.
HIP STRAP—¾ inch.
SIDE STRAPS—⅞-inch, with creased box loops.
TURNBACK—⅞-inch, scalloped, round crupper.
SADDLE—Flexible, 3-inch, half track, ring back band, enameled leather pad. Urbana check hook.

SHAFT TUGS—1-inch, with creased box loops.
BELLYBAND—"Griffith," folded, with long straps to wrap around shafts.
LINES—1-inch, steel spring billets; 1⅛-inch hand parts; made smooth, round edges, no creasing; flat russet lines, if preferred. Hitch strap. We furnish lines with beaded fronts, if preferred, for $1.50 extra.

No. 16½—FINE SINGLE STRAP HARNESS WITH FLEXIBLE SADDLE AND CURVED BREAST COLLAR

PRICE
{ Cash with order, with nickel, imitation rubber or brass trimmings...............$15.60
{ C. O. D., with nickel, imitation rubber, or brass trimmings..................... 16.00
{ Genuine rubber trimmings, if preferred to the regular trimmings, add........... 2.00

Our No. 16½ is a very desirable single strap harness. It is made in single strap work throughout, except the saddle. We cut this harness from the best of stock and it is well finished and trimmed. We know it is as good as usually sells for fully $8.00 more than our price, and we are glad to ship for examination and approval with the understanding it may be returned at our expense if not found all we claim.

BRIDLE—⅝-inch, overcheck has five buckles and nose band, same as shown in cut; box loops, round winker stays, layer on crown.
BREAST COLLAR—3-inch, curved. We furnish Swiss style neck piece same as No. 16¾ for 50c extra.
TRACES—1¼-inch, stitched to breast collar.
BREECHING—1¾-inch. Will furnish double hip strap breeching for 50c extra.
HIP STRAP—¾ inch.
SIDE STRAPS—⅞-inch, with creased box loops.
TURNBACK—⅞-inch, scalloped, round crupper.

SADDLE—Flexible, 3-inch, half track, ring back band, enameled leather pad. Urbana check hook.
SHAFT TUGS—1-inch, with creased box loops.
BELLYBAND—"Griffith," folded, with long straps to wrap around shafts.
LINES—1-inch, steel spring billets; 1⅛-inch hand parts; made smooth, round edges, no creasing; flat russet lines, if preferred. Hitch strap. Will furnish lines with beaded fronts for $1.50 extra.

No. 16¾—FINE SINGLE STRAP BUGGY OR LIGHT SURREY HARNESS

PRICE
{
Cash with order, with nickel, imitation rubber or brass trimmings.............$16.50
C. O. D., with nickel, imitation rubber, or brass trimmings....................17.00
Genuine rubber trimmings, if preferred to the regular trimmings, add............2.50
}

Our No. 16¾ is a very desirable style single strap harness. It has the Swiss style neck piece and double hip straps and is a very appropriate harness for buggy, road wagon, Stanhope or light surrey use. We know this harness is as good as usually sells for $8.00 to $10.00 more than our price. We are glad to ship for examination and approval.

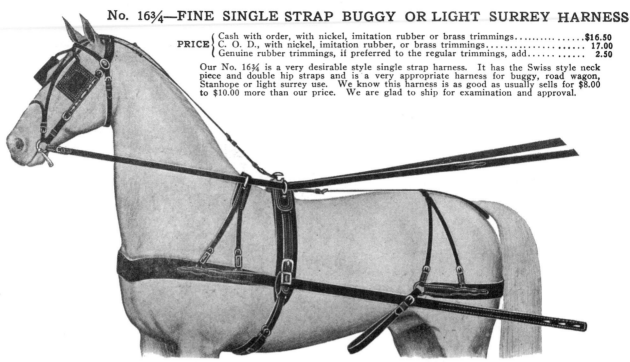

BRIDLE—⅝-inch, overcheck, with five buckles and nose band; box loops; round winker stays and layer on crown.
BREAST COLLAR—Wide curved breast collar, 3-inch, with Swiss style neck piece.
TRACES—1¼-inch, stitched to breast collar.
BREECHING—1¾-inch, with ⅞-inch side straps.
HIP STRAPS—Double, ⅝-inch.

TURNBACK—⅞-inch, scalloped, round crupper.
SADDLE—3-inch full track style, leather-covered seat and ring back band; enameled leather pad. Urbana check hook.
BELLYBAND—Double, with billet shaft tugs. We furnish "Griffith" style bellyband with long straps to wrap around shafts, if desired.
LINES—1 inch, steel spring billets, 1⅛-inch hand parts; flat russet lines, if preferred. Hitch strap.

No. 17—FINE SINGLE STRAP HARNESS WITH HALF TRACK KAY SADDLE

PRICE
{
Cash with order, with nickel or brass trimmings.............................$16.50
C. O. D., with nickel or brass trimmings.......................................17.00
Genuine rubber trimmings, if preferred to the regular trimmings, add............2.00
}

Our No. 17 is made up from choice material and it is well finished and trimmed throughout. We know this harness is as good as usually sells for $8.00 to $10.00 more than our price, and we are glad to ship for examination and approval, with the understanding it may be returned at our expense if not found all we claim.

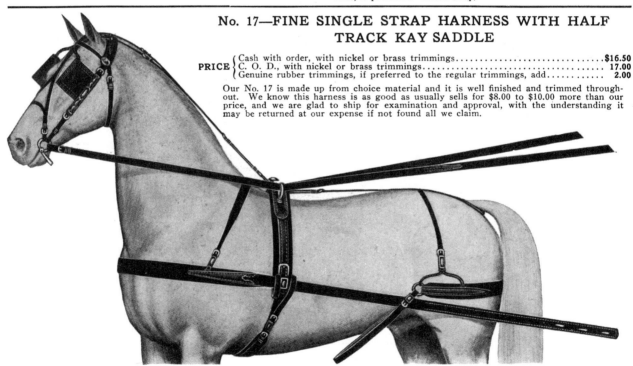

BRIDLE—½-inch; five-buckle overcheck, with patent leather nose band, round winker stays, layer on crown. Can furnish with light open bridle instead of bridle with blinds, if preferred.
BREAST COLLAR—1¾-inch.
TRACES—1⅛-inch, stitched to breast collar.
BREECHING—1⅝-inch, side straps, ⅞-inch.
HIP STRAP—⅝-inch.
TURNBACK—⅝-inch, scalloped, round crupper.

SHAFT TUGS—⅞-inch.
SADDLE—Kay, 2¾-inch, half track leather covered seat. Urbana check hook.
BELLYBAND—Folded, with long straps to wrap around shafts. Box loops throughout; made smooth; round edges; no creasing.
LINES—⅞-inch, steel spring billets; 1⅛-inch hand parts; flat russet lines, if preferred. Hitch strap. We furnish lines with beaded fronts for $1.50 extra.

We make an additional charge of $1.50 for harness large enough to fit horse weighing 1250 to 1500 pounds.

No. 17½—FINE LIGHT SINGLE STRAP HARNESS

PRICE
{ Cash with order, with nickel or brass trimmings.................................$18.50
{ C. O. D., with nickel or brass trimmings... 19.00
{ Genuine rubber trimmings, if preferred to the regular trimmings, add.............. 2.00

Our No. 17½ is made from A number one stock and is as fine in quality of workmanship and material throughout as similar harness sold for fully $8.00 to $10.00 more than our price. It is strictly up-to-date in style, and a harness that we know will please you. We are glad to ship it for full examination and approval.

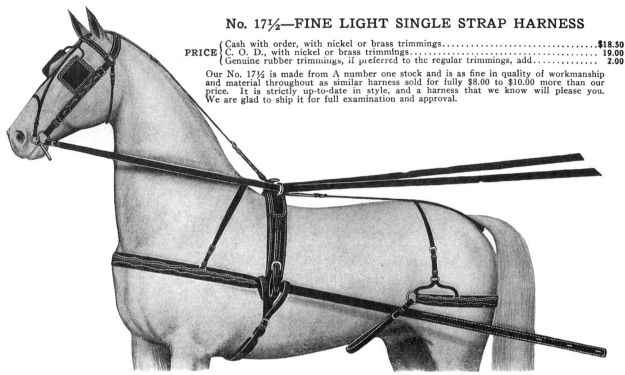

BRIDLE—½-inch; five-buckle overcheck, with patent leather nose band; round winker stay; crown, folded with layer. We furnish light open bridle, if preferred.
BREAST COLLAR--Enameled leather fold, with waved raised layer extending on traces; neck piece, folded same as breast collar, and reversed ends.
TRACES—1⅛-inch single strap traces, stitched to breast collar. Will furnish 1-inch full lined double and stitched traces to buckle to breast collar, if preferred.
BREECHING—Enameled leather fold, with waved raised layer.
SIDE STRAPS—⅞-inch.

HIP STRAP—⅝-inch reversed.
TURNBACK—⅝-inch, scalloped, soft round crupper.
SADDLE—2½-inch, half track; full patent leather; leather covered seat; enameled leather pad. Urbana check hook. Will furnish flexible saddle with two minute dee bearers, if desired.
SHAFT TUGS—⅞-inch.
BELLYBAND—Inside enameled leather fold with layer; outside single attached with long straps to wrap around shafts.
LINES—⅞-inch, steel spring billets; 1⅛-inch hand parts; flat russet lines, if desired. Will furnish lines with beaded fronts, if preferred, for $1.50 extra. Hitch strap.

No. 18—FINE SINGLE HARNESS WITH HALF TRACK SADDLE

PRICE
{ Cash with order, with nickel or brass trimmings.............................$18.50
{ C. O. D., with nickel or brass trimmings.................................... 19.00
{ Genuine rubber trimmings, if preferred to the regular trimmings, add........... 2.00

Our No. 18 is made up in A number one style throughout. There is a good deal of work about this harness which cannot be shown at all in picture, and one must see the harness to appreciate its value for price charged. We know this harness is as good as usually sells for $5.00 to $8.00 more than our price. We are glad to ship it for examination and approval.

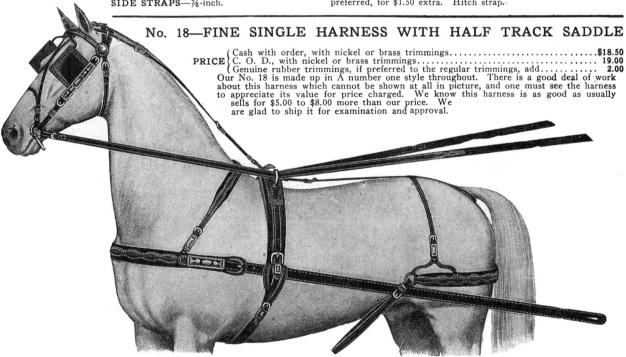

BRIDLE—⅝-inch; overcheck has five buckles, with nose band, same as shown in cut; box loops, round winker stays, layer on crown. Will furnish an open bridle, if preferred to blind bridle, without extra charge.
BREAST COLLAR—Glove finished leather fold, scalloped raised layer, box loops, safe underbuckles; neck piece glove finished leather fold.
TRACES—1⅛-inch; raised, double and stitched; round edges.
BREECHING—Glove finished leather fold, scalloped, raised layer.
HIP STRAP—⅝-inch.

SIDE STRAPS—⅞-inch, with creased box loops.
TURNBACK—⅞-inch, scalloped round crupper.
SADDLE—3-inch, half track; leather covered seat and ring back band; enameled leather pad. Urbana check hook.
SHAFT TUGS—1-inch, with creased box loops.
BELLYBAND—Inside folded with layer; outside single attached, with long straps to wrap around shafts.
LINES—1-inch, flat russet, steel spring billets; 1⅛-inch hand parts; black lines, if preferred. Hitch strap. We will furnish lines with beaded fronts for $1.50 extra.

We make an additional charge of $1.50 for harness large enough to fit horse weighing 1250 to 1500 pounds.

No. 18½—FINE LIGHT SINGLE COLLAR AND HAME BUGGY HARNESS

PRICE
{ Cash with order, complete with collar, nickel or brass trimmings................$20.50
{ C. O. D., complete with collar, with nickel or brass trimmings.....................21.00
{ Genuine rubber trimmings, if preferred to the regular trimmings, add.............. 2.00

Our No. 18½ is one of the best styles of light collar harness we are manufacturing. It is made up in A number one shape throughout and is well finished and nicely trimmed. This harness is very suitable for top buggy, driving wagon, Stanhope, trap or light surrey. We know it is as good as usually sells for $5.00 to $8.00 more than our price, and we are glad to ship it with the understanding it may be returned at our expense if not found satisfactory and all we claim.

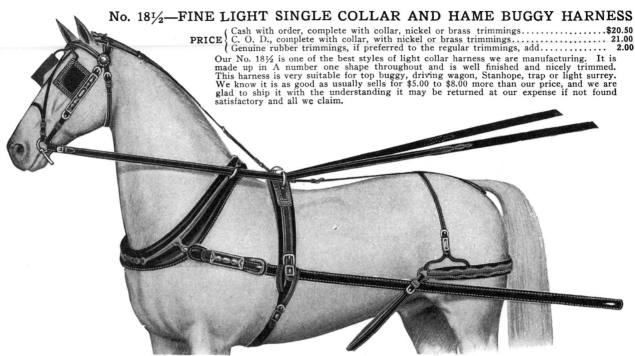

BRIDLE—⅝-inch, five-buckle overcheck, with nose band; box loops; round winker stays; layer on crown. We will furnish open bridle, if preferred to blind bridle, without extra charge.
COLLAR—Full patent leather.
HAMES—Full nickel plated.
HAME TUGS—Patent leather; box loops with safe under-trace buckles.
TRACES—1⅛-inch, raised, double and stitched, round edges.
BREECHING—Glove finished leather fold, scalloped, raised layer.
HIP STRAP—⅝-inch.
SIDE STRAPS—⅞-inch, with creased box loops.

TURNBACK—⅞-inch, scalloped, round crupper.
SADDLE—3-inch, half track; leather covered seat and ring back band; enameled leather pad. Urbana check hook.
SHAFT TUGS—1-inch, with creased box loops.
BELLYBAND—Inside folded with layer; outside single attached, with long straps to wrap around shafts. Will furnish double bellybands with billet shaft tugs, if preferred.
LINES—1-inch, steel spring billets; 1⅛-inch hand parts; flat russet lines, if preferred. Hitch strap. We will furnish lines with beaded fronts for $1.50 extra.

No. 19—FINE LIGHT RUBBER TRIMMED SINGLE STRAP HARNESS WITH KAY SADDLE

PRICE
{ Cash with order, with genuine rubber trimmings.............................$25.50
{ C. O. D., with genuine rubber trimmings....................................26.00
{ Solid aluminum gold bronze saddle trimmings, if preferred to rubber.

Our No. 19 is cut from the best of stock throughout, is finely finished and trimmed and as good a harness in every particular as light single strap harness sold by other manufacturers for fully $35.00. We are very glad, at any rate, to send this harness for examination and approval, and if not found a fine light harness and all we claim we will take it back at our expense.

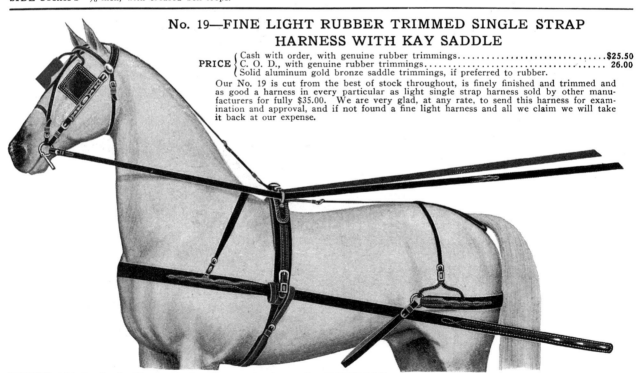

BRIDLE—½-inch; five buckle overcheck, with nose band; round winker stays; crown, enameled leather fold with layer. Fine light open bridle, same as No. 19½, if preferred.
BREAST COLLAR—1⅝-inch, beveled on inside, with reversed neck piece.
TRACES—1-inch, stitched to breast collar, with ends raised, double and stitched.
BREECHING—1½-inch, beveled on inside.
SIDE STRAPS—¾-inch.
HIP STRAP—½-inch, reversed style.

TURNBACK—⅝-inch, scalloped, soft round crupper.
SADDLE—2½-inch; half track, full patent leather, "Kay," with running back band. Urbana check hook.
SHAFT TUGS—⅞-inch.
BELLYBAND—Enameled leather fold, with layer; straps to wrap around shafts.
LINES—⅞-inch, steel spring billets; 1⅛-inch hand parts; flat russet lines, if preferred. Hitch strap. Will furnish lines with beaded fronts, if preferred, for $1.50 extra.

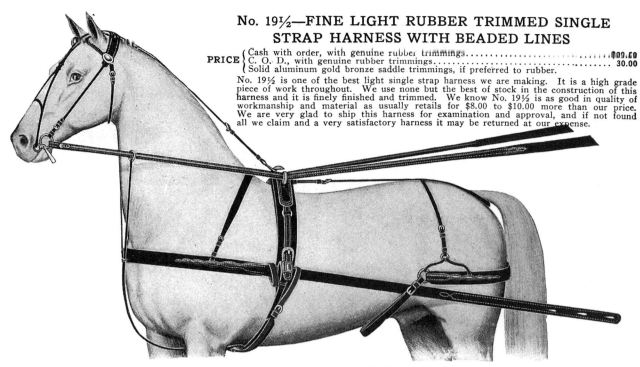

No. 19½—FINE LIGHT RUBBER TRIMMED SINGLE STRAP HARNESS WITH BEADED LINES

PRICE {
Cash with order, with genuine rubber trimmings.............................$29.50
C. O. D., with genuine rubber trimmings.. 30.00
Solid aluminum gold bronze saddle trimmings, if preferred to rubber.
}

No. 19½ is one of the best light single strap harness we are making. It is a high grade piece of work throughout. We use none but the best of stock in the construction of this harness and it is finely finished and trimmed. We know No. 19½ is as good in quality of workmanship and material as usually retails for $8.00 to $10.00 more than our price. We are very glad to ship this harness for examination and approval, and if not found all we claim and a very satisfactory harness it may be returned at our expense.

BRIDLE—Fine open ½-inch; five-buckle overcheck, with nose band; crown, enameled leather, folded with layer; solid round cheeks and throat latch entirely hand made. We furnish fine light bridle with blinds, if preferred to the open bridle.
BREAST COLLAR—1⅝-inch, beveled on inside, with reversed neck strap.
MARTINGALE—Single strap ring martingale with round forks, with rings to match trimmings.
TRACES—1-inch, stitched to breast collar, with ends raised, double and stitched.

BREECHING—1½-inch, beveled on inside, with ¾-inch side straps.
HIP STRAP—½-inch, reversed style.
TURNBACK—⅝-inch, scalloped, soft round crupper.
SADDLE—2½-inch, half track; full patent leather; flexible, ring back band, enameled leather pad. Urbana check hook.
BELLYBAND—Enameled leather, folded with layer; long straps to wrap around shafts; ⅞-inch shaft tugs.
LINES—1⅛-inch hand parts, with beaded fronts and steel spring billets. Hitch strap.

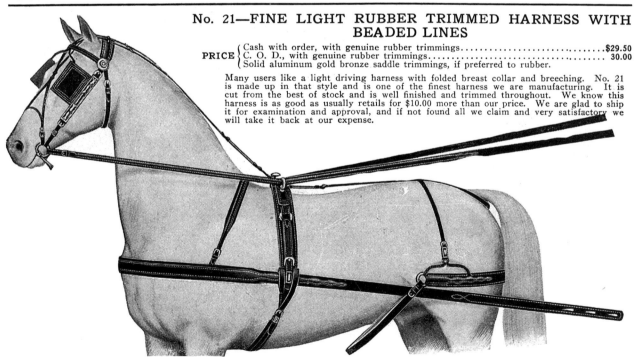

No. 21—FINE LIGHT RUBBER TRIMMED HARNESS WITH BEADED LINES

PRICE {
Cash with order, with genuine rubber trimmings.............................$29.50
C. O. D., with genuine rubber trimmings.. 30.00
Solid aluminum gold bronze saddle trimmings, if preferred to rubber.
}

Many users like a light driving harness with folded breast collar and breeching. No. 21 is made up in that style and is one of the finest harness we are manufacturing. It is cut from the best of stock and is well finished and trimmed throughout. We know this harness is as good as usually retails for $10.00 more than our price. We are glad to ship it for examination and approval, and if not found all we claim and very satisfactory we will take it back at our expense.

BRIDLE—½-inch; five-buckle overcheck, with nose band; round winker stay; crown, enameled leather fold with layer. We furnish fine light open bridle, same as on No. 19½, above, if preferred.
BREAST COLLAR—Enameled leather fold, anti-chafe, with wide oval layer, waved point stitched on traces; neck piece, enameled leather fold, same as breast collar.
TRACES—1-inch single strap traces, stitched to breast collar. Will furnish fine double and stitched traces to buckle to breast collar, if preferred.
BREECHING—Enameled leather fold; anti-chafe with wide oval layer.

SIDE STRAPS—¾-inch.
HIP STRAP—½-inch.
TURNBACK—⅝-inch, scalloped, soft round crupper.
SADDLE—2½-inch, half track; full patent leather; flexible, ring back band, enameled leather pad. Urbana check hook.
SHAFT TUGS—⅞-inch.
BELLYBAND—Enameled leather fold; anti-chafe, with wide oval layer; straps to wrap around shafts.
LINES—Beaded fronts, steel spring billets; 1⅛-inch hand parts; folded russet hand parts, if desired. Hitch strap.

No. 30—FINE RUBBER TRIMMED SINGLE COLLAR HARNESS FOR DRIVING WAGON, STANHOPE OR SURREY

PRICE { Cash with order, complete with collar, with genuine rubber trimmings...........$32.00
C. O. D., complete with collar, with genuine rubber trimmings..................32.50
Full brass trimmings instead of genuine rubber, if desired.

Our No. 30 is a very desirable style harness for Stanhope, phaeton, Goddard or surrey use. It is also often used with open driving wagon. We know No. 30 is as good in quality of workmanship and material throughout as usually sells for $10.00 more than our price. We are glad to ship it for examination and approval, and if it is not found perfectly satisfactory and all we claim it may be returned at our expense.

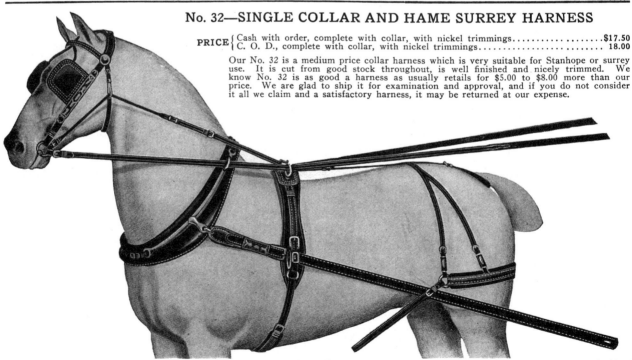

BRIDLE—½-inch; small space loops, round side check, double and stitched nose band and winker brace, patent leather face drop.
TRACES—1⅛-inch, raised, double and stitched, running to hames; patent leather points.
MARTINGALE—¾-inch, with patent leather drop.
BREECHING—1¼-inch, double and stitched, raised on inside; side straps ⅞-inch.
HIP STRAPS—½-inch, double and stitched.
TURNBACK—¾-inch, English style with heavy round crupper to buckle.

SHAFT TUGS—1-inch, raised.
BELLYBAND—Inside enameled leather fold, with layer; outside single attached, with straps to wrap around shafts.
LINES—⅞-inch fronts, with 1⅛-inch hand parts; folded russet hand parts, if preferred. We furnish lines with beaded fronts, if preferred, for $1.50 extra.
SADDLE—3½-inch; hand laced, enameled leather pad, tapered patent leather skirts, leather covered seat, running back band.
COLLAR—Full patent leather, closed bent top. Hitch strap. Directions for measuring collar on page 148.

No. 32—SINGLE COLLAR AND HAME SURREY HARNESS

PRICE { Cash with order, complete with collar, with nickel trimmings...................$17.50
C. O. D., complete with collar, with nickel trimmings........................ 18.00

Our No. 32 is a medium price collar harness which is very suitable for Stanhope or surrey use. It is cut from good stock throughout, is well finished and nicely trimmed. We know No. 32 is as good a harness as usually retails for $5.00 to $8.00 more than our price. We are glad to ship it for examination and approval, and if you do not consider it all we claim and a satisfactory harness, it may be returned at our expense.

BRIDLE—⅝-inch throughout; box loops, round rein and winker stays.
HAME TUGS—Box loops, japanned iron hames.
TRACES—1¼-inch, double and stitched, round edges.
BREECHING—Folded, with layer; ¾-inch double hip straps; side straps 1-inch.
TURNBACK—⅞-inch, round crupper to buckle.

SADDLE—3½-inch, leather lined, patent leather jockey and skirts.
BELLYBAND—Inside folded, outside single.
SHAFT TUGS—With dees.
LINES—1-inch, buckle and billet; flat russet lines, if preferred.
COLLAR—Half patent leather. Hitch strap. Directions for measuring collar on page 148.

No. 33—SINGLE SURREY HARNESS

PRICE
- Cash with order, complete with collar, with nickel or brass trimmings............$21.00
- C. O. D., complete with collar, with nickel or brass trimmings.............. 21.50
- Genuine rubber trimmings, if preferred to the regular trimmings, add............. 3.00

No. 33 is one of the best style surrey harness we are making. It is cut from A number one stock throughout, is nicely finished and well trimmed. We unhesitatingly recommend this harness and are glad to ship it for examination and approval, and if it is not found as good as usually sells for $28.00 to $30.00 it may be returned at our expense.

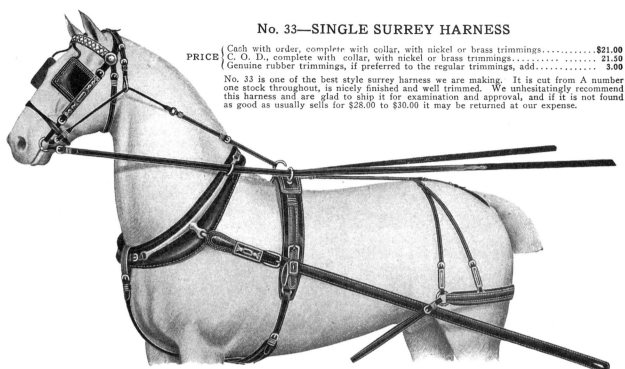

BRIDLE—⅝-inch, round side check, box loops, round winker stays, layer on crown, nose band.
HAME TUGS—Patent leather, box loops, full nickel plated hames, safe under-trace buckles.
TRACES—1¼-inch, raised, double and stitched round edges.
BREECHING—Folded, with straight raised layer, side straps, ⅞-inch.
HIP STRAPS—Double, ⅝-inch.
TURNBACK—⅞-inch, double reversed, round crupper to buckle.

SADDLE—3½-inch, leather covered seat, enameled leather pad.
SHAFT TUGS—1⅛-inch, with dees and creased box loops.
BELLYBAND—Inside folded, with layer; outside single, attached.
LINES—⅞-inch, buckle and billet, 1⅛-inch hand parts; flat russet lines, if preferred.
MARTINGALE—⅞-inch.
COLLAR—Half patent leather, closed top. Buckle top collar if preferred. Hitch strap. Directions for measuring collar on page 148.

No. 34—SINGLE STANHOPE OR SURREY HARNESS WITH SWISS BREAST COLLAR

PRICE
- Cash with order, with brass or nickel trimmings................................$21.00
- C. O. D., with nickel or brass trimmings..................................... 21.50
- Genuine rubber trimmings, if preferred to the regular trimmings, add............ 3.00

No. 34 is a very popular style harness and one that gives the best of satisfaction everywhere. This harness is appropriate for driving wagon, Stanhope, Goddard or surrey use. It is cut from good stock throughout, is nicely finished and well trimmed. We know No. 34 is as good as usually sells for $8.00 to $10.00 more than our price, and we are glad to ship it anywhere for examination and approval, with the understanding that it may be returned at our expense if not found all we claim and satisfactory.

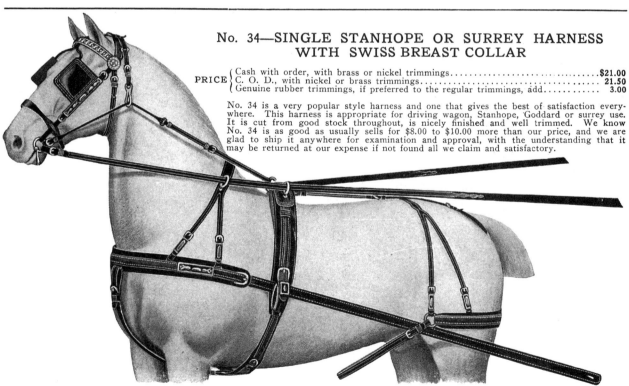

BRIDLE—⅝-inch, round side check, box loops, round winker stays, layer on crown, nose band.
BREAST COLLAR—Wide single leather, folded; open bottom; Swiss style box loops; neck strap has swivel terrets.
TRACES—1¼-inch, raised, double and stitched, round edges.
BREECHING—Folded with straight layer, side straps ⅞-inch.
HIP STRAP—Double, ⅝-inch.

TURNBACK—⅞-inch, double reversed, round crupper to buckle.
SADDLE—3½-inch, leather covered seat, enameled leather pad.
SHAFT TUGS—1⅛-inch, with dees and creased box loops.
BELLYBAND—Inside folded, with layer; outside single, attached.
LINES—⅞-inch, buckle and billets, 1⅛-inch hand parts; flat russet lines, if preferred. Hitch strap.

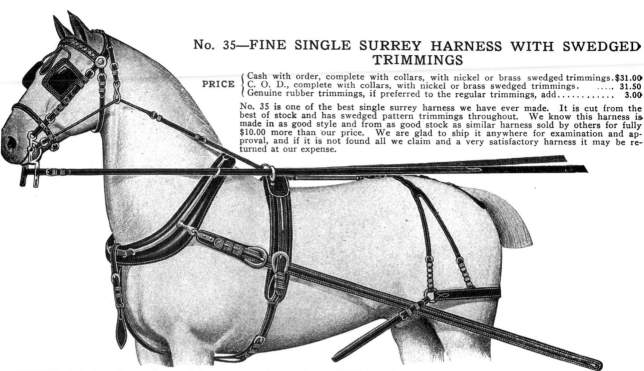

No. 35—FINE SINGLE SURREY HARNESS WITH SWEDGED TRIMMINGS

PRICE { Cash with order, complete with collars, with nickel or brass swedged trimmings.$31.00
C. O. D., complete with collars, with nickel or brass swedged trimmings. 31.50
Genuine rubber trimmings, if preferred to the regular trimmings, add............ 3.00

No. 35 is one of the best single surrey harness we have ever made. It is cut from the best of stock and has swedged pattern trimmings throughout. We know this harness is made in as good style and from as good stock as similar harness sold by others for fully $10.00 more than our price. We are glad to ship it anywhere for examination and approval, and if it is not found all we claim and a very satisfactory harness it may be returned at our expense.

BRIDLE—⅝-inch, with small spaced loops, patent leather face drop, round reins, double and stitched winker stays and nose band, elbow bit with curb strap.
HAME TUGS—Patent leather ends, spaced loops, double and stitched safe under-buckles, full nickel hames with face clips.
TRACES—1¼-inch double, and four rows stitching, raised round edges.
BREECHING—1⅜-inch, double and stitched, raised on inside, side straps, 1-inch.
HIP STRAPS—Scalloped center, with ⅝-inch points.
TURNBACKS—⅞-inch, English style, with heavy round crupper to buckle.

COLLAR—Full patent leather, closed bent top, fair face, turned edge. Hitch strap. Directions for measuring collar on page 148.
SADDLE—4-inch, hand laced, enameled leather pad; tapered patent leather skirts, covered seat, running back band.
BELLYBAND—Inside enameled leather fold with layer; outside single, attached.
SHAFT TUGS—1⅛-inch, with dees, raised on inside.
LINES—1-inch fronts, with buckle and billets; 1⅛-inch hand parts. Folded russet hand parts, if preferred. We furnish lines with beaded fronts, if preferred, for $1.50 extra.
MARTINGALE—1-inch, with patent leather drop.

No. 36—SINGLE SURREY HARNESS WITH SWISS BREAST COLLAR AND FULL SWEDGED TRIMMINGS

PRICE { Cash with order, with nickel or brass swedged trimmings.....................$31.00
C. O. D., with nickel or brass swedged trimmings............................. 31.50
Genuine rubber trimmings, if preferred to the regular trimmings, add............ 3.00

A great many users prefer the Swiss style breast collar for Stanhope and surrey use, and our No. 36 is one of the finest and richest style Swiss breast collar harness we are making. It is cut from the best stock throughout and the trimmings are all swedged pattern. We know No. 36 is as good as usually sells at retail for $10.00 to $15.00 more than our price. We are very glad to ship it for examination and approval, and if not found all we claim and a satisfactory harness we will take it back at our expense.

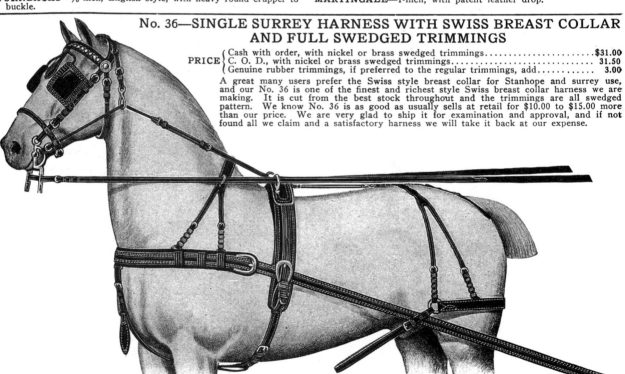

BRIDLE—⅝-inch, with small spaced loops, patent leather face drop, round reins, double and stitched winker stay and nose band, elbow bit with curb strap.
BREAST COLLAR—Wide single leather, folded; open bottoms; Swiss style, spaced loops; neck strap has swivel terrets.
TRACES—1¼-inch, double and four rows of stitching, raised round edges.
BREECHING—1⅜-inch, double and stitched, raised on inside; side straps, 1-inch.
HIP STRAPS—Scalloped center, with ⅝-inch points.

TURNBACK—⅞-inch, English style, with heavy round crupper to buckle.
SADDLE—4-inch, hand laced, enameled leather pad, tapered patent leather skirts, covered seat, running back band.
BELLY BAND—Inside enameled leather fold with layer; outside single attached.
SHAFT TUGS—1⅛-inch, with dees.
LINES—1-inch front, with buckle and billets; 1⅛-inch hand parts; folded russet hand parts, if preferred. Hitch strap. We furnish lines with beaded fronts for $1.50 extra.
MARTINGALES—1-inch, with patent leather drop.

No. 38—SINGLE EXPRESS OR DELIVERY HARNESS

PRICE { Cash with order, complete with collar, with nickel or brass trimmings..........$19.00
{ C. O. D., complete with collar, with nickel or brass trimmings.................. 19.50

No. 38 is just right for delivery work and light express wagon. This harness is cut from good stock throughout, is well made up and nicely finished and trimmed. We know it is as good as usually sells for several dollars more than our price, and we are glad to ship it for examination and approval, with the understanding that it may be returned at our expense if not found perfectly satisfactory.

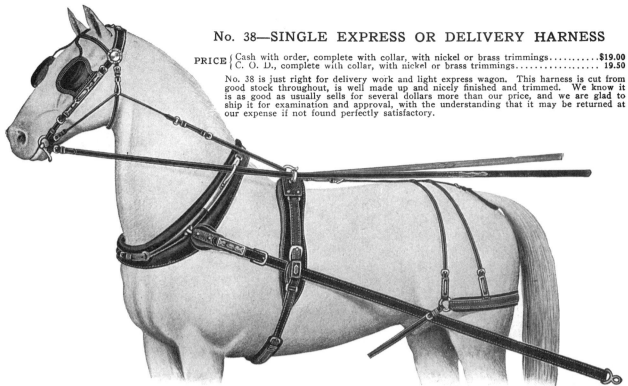

BRIDLE—¾-inch, sensible blinds, box loops, round side check and winker stays.
HAME TUGS—Box loops, sensible trace buckles.
HAMES—Low top, wood.
TRACES—1¼-inch, double and stitched, round edges with cockeyes. Furnished with dart holes in ends in place of cockeyes, if preferred.
BREECHING—Folded with layer, ¾-inch double hip straps.

SIDE STRAPS—1-inch.
TURNBACK—⅞-inch, round crupper to buckle.
SADDLE—4-inch, full kersey pad.
SHAFT TUGS—1¼-inch, with dees.
BELLYBAND—Folded.
LINES—1-inch. Hitch strap.
COLLAR—Kip. Directions for measuring collar on page 148.

No. 41—SINGLE EXPRESS OR DELIVERY HARNESS

PRICE { Cash with order, complete with collar, with nickel or brass trimmings...........$22.00
{ C. O. D., complete with collar, with nickel or brass trimmings.................. 22.50

No. 41 is one of the greatest values in the single express harness line we have ever manufactured. This harness is cut from good stock throughout and is well finished and nicely trimmed. We know it is as good as usually sells for $30.00. We are very glad to ship for examination and approval, with the understanding it may be returned at our expense if not found highly satisfactory.

BRIDLE—¾-inch, patent leather sensible blinds, box loops, round rein and winker stays, and nose band.
HAME TUGS—Box loops, Champion trace buckles, red ball top hames; will furnish low hames, if ordered.
TRACES—1¼-inch, double and stitched, round edges.
BREECHING—Folded with layer, ¾-inch hip straps.
SIDE STRAPS—1-inch.
TURNBACK—⅞-inch.

SADDLE—4-inch, harness leather skirts, kersey pad.
SHAFT TUGS—1¼-inch, with dees.
BELLYBAND—Folded.
LINES—1-inch
MARTINGALE—1-inch.
COLLAR—Imitation Scotch. Hitch strap. Directions for measuring collar page 148.

We make No. 41 extra heavy, with 1½-inch traces, 1-inch turnback, 4½-inch saddle, ⅞-inch hip straps, 1⅛-inch side straps and 1½-inch shaft tugs for $1.50 additional charge. Harness made extra large for horse weighing 1250 to 1500 pounds, $1.50 extra.

No. 42—LIGHT DOUBLE HARNESS

PRICE { Cash with order, complete with collars, with nickel or imitation rubber trimmings..$24.00
C. O. D., complete with collars, with nickel or imitation rubber trimmings........ 24.50

Our No. 42 is a well made, well finished harness at a price from $6.00 to $8.00 less than the same style and grade usually sells for. We are very glad to send No. 42 for examination and approval, and if not found all we claim and a very satisfactory harness it may be returned at our expense.

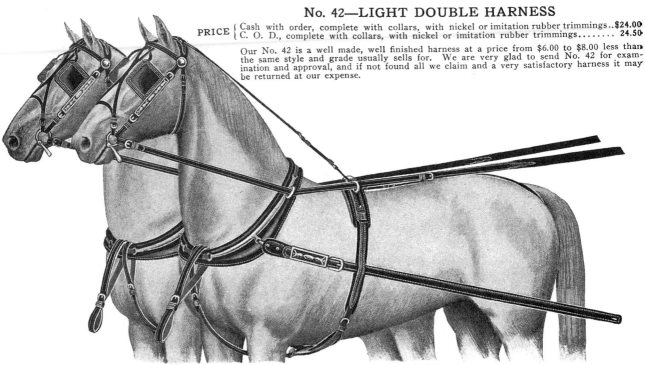

BRIDLES—⅝-inch, overcheck reins, with nose band, unless round sidecheck reins are ordered, box loops, round winker stays, layer on crown.
HAME TUGS—Box loops, iron hames with nickel terrets and draft eyes.
PADS—Straight, enameled leather bottoms, skirts, double and stitched, bearers raised.
TURNBACKS—⅞-inch, scalloped and wave stitched, round cruppers.

BELLYBANDS—Folded.
TRACES—1⅛-inch, 6 feet 6 inches, double and stitched, round edges.
LINES—⅞-inch, 1-inch hand parts.
NECKYOKE STRAPS—1¼-inch.
MARTINGALES—⅞-inch.
COLLARS—All kip, buggy. Two hitch straps. Directions for measuring collars page 148.

No. 43—LIGHT DOUBLE HARNESS

PRICE { Cash with order, complete with collars, with nickel or imitation rubber trimmings..$27.00
C. O. D., complete with collars, with nickel or imitation rubber trimmings........ 27.50

No. 43 double buggy harness is a good seller with us and a style that gives the best of satisfaction everywhere. It is made of good stock throughout and is well finished and trimmed. We know this harness is as good as usually sells for $35.00. We are glad to send it for examination and approval and if not found all we claim it may be returned at our expense.

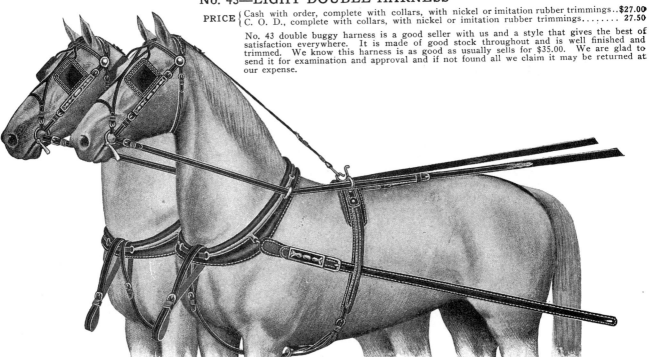

BRIDLES—⅝-inch, overchecks with nose-bands, or round sidecheck reins, if preferred; box loops, round winker stays; layer on crown. We furnish bridles without blinds, if preferred.
HAME TUGS—Patent leather, box loops, iron hames, with nickel terrets and draft eyes.
PADS—Straight, enameled leather bottoms, skirts and bearers raised, double and stitched.
TURNBACKS—⅞-inch scalloped and wave stitched, round cruppers.

BELLYBANDS—Folded.
TRACES—1⅛-inch, 6 feet 6 inches, raised, double and stitched; round edges.
LINES—⅞-inch, 1-inch hand parts.
NECKYOKE STRAPS—1¼-inch.
MARTINGALES—⅞-inch.
COLLARS—Buggy, kip. Two hitch straps. Directions for measuring collars page 148.

164

No. 43½—DOUBLE BREAST COLLAR HARNESS

PRICE { Cash with order, with nickel or imitation rubber trimmings....................$27.00
C. O. D., with nickel or imitation rubber trimmings......................... 27.50

Our No. 43½ is a very desirable style double buggy harness, because the breast collars can be used on any size horse, thus making it suitable for harness to be used with different size teams. We know this harness is as good in quality of workmanship and material as usually sells for $8.00 to $10.00 more than our price. We are glad to ship it for examination and approval, and if not found all we claim and a satisfactory harness it may be returned at our expense.

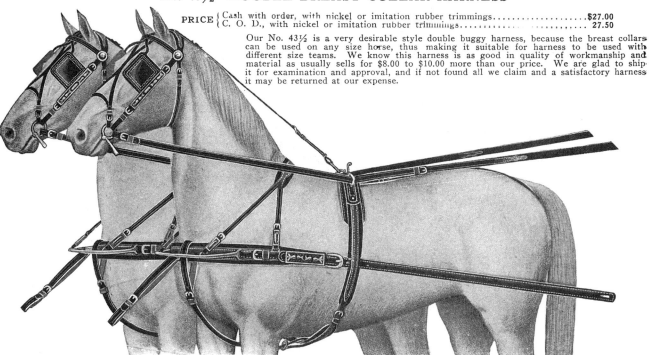

BRIDLES—⅝-inch, overchecks with nose bands or round side-check reins, if preferred; box loops, round winker stays; layer on crowns.
BREAST COLLARS—Folded, with layer; box loops.
PADS—Straight, enameled leather bottoms, skirts and bearers raised, double and stitched.
TURNBACKS—⅞-inch, scalloped and wave stitched, round cruppers.

BELLYBANDS—Folded.
TRACES—1⅛-inch, 6 feet 6 inches, raised, double and stitched, round edges.
LINES—⅞-inch, 1-inch hand parts.
NECKYOKE STRAPS—1¼-inch.
MARTINGALES—⅞-inch. Two hitch straps.

No. 44—LIGHT DOUBLE HARNESS

PRICE { Cash with order, complete with collars, with nickel or imitation rubber trimmings. $27.00
C. O. D., complete with collars, with nickel or imitation rubber trimmings....... 27.50

Many of our users prefer collar double harness with single strap traces running through to the hames. To meet this demand we are making No. 44, and it is a very popular harness. We know this harness is made from as good stock and is as well finished and trimmed as similar styles sold by others for $8.00 to $10.00 more than our price. We are glad to ship this harness for examination and approval and if not found all we claim and a satisfactory harness, it may be returned at our expense.

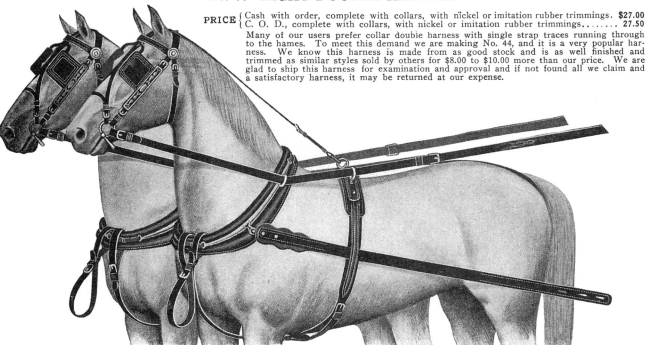

BRIDLES—⅝-inch, overchecks with nose bands, box loops, round winker stays, layer on crown. We furnish open bridles instead of blind bridles, if preferred.
HAMES—Iron, with nickel terrets and draft eyes.
TRACES—1¼-inch, 7 feet 2 inches, single strap, attached to hames.
PADS—Straight, enameled leather bottoms, skirts and bearers raised, double and stitched.
TURNBACKS—⅞-inch, scalloped, round cruppers.

BELLYBANDS—Folded.
LINES—⅞-inch, 1-inch hand parts.
NECKYOKE STRAPS—1¼-inch.
MARTINGALES—⅞-inch.
COLLARS—Kip, buggy. Two hitch straps. If double breast collars are preferred to the hames and collars, we furnish them in place of collars with this harness without extra charge. Directions for measuring collars on page 148.

No. 50—DOUBLE BUGGY OR CARRIAGE HARNESS

PRICE { Cash with order, complete with collars, with nickel or brass trimmings............$31.00
C. O. D., complete with collars, with nickel or brass trimmings....................31.50

Our No. 50 is a very desirable style double harness and one that has always given our customers the best of satisfaction. It is a trifle heavier than the ordinary double buggy harness. It is neatly made up, well finished and trimmed throughout. We know this harness is as good in quality of workmanship and material as usually sells for $8.00 to $10.00 more than our price. We are glad to ship same for examination and approval, and if not found all we claim and very satisfactory it may be returned at our expense.

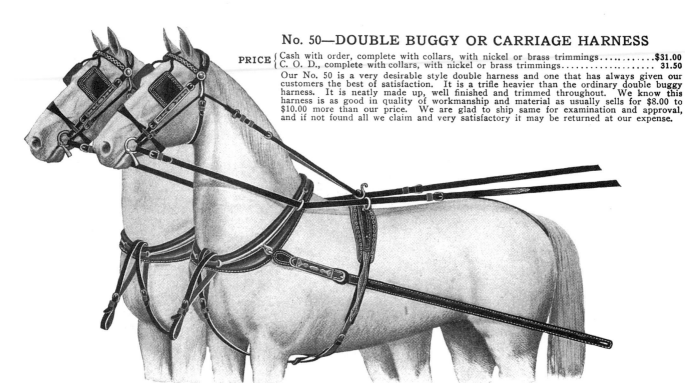

BRIDLES—⅝-inch, round side check reins and nose bands, or overcheck if preferred; box loops; round winker stays; chain fronts.
HAME TUGS—Patent leather, box loops, iron hames, with nickel terrets and draft eyes.
PADS—Straight, raised tops, leather facings, patent leather bottoms and chain housings, skirts single, bearers raised, double and stitched.
TURNBACKS—⅞-inch, scalloped and wave stitched, round cruppers. We furnish hip straps with patent leather drops for $1.50 extra.

BELLYBANDS—Folded.
TRACES—1⅛-inch, 6½ feet, raised, double and stitched, round edges.
LINES—1-inch, with 1⅛-inch hand parts.
NECKYOKE STRAPS—1¼-inch.
MARTINGALES—1-inch.
COLLARS—Half patent leather, closed top. Buckle top collars if preferred. Two hitch straps. Directions for measuring collars on page 148.

No. 51—FINE DOUBLE BUGGY OR CARRIAGE HARNESS

PRICE { Cash with order, complete with collars, with nickel or brass trimmings............$36.00
C. O. D., complete with collars, with nickel or brass trimmings....................37.00
Genuine rubber trimmings, if preferred to the regular trimmings, add..............3.00

Our No. 51 is a light double buggy or surrey harness. It is made from A number one stock throughout, is nicely finished and well trimmed. We can unhesitatingly recommend this harness and will be glad to ship it for examination and approval, with the understanding that it is to be found as good as usually sells for fully $10.00 more than our price or we will take it back at our expense. You are out nothing if not satisfied.

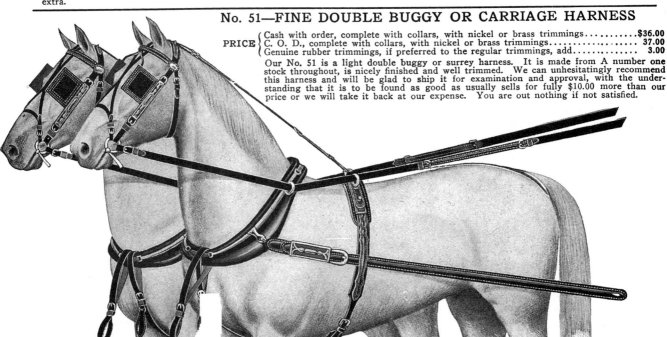

BRIDLES—⅝-inch, five-buckle overcheck with nose bands, or round side check reins if ordered; box loops, round winker stays, layer on crown. Light open bridles instead of blind bridles, if preferred.
HAME TUGS—Patent leather, box loops, safe under buckles, full nickel hames.
TRACES—1⅛-inch, 6 feet 6 inches, double and stitched, raised round edges.
PADS—Straight, raised tops, leather facings, patent leather bottoms, 3-inch beaded edge housings, skirts and bearers raised, double and stitched.

TURNBACKS—¾-inch, scalloped and wave stitched, soft round cruppers.
BELLYBANDS—Glove finished fold, with layer.
LINES—1-inch, 1⅛-inch hand parts to buckle, with double and stitched couplings. We furnish lines with beaded fronts for $3.00 extra.
NECKYOKE STRAPS—1¼-inch.
MARTINGALES—⅞-inch, with patent leather drop.
COLLARS—Full patent leather, closed bent top, turned edges, fair face. Two hitch straps. Directions for measuring collars page 148.

We make this harness large enough for horses weighing 1250 to 1500 pounds for $3.00 extra.

No. 52—FINE DOUBLE CARRIAGE HARNESS

PRICE { Cash with order, with collars, with nickel or brass trimmings..................$41.00
{ C. O. D., complete with collars with nickel trimmings.............................. 42.00

Our No. 52 is a medium heft carriage harness and very suitable for surrey, carriage or hack. It is made from the best of stock throughout, is well finished and nicely trimmed. We unhesitatingly recommend this harness and are glad to ship it anywhere for examination and approval, and if it is not found all we claim and as good as usually sells for fully $10.00 more than our price, we will take it back at our expense.

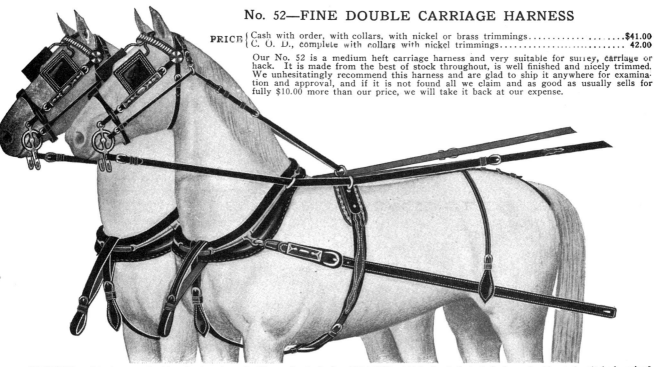

BRIDLES—⅝-inch, round side check reins, double and stitched winker stays and nose bands, box loops, patent leather face drops, chain fronts. Liverpool bits with curb straps.
HAME TUGS—Patent leather, box loops safe under buckles, close plate hames.
PADS—Straight, raised tops, patent leather bottoms, chain housings, skirts and bearers double and stitched.
TURNBACKS—⅞-inch, double, reversed, round cruppers to buckle.
HIP STRAPS—⅞-inch, with patent leather drops.

TRACES—1¼-inch, 6 feet 6 inches, double and stitched, raised, round edges.
LINES—1-inch, 1⅛-inch hand parts.
MARTINGALES—1-inch, with patent leather drops.
BELLYBANDS—Folded with layer.
NECKYOKE STRAPS—1¼-inch, double and stitched.
COLLARS—Half patent leather, close bent top, fair face, turned edges. Buckle top collars if preferred. Hitch strap. Directions for measuring collars page 148.

No. 54—FINE COACH OR CARRIAGE HARNESS WITH FULL SWEDGED TRIMMINGS

PRICE { Cash with order, complete with collars, with nickel or brass swedged trimmings....$56.00
{ C. O. D., complete with collars, with nickel or brass swedged trimmings.......... 57.00

Our No. 54 is one of the finest harness for the money to be found anywhere. It is cut from our best stock, is well made and well finished throughout. It is just as good in every particular as similar style coach and carriage harness sold from city repositories for fully $75.00. We are very glad to ship it for examination and approval, and if not found all we claim and a very satisfactory harness it may be returned at our expense.

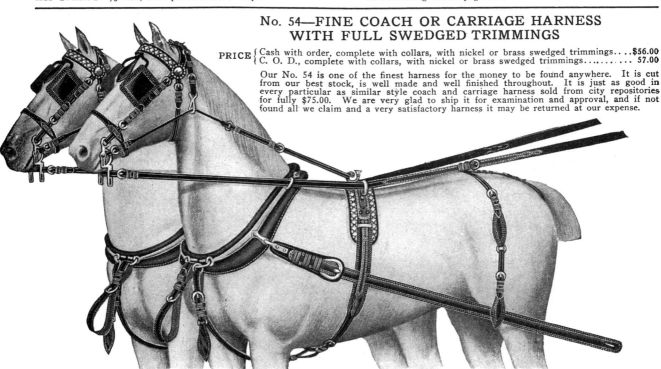

BRIDLES—¾-inch, with small spaced loops, patent leather face drop, round reins, double and stitched winker stays and nose bands, elbow bits with curb strap.
HAMES—Full nickel, with face clips, kidney links and rings.
HAME TUGS—Patent leather ends, spaced loops, double and stitched safe under buckles.
PADS—Straight, raised tops, patent leather facings and bottoms, chain housings, skirts and bearers raised, double and stitched.
TURNBACKS—⅞-inch, English style, heavy round cruppers to buckle.

HIP STRAPS—⅞-inch, with patent leather drops.
TRACES—1¼-inch, 6 feet 9 inches long, with four rows stitching raised with round edges, dart holes or whiffletree loops.
LINES—1 inch, front, 1⅛-inch hand parts, with double and stitched couplings.
MARTINGALES—1-inch, with patent leather drops.
BELLYBANDS—Folded with layer.
NECKYOKE STRAPS—1¼-inch, double, with four rows stitching.
COLLARS—Full patent leather, closed bent top, fair face, turned edge. Two hitch straps.

We furnish this harness made extra large for 1250 to 1500 pound horses for $3.00 additional charge.

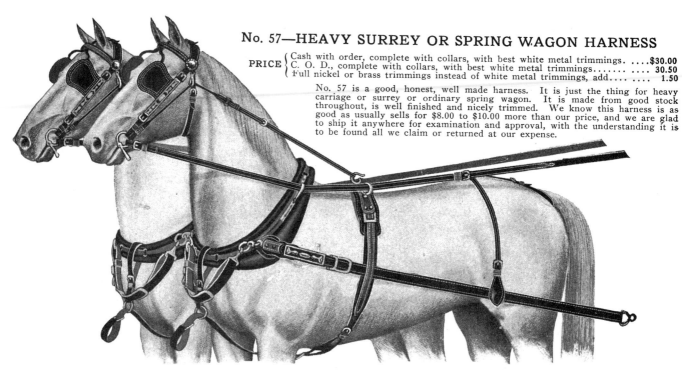

No. 57—HEAVY SURREY OR SPRING WAGON HARNESS

PRICE
{ Cash with order, complete with collars, with best white metal trimmings. $30.00
{ C. O. D., complete with collars, with best white metal trimmings.......... 30.50
{ Full nickel or brass trimmings instead of white metal trimmings, add........ 1.50

No. 57 is a good, honest, well made harness. It is just the thing for heavy carriage or surrey or ordinary spring wagon. It is made from good stock throughout, is well finished and nicely trimmed. We know this harness is as good as usually sells for $8.00 to $10.00 more than our price, and we are glad to ship it anywhere for examination and approval, with the understanding it is to be found all we claim or returned at our expense.

BRIDLES—¾-inch, box loops, round side check reins and winker stays, patent leather sensible blinds.
HAME TUGS—Box loops, Champion trace buckles, oval, iron bound wood coach hames.
PADS—Swell, inserted housings, harness leather bottoms, skirts and bearers double and stitched.
TURNBACKS—⅞-inch, scalloped and wave stitched, heavy round cruppers to buckle.
HIP STRAPS—⅞-inch, with patent leather drops.
BELLYBANDS—Folded.

TRACES—1¼-inch, 6 feet 6 inches, raised double and stitched, round edges with cockeyes, unless ordered without. We will furnish 1½-inch traces instead of 1¼-inch for $1.00 additional charge.
LINES—Flat, 1-inch, 1⅛-inch hand parts.
BREAST STRAPS—1¼-inch, with snaps and slides. Breast straps and martingale same as No. 50 if preferred.
MARTINGALES—1¼-inch.
COLLAR STRAPS—¾-inch.
COLLARS—Kip, coach, all black. Two hitch straps. Directions for measuring collars page 148.

No. 62—FARM HARNESS

PRICE
{ Cash with order, complete with collars, with best white metal trimmings...$30.00
{ C. O. D., complete with collars, with best white metal trimmings......... 30.50
{ Deduct $4.00 if collars are not wanted.

Our No. 62 is a very desirable harness. We know this harness is as good in quality of workmanship and material as usually sells for several dollars more than our price. It is complete with collars. We are glad to ship it for examination and approval, and if not found all we claim and a satisfactory harness it may be returned at our expense.

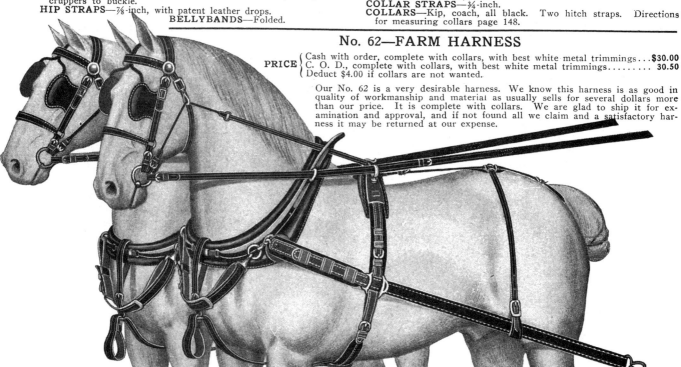

BRIDLES—¾-inch, with nose bands, round reins and winker stays, sensible blinds.
HAMES—Red X C iron overtop, have metal loops for hame straps, which allow them to lie flat on top of collars. We furnish oiled steel bound Concord bolt hames for $1.50 extra. Red steel bound Concord bolt hames with large brass ball tops, $3.00 extra. If the Moellor style hame tug is desired we furnish it without extra charge.
PADS—Self adjusting, short skirts, patent leather housings. Can furnish long skirt, slip tug, if preferred.
TURNBACKS—1-inch, with trace carriers. We furnish single hip strap shifting breeching for $3.00 additional charge. Double hip strap breeching, $4.00 additional charge.

HIP STRAPS—1-inch.
TRACES—1½-inch, 6 feet, double and stitched; 1¾-inch traces in place of 1½-inch traces, $1.50 additional charge.
LINES—1-inch, 18 feet, with snaps. 22-feet lines instead of 18 feet, 50c extra. Lines with round front parts instead of flat, $1.00 extra.
BREAST STRAPS—1½-inch, with slides and snaps. Two roller snaps furnished instead of slides, 25c extra.
MARTINGALES—1½-inch.
COLLAR STRAPS—⅞-inch.
COLLARS—Fine heavy team; spread straps and rings. Two hitch straps. We furnish collars open at throat instead of regular open top collars for 75c extra. Half Sweeny shaped collars instead of regular collars, 50c extra. Directions for measuring collars, page 148.

We make an extra charge of $3.00 for large harness to fit horses weighing 1250 to 1500 pounds.

THE CARGILL COMPANY, GRAND RAPIDS

QUESTIONS AND ANSWERS

Do you change the color of painting from the regular colors described for different styles in catalogue? Yes, we are glad to change the color of painting of gear or even body on any of our carriages, surreys, phaetons, stanhopes, traps, or top buggies, but we cannot make such changes and ship as promptly as when painted regularly.

Do you allow special discount when more than one vehicle or harness is ordered? No, we do not.

How shall I send money? Either bank draft, post-office money order, express money order, or registered letter.

How many spokes in your wheels? Banded hub wheels have 14 spokes, Sarven patent 16.

What is meant by leather quarter top? Our leather quarter tops have the strength and appearance of a full leather top; side quarters and back-stays are leather; roof, back curtain and side curtains are rubber.

Do you furnish four-bow top if desired where cut shows three-bow? Yes, we furnish four-bow top when wanted. No additional charge.

What kind of oil is the best to use on spindles? Good castor oil.

Do you sell on time or on the installment plan? No, we do not. All goods not paid for in advance are shipped by freight C. O. D. Our prices are so low for the quality of the work that we cannot vary from the above; we believe our friends will find it to their interest to borrow the money and buy from us. The saving in price will much more than pay interest.

Do poles have neck-yokes and whiffletrees? Yes, they do. We also furnish stay straps with all poles.

Are the tops on all your top buggies removable? Yes, the tops on all top buggies are attached to seat with shifting rail and can be easily removed if an open driving wagon is desired. We can furnish leather seat fenders to attach to ends of seats when top is removed, if fenders are desired, for $2.00.

Do you furnish the Cateley patent top levers, with spring for top rests, for raising and lowering buggy top when curtains are attached? Yes, we furnish the Cateley patent levers for lowering top on any of our top buggies for $1.00 extra. See small cut, page 9.

What is meant by leather trimmings? By leather trimmings we mean the cushions and backs are covered with leather instead of cloth.

Do you furnish brakes when ordered? We furnish brakes on any of our spring wagons or delivery wagons for $4.00 extra charge; on surreys, phaetons and top buggies, $5.00 extra charge.

Do you furnish breast straps with pole? No, they belong with harness.

Will you make changes in your regular styles? Yes, we are glad to make changes in our regular styles and will quote price on any changes desired or will gladly figure on special work made to order and according to your own ideas. We perhaps build more special work to order than any manufacturer in the United States.

Are the dashes on your road wagons and spring wagons patent leather? Yes.

Do you furnish either pole or shafts with any of your vehicles? On buggies priced with shafts it is extra for pole instead of shafts. When priced with either pole or shafts we send what is ordered.

How do you measure width of track? Track is measured from outside to outside of tire along the ground. The regular widths are 4 feet 8 inches and 5 feet 2 inches. Bodies are the same width for both tracks.

Do you furnish your different style vehicles on any other width track than 4-ft. 8-in. and 5-ft. 2-in.? Yes, we can furnish any width track desired, but we do not carry any other widths than the 4-ft. 8-in. and 5-ft. 2-in. in stock. In wide track or 5-ft. 2-in. localities an extra narrow 4-ft. 4-in. track is often used where a light weight buggy is desired. This width works very well in wide track localities and is preferable with many users for light open driving wagons and top buggies to the 5-ft. 2-in. track. In localities in Massachusetts and Rhode Island the width of track is even wider than 5-ft. 2-in. track and we make these extra wide tracks for localities where they are required.

Do you pay freight? No, we do not. Prices quoted in our catalogue are for goods crated on board cars at Elkhart. If for any reason you are not pleased, and what you order is returned, then we pay freight both ways.

Do you furnish storm apron with carriages and road wagons without tops? We do not furnish storm apron with open vehicles unless ordered extra at $1.00.